DEMOCRATIC CRISIS AND GLOBAL CONSTITUTIONAL LAW

Democratic Crisis and Global Constitutional Law explains the current weakness of democratic polities by examining antinomies in constitutional democracy and its theoretical foundations. This book argues that democracy is usually analysed in a theoretical lens that is not adequately sensitive to its historical origins. The author proposes a new sociological framework for understanding democracy and its constitutional preconditions, stressing the linkage between classical patterns of democratic citizenship and military processes and arguing that democratic stability at the national level relies on the formation of robust normative systems at the international level. On this basis, he argues that democracy is frequently exposed to crisis because the normative terms in which it is promoted and justified tend to simplify its nature. These terms create a legitimising space in which anti-democratic movements, typically with a populist emphasis, can take shape and flourish.

CHRIS THORNHILL is Professor in Law at the University of Manchester. His publications include *A Sociology of Constitutions* (2011), *A Sociology of Transnational Constitutions* (2016) and *The Sociology of Law and the Global Transformation of Democracy* (2018). His works have been translated into many languages, including Chinese, Japanese, Portuguese, Russian and Spanish. He is a member of the Academia Europaea.

GLOBAL LAW SERIES

The series provides unique perspectives on the way globalization is radically altering the study, discipline and practice of law. Featuring innovative books in this growing field, the series explores those bodies of law which are becoming global in their application, and the newly emerging interdependency and interaction of different legal systems. It covers all major branches of the law and includes work on legal theory, history, and the methodology of legal practice and jurisprudence under conditions of globalization. Offering a major platform on global law, these books provide essential reading for students and scholars of comparative, international, and transnational law.

Series Editors

M. E. A. Goodwin
Tilburg University

Randall Lesaffer
Tilburg University

David Nelken
King's College London

Han Somsen
Tilburg University

Books in the Series

Intimations of Global Law
Neil Walker

Legalized Families in the Era of Bordered Globalization
Daphna Hacker

Transnational Sustainability Laws
Phillip Paiement

The Sociology of Law and the Global Transformation of Democracy
Chris Thornhill

Authority and the Globalisation of Inclusion and Exclusion
Hans Lindahl

The Law of the List: UN Counterterrorism Sanctions and the Politics of Global Security Law
Gavin Sullivan

Democratic Crisis and Global Constitutional Law
Chris Thornhill

DEMOCRATIC CRISIS AND GLOBAL CONSTITUTIONAL LAW

CHRIS THORNHILL
University of Manchester

CAMBRIDGE
UNIVERSITY PRESS

University Printing House, Cambridge CB2 8BS, United Kingdom

One Liberty Plaza, 20th Floor, New York, NY 10006, USA

477 Williamstown Road, Port Melbourne, VIC 3207, Australia

314–321, 3rd Floor, Plot 3, Splendor Forum, Jasola District Centre, New Delhi – 110025, India

79 Anson Road, #06–04/06, Singapore 079906

Cambridge University Press is part of the University of Cambridge.

It furthers the University's mission by disseminating knowledge in the pursuit of education, learning, and research at the highest international levels of excellence.

www.cambridge.org
Information on this title: www.cambridge.org/9781108496087
DOI: 10.1017/9781108865869

© Christopher Thornhill 2021

This publication is in copyright. Subject to statutory exception and to the provisions of relevant collective licensing agreements, no reproduction of any part may take place without the written permission of Cambridge University Press.

First published 2021

A catalogue record for this publication is available from the British Library.

Library of Congress Cataloging-in-Publication Data
Names: Thornhill, C. J. (Christopher J.), 1966– author.
Title: Democratic crisis and global constitutional law / Christopher Thornhill, University of Manchester.
Description: Cambridge, United Kingdom ; New York, NY : Cambridge University Press, 2020. | Series: Global law series | Includes bibliographical references and index.
Identifiers: LCCN 2020028709 (print) | LCCN 2020028710 (ebook) | ISBN 9781108496087 (hardback) | ISBN 9781108791120 (paperback) | ISBN 9781108865869 (ebook)
Subjects: LCSH: Representative government and representation. | People (Constitutional law) | Democracy. | Legitimacy of governments – History.
Classification: LCC K3289.5 .T46 2020 (print) | LCC K3289.5 (ebook) | DDC 342–dc23
LC record available at https://lccn.loc.gov/2020028709
LC ebook record available at https://lccn.loc.gov/2020028710

ISBN 978-1-108-49608-7 Hardback
ISBN 978-1-108-79112-0 Paperback

Cambridge University Press has no responsibility for the persistence or accuracy of URLs for external or third-party internet websites referred to in this publication and does not guarantee that any content on such websites is, or will remain, accurate or appropriate.

For Atina, Grace and John

CONTENTS

Acknowledgements   *page* viii

Introduction   1
1   Democratic Subjects and Social Process   16
2   Democracy and Militarization   41
3   Democracy and Global Law   118
4   Populism as Misunderstood Democracy   187
Conclusion   217

Bibliography   222
Index   262

ACKNOWLEDGEMENTS

The idea for this book first occurred to me in the summer of 2018, when I spent a very stimulating semester as Niklas Luhmann Professor of Sociological Theory at the Universität Bielefeld. I would like to thank all colleagues in the Faculty of Sociology at Bielefeld for inviting me to work there, for their warm reception and for enabling me to begin my research for this book in their magnificent library. Since 2018, I have conducted further research for this book at the British Library (London and Boston Spa) and at the Zentrum fur Militärgeschichte und Sozialwissenschaften der Bundeswehr in Potsdam. Additionally, I benefited from guest professorships at the University of Flensburg, the Federal University of Parana (Curitiba), UNISINOS, the Federal University of Pernambuco (Recife) and the University of São Paulo, all in spring and summer 2019. I am grateful to colleagues at these institutions for their assistance in my research and for engaging me in debates relating to the questions addressed in this book. During this period, I have also profited from discussions with colleagues at numerous conferences, most notably in Athens (2018), Lisbon (2018), Nottingham (2019) and Brussels (2019). More informal conversations with many friends, relatives and colleagues have been very important in shaping my thoughts, and I wish to thank the following people in particular for taking time to engage in discussions with me: Guilherme Azevedo, Juliano Benvindo, Gilberto Bercovici, Paul Blokker, Alfons Bora, Hauke Brunkhorst, Carina Calabria, Lucas Delgado, Pierre Guibentif, Gorm Harste, Kirsty Keywood, Poul Kjaer, Atina Krajewska, Andreas Krampe, Ben Morris, Darrow Schecter, Rainer Schützeichel, Maria Smirnova, Gunther Teubner, Grace Thornhill, John Thornhill, Amit Upadhyay, Rustamjon Urinboyev and Rafael Valim. As ever, I owe special thanks to students at different universities for their intellectual engagement in the courses I have taught. Particular gratitude is due to students who took my course on the sociology of law at Manchester University in 2019, to students who took my short course on militarism and democracy in Recife in August 2019 and to students who attended my PhD seminar on the global legal system in Bielefeld in summer 2018. My warmest gratitude is reserved for Finola O'Sullivan at Cambridge University Press.

Introduction

The Hybridization of Democracy

In its broad conception, this book is an attempt to understand the weakening of democracy that is currently observable in different societies, especially in societies affected by the recent rise of populist movements and parties. It is an endeavour, built on broad sociological foundations, to comprehend why constitutional democracy appears to have become unsettled or even imperilled at the moment of its widest diffusion, as it approached the status of a global legal norm. It proposes a general theoretical model to account for this widespread process of democratic destabilization.

The decades since the 1980s have witnessed the global proliferation of democracy, in a variety of constitutional forms. Before 1945, few democracies existed for long, and most democratic experiments ended in catastrophe. Moreover, the few polities that appeared to have reached stable democratic form before 1945 fell short of satisfying criteria that are now used to define democracy. For example, the United Kingdom was often seen as a democratic state before 1945. However, it had a weighted franchise until 1950, and it would not, in its pre-1950 form, be seen as a full democracy today. Likewise, the United States was often seen as a democracy before 1945, but it remained an apartheid democracy until the 1960s. After 1945, the principle was slowly accepted that only fully democratic governments, based in equal enfranchisement of adult citizens and regular organization of competitive elections, should be viewed as legitimate. Initially, this principle did not produce many polities that can be defined as completely democratic. Between the late 1940s and circa 1960, a small cluster of polities, mainly in the north of Europe, could be classified as relatively solid democracies. By the mid-1960s, the United States joined the category of comprehensively democratized polities, as legislation was introduced to enforce equal voting rights for all population groups. Some Latin American states underwent short-lived experiments in increased democracy from the late 1940s to the 1960s. However, from the 1960s to the 1980s, much of Latin America was governed either by hard or by soft authoritarian regimes. Even Latin American polities that preserved some democratic procedures were only partial democracies. For example, Colombia had a democratic system from 1958, but, until the 1970s, rotation of government office was conducted in pre-agreed sequences. Party-based polities in Eastern Europe after 1945 possessed some representative mechanisms, such as arrangements for intra-party delegation and local consultation (Kahn 1988: 80). But hard or soft authoritarianism was the dominant mode of government in this region until the reforms initiated in the late 1980s. In Africa, in the wake of decolonization, many polities experimented in democratization for a short period. By the 1970s, however, sitting governments were normally ousted by military intervention.

Since the 1990s, by contrast, it has become possible to speak of democracy, or of some kind of democracy, as a globally consolidated pattern of government. The emergence of democracy as a global institutional reality, distinct from a tentative normative expectation, obtained the strongest impetus in the regime transitions in Argentina in 1983 and Brazil in 1985. These transitions reverberated through other Latin American polities, leading either to the overthrow of authoritarian governments or to the reinforcement of existing instruments for democratic representation. Democracy was then strengthened as a generalized political phenomenon in Eastern Europe from the late 1980s to the 1990s, following the reduction of Soviet influence in Eastern Europe and the dissolution of the Soviet Union. At the same time, many African polities embarked, in different ways, on pathways to renewed democratization. By the late 1990s, democracy could, with reservations, be seen as a global political form. Major regional exceptions persisted in North Africa, the Middle East, Central Asia and China, but the promotion of democracy no longer appeared as a singular or localized commitment. In most parts of the world, the legitimacy of government was measured by criteria linked to democracy.

Many reasons have been provided to explain the trans-regional growth of democracy, and it is not necessary to see this, without qualification, as a beneficial occurrence. In particular, the fact that in Africa and Latin America democratization was often flanked by the imposition of deep, globally mandated fiscal cuts meant that the benefits of democracy may have appeared dubious to those blessed by it (Brysk and Wise 1997: 82). Yet, by the 1990s, the citizens of most polities, even those deeply dissatisfied by the governments under which they lived, at least had access to some democratic instruments in order to express their dissatisfaction.

Within a short period, however, it became clear that the step-wise globalization of democracy that gathered pace in the mid-1980s was unlikely to give rise to a uniform set of fully evolved democratic polities. At a manifest level, this should not have been surprising. Most democracies formed after 1945 had required several decades to stabilize democratic procedures. Polities such as India, Italy and Japan that became democracies in the years immediately after 1945 persisted for decades in a state of protracted transition, and rotation of government remained weakly institutionalized. There is little historical evidence of immediate success in abrupt large-scale democratic transitions. In many societies that entered democratic transitions in the 1980s or 1990s, accordingly, political reforms soon had results that differed from textbook definitions of democracy. In many societies, the shift towards democracy either stalled completely or generated atypical political systems, combining clearly democratic features with some attributes not commonly associated with democracy. By the first decade of the twenty-first century, it was difficult to overlook the fact that the global expansion of democracy had created a condition in which democracy had developed many new strains and variants (see Carothers 2002; Diamond 2002). In most cases, democratization led, not to the creation of democracy in simple form, but to the formation of distinctive democratic hybrids, positioned at intermediary points on the spectrum between democracy and authoritarianism.

Such hybrid democratic polities assumed a number of different characteristics, not all of which can be examined here. Generally, however, a hybrid democratic polity can be defined as a polity with the following broad features: (1) at a formal level, it attaches the production of legitimacy for political functions to the subjects that classically authorize constitutional-democratic rule, reflecting the assumption that legitimacy results from the fact that *sovereign citizens* articulate their will, freely, through *sovereign institutions*; (2) the actual accountability of political institutions to citizens is curtailed, and the procedures enabling citizens to exercise sovereignty are either weakly developed or subject to restriction.

In many cases, the institutional characteristics of hybrid democratic polities are historically determined, and they can be linked to structural dispositions of the societies in which they appear. For example, some polities acquired hybrid characteristics because they reverted to a condition in which distinctive pre-transitional features reappeared, such that democratic institutions could not acquire a primary role in the polity as a whole. The most obvious example of this is the Russian Federation. Of course, it is widely argued that the Russian polity has now, once again, become simply authoritarian, replicating elements of the Soviet-era polity in both domestic political management and in international policies (Hale 2015: 20). However, the Russian polity still preserves some democratic institutions, although, partly owing to international pressures, these institutions are subject to increasing strain. In parallel, some polities acquired hybrid characteristics because organizations for mediating between government and society are weakly consolidated. As a result, such polities are often typified by semi-detached presidential executives, and long-term coordination of oppositional movements is difficult. This is a common phenomenon in Latin America. Alternatively, some polities acquired hybrid characteristics because their institutions lack the force required for deep societal penetration, such that government policies have limited societal effect. This phenomenon is common in Africa and Latin America. In such polities, private actors are able to isolate themselves from the state, and informal regional control, often based in patronage or private violence, becomes a dominant governmental feature. Colombia might be viewed as the paradigmatic example of this type of polity.

Overall, hybrid democracy displays many variations. The above list only claims to be exemplary, not exhaustive. As part of the tendency towards democratic hybridization, however, we can observe one institutional process which has become globally generalized in recent years. This process generates a relatively uniform pattern of democratic hybridity, with some independence of the structural features of the societies in which it occurs. That is to say, many polities, at different points on the spectrum of democratization, are currently susceptible to destabilization by movements that can be defined as neo-populist or neo-nationalist, usually combining aspects of populism and aspects of nationalism. In addressing this point, some nuance is required. Populism is not an essentially new phenomenon, as precursors of contemporary populist movements have a long history, especially in Latin America and, to a lesser degree, in the United States. Further, populist governments are not always neatly distinguishable from non-populist governments. Nonetheless, in recent years, some brand of populism has, for the first time, become a widespread governmental type. Populism is now or has recently been institutionalized at the governmental level in a number of polities, including Bolivia, Brazil, Hungary, India, Italy, Poland, the United States, the United Kingdom, and Venezuela. In addition, parties with strong populist elements are influential in a much larger sample of polities. Nationalism and populism at times combine in ungainly form, and populist parties are not necessarily nationalist. In most cases, however, populism tends, with variations, to coalesce with nationalism, and the recourse to 'the people' that supports populism typically implies a recourse to 'the nation'. Such populism is now a common expression of democratic hybridization, and it appears in polities once thought immune to the populist appeal.

In general terms, populism is defined by the fact that it challenges established democratic institutions, and it weakens the liberal-procedural elements of representative democracy. Although typically a movement of the right, it may also express social motivations usually associated with the left. Some populist governments, for example, in Venezuela and Bolivia, have adopted policies clearly typical of movements of the left. As discussed in Chapter 4, contemporary populism tends to appear as a movement, as a group of movements or as a governing regime that (a) premises the legitimate exercise of power on the immediate expression of the sovereign will of the people, often inciting popular mobilization to discredit governmental elites, and claiming to oppose entrenched elite interests; (b) shows the capacity to change ideological position very quickly, depending on its interpretation of popular interests and its pursuit of electoral support; (c) attributes a certain shared identity to the sovereign people, such that popular interests are often defined in exclusive terms; (d) endorses extreme majoritarianism and condemns institutions imposing normative standards that obstruct the direct expression of the sovereign will of the people in national legislative bodies. For this reason, populism also tends (e) to be hostile to international norms, to international organizations with supra-jurisdictional force and to domestic courts tending to interact closely with international norm providers.[1]

In each attribute, populist movements and governments strain established systems of democratic organization. For example, populist politicians are often able to circumvent standard conventions for legitimating legislation by claiming a direct mandate from the people. For this reason,

---

[1] On populist hostility to institutions of global governance, see Drolet and Williams (2018: 287)

populist governments tend to transfer power from complexly balanced representative bodies to more personalized executives. In addition, populist governments are able to reduce the standing of opposition parties by claiming strong foundation in the popular will, so that inter-fractional consensus becomes less important as a source of legitimacy. Frequently, populist politicians are able to exercise political influence on the judicial branch of government, tending to politicize judicial functions. Overall, populism contains a strong impetus towards executive personalism, which sits very uneasily both with the procedural and with the moderated, consensus-based aspects of representative democracy. In these respects, states ruled by populist politicians normally belong to the family of democratic polity types, and the populist questioning of established democratic institutions is conducted, at least ostensibly, in the name of democracy. However, populist rule reflects pronounced, yet not fully corrosive authoritarian propensities.

Populism and Constitutional Sociology

Important commentators have noted that modern populism has not yet been subject to wide-angled analysis, and we lack a sociological perspective for explaining the prevalence of populism in contemporary society (Jansen 2011: 90). The objective of this book is to propose a broad sociological model for analysing populism, and to isolate the deep-lying social causes that create legitimational opportunities for populist movements in contemporary society.

At one level, the phenomenon of democratic hybridity can itself provide a sociological key to understanding populism. Most recent cases of populist mobilization can be partly explained as variants on the widespread hybridization of democratic institutions, and the growth of populism can be observed as part of a broader climate of democratic debility. In some ways, in fact, the upsurge of populist movements in the last decade might be attributed to the fact that, in more recent transitions, democratization was often conducted on foundations not imagined in classical accounts of democracy. Many democracies created since the 1980s were established in procedures that weakened the popular or collective aspect of institution building, and it is arguable that, because of this, these democracies were intrinsically pre-disposed to the particular form of hybridity now expressed in populism.

First, in most polities, recent processes of democratization were strongly linked to the influence of international organizations and norm setters. In some societies, architects of new democracies worked in close conjunction with international human rights bodies, and democracy was deliberately designed to signal compliance with international human rights norms.[2] In some societies, new democracies were created as politicians endorsed democratization as a precondition for accessing economically promising international organizations. This began in Spain after 1975. But most Eastern European states after 1989 exemplify this. In these polities, democratic transition was partly conducted as a process in which domestic constitutional principles were aligned to global standards of political democracy, based in human rights, so that the polities in question could eventually acquire membership in the European Union (EU). Few current Member States of the EU were fully consolidated as democracies before they were integrated in the EU. More intangibly, in societies in which strongly authoritarian features persist, elements in the polity that retain a democratic component are preserved largely because some institutions are functionally linked to international norm setters, so that globally defined norms are still able to penetrate into the polity. One very important example of this is the Russian Federation, where, despite the increasingly authoritarian nature of the polity as a whole, the judiciary still links domestic institutions and political practices to international normative expectations.

Second, in many settings, democratic government has been led by institutions that are only indirectly connected to popular representation. Notably, recent patterns of democratic polity building are strongly marked by the fact that judicial institutions play a leading role in defining legislation, and, in many cases, even basic constitutional laws have been established by actors in the judiciary. This judicial prominence is particularly visible in polities created after the 1980s. Many polities assumed democratic form in and after the 1980s at the same time that they entered international human rights systems and accepted the jurisdiction of international human rights courts. The causal connection between these two processes is not always immediate. Yet, the temporal coincidence between democratization in Latin America, Eastern Europe and Africa and the consolidation of the power of the courts and commissions attached to the American, the European and the African human rights systems is difficult to contest. This coincidence frequently meant that judicial bodies within national polities assumed a hinge role in democratization, overseeing transitional processes and legitimating acts

[2] See p. 175.

of legislation by mediating international law into domestic law. This judicial prominence is also clear in polities with longer democratic pasts. Some polities – for example, India and the United Kingdom – that have democratic histories that long pre-date the 1980s have, to some degree, acquired their present democratic form because of an increase in the influence of judicial bodies. In both cases, this is partly caused by the linkage between domestic and international norm setters (see Thornhill 2018: 323–350, 478–479). Similarly, the United States is a polity in which the current form of democracy was partly crafted by judicial bodies which transferred global norms into national constitutional law.[3]

In these different ways, most contemporary democracies have taken shape as part of a process in which constitutional norms have been established on global preconditions, or they have at least been coloured by deep interaction between international and national processes of norm construction. Few democratic polities have been built through classical expressions of democratic volition, in which sovereign peoples simply create and obtain legislative force within institutions that they have designed for themselves. Few democracies rely on legitimacy resulting from collective decisions of a national people. In most democracies, basic citizenship roles have been determined, at least in part, by external expectations, and they express globally convergent processes of constitutional formation.

The fact that many contemporary democracies have such atypical origins creates a terrain that is generally propitious for hybrid regime formation. The more authoritarian hybrid regimes, such as those currently found in Russia and parts of Central Asia, have clearly taken root in conditions in which democratic institution building was not led by popular commitment. In such settings, the recurrence of authoritarianism is demonstrably influenced by the fact that classical citizenship roles were not strongly embedded in society.[4] This background also provides a context in which populism can easily take form and flourish. Populism is usually driven by the claim that political institutions lack deep roots in society, and that the patterns of political subjectivity – or sovereign citizenship – required to bring legitimacy to democracy are not solid. As mentioned, the essential vocabulary of populism is focused on the claim that representative mechanisms favour elites and weaken popular engagement. A common emphasis in contemporary populism is that it

---

[3] See p. 140.
[4] See background in Brubaker (1994).

shows a strong hostility towards international norms and towards institutions in domestic societies that align political procedures to international principles. In this respect, strictly observed, populism expresses the accusation that the polities that it criticizes are themselves of a hybrid nature. Populism is a mode of hybrid democracy that proposes itself as an attack on democracies that it perceives, rhetorically, as possessing hybrid features, and it gains legitimacy by asserting that the polities in which it emerges are not fully democratized. In its critique of contemporary democracy, populism is specifically propelled by, and it derives legitimacy from, the insistence that the classical democratic concepts of *national citizenship* and *popular sovereignty* must be placed, ineradicably, at the centre of democracy. In this light, populism reflects a way of thinking about governmental legitimacy that deeply rejects the premises on which much contemporary democracy has been built.

For these reasons, analysis of populism can be productively framed within a wider political-sociological discussion of democratic hybridization and its implications. At an immediate level, it can be observed that democracy itself became a global form as a hybrid form, such that most democracy is now hybrid democracy. Populism can be seen, thus, as one hybrid among many others, taking its place in a legitimational environment caused and defined by democratic hybridity. At a deeper level, however, the fact that populism proposes itself as a remedy to defective democracy raises questions that cannot be simply explained through comparative discussion of democratic hybridization. What is distinctive about populism in contrast to other patterns of hybrid democracy is that it seeks to establish an emphatically legitimated model of democracy, based in classical sources of democratic agency. As a result, populism raises questions about the basic preconditions of democracy, and it draws into light some antinomies in democracy that would not otherwise become visible. Populism discloses a deep paradox at the core of modern democracy, comprehension of which requires broad global-sociological analysis. This paradox is expressed, simply, in the fact that populist movements frequently assume influence in polities that are deeply defined by global-constitutional processes, and they acquire legitimacy by denouncing such polities as hybrids. However, where they react against the depleted patterns of democracy (allegedly) caused by such global-constitutional patterns of norm construction, populist movements normally weaken democracy further.[5] In other words, populism

---

[5] See Huber and Schimpf (2016: 873–874) and analysis on pp. 204–214.

appears as a constitutional form that reacts critically against the promulgation of constitutional norms at the global level to establish democracy. Yet, its reaction to such global norms leads to the erosion of democracy at the national level. The populist demand for *more democracy*, or for *less global democracy*, usually creates *less national democracy*.

In this respect, the rise of populism reflects and presents a sociological problem that extends beyond discussions of hybrid democracy. First, populism raises a question about the relation between national and global constitutionalism. It implies that this relation has been misunderstood, or least that some greater clarification of this relation is needed, for the sake of democracy. Since the 1980s, democratic constitutionalism has widely evolved on two separate axes, one national and one global. These separate axes generate conflicting normative expectations in society, and they are not easily brought into alignment. The normative friction between these domains is often expressed in populism, and it is clearly critical for the future of democracy. The terms of articulation between these domains requires hard sociological clarification. Second, populism raises a deep question regarding the essential normative conception of democracy. Populist movements assert classical democratic subjects as the essential substructure of democracy, and they insist on extracting support from strong projections of popular sovereignty. In so doing, however, populism exacerbates democratic weakness. As a result, populism implies that classical concepts of democracy are, in some conjunctures, detached from the actual sociopolitical premises of democracy. In most settings, classical concepts of democracy fail to describe the processes by which democracy has been created, and, when applied as measures of legitimacy, they lead to the weakening of democracy. In populism, by consequence, we see a political reality, in which democracy destabilizes itself through the invigoration of its core normative claims and concepts. Consequently, some critical scrutiny of these normative claims and concepts is needed, and a broad inquiry is required to determine why the assertion of democratic concepts so often undermines democracy. In sum, the problem of populism displays two antinomies in the stock self-comprehension of democracy: it raises a question about the conflict between national and global patterns of democratic constitution making; it raises a question about the conflict between conventional understandings of democracy and the actual sociological form and preconditions of democratic rule.

This book addresses populism by examining these antinomies in democracy, and it attempts to elucidate reasons for the spread of populism by conducting an investigation into democracy itself. To address the problem of populism, it deploys a global-sociological method to analyse democracy and its constitutional foundations and weaknesses. It uses this approach to isolate the objective processes through which, typically, democracy has been formed, its founding concepts have come into being, and, with variations, it has been able to strike roots in different societies. In particular, it argues that populism is often able to gain influence because understandings of democracy display sociological deficiencies, so that democracy is judged from a false perspective. It argues that, seen through a global-historical lens, democracy should be construed, not as the outcome of subjective political choices or actions, but as the variable result of deep-lying processes of integration, the balancing of which is fundamental to the overall organization of modern society. On this account, democracy is the product of two embedded integration processes, one of which has an institutional focus and one of which has a normative focus, which reach back to the origins of modern societal form and shape all national societies. Democracy emerges through a process in which society as a whole is transformed into a system of legal integration, and democracy depends on the fact that a polity is able to support this process by consolidating in society a general *system of institutional integration* and a general *system of normative integration*. That is to say, democracy assumes reality in society as the polity extends and sustains the form of society by integrating citizens into the functions of political institutions and by establishing legal norms that are recognized by and applied to all members of society. Democracy cannot easily exist without these two integrational processes and it cannot easily come into being where these integration processes do not shape society. To sustain these integrational processes, a democratic polity must: (a) build institutions capable of upholding an immediate interactive connection with individual citizens, consolidating citizenship roles to perpetuate such interaction; (b) establish a normative order in which citizens are connected to each other and to the government by laws whose origin they recognize as legitimate; (c) construct normative legitimacy for laws, able to support the application of law across society; (d) ensure, as far as possible, that the process of institutional integration and the process of normative integration on which democracy relies do not conflict with or unsettle each other. By advancing an integrational account of democratic formation, this book argues that democracy has preconditions that are widely misinterpreted. Moreover, it argues that, seen as part of the integrational form of society as a whole, democracy usually results from the articulation between national polities and global processes of norm construction. Misunderstanding of these facts frequently causes democratic instability, and such instability is often reflected in populism.

On this basis, this book attempts to explain populism by presenting a global-sociological analysis of the articulation between the core norms of national constitutional law and the core norms of global constitutional law. Its claim, in this regard, is that a deep conceptual misconstruction of the relation between these domains creates the environment in which populism evolves. Underlying this analysis is the further claim that the basic vocabulary in which democracy is defined and promoted exacerbates integrational problems in society, and it underlies democratic crises more generally. A wide sociological reconstruction of the emergence of democracy and the formulation of democratic concepts is required both to clarify the actual nature of democracy, and to avert the tendency of democracy to collapse into populism.

Research Context

In fusing global sociology and sociological analysis of democracy, populism and constitutionalism, this book refers to three separate fields of research.

First, this book takes up a position in the growing body of research that addresses atypical patterns of constitutionalism, and it engages in critical dialogue with claims expressed in this research. There is now a growing body of very important literature that analyses *authoritarian constitutionalism* as a distinct phenomenon, created by the partial failure of recent constitution-making experiments (Law and Versteeg 2013; Tushnet 2015; Ginsburg and Huq 2018). This book aims to contribute to this field of inquiry by examining the social foundations of constitutional crisis in democratic polities. Within this field, there also exists a more specialized body of research which focuses on the constitutional dimensions of populism. It is now frequently argued that populism has become a distinct constitutional form, expressing problems of a specific constitutional nature, and demanding explanation in constitutional categories (Landau 2018; Blokker 2019; Bugaric 2019). This book develops and extends this line of analysis. It also shows how populism evolves as an expression of antinomies inherent in constitutional democracy. Yet, it differs from other attempts to interpret populism as a category of constitutionalism. It does so, most obviously, in that it claims that the reason why contemporary democracy appears fragile is attributable, largely, to the literal diction of democratic constitutionalism itself: it claims that democratic crisis is caused by the constitutional categories in which the foundations of democracy are articulated. Central to the problem of populism, which widely reflects and causes democratic crisis, is a problem internal to democracy. This problem is expressed in the increasingly intense contradiction between the constitutional construction of the subjects that are expected to underpin legitimate democratic formation and the real procedures that actually establish and stabilize democracy. This reveals a deep paradox at the core of constitutional democracy.

Second, this book takes up a position in the field of research concerned with *global sociology* or *global legal sociology*. In promoting a global-sociological approach to constitutional problems, this book understands global sociology in a distinctive fashion. That is, it attempts to explain democratic crisis by identifying common normative and institutional conjunctures, which, over long periods of time, have sustained democratic polities in different parts of the globe. In this regard, it shares some common ground with lines of theoretical sociology that utilize models of the world polity, world culture or world society as explanatory matrices. Like such approaches, it isolates and explains generalized or isomorphic tendencies in global society that support democratic consolidation.[6] It argues in fact that the processes that sustain democratic statehood are relatively consistent across the globe, and most states have acquired democratic form on broadly uniform premises. However, this book differs from other approaches by virtue of its historical focus. In addressing global processes that form and affect democracy, it places emphasis on identifying and explaining the original, the most distilled or the paradigmatic expressions of such processes, and it attempts to reconstruct the impact of global processes by evaluating the contexts in which they were first expressed and conceptually elaborated. In examining democracy and democratic constitutionalism through a global-sociological lens, therefore, this book focuses first on the European heartlands of early democracy and early constitutionalism. Much of its early analysis focuses on France and some German states, where the concepts of citizenship that have defined modern society first acquired expression. It adopts this focus because it is in these settings that the

---

[6] For different versions of such theory, see Meyer (1980); Meyer, Boli, Thomas and Ramirez (1997); Stichweh (2000). The latter's analysis of the transformation of national polities through the growth of transnational norms in world society overlaps with my own (2000: 43).

forces that shaped democratic polity building became evident, and that the complex societal implications of democratic concepts can be most clearly analysed. This does not imply a privileging of one geographical location over others. However, it reflects an attempt to trace global political processes to their origins, and it analyses the initial manifestations of global processes as possessing heightened and generalizable explanatory value. In this respect, this book reflects the claim, originally articulated in systems-theoretical analysis of global society, that global legal-political processes are usually connected to experiences of social differentiation, and global processes can be most accurately captured through inquiry into the patterns of differentiation that shaped their first emergence. As a result, the approach to global social formation proposed here is informed by recent research in historical sociology. In particular, it engages with research that examines the position of the military system in the processes of differentiation that accompanied the first rise of democracy (Hoeres 2004: 344; Kuchler 2013; Harste 2016). The global-sociological emphasis of the book is expressed in its attempt to reconstruct occurrences that have shaped the form of democracy across a broad spectrum of national societies. It also addresses contextual variations in such global processes. However, it proceeds from the assumption that patterns of differentiation that eventually acquired global relevance for democracy are best understood through analysis of their beginnings.

Third, this book contributes to a body of research that can broadly be categorized as the *sociology of concepts*. This book attempts to reconstruct contemporary crises of democracy by showing how normative principles that shape democratic and constitutional theory are reflections of deep-lying social forces and pressures. In this respect, it expands on ideas developed in the context of conceptual history, and it utilizes aspects of systemic sociology that help to illustrate how normative ideas are formed by, and how they in turn help to form, processes of social evolution. The sociology of concepts is not fully established as a sub-field of sociology. However, aspects of a sociology of concepts were already present in the thought of Hegel, who observed concepts as structural refractions of historical processes. More recently, a range of theorists have endeavoured to show how political concepts structure, direct and reinforce lines of historical development. Such outlooks are evident in different aspects of Bielefeld historiography, exemplified by Reinhart Koselleck (1979: 113) and Niklas Luhmann (1980: 49). This book expressly attaches itself to the claim, articulated in such thought, that theoretical concepts and social processes are structurally intertwined. However, it differs from such approaches in that, centrally, it insists that sociological construction of concepts is fundamental to adequate political debate, and it explains how overly literal or sociologically unreflected interpretation of political and constitutional concepts has adverse consequences for democracy as material reality. On this premise, this book argues that the objective reality of democracy cannot be understood through the conceptual models in which democracy has been explained through its historical development. Crises in democracy often result from lack of sociological reflexivity in the interpretation of normative concepts.

On this threefold foundation, this book offers a sociological account of the reasons why modern democracies show a propensity to subside into populism. It argues that the reasons for this need to be sought in the origins of modern democracy, in patterns of societal differentiation that underlie democracy, and in normative problems created by the conceptual self-comprehension of democracy.

1

Democratic Subjects and Social Process

Introduction

The model of political order known as 'democracy' has developed around the assumption that the exercise of political power becomes legitimate when a political system institutionalizes procedures for the equal representation of members of the population that is subject to it. On this basis, the essential indicator of democratic legitimacy is that a political system expresses the principle of *popular sovereignty*, and political systems are considered legitimate to the extent that they give effect to the *sovereign will of the people*. This construction of the legitimate political system first became widespread in the constitutional revolutions that occurred in Europe and America at the end of the eighteenth century. After this time, decisions of the sovereign people were posited as the essential legitimational foundation of government, forming the primary source of binding legal and political norms in a given polity.

The legitimational idea of the sovereign people was, from the time of its first projection, closely associated with the concept of *citizenship*, a concept used to describe the bundle of rights and duties by which members of society construct and recognize the legitimacy of the governmental bodies that exercise authority over them. The concept of citizenship contains a number of meanings, and it acquired different implications at different stages in its formation. Initially, an inchoate concept of the citizen took shape which envisaged citizenship as a social condition, in which persons in society obtained rights and duties towards government because of their membership in a distinct territorial community. This early idea of citizenship implied that persons were bound to recognize their governments as legitimate if governments provided them with a certain number of subjective legal protections (rights), flowing from their territorial affiliation. Usually, such rights included protection for occupancy of property – including rights of residency on land – and, most importantly, protection for procedurally fair treatment under law. These legal principles of citizenship were already partly consolidated in Europe in the eighteenth century, before the revolutionary *époque*. However, in the late eighteenth century, a thickened concept of citizenship was established. At this point, citizenship was defined as a condition in which, in a given territorial context, individual persons were expected to see their governments as legitimate if they participated, usually through electoral representation, in creating the norms that define the polity as a whole and the laws that shape everyday life. The conception of the modern democratic polity resulted, in essence, from the fusion of the concept of popular sovereignty with the concept of the citizen, through which the citizen was defined as a strongly engaged political agent. Immanuel Kant spelled this out in paradigmatic terms. He declared that the citizen (*Staatsbürger*) is defined by the exercise of popular sovereignty, and the state's legitimacy flows directly from the sovereign will of citizens (Kant 1977a[1797]: 432). On this basis, the modern polity was concentrated in one dominant model of political subjectivity – the sovereign citizen, or the national citizen as agent of popular sovereignty.

The fusion of these conceptual subjects, the sovereign people and the citizen, is still fundamental to the categories in which the legitimacy of modern states is evaluated. To be sure, in recent years, much theoretical analysis has been conducted that questions the essential correlation between popular sovereignty, national citizenship and democratic legitimacy. Scholars such as Jürgen Habermas and Hauke Brunkhorst insist on the possibility of post-sovereign democracy or post-national citizenship, in which acts of popular participation historically linked to national populations are transferred to supranational practices and organizations. Nonetheless, the projection of the primary subjects of democracy has remained largely unchanged since the eighteenth century. The essential assumption that a political system is legitimated by the fact that it produces laws that originate in acts of sovereign peoples, enfranchised in the role of citizens, remains at the core of democracy. Few theories of democracy challenge this subjectival architecture of democracy. Crucially, this understanding of democratic subjects crosses the spectrum of currently influential accounts of representative democracy. It is a central wellspring both of theories that defend liberal patterns of democracy and of theories, usually with a populist emphasis, that advocate stronger assertions of collective agency as the basis of the legitimate polity. As mentioned, many authoritarian political forms that are emerging in contemporary society generate normative appeal because they radicalize the constructs of political subjectivity around which democracy originally explained itself.

This chapter aims to examine the crises of contemporary democracy by analysing the conceptual subjects – citizens and sovereign peoples – by which democracy explains its legitimacy. As a point of departure, it explains how the formation of these subjects was linked to multiple societal causes. In their origins, these subjects were determined by distinct societal pressures, and they served quite specific functional objectives. In particular, this chapter explains how these subjects were articulated as principles to stabilize deep-lying functional preconditions for modern society, and their early expression was closely attached to processes of social integration, institution building and legal inclusion.

On this basis, this chapter sets out the claim that the basic conceptual architecture of democracy is a contingent social construct. In developing this claim, first, it indicates that the subjects imputed to democracy should be seen not simply as descriptions of real persons or as real norm producers in society but as articulations of ingrained social processes. In many cases, these subjects acted to consolidate pre-existent lines of social formation, and the normative substance attributed to them was not strictly independent of the broader social constellation in which they assumed contours. Further, second, this chapter argues that the basic subjects of democracy have acquired the authority to define conditions of legitimate government, in part, because theorists of democracy have not adequately identified and interpreted the social processes that are reflected in and consolidated by them. As a result, norms arising from such subjects have been construed in rather simplified fashion, in abstraction from their social origins, without full awareness of their implications. In some respects, these subjects were constructed by processes that do not provide a strong foundation for democratic government. This means that democratic subjects are often burdened with normative expectations that are not aligned to their original social position. On this basis, third, this chapter sets out a theoretical framework for a more critical engagement with problems of contemporary democracy, showing that a lack of sociological sensitivity, reflected in the common construction of the subjective sources of democracy and democratic norm production, lies at, or close to, the core of the crises inherent in many democratic polities today. In other words, it argues that the basic diction of democracy has been rather simplistically formulated, and it has transposed historical processes of subject formation into contemporary society in rather unreflected fashion. This simplicity creates a legitimational space that can easily be occupied by movements hostile to democracy. In this respect, fourth, this chapter proposes a foundation for a deep critique of populism. In making these points, it aims to direct debate about democracy and populism towards more sociologically refined analyses, and it creates a lens to observe how, in some respects, crises of democracy, now manifest in populism, are induced by sociologically under-reflected approaches to democracy itself.

Social Integration and Political Subjectivity

As mentioned, the conviction that defines modern citizenship – namely, that citizens possess certain rights that allow them to engage in sovereign will formation and that the exercise of such rights legitimates the political system – was elaborated in the revolutionary period at the end of the eighteenth century. However, this conviction did not appear without cause. Certain norms of citizenship, mainly expressed in the formalization of legal rights, permeated European societies and societies open to European influence long before this point. In a number of ways, the basic form of society had already been defined by legal principles of citizenship, and the emergence of the modern figure of the political citizen resulted from processes of social formation that had been deeply shaped by notions of citizenship. In particular, the modern construct of the citizen evolved in a social environment that was profoundly marked by patterns of integration expressed in pre-existing, less emphatically political norms of citizenship. This construct took shape at a crucial point in the development of modern society, and it assumed a position at the centre of a long-standing trajectory, in which society was increasingly defined by processes of institutional integration and normative integration. That is, this construct emerged as part of a process in which institutions penetrated more deeply into society, and the legal order of society expanded its societal reach and consistency. As examined later, it is possible to observe a number of ways in which earlier legal forms of citizenship had promoted rising integration in the institutional dimension and in the normative dimension of society. These processes created the location in which the modern political construct of the citizen appeared, and this construct grew directly out of earlier forms of citizenship. To understand the modern political citizen as a figure that simply spelled out new norms of participation for defining the legitimacy of a political system is, therefore, deeply to simplify the role of theoretical concepts.

First, by the eighteenth century, the early legal construct of the citizen had enlarged the integrational form of society because it imprinted secular features on European governmental systems. On the one hand, to be sure, in early modern Europe most states possessed an express religious bias. The rise of modern structures of government began in the Reformation, and it was cemented, most notably, in the Religious Peace of Augsburg (1555). In this period, it became distinctive for state institutions that they imposed uniform confessional obligations on their populations, so that citizenship in a particular state implied acceptance of a particular religion. Some states prohibited confessional diversity until the late eighteenth century. The most important case of such prohibition is the Edict of Fontainebleau in France (1685), which repealed earlier provisions for religious tolerance. Despite this, however, most European states were shaped, both conceptually and functionally, by the fact that their legitimacy was not defined on religious grounds. They developed as institutions with free-standing administrative orders to regulate judicial, fiscal and military matters, which were not justified by religious ideals and models of legitimation.[1] Even states that imposed religious uniformity developed administrative systems that strictly detached governmental functions from religious functions.

Over a longer period of time, this process of governmental secularization was reflected in the fact that governments sought to legitimate their activities in principles derived from *natural law*. Natural law evolved as a vocabulary for explaining the actions of government in which states projected their legitimacy on formal premises, so that the authority to legislate was supported by norms of a rationally accountable nature. In some theories, natural law still referred to metaphysical constructions of the polity, implying that the polity was authorized by its proximity to the divine will (Locke 1960[1689/1690]; Domat 1705a: 2; Wolff 1754: 113; Leibniz 1885: 39–40). In some cases, natural law was close to early positivism, accounting for governmental legitimacy through the reasoned interpretation of human behaviour (Thomasius 1699: 107). In some polities, natural law theory gradually incorporated classical constitutional principles, stating that all law in society must be determined by higher normative principles, or *fundamental laws*: that is, by laws that were recognized as valid by all citizens and that could not be arbitrarily contravened by persons in whom political power was physically vested. The doctrine of fundamental laws was widely endorsed in the Holy

---

[1] See pp. 23, 35. See Carl Schmitt's claim that early modern states underwent a threefold process of secularization. This entailed the establishment of central legislative, administrative and judicial organs; the suppression of religious civil wars; and the organization of society as a territorial unit (1950: 98–99).

Roman Empire by 1700; it was accepted in France by the same time, and it was strongly promoted by 1750; it appeared in England during the era of the Civil War, and it was a constitutional commonplace by the 1760s; it became political orthodoxy in Prussia after 1750; and it played a vital role in the background to the American Revolution.[2] In some respects, this doctrine protected the constitutional interests of privileged actors in the state, as it was often used to prescribe consultation with noble estates as the precondition for legitimate legislation. Across variations, however, doctrines of natural law converged around the claim that legitimate law originated in higher normative obligations, separate from particular human subjects. Governmental legitimacy obtained through recognition of natural law was expected to gain reflection in the fact that, within justified constraints, rulers passed the same laws for all people, and all persons were treated equally under law. For example, John Locke argued that the most essential quality of a polity governed by natural law is that judges apply 'settled, known law' in equal fashion (Locke 1960[1689/1690]: 369). Before 1720, D'Aguesseau, chancellor of France, declared indicatively that laws to which obedience is due have two features: they are applied commonly to all people; they are imposed on all people by a 'superior will' giving expression to 'natural revelation' (1819: 187).

In different ways, natural law theory implied a broad legal order for the state, which attached the premise of law's authority to rationally acceded norms. It also created a broad legal order, in which the enforcement of law across society was tied to expectations of uniformity and consistency. In both respects, principles of natural law were vital to the integrational form of modern society, and natural law established the foundations for a legal order that could incorporate all parts of society. Importantly, the connection between natural law and legal integration became visible in the fact that natural law doctrines promoted the principle that persons under law should be treated as *legal subjects*, endowed with certain legitimate expectations regarding their treatment by persons applying law.[3] By the late eighteenth century, the idea was widespread that all

---

[2] For this theory in the Holy Roman Empire, see Limnaeus (1699: 7, 12); in France, see the early expression (1519) in de Seyssel (1961: 113) and the later expression of this theory in Holbach (1776: 17); for England, see Blackstone (1979[1765-69]: 124); in America, this doctrine underpinned revolutionary thought and practice in the late eighteenth century. The great Dutch jurist Ulrich Huber defined *constituties* as fundamental laws (*leges fundamentales*) that define the structure of the state (1684: 125).

[3] Wolff claimed that the human being is a 'moral person' or a 'subject with certain obligations and certain rights' (1754: 59). Later, Kant claimed that the human being

persons possessed certain common legal rights. This idea flowed directly from the assumption that certain higher (natural) laws existed prior to the order of state, so that all persons had claim to protection for certain attributes and liberties. In this regard, natural law promoted an early concept of citizenship. It implied that legitimate law was law applied equally to all people, demonstrating its inherent rationality and legitimacy through its equal protection of natural liberties. This aspect of natural law contributed deeply to the formation of society as a system of legal integration. It implied that, if proportioned to persons as legal subjects, law could be utilized in different societal domains, and it possessed an intrinsic, general justification. Overall, secularization, legal integration and early norms of citizenship were closely entwined at the origins of modern European society.

Second, by the eighteenth century, the early legal construct of the citizen had expanded the integrational form of society because it reduced the dependence of European governments on organizations based in private or familial attachments. In particular, this construct curtailed the extent to which aristocratic families with dominion over particular persons and regions in society could engage, on their own authority, in matters of government. By the eighteenth century, governments promoted practices of negotiation with traditional familial elites in terms that subordinated these elites to the force of territorial states.[4] Sometimes, this occurred in prerogative manner, as emergent national governments used coercive means to eliminate the countervailing power of noble families. At times this occurred in more consensual fashion, as regents offered members of the aristocracy privileges of a social or economic nature (i.e. public status, remuneration, sinecures) that compensated for their loss of immediate political influence.[5] Fundamental to these processes was the general fact that offices of state were defined, incrementally, in accordance with public norms, and the use of public power by individual persons was expected to comply with laws of a publicly prescribed nature. Political offices were separated, in principle, from patrimony or benefices, which had historically been distributed amongst members of the aristocracy. In these respects, governments began to impose a distinctly national structure on their societies, in

---

must be treated as a 'subject of moral-practical reason', whose essential dignity must be recognized under law (1977a[1797]: 569).

[4] See p. 52.
[5] See p. 51.

which all subjects were integrated, in increasingly uniform manner, in the same administrative order.

This separation of government from traditional sources of local or private power was partly effected through a legal process in which the use of political authority was subject to universally accepted constraints. As part of this process, norms were adopted to determine the competences attached to public offices and to decide which persons were authorized to enforce public power. Indicatively, the primary norms of early administrative law began to acquire definition in the eighteenth century.[6] In addition, norms were adopted to decide how public authority should be applied in society. At this time, the assumption was increasingly formalized that public office-holders should use their power in reasonable procedures, without express privileging of particular persons.[7] The idea that the citizen is an individual person with general legal rights appeared as a construction of legitimacy in this context, and the centralization of authority in formal offices and institutions was reinforced by the (still only semi-articulated) belief that political power must be used in a legal form that is adapted and equally applied to single social agents. In each respect, the construction of the state as an integrated institutional order able to enforce authority in generalized form across society depended, formatively, on the concept of the citizen as legal person.

In these respects, third, by the eighteenth century, the early legal construct of the citizen had strengthened the integrational form of European society because it promoted a process of intense *territorialization*. By this time, the functions of government were typically identified with one ruling administration, and the powers of the state extended in (notionally) equal fashion across all parts of the physical region subject to this administration. As a result, society was increasingly transformed into one integrated territory, in which internal political and regional subdivisions lost some of their importance, and families or organizations with authority concentrated in particular localities lost some of their authority. In this respect, governments in pre-revolutionary Europe promoted concepts of societal membership that clearly prefigured later ideas of citizenship. The construction of society as a uniform territory was realized through the principle that all persons in society were equally subject to law, and all persons in society obtained certain rights in law, which emanated directly, not from local families, but from national

---

[6] See p. 64.
[7] See p. 66.

governments. These legitimational concepts impacted transformatively on the basic geographical form of society, turning society normatively (although not yet materially) into one single and inclusive national domain.

Fourth, more broadly, the early legal construct of the citizen had the consequence that it stimulated and deepened a process of legal systematization which defined the substance of personal relationships in European society. At the core of eighteenth-century government in Europe, as discussed, was the increasingly pervasive principle that laws extracted their legitimacy from underlying norms, so that all persons were governed by the same laws, sustained by overarching principles. On this foundation, by the late eighteenth century, society as a whole approached the end of a century-long process of structural transformation, connected to the dissolution of feudalism. In key respects, societies of eighteenth-century Europe experienced the latter stages of a deepening trajectory of legal solidification, in which law became the dominant medium for defining social and political rights and duties and for structuring interpersonal relations. Through this process, society as a whole was transformed into a system of integration, in which legally articulated obligations replaced obligations of a more informal or personal nature, typically rooted in personal, often land-based patterns of authority surviving from feudal social order. As a result, many societies in the eighteenth century experienced far-reaching processes of legal and judicial codification, in which dispensation of justice was placed on more uniform foundations and the common public origin of legal expectations was accentuated. The formalization of law and justice at this time was intended to cut through the mass of customary duties in society, to place limits on the judicial powers of the nobility and to consolidate the legal system as a shared normative order. In such processes, new legal codes were increasingly based on the normative principle that the essential addressee of the law is the individual subject, separated from intermediary bodies or corporate affiliations, and that law's force depends on the construction of the legal person, in essence, as a holder of certain uniform entitlements. As discussed later, the idea of the citizen as a holder of publicly defined rights was not fully consolidated prior to the revolutionary period. However, legal innovations at this time were strongly informed by the sense that the law was intended to be applied to single citizens, with similar legal claims. The legal principle of citizenship gave strong impetus to the ordering of society in one legal system.

Examples of such developments can be found in different legal systems in eighteenth-century Europe. In Prussia, for example, the middle of the eighteenth century saw reforms to judicial procedure. Then, the Land Law of 1794 marked an attempt to organize society on legal premises shaped by common rights of citizenship. It is surely not accurate to claim, as some sociologists have done, that Prussia evolved as a polity based in arbitrary rule (Downing 1992: 77, 92). On the one hand, the Prussian Land Law defined persons as 'free citizens of the state', entitled to equal legal protection. Yet it also ensured that freedoms of citizens could only be exercised in limited form within private noble estates.[8] Consequently, it permitted the continued existence of serfdom, and it even sanctioned the persistence of aristocratic courts.[9] As a result, a two-level pattern of citizenship was established under the Land Law, in which persons subject immediately to the state were freed but those subject to aristocratic authority were not.[10] Despite this, the authors of the Land Law pursued a vision of legal order, in which all jurisdiction was derived from the authority of the regent, and the same law was valid and binding for all people. The Land Law stated clearly that, in cases of conflict, the law of the state must prevail over obligations of a feudal nature.[11] This vision was closely tied to the assumption that the law is based in subjective rights, claimed by equally entitled citizens, which 'must be respected in all constitutions of state' (Svarez 2000: 72). In Austria, legal regulations implemented in the late eighteenth century were intended to reduce the effects of serfdom and to provide legal protection for all citizens. The Civil Law Code introduced by Joseph II in 1786/87 accentuated the position of the person subject to law as that of a holder of certain common rights, and it stated (Section I, §1) that the primary duty of the regent is 'clearly to determine the rights of subjects' and to ensure that their actions promote public well-being. In England at this time, Blackstone drew up a body of laws that projected the single person as the focus of legal entitlement and defined legal obligations in terms of general personal rights and duties (1979[1765–69]: 125). In France, a relatively uniform legal order was promoted under Louis XIV, who introduced a number of legal codes, most notably the *Code Louis* of 1667. More generally, from the late seventeenth century on, France saw

---

[8] This was set out in the Prussian Land Law (1794) II, 7, §147.
[9] On the persistence of informal courts after the revolutionary period, see Wienfort (2001: 80–117).
[10] For a yet more critical view, see Breuer (1983: 207).
[11] Prussian Land Law (1794) II, 7, §136.

repeated attempts by the monarchy to limit the jurisdictional privileges of the nobility and to establish a legal order that could integrate noble courts into the national judicial system.[12]

In these examples, different societies in eighteenth-century Europe witnessed a process in which the law developed as an overarching system of integration. This was propelled by the fact that, however incompletely, the individual person, defined in relatively uniform categories, was established as the point of reference for law. In most societies, the idea that law assumed authority on the grounds that it was applied immediately to individual persons played a role in a far-reaching process of centralizing legal reform and general legal integration. Through such legal individualization, society as a whole assumed the form of a shared legal order, centred around state institutions and able to extend beyond or to override traditional or local legal norms in society.

In such innovations, the organization of modern law was driven by an implied, although self-evidently unrealized, alliance between parties located within the state – that is, regents, rulers and their administrators – and non-noble members of society. The construction of persons as individual legal subjects in eighteenth-century Europe was specifically intended to direct legal obligations away from aristocratic landholders, towards the state, and to ensure that the immediate relation between subject and state should form the core of legal obligations. Most law reforms were flanked by policies to protect the property rights of peasants, to control taxation arrangements between peasants and lords, and to utilize the law as a means of curtailing local noble authority. In France, for example, legal reforms in the eighteenth century were intended directly and uniformly to connect the peasantry to the monarchy (Mauclair 2008: 47). One important account explains how this led to the reinforcement of peasant communities as legal persons with access to law, so that their willingness to litigate against their lords increased (Root 1987: 203). In Austria, the Civil Code of 1786/87, which stated that all persons had equal legal rights, followed earlier legislation, beginning in 1781, to abolish serfdom and to reinforce the legal position of peasants in Habsburg lands. In regions now in southern Poland, eighteenth-century law reforms did not uniformly abolish serfdom, but they brought greater legal protection to peasants (see Kieniewicz 1969: 38). In regions now in the Czech Republic, earlier legislation had been introduced, notably in 1775, to protect peasant property and to control labour duties paid by

[12] See pp. 62–65.

peasants (Grünberg 1894: 244, 223; Wright 1966: 55). In Prussia, 1748–49 saw the introduction of policies to defend the property of peasants from noble expropriation (Knapp 1927: 314; Kaak 1991: 411). In each case, processes of legal and judicial systematization brought important reforms to the legal status of peasants. In each case, legal reform was intended to heighten the legal immediacy between the central administration and the individual legal person, and, in so doing, to liberate social agents, especially peasants, from full aristocratic control. Overall, the early legal construct of the citizen became the focal point in a broad process of legal integration, in which the construction of all subjects, including serfs, as personal bearers of legal subjectivity, propelled the integration of society in its entirety. In this quality, the legal form of the citizen proved the central axis in the growth of the state's integrational power.

For these reasons, fifth, the early legal construct of the citizen heightened the integrational unity of society because it strengthened the basic authority of state institutions. Governments that took shape in the eighteenth century tended to acquire significantly reinforced powers in society, and they were able to dislodge organizations with authority rooted in private or familial power. Central to this aspect of government was the fact that, to an increasing degree, governmental actors assumed a position in society in which they engaged with persons on an immediate, individual basis, through unobstructed lines of communication. As mentioned, the development of common national legal codes implied that individual persons were addressed directly by actors in state institutions. This meant that persons in society began to construct the regulatory horizon of their lives, not around obligations to families or to economic corporations, but to office-holders within the state administration. As persons were positioned in this individualized legal relation, national states began to operate as sovereign organizations in society, and they defined social obligations without recognition of, or at least with diminishing regard for, the powers attached to other bodies and other membership units. Of course, this process of individualized integration only began in the eighteenth century. In many societies, intermediary organizations between the state and particular social agents remained influential for at least a century after 1800. Nonetheless, by 1750, state institutions in much of Europe had begun to approach a position in which, simultaneously, they assumed unprecedented authority in society and they applied this authority directly to single persons. In fact, state institutions were formed through a process in which national governments isolated their subjects from intermediary corporations, and, especially in legal, military and fiscal matters, drew them into a simple relation to their own institutions and offices. In this respect, as Durkheim observed, the rise of the sovereign state and the increasing individualization of the legally protected citizen were two sides of the same process (1928: 93). The construction of modern sovereign states necessarily relied on the capacity of actors within states to reach beyond traditional and familial organizations and to tie their authority to single legal persons (citizens), whose legal individualization and recognition as individual legal subjects they constantly reinforced as a precondition of their sovereign power.

This description of the processes of legal and political integration underlying modern society does not presume to be more than an ideal-typical account of the lines of institution building and norm construction that underscored early European polities and societies. These processes were not uniformly articulated across different regions, and, before the revolutionary period, all merely appeared as incipient patterns of social and institutional formation. Nonetheless, by the late eighteenth century, the legal principle of citizenship, entailing the assumption that each individual person had some claim to legal subjectivity and recognition, was reflected across Europe, and beyond. This principle formed a powerful material determinant of societal structure: it underpinned a series of secular integration processes that we now identify as fundamental to modern society. Expectations attached to this principle of citizenship supported trajectories of centralization in society, which slowly gave rise to legal and political institutions able to exercise (notionally) sovereign force – that is, to incorporate all social agents, and to ensure a direct nexus between state institutions and individual persons at different locations in society. Expectations attached to legal citizenship stabilized patterns of legal integration that connected members of society as nations and separated social actors from private obligations. In both respects, the legal construct of the individual citizen emerged as the pivotal term in a long process of societal reorganization. This process reflected the deep transformation of modern society from its medieval condition as a set of relationships based in normative expectations of an essentially private nature into an encompassing system of interaction, based in laws rooted in public sources of authority and capable of integrating all society. The individual citizen, appearing initially as a simple form of legal personality, defined the core normative axis in this process. The basic structural occurrences that are formative of modern society were created through the initial projection of the societal agent in the form of the legal subject (citizen).

As they approached national form, emergent modern societies conducted integrational processes in two broad dimensions: in a general normative/subjective dimension, in which overarching norms to control social interactions and to legitimate legal obligations were consolidated, and in a general institutional/functional dimension, in which individual persons released from local life-horizons were incorporated in formal institutions. In the first instance, the figure of the citizen as an individual legal subject underpinned both processes, and it created a deep link between the normative and the institutional dimensions of societal integration. This figure emerged as a norm of governmental legitimacy that promoted the production of law in general form and stabilized the institutions of government, by which the law was applied. Distinctively, the legal construct of the citizen provided an image of legitimacy for law in which legislators were able to find immediate support for processes of institutional integration. Vitally, legislators were able to utilize this figure as a premise for the formation of states as sovereign entities, able to extend their integrational reach into society. In this figure, accordingly, the normative and the institutional elements of societal integration processes were brought into close alignment. The recognition of the person as individualized legal subject implied in early citizenship initially appeared as a key figure, or a *functional norm*, in the integrational transformation of society as a whole. The figure drove both processes of integration in the core moment in early European state building which occurred in the eighteenth century.

Social Process and Modern Citizenship

During the revolutions of the late eighteenth century, as mentioned, early legal principles of citizenship were incorporated in a thickened concept, in which subjective guarantees of legal personality were extended to include rights of broad political participation. From the revolutionary era on, public institutions claiming legitimacy were required to create laws that could be explained as laws to which persons, qua citizens, had rationally acceded – or to which they would necessarily accede if they were able adequately to exercise their essential faculties of practical reason. Laws signalled legitimacy, thus, if they could be presented as laws created by the persons to whom they were applied, reflecting the essential subjective dispositions of citizens. To be clear, no polities acquired democratic legitimacy at this time. After the revolutionary decades, democratic experiments were rapidly terminated in most societies, and it took well over one hundred years until political systems close to democracy became a common institutional phenomenon. In most European societies, rights of active political citizenship allotted in the earlier nineteenth century were very limited indeed.[13] At this time, nonetheless, political citizenship began to acquire force as a legitimational norm, and most polities began to design their legitimacy as the expression of constitutionally implicated, sovereign citizens. This was illustrated, evidently, in the constitutional revolutions in America and France. However, even polities with only limited provision for political representation began to project their legitimacy in reference to publicly defined norms. This was illustrated by German states that underwent structural and constitutional reform after the French Revolution and under Napoleonic influence. From this point on, polities could not restrict citizenship to a simple set of thin legal rights. *The granting of citizenship rights necessarily meant that the recipient of such rights was transformed into an inherently political actor, with potential and contestable claims to a role in the creation of law.* After 1848, indicatively, procedures for electoral representation were gradually re-established in most of Europe.

The emergence of the modern form of political citizenship is often seen as the defining caesura in the formation of modern society, after which political institutions were envisioned in terms that broke categorically with previous understandings of social obligation (Dahrendorf 1965: 79; Shklar 1991: 1). As discussed, this conceptual construct gave rise to a normative outlook that, still today, is used to measure the legitimacy of government. In many respects, however, the formation of the political citizen was not an occurrence of a revolutionary nature. Importantly, the norms articulated by this concept cannot be easily separated from the aggregated integrational processes described above. If observed carefully, the construct of citizenship in its modern political form evolved from the functional substance of earlier legal constructs of the citizen, and it projected an image of government that brought existing integrational trajectories, linked to citizenship, towards a heightened degree of articulation. Early democratic revolutions took place in a conjuncture defined by citizenship, and their primary effect was to expand the system of integration already created by principles of citizenship. In key respects, early democratic citizenship proposed legitimational *norms* of government that hardened the emerging *institutional* form of society, and, in so doing, it created a societal environment in

[13] See p. 106, note 97.

which rights attached to democratic citizenship could be exercised. To this extent, as examined later, the modern construct of democratic subjectivity expressed a *functional norm* for society. Like earlier patterns of citizenship, this idea spelled out a norm that actively promoted the institutional structures required for its realization.

Political Citizenship and Institutional Integration

Governments created after the 1780s that derived legitimacy from the construct of the sovereign political citizen usually intensified processes of institutional centralization and legal integration that had existed in pre-revolutionary polities. Indeed, extraction of legitimacy from the political citizen played a fundamental role in promoting the institutional expansion of government.

The strongest link between active political citizenship and institutional integration can be seen in the fact that post-revolutionary governments increased their interaction with individual citizens. In most polities legitimated by active citizenship, the attachment between government and single members of society was deepened, and institutional divisions within national societies were weakened. This became evident in the representative organizations that accompanied the first formation of revolutionary polities. Polities that extracted legitimacy from the concept of the sovereign citizen began to establish institutions to facilitate the production of legitimacy for government, most typically in the form of electoral consent. As a result, political systems legitimated by active citizens usually evolved representative institutions, such as parliaments and other organs of popular delegation, through which the relation between citizens and state was translated into a material fact: citizens became immediately represented actors in the political system. The link between political citizenship and integration also became evident in the fact that most political systems legitimated by active citizens began to establish organizations whose function was to connect representative institutions with citizens at different points in society. In consequence, early democratic political systems generally saw the emergence of political parties, capable of transmitting prerogatives from different social milieux into the state and of imprinting a more strongly nationalized form on society as a whole. Political parties played a particularly crucial role in constructing citizens as national agents and in linking citizens, in different geographical domains, to national political institutions (see Caramani 2004). The link between political citizenship and integration also became visible that, in most polities of the revolutionary period, the institutional density of the state was rapidly intensified, and the administrative capacities of government grew exponentially. For example, revolutionary France witnessed rapid institutional centralization and the creation of an enlarged class of salaried state officials (Bosher 1970: 231, 276; Brown 1995: 282–283). In the same period, Prussia and other German states witnessed the expansion of the civil service, which imposed a uniform administrative order on society (Cancik 2007: 226). In most settings, the growth of the civil service was propelled by the fact that state agencies engaged with citizens more immediately.

The connection between active citizenship and institutional integration in the revolutionary era assumed particular importance because of the wider transformation of society in which it occurred. In many settings, both within and outside Europe, the rise of political citizenship coincided, either immediately or over a longer period of time, with the final abolition of private ownership of persons – that is, depending on the geographical context, of serfdom or slavery. The expectation of immediacy in the relation between person and state in the modern construct of the citizen typically brought to an end the local/personal administrative organizations typical of serf-based or slave-holding economies, and it replaced these with more formally integrated systems of personal regulation.[14] In this respect, the modern figure of the citizen accelerated processes of integration expressed in earlier concepts of the citizen, and it dramatically transformed the institutional structure of society. As examined later, the legitimacy of political institutions established through modern citizenship often depended on their capacity to integrate the large population groups released from serfdom or other patterns of forced labour. From the late eighteenth century, states progressively internalized the judicial, educational and military functions originally performed by feudal lords and serf or slave holders. This led to the rapid functional expansion of government.

In these respects, the emergence of the basic subject – that of the sovereign political citizen – that shaped early democracy appears as one element in a process of integration that pre-existed, and was in some

---

[14] My analysis does not in any way equate serfdom and slavery, as slavery clearly formed a much more extreme form of bondage than serfdom. Yet, by the eighteenth century, some European societies had developed patterns of serfdom, withdrawing personal and proprietary rights from serfs, which shared some features with slavery. On this relation, see Grünberg (1894: 29–30); Knapp (1927: 25, 80); Blum (1978: 36–38). The Prussian Land Law of 1794 defined serfdom as a 'kind of personal slavery' (II, 7, §148).

respects independent of, democracy itself. In many instances, this process of integration possessed emancipatory implications for members of society, as it was reflected in the reduction of private power, and the abrogation of physical privileges attached to land-based labour regimes (serfdom or slavery). Yet, this process was driven by deeper-lying forces in society. It both reflected and intensified processes of institutional integration and political capacity building, underscored by patterns of legal individualization, which were already fundamental to the form of society. In this regard, the political citizen evolved, not solely as a legitimational principle but as a functional norm that accompanied and consolidated the institutional expansion of society as a whole. The concept of the political citizen attached a principle of legitimacy to the state, in which persons increasingly entered a direct and individual relation to state institutions, and the state became the dominant institutional unit in society. The basic form of the modern sovereign state emanated directly from the construct of the sovereign citizen.

Political Citizenship and Normative Integration

The most profound social process connected to the rise of the political citizen is reflected in the legal system of modern society. In fact, the underlying construction of the modern legal system is difficult to comprehend without the rise of political citizenship.

As discussed earlier, the essential features of modern society were determined by deep-lying processes of centralization, institutional expansion and social integration. Each of these processes was accompanied, at a fundamental level, by the gradual erosion of private power, and in particular by the abolition of social orders in which private persons were able to exercise physical dominion over others. These processes were linked, constitutively, to the fact that, throughout the longer formation of modern society, the law itself was severed from personal privileges, originating in patterns of private dominion attached to land. Accordingly, the legitimational norms bringing authority to the legal system were transferred from customs underpinned by local position or personal rank onto premises in which the legal system acquired force of a more formally generalized nature, and laws could acquire legitimacy without reliance on immediate personal gifts, privileges or acts of coercion. In these respects, the processes of institutional integration and normative integration underlying modern society were integrally connected.

This underlying process of normative integration also acquired distinctive expression in the emergence of the figure of the political citizen. The political citizen, established as a norm of recognition for the law, articulated a positive form around which the transformation of society into a shared system of legal integration was intensified. This principle instilled a general definition of legitimacy within the legal system itself, separating the law from external sources of power and legitimacy. The result of this was that law was abstracted against particular persons and particular patterns of influence, so that laws emanating from the state could be accorded a higher distinction, higher legitimacy and higher integrational force than other laws.

This increase in law's integrational force became clear, in different ways, in the revolutionary contexts in which democratic citizenship was first elaborated as a legally constitutive norm. In revolutionary France, law's increasing integrational force was expressed in the doctrine of the sovereignty of the legislature, in which exclusive authority to pass laws was concentrated in legislative assemblies, elected by the enfranchised community of citizens. Through this doctrine, all formal and informal counterweights to public authority, which remained from the structure of the *ancien régime*, were eradicated. In the United States, law's increasing integrational force was expressed, even more simply, in the concept of constitutional sovereignty. As set out in *Federalist 33*, this doctrine implied that the new federal constitution served as the original authority for all law in all parts of society (Madison, Hamilton and Jay 1987[1787–88]: 226). In both contexts, the emergence of state institutions claiming legitimacy directly from citizens meant that the law was organized on a simple normative basis, and the grounds of law's authority could be made clearly visible throughout society. As a result, the legal system was able to generate norms to support its position as one broad integrational order which could penetrate into different domains of social exchange. Accordingly, the processes of legal codification begun in the eighteenth century acquired renewed momentum after 1789, and the principle that law's authority was extracted from citizenship led, frequently, to the codification of law in different social spheres. The codification of criminal law was widespread in revolutionary France and post-revolutionary states. Initiatives for the codification of French civil law began in 1791, which moved towards definitive form in 1804. These patterns of legal codification were then emulated in much of Europe. After 1789, most polities began, progressively, to codify public law in constitutional form. In constitutions created at this time, the citizen was defined as the primary author of all law, so that all legislative processes were required to reflect the general interests of citizens. In each respect, law's integrational force, linked to the remote authority brought to law by the citizen, was dramatically extended.

The connection between active citizenship and normative integration can also be seen in the fact that political systems legitimated by the will of active citizens tended to develop systems of administrative law, through which they organized exchanges with their citizens. As mentioned, the growth of political systems based in democratic citizenship triggered a rapid extension of the state administration. At the same time, the growth of the state administration was frequently accompanied by the consolidation of stricter principles of normative accountability for public office-holders, which meant that state officials were required to communicate with persons in society within a set of strict normative constraints. In many settings, as discussed, the growth of administrative law predated the effective emergence of constitutional law. By the middle of the eighteenth century, some rudimentary body of administrative law was present in many European societies, especially in the fiscal domain, and procedures for reviewing monetary extraction were widespread.[15] However, the revolutionary period brought a significant thickening of administrative law. This is exemplified in the longer revolutionary period in France, which saw the elaboration of a free-standing corpus of administrative norms. In 1790, a law was introduced to facilitate submission of administrative appeals. After 1800, specialized bodies, *conseils de préfecture*, were established to address administrative complaints. By 1806, a separate organ for administrative litigation had been added to the *Conseil d'État*, the highest administrative tribunal. Mechanisms to ensure that administrative exchanges were subject to judicial control were created in Prussia throughout the revolutionary period (Poppitz 1943: 185; Schrimpf 1979: 66). These mechanisms included a regulation in 1797 to promote the separation of the judiciary from the state administration in some parts of Prussia, and further more restrictive legislation in 1808.[16] In such laws, the administrative expansion of the state imposed a pervasive legal grammar on persons that interacted with it, and interactions between state and society were incorporated within a defined legal order.

---

[15] See pp. 63–65.
[16] The final point in this process was the *Verordnung wegen verbesserter Einrichtung der Provinzial-, Polizei- und Finanz-Behörden* (26 December 1808).

Observed in this wide functional context, the modern figure of the democratic citizen was established, in the late eighteenth century, as a culminating position in a long socio-conceptual process. In this figure, the formative legal trajectory of modern society – the separation of legal obligations from land-based privilege and personal power and the translation of these obligations into relatively generalized legal structures – approached completion. The concept of the democratic citizen acquired shape as a subjective form that, in many respects, dramatically accelerated the production of law, intensified the integrational force of law, and ensured that for most persons the attachment to national states was the primary source of legal obligation in society. This concept placed the law on free-standing foundations, so the legal system as a whole became relatively differentiated, and laws could be transmitted across society at a high level of autonomy. This concept made it possible for society as a whole to stabilize itself as a set of integrational affiliations which were not fundamentally bound to one physical location, or to persons occupying distinct positions within a geographical territory. The essential form of modern society was defined as persons began to account for their obligations towards each other as shared subjective legal obligations. This was reinforced as persons defined their obligations as legal results of their own collective decisions. Each aspect of these processes presupposed the figure of the citizen, first as legal subject, then as democratic agent. The concept of the political citizen created a strong line of normative integration around the state, in which persons were increasingly subject to the same laws and all persons were directly assimilated within the same legal order.

An important implication of these analyses is that a certain sociological nuance is required in any examination of the political concepts and normative constructs that took shape in revolutionary Europe, and which subsequently shaped understandings of democracy. In the revolutionary époque, the figure of the citizen underwent a deep conceptual transformation, and it appeared in a form that sharply accelerated the different integrational processes to which the principles of citizenship had, from their first conception, been linked. This concept created the basic form for the modern polity, and it gave rise to a dual process of institutional and normative integration around the political system. However, this transformation did not create a radically new subject, and it did not initiate an entirely new bundle of social processes. Although the concept of the political citizen deviated at a normative level from earlier principles of legal personality, it reinforced the results of these principles at a functional level. At core, modern democracy, attached to conceptually constructed democratic subjects, developed as a form of political system in which preceding processes of integration could be sustained and reinforced. Early democracy took shape in sociopolitical realities defined by increasing institutional centralization and heightened legal integration: the figure of the political citizen could only acquire force in a national political reality of this kind. Once it became established, then, early democratic citizenship both structurally relied on, and in turn solidified, these same processes of institutional and normative integration. The figure of the political citizen provided a legitimational construct around which these processes and structures could be solidified in society, and it reinforced the foundations on which, originally, it itself progressively came into being. The concept of political citizenship that appeared around 1789 emerged with a certain conceptual necessity, resulting from existing patterns of normative individualization, and propelling the processes of national institutional centralization and legal integration already promoted by existing legal-political constructs. As a result, the figure of the political citizen expressed a deepening linkage between the normative dimension and the institutional dimension of societal integration. It projected a set of norms that directly cemented the institutional structures required for societal integration, and required for the realization of democratic citizenship.

Conclusion

Our understanding of modern democracy is attached to a number of concepts, or to a number of *conceptual subjects*. Democracy is seen, in general, as a system of political organization in which a distinct subject, usually expressed as the sovereign citizen, takes central position as an actor that defines the deep architecture of government. However, this subjectival comprehension of democracy revolves around a reductive understanding of social process, and it reflects a reluctance to observe how the conceptual subjects to which acts of democratic norm formation are imputed are affected by underlying social forces. It can be observed, first, that the subjects of democracy are not simply real-material agents that came into being at the origins of modern democracy. On the contrary, these subjects evolved as articulations of social processes that long pre-dated political citizenship and democracy. It can be observed, second, that the subjects of democracy were extracted from functional trajectories, assuming central importance for modern society.

Amongst the functions served by these subjects is, most importantly, the promotion of reliable processes of normative and institutional integration, likely to stabilize social relations in a societal order defined by the dissolution of feudalism. As discussed, the conceptual architecture to support these processes was already established, in more inchoate form, before the rise of democratic citizenship. Originally, these processes were reflected in a concept of the citizen formed within the law, as a legal subject. However, these processes are now structurally linked to political citizenship. Modern democratic citizenship originally appeared as a *functional norm* to carry forward these processes, and democratic citizenship developed by consolidating these processes.

From this standpoint, we can observe democracy from a dual perspective. At one level, democracy can be examined from a perspective that accentuates its emphasis on subjective norm formation: we can argue that democracy is designed to express the collective interests of the constitutional subjects (sovereign populations, national citizens) that are imputed as its foundation. This is the dominant normative view of constitutional democracy. At a different level, democracy can be examined from a perspective that accentuates its position within a complex mass of functional processes, identifying a certain historical-conceptual contingency in the subjects that have been created to stabilize democracy. On this basis, the citizen always acts in two integrational dimensions – the normative/subjective and the functional/institutional. It is required both to project norms for democratic government and democratic legislation and to solidify the functional-institutional conditions in which democratic government can be conducted. The normative and the institutional dimensions of the citizen are always inseparable, and the normative aspect of citizenship is both the precondition and the result of the functional processes that sustain democratic institutions.

On this analysis, democracy may appear as a political order in which the liberties and interests of democratic subjects are effectively realized. In democracies, persons may exist in large expansive communities, their interests may be included in collective processes of law making, and social affiliations may be structured around relatively impersonal modes of recognition, in which immediate physical coercion or immediate private privilege play a reduced role in defining social obligations. Indeed, democracy can be seen, in its origins, as a political order in which norms of human subjectivity were closely aligned to functional developments in society, and these norms helped to establish a reality in which expansive processes of integration could be stabilized. Nonetheless, these democratic subjects have a certain functional independence of democracy. The evolution of the social reality of democracy was shaped by underlying realities, in which the democratic citizen made a late appearance, and in which the figure of the sovereign citizen supports conditions of integration that first developed without obvious popular volition or normative selection. Overall, democracy can be observed as a system of governance which exists in two dimensions. Democracy exists as a system of institutional integration, serving the material incorporation of society in the sphere of governmental authority. Democracy exists as a system of normative integration, defining legitimational premises for the translation of human obligations into shared legal relations. These dimensions are dialectically attached to each other. The normative dimension of democracy consolidates the institutional dimension of democracy, but it also – historically and structurally – relies on the institutional dimension of democracy. The figure of the democratic subject first acquired form in an integrational reality created by earlier constructs of citizenship, and it acted to connect the institutional and the normative dimensions of society. This subject cannot easily exist outside the integrational realities – centralized institutions, integrated societies, positively formed legal systems – in which it first developed. Early democratic polities at once *grew out of*, constantly *presupposed*, and then in turn *reinforced* the patterns of integration that had developed in pre-democratic periods of history.

If viewed in this dual sociological perspective, it is only with a certain degree of caution that the concept of the political citizen can be identified as the categorical focus for a firm normative account of the political system and for a categorically binding set of legal-political expectations. The extent to which political subjects, such as sovereign peoples and citizens, can be simply extracted from the social processes that produced them, and projected as immutable measures of legitimacy, is at least questionable. In democratic theory, the core subjects of democracy – national citizens and sovereign populations – are seen as the authors of norms that categorically define legitimate government. However, this relation can be inverted. In many respects, the subjects of democracy came into being as reflections of the emergent integrational form of society, and they articulated patterns of norm construction, deeply linked to society's functional evolution, which were already very well advanced. It is disputable whether, given their structural linkage, these subjects can be isolated against the processes with which they were formatively correlated, or whether in fact they were ever fully attached to real subjects.

Within this dual perspective, above all, there is always a possibility that the normative or subjective aspect of democratic integration will conflict with the functional or institutional aspect of democratic integration. That is, democracy as a subjective-normative construction may present principles for the authorization of law that undermine the prerequisites of democracy as a functional reality. The constructs of subjectivity imputed to democracy may, in certain circumstances, generate conditions in which democratic freedoms become improbable, and in which the institutional order presupposed for the exercise of democratic subjectivity becomes precarious. Although theorists of democracy have identified the normative subjects of democracy as the absolute preconditions of democratic legitimacy, these subjects are not necessarily constitutive of democracy as a functional reality. In fact, it is by no means certain that the normative subjects identified as the core of democracy are fully adequate to the task of preserving democracy as a system of legal integration, based in stable patterns of legitimation and law production. There is no reason to presume that these subjects remain a perennially apt description of democracy. To attribute democracy exclusively to the subjects that originally crystallized around it always entails a simplification of the first emergence of democratic politics.

Chapter 2 examines ways in which the normative subjects in relation to which democracy has been envisaged at times conflict with and subvert the functional processes that underlie democracy. It extends its conceptual-sociological method to investigate how principles of democratic subjectivity have, at times, challenged democracy itself, and how the social elaboration of these principles has formed a strong obstruction to democracy. It uses this method to show that, in its actual historical articulation, the modern concept of the sovereign political citizen did not provide a solid foundation for the normative integration of society. Owing to the first conditions of its construction, this concept did not provide a focus of normative integration for society and it weakened the basic functional order required for its own implications to become reality. In many respects, the figure of the sovereign political citizen eroded the realities of collective integration, shared legal formation, robust institutionalization and even nationhood itself, which it proposed as its own essence.

2

Democracy and Militarization

The End of Feudalism and Social Violence

As mentioned earlier in this book, modern society was constructed, in large part, by a process, which lasted many centuries, in which basic sources of legal validity were separated from personal authority attached to land tenure. Through this process, society as a whole moved towards a form defined by *legal integration*: law was detached from feudal bonds, the instruments for creating and applying law were removed from the hands of the landed aristocracy and persons in society were progressively connected to each other through more uniformly defined obligations. This transformation was primarily conducted by emergent states, and general legal integration presupposed the rise of national state institutions with sovereign power and deep societal penetration in a given territory. This transformation was not a uniform historical occurrence, and it varied greatly from region to region. Moreover, it was far from completion by the time of the revolutionary upheavals in the last decades of the eighteenth century. In many regions, the aristocracy retained some, albeit limited, control of judicial and fiscal bodies into the nineteenth century. In many regions, serfdom remained entrenched long after 1789. Slavery of course persisted far longer, and legal orders reflecting extreme status variations, resulting from colonial servitude and indirect rule, survived until after World War II. Nonetheless, over a long time period, this process of legal transformation shaped the structure of most societies. The rise of the citizen, and ultimately the rise of the democratic citizen, appeared as key moments in this transformation, placing the law on free-standing integrational premises and attaching political institutions directly to individual persons. In its original manifestation, importantly, this process of legal integration was not a solitary phenomenon, and it was flanked by parallel trajectories in other parts of society. Closely linked to the integrational transformation of the law was a simultaneous development in the *military dimension* of society, which mirrored the transformation of society's legal form.

The feudal societies of medieval Europe were characterized not only by the fact that the law reflected status variations attached to land tenure but by the deep connection between land and military force. As a mode of social organization, feudalism evolved as a complex constitutional mechanism to facilitate military levying, and its original function was to support the recruitment of soldiers for feudal lords. In feudal societies, persons with high social standing were typically persons who received land or offices in the form of fiefs or regalia from higher-standing territorial rulers, or regents. Possession of fiefs typically brought legal authority within lands granted as fiefs, and it meant that holders of fiefs acquired personal rights to exercise jurisdiction over inhabitants of their domains. At the same time, receipt of land committed fief-holders to ensure that they and persons subordinate to them, within their own fiefdoms, would provide military service and recruits to the original donor of the fief, if required for war or for territorial consolidation and defence. The fiefs that supported feudal society were granted, in essence, as contracts to facilitate the engagement of troops and to bolster the military authority of persons in highest positions of power.[1] The supply of military force acted as a tax in blood, which constitutionally linked the nobility to government.

Although essentially hierarchical, feudal obligations established a broad constitutional equilibrium between leading actors in society, in which, ideal-typically constructed, regents were bound to recognize rights of lords on whom they relied for military service, and even to include such lords in political decision-making procedures. In fact, performance of military functions often created the right for important vassals to participate in deliberations concerning matters of high public importance. Most feudal polities developed consultative organs in which some higher-ranking vassals required to fight or to provide soldiers were also entitled to a voice in affairs of state (Kaeuper 1988: 151).[2] These organs eventually developed into early parliaments or representative assemblies, whose main decisions concerned military matters,

---

[1] See Weber (1921/22: 136); Huber (1937a: 44–45); Lyon (1957: 232–33). One analysis sees feudalism as centred on a contractual offer of land for military service (Hofbauer 2015: 84). One early account of this phenomenon states that obligations of vassalage first resulted from the fact that lords granted land in return for cavalry service (Brunner 1887: 28).

[2] See analysis of this process in England in Baldwin (1913: 308); in France in Aubert (1977: 259); in Spain in O'Callaghan (1989: 19).

particularly the raising of armed forces and monetary resources for war. It is often noted that feudal techniques for military recruitment created expanded provisions for political representation in times of war. To this degree, armies always promoted rudimentary constructions of citizenship, and polities marked by shared military duties tended to extend political rights to a widened circle of notables.[3] One historian has explained that, in medieval Europe, the source of constitutional representation 'was in the first instance the army', and persons providing military resources were the first to establish a constitutional order for the nation or the people (Bisson 1966: 1200). In each respect, the primary social relation in feudal and late-feudal society, underpinning the legal obligations that bound persons and defined their political rights, was the military relation. This relation was originally based in fiefs, which were normally attached to grants of land (Blum 1957: 808).

In discussing these matters, some circumspection is required. In most regions marked by feudal structures, feudal laws sat alongside legal norms of a less personalized nature, created by corporative associations or established as simple laws for all residents of a territory. In some respects, feudal law developed as a normative order that was superimposed on earlier, laterally formed constructions of legal duty. Feudal law was always part of a heterogeneous legal order, sitting alongside normative principles that recognized individual persons as holders of less personal rights and as subjects of less personal constraints (Droege 1969: 55, 77–78; Keitel 2000: 244). Indicatively, some law codes of medieval Europe divided the law as a whole into separate provisions, distinguishing between the law of fiefs and related personal obligations and the more general body of civil and criminal law. This meant that residents of a territory were subject to two legal orders, with different origins.[4] Some non-feudal aspects of medieval law survived into the early modern era, including in the military sphere. However, it was feudal law that most pervasively shaped society in medieval Europe. It organized society around a set of hierarchical legal duties, and it construed rights of persons as claims mediated through personal fiefs and personal military responsibilities.

For a number of reasons, feudalism impeded the formation of national political systems and the consolidation of national society as an

---

[3] The *locus classicus* for the association of military participation and popular representation is the work of Max Weber (1921/22: 734–735). But see also Downing (1992: 25).

[4] This is the case in the *Sachsenspiegel*, which contained a book for the law of land and a book for the law of fiefs.

integrated order. The military principles of feudalism formed the strongest obstruction to the establishment of institutions and legal norms with broad integrational force in society. For example, the feudal military system was based in arrangements in which territory was privatized in return for arms, and powerful suppliers of military force were able to position themselves outside the full authority of national political institutions. Such arrangements meant that military mobilization was strongly shaped by local prerogatives, and local fief-holders possessed independent military resources, which they could easily use against each other. This imprinted a deep propensity for localized violence on feudal society. Such arrangements also meant that armies could only be raised unreliably, and the military system depended on complex negotiations and patronage between regents and powerful vassals. Moreover, feudal recruitment could only be sustained if land was plentiful, such that regents who could not offer gifts of land could not stabilize military support across society.

Most importantly, feudal models of military recruitment were dependent on the institution of serfdom. The levying of soldiers in feudal societies did not necessarily require the direct military participation of peasants in combat. In some earlier feudal societies, all fit men, including serfs, were subject to levying, so that military service was tied to residence in a particular territory. Ultimately, however, vassalage became the basis for military service, and, in some feudal societies, it was prohibited for serfs to bear arms, except when pressingly needed for local or national defence (Fehr 1914: 162; Bisson 2009: 64; Hofbauer 2015: 47). Nonetheless, in many medieval settings, armies were formed through summons, militia musters and acts of conscription that reached deep into the poorer sectors of population. Moreover, the feudal military system presupposed that, in times of war, the subsistence needs of society would be covered by peasants working in agricultural production and paying duties, so that military mobilization was not possible without serfdom.[5] This meant that persons with the authority to raise troops presided over a local administrative machinery, which cemented the personal power of the nobility over serfs. In fact, the intensification of reciprocal duties between high-ranking vassals and regents in times of war usually strengthened the institution of serfdom in domains owned by the vassal, such that any expansion of constitutional influence caused by war did not necessarily include the peasantry. At the constitutional centre of feudal

---

[5] See on this point Lampe (1951: 4); Hellie (1971: 146).

society was a radical denial of equal legal status in the relation between lords, warriors and serfs. The military order of feudal society hinged on the entrenchment of variable legal positions, in which primary suppliers of military force obtained elevated legal and jurisdictional authority and rights of personal control over their inferiors. This meant that society as a whole acquired a deeply centrifugal form.

Significantly, long after members of the nobility had renounced their original military roles, the residues of feudalism frequently remained visible in some parts of Europe in the fact that lords who had acquired lands as fiefs transformed their lands into private estates. In their estates, members of the nobility used the rights and powers emanating from fiefs to cement their personal jurisdiction over peasants working on their lands, and to extract taxes from the peasant economies that they controlled. As a result, the initial military order of feudalism eventually gave rise to a secondary pattern of feudal organization, which became widespread in some of Europe from the fifteenth century onwards. This pattern of feudalism differed from the original feudal order as it coexisted with processes of institutional centralization, which reduced the political role of the aristocracy. Where this system was established, however, the local nobility managed to elicit social privileges from emerging territorial states, to arrogate judicial functions in its domains and to establish serf-based aristocratic economies, functioning as semi-autonomous administrative and fiscal units within different regions. By circa 1650, much of Central and Eastern Europe was organized in a neo-feudal system of agrarian management, in which peasants were held in a condition of intensified subjection, often with some similarities to slavery. This system was less strongly consolidated, but not absent, in Western Europe. In this system, the aristocracy placed deep restrictions on the vital rights of peasants, especially the right to own land, the right to change employment and the right to seek legal redress.[6] The period circa 1650–1750 witnessed a stringent reinforcement of serfdom across much of Europe, long after the primary military function of vassalage had disappeared.

---

[6] These processes were especially intense in Central and North Eastern Europe, including regions now in Germany, Poland, the Czech Republic and Slovakia. For comments, see Grünberg (1894: 91); Bornhak (1884: 116); Knapp (1927: 50); Wright (1966: 10–15); Kieniewicz (1969: 3); Kaak (1991: 3–6, 45); Schmidt (1997: 22–29); Lemarchand (2011: 101). For similar analysis of regions now in Austria, see Feigl (1964: 320). For analysis of France, where this process can also be observed, see Saint Jacob (1960: 62); Soboul (1968: 983); Hayhoe (2008: 17, 48–49). For general analysis, see Blum (1978: 71, 197–199).

Feudal methods of military mobilization underwent a deep transformation as European societies began to assume a more obviously national form in the later Middle Ages. This period witnessed a process of gradual societal convergence around state institutions which was both mirrored in, and propelled by, events in the military system. Through the medieval period, recruitment through fiefs attached to land tenure typically gave way, in part, to recruitment by monetary fief and then, eventually, to military indenture. In both stages, military contracts attached to land were supplanted by contracts of a pecuniary nature, so that late medieval armies were largely filled with mercenaries, of one kind or another.[7] In discussing this point, suggestions of neat caesura should be avoided. The recruitment of mercenaries had already begun at an earlier stage in feudal society, and feudal armies always included hired soldiers. Moreover, as late as the sixteenth century, some states, notably England, still recruited some soldiers using partly feudal levies. However, the tendency towards the formation of contract armies was strengthened in later feudal polities. By this time, the basic value of soldiers was increasingly calculated in monetary terms, and armies were supported by fiscal grants. In such contexts, indicatively, military obligations were often viewed as a type of taxation, and some payment for war was transacted in blood and some payment for war was transacted in money (Harriss 1976: 1950; Henneman 1983: 2). By the late Middle Ages, direct aristocratic involvement in military organization was limited.[8]

The outcomes of these changes for political institutions were often ambiguous, and partly undermining. This process meant that late-feudal regents could engage substantial armies using finance raised through early taxation regimes, and, in so doing, they enhanced the general sovereign power of central institutions (Lyon 1957: 11). In some ways, this process meant that states began to engage more immediately with their subjects, and late-feudal polities often saw the expansion of popular mobilization, at least for national defence. However, this process also meant that powerful lords could employ large armed retinues, which reinforced their independence and often led to civil conflict and heightened social violence. It meant that members of the nobility often acquired powerful positions as military retainers and as captains of mercenary armies, creating new military leadership positions for the aristocracy.

---

[7] See Sczaniecki (1946: 27). On the elision of the fief into the contract see Lyon (1954: 511).

[8] On one calculation, the proportion of the French aristocracy involved in military service had declined in some regions to below 20 per cent by the sixteenth century (Le Roux 2015: 77). For similar claims about England, see Gunn (2018: 54).

Across Europe, further, as regents waged war with large paid armies, they became reliant on representative institutions in which the nobility and other estates obtained power to control military finance.

Ultimately, the feudal military order was widely replaced by a contracting system, in which enlistment and military administration were conducted by professional recruiters or military entrepreneurs, often of aristocratic origin. This system of recruitment hinged on a direct contractual relation between regents and military entrepreneurs, and it enabled regents to hire large numbers of mercenaries, and even entire private armies, to support their wars (see Redlich 1964a: 53; Lynn 1997: 6).[9] This meant that the raising of armies lost some significance as a direct constitutional lever for the aristocracy to acquire political rights and to shape the exercise of royal power. Where this system developed, however, regents often struggled to institutionalize adequate fiscal mechanisms to support their armies. In most cases, they were forced to deploy techniques for supporting their armies that weakened their ability to exert control over military organization, and frequently undermined their basic sovereignty.

Each stage in the dissolution of feudalism saw a change in the contractual basis of the army. Each change in the contractual basis of the army was refracted in the contractual basis of the state, as states secured military capacity by changing the terms of their articulation with leading subjects. By consequence, each stage in the dissolution of feudalism also brought a change in the constitutional position of the nobility. Through the monetarization of military contracts, the nobility lost some of its traditional constitutional strength, as it was less strongly required as a direct provider of military force. As discussed later, however, the nobility still retained constitutional influence because, as the feudal levy was abandoned, it was strongly required as a provider of taxation. The constitutional axis of noble power was moved into the fiscal domain. At each stage in this process, however, the constitutional legacy of feudalism, linking military supply to legal authority, frequently pulled against the growth of a robust integrational order in society. The consequences of the displacement of the nobility from its original military-constitutional position, and the resultant need to create an alternative foundation for

---

[9] In England, it is argued that private contractors replaced more traditional sources of military force in the course of the Hundred Years War (Powicke 1962: 166; Hewitt 1966: 33). This was due to the increasing size of the armies raised at this time.

the army, long remained one of the most sensitive aspects of post-feudal polity building.

In some contexts, the transition from feudal armies to contract armies caused a deep crisis in the process of national state formation. The monetarization of military recruitment was already well established by the fifteenth century. By the late Middle Ages, the reliance of regents on privately recruited armies decisively conditioned the social implications of war. At this time, exploitation of conquered lands became a primary means of rewarding military leaders and their soldiers, and longer periods of combat frequently led to endemic violence and extreme social crisis as armies escaped public control. However, such monetarization approached an interim apotheosis in the religious and dynastic wars, known commonly as the Thirty Years War, that occurred in Europe in the seventeenth century. In these wars, France formed a distinct model, emulated later, as the French army was more officially controlled. Typically, however, these wars were fought by mercenary armies, led by independent entrepreneurs. Owing to the scale of combat in many regions, such armies could only be partly funded from princely coffers. At this time, it was often only possible to keep armies in the field through the raising of levies and contributions that were extorted directly by military commanders in the lands where troops were located. The extraction of contributions became central to the contractual basis of many armies at this point, as it created private revenue to pay for troops, in contexts in which most governments lacked robust institutions to support military financing and soldiers often went unpaid. On this contractual basis, mercenary armies developed as organizations with highly autonomous legal structures. Different military units, hired by entrepreneurs, acted as free-standing corporations, positioned outside both feudal and national-political systems of obligation.[10] Such armies, comprising soldiers from many countries, were often bound together by agreements, declared as oaths on recruitment by members of individual units, in which the laws binding the unit and the jurisdictional force to impose such laws were established on a collective basis.[11] The fact that they were not financed through stable fiscal arrangements meant that armies and their commanders were able to exercise extraordinary power

---

[10] See excellent discussion of the legal characteristics of late-medieval armies in Möller (1976: 5); Burschel (1994: 129).

[11] For analysis of this, see Redlich (1964b: 61); Möller (1976: 40); Baumann (1994: 79); Huntebrinker (2010: 35); Krüssmann (2010: 661); Parrott (2012: 104).

in the territories in which they were located, inflicting acute hardship on the regions where they were stationed.

The growth of mercenary armies in late-feudal and early modern Europe formed a key intermediary point on the path towards the consolidation of the modern military apparatus and the modern state as a whole. As mentioned, these armies led to the separation of military resources from persons constitutionally privileged by feudalism, creating a societal condition in which the state's constitutional dependency on the nobility declined. In this constitutional transformation, however, regents frequently lost control of the means of violence in society, and mercenary armies caused much greater instability than feudal armies.

After the religious wars, the authority exercised by states over their armies was substantially reinforced. Although armies were still composed of mercenary corps, often recruited abroad, states assumed greater power over military recruitment and supply. The period after 1648 witnessed the expansion of permanent standing armies, which profoundly shaped the modern state and modern society. The basic integrational form of modern society was decisively shaped by standing armies.

The position of standing armies in early modern Europe needs to be assessed in a nuanced manner. Such armies cannot always be neatly separated either from previous or from subsequent patterns of military organization. For example, central to the creation of standing armies was the principle, typical of later military systems, that soldiers were positioned in an immediate relation to the state, so that soldiers lost the contractual independence that they possessed in feudal and earlier mercenary armies. The rise of standing armies reflected a process in which the claims placed by territorial states on individual subjects were intensified, and interactions between subject and government expressed an immediate set of personal obligations. In fact, recruitment for standing armies relied in part on involuntary mobilization of military personnel, through crude forms of military conscription, and the establishment of early standing armies was accompanied by the increased use of militias. In France, mandatory militia service was, from 1726, an important and constant aspect of military recruitment (see Blanton 2009: 6).[12] One historian describes the eighteenth century in France as the 'century of militias' (Gebelon 1882: 73). Militia recruitment increased significantly in late eighteenth-century England, following the Militia Act of 1757 (Western 1965: 205; Brewer 1989:

---

[12] The origins of the militias in France lie considerably earlier, and the militia existed as a regular institution by 1688 (Girard 1921: 163).

32–33). Mandatory military recruitment was established in Prussia through the imposition of the cantonal system, finalized in 1733, which established mechanisms for raising armies that had some features of general military conscription (see Bornhak 1885: 6; Sikora 1996: 146). This has led some historians to argue that the growth of the Prussian standing army led to the deep militarization of Prussian society as a whole.[13] Variants on the cantonal system were introduced in other German-speaking regions, including some Habsburg territories from 1771. In these respects, standing armies both looked forward to later recruitment processes, but they also echoed procedures used for territorial defence and militia mobilization in feudal societies. Analysis of the distinctive character of standing armies needs to proceed with caution.

Nonetheless, the standing armies that became widespread in Europe in the decades after 1648 reflected a distinct model of social and institutional order which had deep implications for the integrational structure of state and society as a whole. Above all, the rise of standing armies meant that checks were placed on military lawlessness, and states increasingly asserted their authority (sovereignty) over persons and organizations able to mobilize military force. The basic construction of the modern state as a sovereign administrative order, able to exercise general powers of integration in society, was partly the result of these processes.

First, the importance of standing armies for the emergence of modern states is seen in the transformation of military roles to which such armies gave rise. On the one hand, the rise of standing armies altered the position of the mercenary. From around 1648, the more loosely formed mercenary troops, which had originally replaced feudal armies, were increasingly incorporated in official regiments of the emerging territorial state. Foreign mercenaries continued to play an extremely important role in most armies, but they were usually employed on a more permanent basis and integrated into the regular army. Above all, the contracts that subordinated soldiers to their commanders acquired a more publicly controlled character, and they attached individual soldiers immediately to the state (Fichte 2010: 55, 231). On the other hand, the rise of standing armies altered the position of military leaders (Redlich 1964b: 46).[14] After 1648, military commanders were increasingly bound by official duties towards the lords, regents and rulers that they served, which meant that

---

[13] This is the theory proposed in Büsch (1962: 73). For a rejection of this theory, see Hanisch (1996: 147); Nowosadtko (2011: 20).

[14] This view is challenged in Parrott (2012). Yet, Parrott also argues that after 1648, 'state-distributed finance' assumed greater centrality in military politics (Parrott 2012: 317). My

the functions performed by military entrepreneurs were absorbed in the state administration (see Schmoller 1921: 113; Burschel 1994: 206). To be sure, military entrepreneurs did not cease to exist. Many historians now recognize that some states continued to depend financially on private supply of military capacity and international military subsidies remained central to warfare (Thiele 2014: 175). Moreover, in some countries, notably France, use of independent entrepreneurs had been less widespread in the earlier seventeenth century and military contractors had often been integrated in the official administration (Parrott 2001: 279, 301). After 1648, however, it was generally the case that the independence of military elites and recruiters was restricted.

Owing to these processes, military office holding in early modern Europe increasingly mirrored office holding in other parts of the state service. Responsibilities relating to warfare were primarily discharged as contractual duties imposed by regents, subject to formal administrative control. This meant, notably, that the military developed an increasingly structured professional order, as different social groups accessed military careers at specific points in an internal professional hierarchy (see Schmidt 1996: 36). Military offices were partly separated from benefits and distinctions of a personal nature (see Lorenz 2007: 7; Guinier 2014: 157).[15]

These processes had clear implications for the constitutional role of the nobility. The formal organization of the army meant that the aristocracy was, in its traditional sphere of influence, increasingly subordinated to the territorial state. In many states, to be sure, positions in the officer corps were reserved for, or at least largely monopolized by, members of the aristocracy. In Prussia, indicatively, positions in the officer corps were almost exclusively held by members of the aristocracy, who obtained very evident social benefits through access to such offices. One classical analysis of Prussia claims that membership in the officers' corps became almost a 'new type of feudal obligation' (Frauenholz 1940: 7). One parallel analysis of France states that before 1789 the army was little more than a 'sinecure system' for the nobility (Feld 1977: 149). In France, recruitment for armies was still coordinated by noble captains until the

---

historical account mirrors Lynn's description of the transition in the 1600s from the *aggregate contract army* to the *state commission army* (1997: 6–9).

[15] Here, some qualifications are in order. In France, for example, important positions of military command could be purchased venally, so that powers of regimental command were in some respects transacted as a private good (see Duruy 1887: 396).

1760s (Blaufarb 2002: 25–26). In some countries, the fact that the aristocracy had easy access to ranked military positions meant that it was insulated against loss of status caused by political centralization, and it retained a protected class position into the twentieth century (see Kunisch 1973: 54). Nonetheless, the fact that the sons of the aristocracy were integrated into formal roles in the army meant that they were inculcated with military skills that made them useful for government and unlikely to demand independent authority. This meant, in effect, that the aristocracy was partly internalized in the emerging civil service (Messerschmidt 1980: 45–46).

In each regard, the rise of standing armies led to the construction of a military system in which persons with military authority lost some legal and constitutional independence, and military agents were placed under tighter, vertical lines of command. As part of this process, indicatively, both monetary and penal aspects of military law were formalized, and the independent military agreements that had previously regulated mercenary units were subject to greater central control (Frauenholz 1940: 8; Messerschmidt 1980: 73; Burschel 1994: 144–145). Well before 1648, attempts had been made to establish a systematic body of principles to regulate military law. Articles to support a uniform military order had been promoted in the Holy Roman Empire in 1570, so that by this time there existed a clear idea of 'general military law' (Laurentius 1757: 97). By the later seventeenth century, military law was increasingly ordered in formal legal articles, and soldiers were bound by increasingly uniform patterns of legal command and obligation. In the Holy Roman Empire, new military articles were published from the 1660s to the 1680s.[16]

The importance of standing armies for the emergence of modern states is seen, second, in the mechanisms deployed to fund military units, and in the implications of military finance regimes for society as a whole.

At an immediate level, states with standing armies usually reduced their dependence on direct contributions as a source of military revenue, and this impacted deeply on society in its entirety. The direct raising of contributions to support armies continued after 1648. Contributions formed a source of military finance throughout the European *ancien régime*, and even the most organized armies relied on armed requisitioning into the eighteenth century (Lynn 1997: 216). In some contexts, this pattern of extraction induced high levels of violence between soldiers and

---

[16] In 1672, the *Articuls-Brief vor die Reichs-Völcker* established an important template for military regulations and the dispensation of military justice.

the civil population (see Lynn 1997: 185–197; Lorenz 2007: 81–82). As discussed later, however, political organization after 1648 was deeply marked by the endeavour to control the violence required to raise and to sustain large armies. Armies were increasingly financed through formal modes of taxation, and they lost some of their power to raise independent levies, through requisitioning and plunder, from theatres of war (Lynn 1997: 197). Indicatively, military laws created at this time emphasized that all goods obtained by troops belonged to the regent. In fact, regents asserted sovereign command over requisitioning as a core part of the process of administrative expansion and sovereign institution building that defined early states more generally.[17] By the eighteenth century, contributions were widely obtained through relatively ordered fiscal mechanisms. In some regions, the distinction between military contributions and regular taxation was erased (Redlich 1956: 66–69; Dickson 1987: 297–298; Hochedlinger 2003: 105). Important contemporary treatises on this subject defined contributions as a form of public duty, 'paid by the state', for 'safety and to avert enemy violence', which 'all subjects [...] must accept' (Beust 1747: 231–233).

In both respects, the modern state began to acquire its characteristic administrative form in a context, deeply linked to the protracted dissolution of feudalism, in which the organization and financing of war had emerged as the defining constitutional problem in society. The state began to emerge as the dominant organization in society as rulers constructed a regulatory order for curbing the extreme violence, exemplified most acutely in the earlier seventeenth century, caused by mercenary armies and weak fiscal regimes.[18] The creation of a contractual

---

[17] Before the late 1600s, military codes had recognized taking of booty from the enemy as part of military business, subject to general laws of war. In 1570, Emperor Maximilian II introduced military articles which were partly intended to suppress uncontrolled plundering. Yet, these articles accepted the right of soldiers to take booty. The early military code of the Netherlands (1590) stated that all booty must be formally registered (Pappus 1674: 664–665). Later, the Brandenburg military code, the *Churfürstliches Brandenburgisches Kriegs-Recht oder Articuls-Brieff* (first version promulgated 1656), defined categories of plunder that belonged to the prince (Pappus 1674: 428–429). Imperial military laws also placed the search for spoils under formal regimentation (see Maldoner 1724: 174–175). Other treatises defined booty as a form of military tax (Beust 1747: 426). Even sceptical discussions of these norms accept that taking of booty for personal benefit had become less frequent by circa 1750 (Rink 2000: 44). Control of booty was also expressed as a principle of the law of nations. This is exemplified in Wolff (1764: 310).

[18] Lynn describes such 'agonies of war' as the 'birth pangs of the modern state' (1997: 184). For similar claims, see Burschel (1994: 318). Even accounts that reject the 'state-building'

system for army recruitment, supported by a politically controlled fiscal regime, was fundamental to this process. Standing armies and attendant fiscal mechanisms formed an apparatus in which, in part, war was incorporated in the public domain, and the conduct of war was separated from persons positioned outside the state. One interpreter captures this phenomenon expertly by explaining how states began to acquire their modern form through a process of administrative expansion, in which they translated the 'social costs' of early modern war (i.e. uncontrolled violence and deep societal militarization) into 'fiscal' costs (Asch 1999: 655). Expressed differently, standing armies and early fiscal regimes were formed together within the state, as the price and condition of social peace. The consolidation of central fiscal regimes allowed regents to obtain sovereign control of their armies, to assert sovereign control over society at large, and to reduce the profusion of violence in society. On this basis, incipiently, *tax replaced blood as the basis of social authority*, and the ability of the state to manage taxation as a mechanism for integrating soldiers became the foundation of its sovereignty.

The Civil Constitution and the Military Constitution

To manage the social impact of military violence, the states that evolved after 1648 eventually subjected their institutions to a deep constitutional revision, which affected all aspects of society. At the core of the European state that took shape at this time was the fact that standing armies changed the fundamental articulation between the civil and the military spheres – between war and society.

Self-evidently, the growth of standing armies hardly meant that interactions between military and civil institutions lost significance. Important sociologists and military historians have argued that increasing professionalization of the army after 1648 led – in part – to the heightened assimilation of the military in general civil life (Corvisier 1964: 98, 848, 990; Redlich 1964b: 160). As discussed, the reorganization of the military formed a key element in the wider process of national state formation, and the basic form of the modern administrative state was partly the outcome of the process in which standing armies were disciplined and placed under civil authority. The early modern state was partly defined by the internalization of military functions, and the fundamental

framework to explain the regulation of military functions in early modern Europe describe intensifying patterns of institutional control at this time (Rowlands 2002: 361).

quality of the modern state as a provider of administrative regulation resulted from the connection between the state and the army. Tellingly, historians of early modern France observe that it was only in the 1750s that the term 'administration' began to be used as a broad description of government functions, and the increase in the volume of administrative offices at this time was stimulated by military exigencies (Mousnier 1979: 321, 326; Bigot 1999: vi). In some cases, early modern armies actually developed as a parallel administrative apparatus, which emerged alongside and then progressively dislodged the administrative structures based in aristocratic estates, thus extending the authority of institutions directly tied to military command. It is often recorded that, during the growth of standing armies, the military appeared as an invasive system of command which marginalized the traditional regulatory institutions of civil life.[19] A defining example of this is Prussia. In Prussia, all matters regarding military administration were, from 1655, centred in a General Military Commissariat, in which military personnel assumed responsibilities for fiscal extraction previously performed by estates (Jany 1928: 153, 308–309; Schmidt 1980: 85). Supreme military and fiscal functions were fused in the creation of the General Directory for financial and military matters in 1722–23 (Issaacsohn 1884: 118–119). As a result, the military administration became the foundation for state responsibilities more widely, and it incorporated other spheres of official interaction into military offices.[20] Consequently, it is possible to see the century prior to 1789 as defined by the distinctive militarization of some European polities, as military functions were separated from private actors and attached to public offices. This theory was famously proposed by Otto Hintze, who argued that *militarism* was the defining structural characteristic of this period (1962: 58). Other observers have argued that the period after 1648 experienced an 'intensification of war', in which the means of violence penetrated more deeply into society (Burkhardt 1997: 571).[21] This view is supported by the fact that the growth of standing armies typically meant that the proportion of national populations serving in the army grew rapidly.

[19] One classical account states that, under early modern government, the military system formed involved 'a completely alien element in the daily life of feudal administrative regions, village communes and towns' (Gneist 1966[1879]): 120). A similar classical account argues that the army appeared as 'an alien body in the state' (Hintze 1962: 70).
[20] See Marwitz (1984: 149–150). See the account of parallel processes in other German states, also explaining how 'the origins of modern bureaucracy lie in institutions serving military purposes', in Böhme (1954: 19).
[21] See for this argument regarding Prussia Büsch (1962). For similar claims, strongly reliant on Büsch, see Downing (1992: 77–78, 95).

Despite this, the more centrally regulated administration of military life that became prevalent after 1648 meant that the army was placed on foundations which, in key dimensions, were separate from civil institutions and civil life more widely. By the eighteenth century, European society was marked by new lines of differentiation between the civil sphere and the military sphere. The basic integrational structure of early modern European society, outlined earlier, was primarily determined by this process.

The separation of the civil and the military domains can be observed at the general interactional level of society. The administration of the army in the eighteenth century created a system of civil–military interaction, in which, at one level, the population as a whole was less intensely integrated in war and military activities. In general terms, interstate wars after 1648 did not become less frequent, and they retained the potential to devastate entire regions. Yet, wars gradually became more demarcated, and the frequency with which they degenerated into uncontrolled domestic conflict was reduced (Lynn 1997: 13; Hewitson 2017: 128). The strategy of conducting ordered technical warfare, less prone to expand into the civil population, became widespread – at least in principle – in the eighteenth century (Demeter 1933: 151; Schmitt 1950: 295; Kunisch 1973: 80; Hewitson 2013: 464). Paradigmatically, Clausewitz argued later that this *époque* witnessed the 'artificial walling off' of military experience from other social exchanges (2008[1832]: 570).

The separation of the civil and the military domains can be observed at the political or *legitimational* level of society. The rise of standing armies meant that, in many polities, offices relating to civil legislation were separated from offices relating to military organization. One historian explains that this period was characterized by a 'division of labour' between civil and military office-holders (Rink 2010: 68).[22] Through the eighteenth century, both the legal system and the military system were, in many polities, brought under the control of a central governmental administration. In this process, both legal institutions and military institutions were removed from the control of powerful noble families, with powers traditionally linked to military capacity. On the

---

[22] See also the claim that before 1789 the military evolved as a distinct 'social system' or a separate 'sub-system' of society, in which interactions between persons in the military and persons outside the military were increasingly differentiated (Pröve 1995b: 220; 2016: 253). Similar claims are expressed in Rink (1999: 42, 71); Paret (2009: 7); Nowosadtko (2011: 138). For discussion of the constitutional particularity of early modern states in this respect, see Papke (1979: 207).

one hand, quite clearly, this process meant that military and legal functions were closely connected within the polity, as the military system was subject to increasingly invasive formal-legal jurisdiction. However, this was also a process in which legal and military functions were located in separate administrative divisions within the state, supported by distinct regulatory principles. In fact, the law acquired distinct functions in formally partitioning the military system against other parts of society and in closing legal roles to military persons, which greatly increased the basic autonomy and the integrational reach of the legal system as a whole. The weakening of noble influence on military and legal functions created a constitution based, in important respects, in the normative separation of war and law, in which legitimacy for legislative processes was withdrawn from persons with constitutional positions supported by military authority. Many features of the modern European state resulted directly from the fact that, owing to the growth of standing armies, the legal system and the military system became relatively differentiated. By the eighteenth century, the legal order in which states articulated their legitimacy was pervasively determined by this differentiation, and the institutions producing law for society were increasingly detached from actors owing their authority to military functions.

This separation of the legal system and the military system was reflected, first, in the fact that, in most European states after 1648, the aristocracy was placed in a functionally subordinate political role, and the contribution of the nobility to military commitments was less strongly articulated in constitutional influence.

In feudal societies, as discussed, the sociopolitical position of the aristocracy was defined as that of a class with military duties, providing military personnel, revenue and expertise for monarchies. As mentioned, their discharge of military duties meant that members of the ancient military class possessed protected constitutional status, through which they exercised legal authority over inhabitants of their lands and assumed influence on governmental policy. During the first construction of modern state-like institutions, the constitutional influence of the nobility often increased, in altered form. In fact, the transition to governmental regimes based in mercenary armies often strengthened the constitutional position of noble families, at least temporarily. This occurred because payment of mercenaries presupposed that the nobility was willing to grant regular gifts of money to rulers. On this basis, the post-feudal governance system developed, slowly, towards an early form of the *fiscal state*, in which public administration was reformed to maximize the state's powers of revenue extraction.[23] In the first tentative stage of its emergence, the post-feudal polity was ordered around a diffuse constitution, based in complex negotiations, in which the instruments for raising armies and the instruments for securing consensus for legislation were deeply and delicately interlinked. As regents were forced to raise mercenary armies through taxation, they relied on the nobility and other estates for fiscal support, and they established a constitutional order to facilitate fiscal extraction. In such contexts, regents typically designed delegatory systems in which members of the nobility, and sometimes of other social groups, were allowed to debate, to approve or to reject taxation policies. One historian describes the power to approve fiscal levies as the 'fundamental right' of the early modern European aristocracy, and this right was usually exercised through assemblies of noble estates (Schotte 1911: 37). This power had its remote origins in the earlier constitutional arrangements that had surrounded the feudal levy. This power survived into the early modern period, and, in core respects, it remained fundamental to the constitutional order of the European state until the late seventeenth century, and beyond. Above all, this power limited the capacity of ruling executives to legislate against the interests of actors with authority originating in feudal privileges. In most societies, rulers of early modern states retained a conciliatory approach to the aristocracy, and they were careful to preserve aristocratic influence and autonomy in certain spheres so that their demands for taxation would be satisfied.[24] In some cases, the authority of noble estates expanded to such a degree that they brought dynastic regimes to crisis. The most important example is the rebellion of the Bohemian estates in 1618. Indicatively, however, the constitutional laws introduced in 1627 to curtail the powers of the rebellious Bohemian nobility did not abrogate the essential right of the estates to approve taxation.

The protected constitutional position of the nobility was usually weakened in the seventeenth century. This position was first weakened in religious wars. As mentioned, during the religious wars, military funding often escaped constitutional control, and some armies became independent corporations, acting almost like mobile states. This position was then further weakened, in a different way, by the growth of standing armies, as, at this time, states consolidated fiscal systems able to support standing

[23] I define the fiscal state as a model of statehood in which the costs of war presuppose the formation of government institutions able to levy increasing revenue, so that war and tax become the primary causes of institutional design (see Bonney and Ormrod 1999: 2).
[24] See pp. 51–52, 68.

armies that reduced the constitutional authority of the nobility. Standing armies were initially recruited through the imposition of increased fiscal burdens on aristocratic estates, which had to be approved through complex transactions between regents and members of the nobility. Progressively, however, regents learned to finance standing armies by establishing instruments for fiscal extraction that permitted them to dispense with express noble approval for the engagement of military forces. In most societies, regents developed techniques to establish taxes with protracted effect, to obtain which recurrent authorization by noble estates was not required, and such taxes formed the basis to support standing armies. This began, proto-typically, in France. In 1439, Charles VII asserted his authority to raise some annual national taxes without specific consent, which meant that the autonomy of the monarchical executive grew proportionately (Marchadier 1904: 131; Wolfe 1972: 33, 51; Lynn 1997: 22). In France, tax laws were subsequently signed into force by the royal courts, the *parlements*, which meant that (with interruptions) the nobility retained some control over public finance. However, the constitutional authority of noble estates was restricted by the weakening of their power to legislate over monetary supply. This process culminated after the 1660s, when the extraction of taxes was placed under tighter royal control. Eventually, similar patterns of extraction were copied across Europe, usually after 1648. From 1653, a new fiscal order was established for the estates in Brandenburg, greatly limited their political powers, such that the monarchy was able to rule without convening full representative assemblies. This proved central to the later consolidation of the Prussian state. In East Prussia, taxes were raised without approval by the noble estates from 1673. Throughout the Holy Roman Empire, an Edict of 1654 declared that all estates had an obligation to provide funds for military purposes. In addition, the constitutional weakening of aristocratic power was reflected in the increased introduction of permanent levies, often in the form of *indirect taxes*, which created revenue for ruling executives without the need to obtain the agreement of estates.[25] This phenomenon is frequently analysed as a distinctive hallmark of the early modern state, and it should be judged with nuance. Indirect taxes were not the sole instrument for securing

---

[25] For analysis of this process at different junctures and in different settings, see Bornhak (1884: 251, 408–409); Schmidt (1980: 88); Brewer (1989: 99–100); Beckett and Turner (1990: 378); Winnige (1996: 61); Lynn (1997: 22); Sahm (2019: 5–7). In some contexts, indirect taxes were introduced specifically to support military forces (Inama-Sternegg 1865: 518).

independent fiscal systems to support standing armies. Many states developed complex portfolios for stabilizing their monetary autonomy, including loans, sale of offices, new direct taxes, subsidies in times of war, permanently serviced debts (Root 1987; 25; Brewer 1989: 126; Asch 1999). Moreover, indirect taxes had been used to finance war long before the seventeenth century. Yet, indirect taxation became an increasingly common means of revenue extraction after 1648, and it meant that regents could impose some forms of taxation without the support of their noble compatriots.

As a result, in much of Europe, the expansion of standing armies meant that aristocratic estates forfeited a portion of their constitutional power.[26] In most polities, the weakening of the estates led, not to the uncompensated political demotion, but to the functional displacement and modified accommodation of the nobility. Regents typically preserved collaborative relations with noble estates, and intricate forms of dependency and clientelism connected regents and nobility throughout the later *ancien régime*. One analysis of this process explains that the standard governmental system in Europe around 1700 was based in the 'reciprocal exchange of goods and services between monarchy and aristocracy' (Lemarchand 2011: 176). The assumption that government in early modern Europe created a unilaterally beneficial system of 'absolutism', in which one ruler simply eradicated all counterweights to royal power, is one of the great myths of modern historiography. As mentioned, the period associated with 'absolutism' was, in many settings, one in which the nobility experienced a resurgence of power. This period intensified the force of feudal law within private noble domains, expressed in tightened control over serfs and imposition of forced-labour regimes. It was only around 1750 that, in different parts of Europe, the powers of the aristocracy within its estates came under concerted attack by national rulers. In many respects, the governmental orders created after 1650 were based in an arrangement of mutual constitutional benefit, in which the political privileges withdrawn from the nobility through the growth of standing armies were transmuted, as compensation, into fiscal, jurisdictional and professional privileges. Yet, as a general tendency, many polities in the long seventeenth century developed constitutional orders, in which estates with traditional military roles lost the power directly to shape legislation.

The fact hardly needs emphasis that there were important national variations in these processes. In England and the Dutch Republic, fiscal

---

[26] See, for commentary, Isaacsohn (1874: 75, 158); Hanse (1979: 456); Willems (1984: 26); Nowosadtko (2011: 20).

systems were created that did not restrict the representation of estates in parliamentary bodies. England saw the growth of a standing army in the later seventeenth and eighteenth century, but the role of parliamentary bodies in approving taxation was not uniformly weakened, which oiled negotiations between monarch and parliament. The parliamentary system in England was sustained by certain rather unusual factors. In particular, it was beneficially affected by relatively low levels of military integration, and by the early emergence of an exchange economy and a banking system able to provide loans for the government (Brewer 1989: 43–45, 182; Carruthers 1996: 77). The latter factor depended centrally on forced labour, as the banking system in England developed, in part, to service slave traders (Inikori 2002: 361). Across Europe, therefore, each constitutional system had its foundation – directly or indirectly – in forced labour. In its typical form, however, the early modern European state was based in a constitutional model, unique in modern history, in which legal obligations and military obligations were not permanently conjoined. This model ensured that persons with power linked to provision of military force lost some constitutional importance in legislative processes. The power to determine the legitimacy of legislation was partly removed from actors with constitutional positions supported by war.

Second, this separation of the legal system and the military system was reflected in the fact that, in the early modern state, both systems underwent separate processes of formalization, and both were organized around more uniform and consistent legal principles. The systematic organization of civil law in the early modern period has been described earlier.[27] However, the rise of standing armies also led to the increased ordering of military law, which was intended to weaken the independent authority of military leaders. In seventeenth-century France, for example, royal *intendants d'armée* were appointed to supervise and manage armies in different regions. The military *intendants* assumed some judicial functions regarding military activities, and one of their duties was to prevent military lawlessness in society (Dareste 1855a: 45; Baxter 1976: 201).[28] Indeed, early military *intendants* were often of bourgeois origin, and they were recruited by the monarchy to curb the powers exercised by members of the aristocracy in the army (Milot 1968: 392). Through the appointment of such *intendants*, military

---

[27] See p. 25.
[28] Functions of the military *intendants* included overseeing supplies, negotiating contracts, receiving complaints about the behaviour of troops, some judicial observation, overseeing inspection of criminality (Rowlands 2002: 94–95).

functions were partly assimilated into an early system of administrative oversight. By the eighteenth century, more generally, military law was viewed as part of public law, as *jus publicum militare*, distinct from the more traditional *jus militare* which had historically formed part of a customary law of nations (Keen 1965: 15). In the earlier part of the century, French military laws were increasingly published in systematic compilations, described as military codes. In eighteenth-century Prussia, military law was defined in general categories of public law, as the body of laws 'that establish the rights and obligations of territorial lords among themselves and between themselves and their subjects' (Müller 1760: 13). Central to such processes was the insistence that military articles, originally agreed between members of particular units, should be established on publicly binding premises, so that they could be enforced by regents.[29] In some contemporary treatises, it was stipulated that military articles had to be separated from corporate oaths and aligned to formal military laws, so that military activity was directly assimilated in the jurisdictional order of the state (Laurentius 1757: 93–94). Military treatises also defined conditions under which soldiers could be recruited, and they were intended to ensure that the recruitment contract formed an official obligation between the recruited soldier and the regent which was subject to legal control (see Müller 1760: 86, 104).

Third, this separation of the legal system and the military system was reflected in the fact that, in most European polities, instruments for military financing were subject to a more centralized system of regulation. In Prussia, as mentioned, powers of military, fiscal and general administrative oversight were partly fused by the early eighteenth century (Schmoller 1921: 90). This meant that the apparatus for generating military revenues was subject to guarded official scrutiny. In *ancien-régime* France, financial *intendants* were appointed to oversee tax collection for military purposes, so that the management of military revenue was placed under a uniform system of administrative control. Generally, a range of *intendants* were appointed in France, amongst which *intendants* with specific military roles formed one category. *Intendants* were official functionaries, whose duty was to ensure that core domains of public administration –

---

[29] Compilers of military law in German states stressed that military articles should be treated as statutes (Müller 1760: 17). Such articles were accorded obligatory force regardless of whether soldiers had sworn an oath to recognize them (Gnügen 1750: 5). This implied that military activities were constitutionally subject to the state, and companies did not possess any autonomous constitutional footing.

especially fiscal and military administration – were conducted in accordance with royal directives. A primary purpose of the *intendants* was to organize an administrative system that weakened the power of the judicial *parlements*, which traditionally represented interests of the aristocracy and tended to express opposition to mandatory taxation. In fact, the *parlements* led early aristocratic revolts against the centralizing plans of the French monarchy, culminating in the *Fronde* that began in 1648, and one of their main demands was the suppression of the *intendants* (Dareste 1855a: 28). The use of *intendants*, thus, was intended to limit the constitutional power of the aristocracy in questions relevant to military finance, and to create a fiscal regime to support the army as a free-standing domain.[30] This endeavour was not ultimately successful, and the French *parlements* eventually re-emerged as opponents of central government and indeed as powerful stimulants of revolution.[31] Nonetheless, *intendants* played an important role in creating a regulatory order, in which procedures for expressing constitutional hostility to military taxation were weakened. Overall, the administrative system of early modern states resulted from pressures caused by military finance, and, in its basic structure, the administrative state came into being because of war. However, the expansion of the state administration meant that vital official functions were withheld from actors with constitutional authority originally arising from war.

Significant in this respect is the fact that, as they sought to separate the administration of taxation from bodies close to the nobility, early modern states began to design alternative, internal procedures by which their functions could be evaluated and legitimated. In some instances, the endeavour to separate public functions from constitutional control by the nobility was accompanied by the growth of a rudimentary body of administrative law.

In France, some procedures for appealing against decisions of public agents, especially in fiscal matters, existed well before the Revolution. Through the later eighteenth century, the *intendants* were increasingly subject to norms of individual accountability, their acts and decisions could be appealed to bodies attached to the *Conseil du roi*, the highest administrative tribunal of the realm, and their rulings were more frequently overturned (Dareste 1855b: 244; Mestre 1999: 94; Pigeon 2011: 232). By the late 1770s, an early system of administrative review was

---

[30] See Frauenholz (1940: 8); Burschel (1994: 318); Pröve (1995: 192). One historian explains how the formation of separate military courts ran parallel to the reduction of aristocratic power over military financing and recruitment (Winter 2005: 202).
[31] See p. 63.

created for regulating public agents, and a separate committee with jurisdictional functions in fiscal appeals, the *Comité contentieux des finances*, was attached to the *Conseil du roi*.[32] At this time, the office of the financial *intendant* was temporarily abolished. The institution of these procedures followed a short attempt in the early 1770s to suspend the ancient *parlements*, which, as mentioned, had historically assumed responsibility for scrutinizing taxation laws, tending to represent interests with a strong noble bias. In eighteenth-century Prussia, the capacity of courts to oversee appeals relating to administrative functions remained weak. In 1749, an Edict was passed to delineate the boundaries of competence between judicial and administrative bodies. This placed very strict limits on the type of claims that could be initiated against agents of the state, and it ensured that matters relating to taxation and the military were not subject to judicial appeal (Loening 1914: 77). However, this period saw the establishment of designated judicial institutions, *Kammerjustizdeputationen*, with some (limited) powers of control in public matters. This period also witnessed the creation of a series of specialized administrative courts, regulating, for instance, tobacco sales and import taxes (Bornhak 1885: 262–263).

To be clear, the normative orders that began to emerge in eighteenth-century Europe should not be seen as strict legal frameworks for regulating public authority. However, some mechanisms of administrative control emerged at this time, as public administration expanded and public officials were increasingly subject to formal appellate procedures. In its most vital constitutional focus, early administrative law developed as a system of internal scrutiny within the state, especially relating to agents with fiscal duties. One function of this system, naturally, was to create a legal order that made it possible for regents to extract taxation more effectively, and to weaken the impact of administrative malfeasance on revenue supply. Yet, in addition, early procedures for administrative control had a crucial legitimational role for the polity as a whole. These procedures served to signal that governmental bodies were supervised by internal norms and office-holders, and they projected an image of government as a consistently rule-bound aggregate of functions. This meant that the state was able publicly to curtail its dependence on external actors for its legitimacy, and it displaced scrutiny of public acts from

---

[32] See discussion in Logette (1964); Antoine (2003: 519). On the functions of the *Conseil du roi* in exercising administrative jurisdiction, see Dareste (1855b: 254). For discussion of administrative law before the Revolution, see Mestre (1976: 141); Bigot (1999: 489–490); Pigeon (2011: 232).

external assemblies to internal review procedures, thus further weakening traditional counterweights to governmental authority. The origins of administrative law can be traced to a context in which princely executives attempted to exclude the nobility from positions of external constitutional influence. Tellingly, in both France and Prussia, the growth of administrative law began, around 1750, in a period in which the conciliatory approach of the government towards noble privileges was waning, and it was promoted as part of an endeavour to increase the revenue of the state. In France, as mentioned, the expansion of administrative oversight coincided with the suspension of the *parlements*, and with attempts to consolidate a uniform fiscal system. In Prussia, the introduction of administrative courts coincided with a (limited) drive to increase fiscal revenue and with policies to improve the legal and economic position of serfs. Important legislation to protect peasants from expansion of feudal tenure was introduced in Prussia in 1749 and 1764 (Knapp 1927:130). In each case, early administrative law was enforced as a distinct constitutional order, acting to place the legitimacy of government on new premises at a time when the nobility was being removed from its traditional constitutional roles. Early administrative law clearly reflected the separation of the legal system from the military system. It allowed the legal system to establish legitimacy for government without dependence on traditionally powerful corporations with constitutional positions tied to war.

Fourth, as discussed, this separation of the legal system and the military system was reflected in the fact that eighteenth-century governments developed a normative conceptual diction to explain their legitimacy that diminished the importance of constitutional agreements with external actors. In this period, the assumption was promoted that public acts of legislation acquired legitimacy if they were proportioned to formal principles of natural law. This assumption contained the implication that the legitimacy of law resulted from higher norms, external to the state, and law demonstrated legitimacy through the fact that it was applied in universal form, without regard for the personality or the standing of its addressees. By the late eighteenth century, this emphasis on universality began, tentatively, to establish the secondary principle that law must recognize persons as individual subjects in society, and persons bound by law must be seen as holders of certain subjective rights.

As discussed, principles of natural law were expressed in philosophies of state in the eighteenth century, which defined the exercise of governmental power as justified by the degree to which it recognized persons subject to power as holders of equal natural rights.[33] These principles also informed the administrative organization of most eighteenth-century states. Much natural law theory implied that the state is legitimated by the fact that it discharges a series of naturally ordained functions, and that each office of state has a defined role within a natural administrative order. This provided the premise for a conception of public office holding as the exercise of a specific rationally allotted function, subject to norms of formal accountability.[34] This conception of public office became fundamental to the growth of administrative states, as it was used to demand 'respect and obedience' for office-holders amongst national citizens (Domat 1705b: 160). Principles of natural law were also expressed in practical processes of legal reform and codification in the eighteenth century. Natural law generally played a central role in the systematic ordering of law at this time, and the emphasis on the universal validity of law formed the basis for national legal codes and authoritative accounts of civil law. By the later eighteenth century, as discussed, natural law had begun, incipiently, to instil an individualistic emphasis in processes of legal codification. Indicatively, one of the most important civil law codes created in the eighteenth century, the Prussian Land Law (implemented 1794), reflected some individualistic principles of administrative jurisprudence. In its final form, this code accorded variable legal status to different societal groups. However, this code was the product of a long process of revision. A preliminary version, the *Allgemeines Gesetzbuch für die Preußischen Staaten* (1791), stipulated clearly (Introduction, §79) that 'laws and ordinances of the state should not restrict the natural freedom and rights of citizens any more than is required by the common purpose'. This expressed the very enduring principle that proportionate recognition of the rights of the single legal person forms the primary determinant of legitimate law.

As discussed, the construction of the individual legal subject as the focus of law emerged as a central point in the stabilization of the modern state, and it played a pivotal role in the transformation of modern society into a system of legal integration. The codification of law as a normative corpus applied equally and consistently to individual subjects implied – clearly – that law possessed fixed authority, and it could be imposed on all actors in the same society. Most distinctively, however, the codification of

---

[33] See p. 21.
[34] On the deep inner connection between early administrative law and natural law, see Voltelini (1910: 67); Hellmuth (1985: 17, 279).

law on premises defined by natural law had the consequence that law could be authorized in formal-universal terms, separate from specific agreements with particular groups in society. In this respect, the natural law construct of the legal subject had the decisive importance in the development of modern society that it supported the legitimation of law in a constitutional order that did not require that law extracted authority from external actors. As mentioned, the promotion of the individualistic concept of legal personality coincided with the introduction of policies by national governments to ensure that peasants on noble estates acquired full legal personality, so that they were able to litigate against their masters.[35] In each respect, the consolidation of the individual subject as the basic focus of law articulated a principle in which the traditional mechanisms in which the nobility had influenced the law were rapidly eroded, and through which government officials could forge immediate normative articulations with single persons in society. In other words, the early concept of the person as legal subject took shape as a figure in which the legal system was detached from persons with constitutional positions linked to the military: it described, paradigmatically, the separation of the civil sphere and the military sphere.

In summary, the basic structure of early modern society was defined by two integrally connected processes. First, society was transfigured by the emergence of the legal system as a free-standing system of integration, in which persons in society were incorporated in the same legal order. Second, society was transformed, in intricately related manner, by the reconstruction of the military as a separate system of interaction, in which the ancient constitutional linkage between military force and feudal tenure was finally broken. Both processes reduced the constitutional nexus between legal authority and military power, which was structural for feudal society. The rising autonomy of the law and the increasingly controlled administration of the army were primary features of early modern society, and both phenomena were connected to the increasing centralization and social abstraction of the institutions of government. In both processes, the legitimacy of government, as a system of normative and institutional integration, was articulated in categories that were not originally tied to war. Accordingly, government was able to perform integrational functions with a strong independent

---

[35] On the expansion of rights to bring legal actions amongst peasants in late eighteenth-century Poland, see Von Mises (1902: 71); Kienewicz (1969: 38); on similar processes in Austria, see Link (1949: 47); on Prussia, see Hagen (2002: 651); on France, see Root (1987: 193).

normative foundation. Both these processes were inseparable from the weakening of serfdom. Both processes presupposed the formation of patterns of interaction between social agents and political institutions in which persons communicated with the polity in individualized form, as citizens, reducing the power of intermediary institutions.

Self-evidently, such differentiation of legal and military functions is outlined here in ideal-typical form. The rise of the modern legal system in France and Prussia was only one variant on a more general process. Less militarized societies, such as England, also witnessed the early formation of an individualized legal system in the late eighteenth century.[36] In England, this process was propitiously affected by the fact that the residues of serfdom were weaker than in other parts of Europe, and levels of military expenditure were lower. The promotion of legal inclusion was achieved within an existing constitutional system. Moreover, across Europe, the military system and the legal system long remained interlocked with other institutional forms. Moreover, neither of these processes of differentiation approached completion in the early modern context. Pre-1789 polities did not typically see the eradication of the judicial powers of the nobility.[37] In France, for example, administration of justice in lower courts remained a seigneurial right throughout the *ancien régime*, and the royal courts were populated through sale of offices to the nobility until 1789. In Prussia, the process of legal codification in the eighteenth century preserved many aristocratic privileges. In both settings, it would be illusory to imagine that uniform patterns of legal subjectivity emerged at this time. In Prussia, further, high-ranking military posts were, as discussed, almost closed to non-nobles. Up to 1790, military posts in France were, despite repeated attempts to prohibit such venality, still acquired by transaction.[38] It cannot, therefore, be plausibly claimed that the army formed a fully differentiated social domain. Despite this, however, most European societies in the eighteenth century witnessed the early construction of the law as a system based in general

---

[36] Early protections for individual persons were established in English law at this time. See Entick v. Carrington [1765] EWHC KB J98.

[37] See the analysis in Blum (1978: 387); Carey (1981: 108–109); Hayhoe (2008: 135); Wienfort (2001: 80–117).

[38] Venal office holding in the army was forbidden in the *Code Michau* of 1629. It was again prohibited in 1776. It was finally prohibited in Art. 9 of the *Décret sur la constitution militaire* (28 February 1790). One account stresses how the consolidation of the French army originally relied on acceptance of venality, as an incentive for recruitment of officers (Rowlands 2002: 167).

principles of validity and the organization of the army as a system with restricted legitimational impact on other governmental functions.

What this meant – in the final analysis – is that, in many settings, the modern state was internally divided into two functional systems: the legal system and the military system, and each system began to acquire its own distinct regulatory order. The legal system obtained, in broad terms, a *judicial constitution*, in which the government organized institutions for legislation and enforcement of legislation. In the long eighteenth century, only limited distinction was made between legislative and judicial functions, and the responsibility of the sovereign for 'administration of justice' was not separable from 'the right to make laws and necessary regulations for the public good' (Domat 1705b: 10).[39] The military system obtained a *military constitution*, in which military functions were internally regulated and separated from institutions with other obligations. Historically, these two systems had been connected by the aristocracy, which had usually been able to harden its influence on the creation and application of the law in times when the polity was externally pressurized, and which typically monopolized institutions for legal enforcement in society. Towards the end of the European *ancien régime*, however, the impact of external wars on domestic law-making processes was weakened. The civil dimension and the military dimension of the state were more clearly demarcated, and both assumed distinct constitutional form.[40] As discussed, this separation was partly caused by the fact that after 1648 interstate wars became less encompassing. However, this separation also occurred because the aristocracy lost constitutional power and legislative influence tied to military recruitment processes. As a result, the military apparatus was primarily connected to the legal system through the executive institutions of the state, usually controlled by single regents or dynastic families, their advisors and their administrators. This meant that the modern state developed principles of legitimacy that specifically reflected and hardened the separation of law and war, and it was able to conduct processes of normative integration

---

[39] For analysis of the 'corollary' link between judicial and legislative functions at this time, see Antoine (1970: 17).

[40] One brilliant analysis explains how the early modern state developed through the separation of the 'civil state' and the 'military state' (Leonhard 2008: 77). For similar arguments, see Rink (1999: 42). An alternative account describes how the modern army was 'constructed on the principle of the separation of the military from civil society' (Guinier 2014: 171). One interpretation describes the 'differentiation of society in a "civil" and a "military" sphere as the core feature of early modern life' (Rink 2010: 68).

separate from war. This is visible in the reliance of eighteenth-century states on principles of natural law, which enabled them to project legitimacy in categories separate from war. This is visible in the fact that persons in society were increasingly integrated in the state as individual rights holders, or at least as holders of basic subjective entitlements. In each respect, the legitimacy of the state was transferred from the nobility as a collective constitutional actor to the individual legal subject. This transformation replicated the transformation of military contracts that occurred at the same time, as the construct of the citizen as a subject under public law mirrored the construct of the soldier as a person bound to the state by public contract. Both soldier and citizen took form at this time as individuals immediately linked to the state by public legal norms. This process of individualization hinged on the constitutional separation of war and law.

As examined, the deep trajectory that shaped modern society is the construction of society as a system of legal integration, in which the uniform production of legal norms and the expansion of state institutions into society occurred as conjoined elements of a basic integrational process. In much of Europe, this process was accelerated in the eighteenth century. The period of state construction in the seventeenth and eighteenth century is habitually reviled as a period of 'absolutist' or authoritarian government. As discussed, this view is justified by the fact that traditional representative mechanisms were weakened in many states (see Downing 1992: 10–11). However, this period can be viewed as one in which the basic focus of citizenship construction was redirected and, in some ways, expanded. At this time, many states lowered constitutional recognition of citizens as active corporate agents, represented, for fiscal purposes, in assemblies and parliaments. This reduced the historically protected powers of members of the nobility, who, as providers of military resources, had been the primary beneficiaries of such representative bodies. In parallel, however, as their fiscal reliance on the nobility decreased, states began to establish legal systems that applied immediately to all persons, and to solidify principles of citizenship that benefited persons positioned outside the aristocracy and promoted more general patterns of legal integration.

As discussed, such processes of legal integration originally depended on the construct of the citizen as an individual legal subject, with a personality recognized under law. At one level, the construct of the legal person promoted an integrational form for law and government because it set out a positive source of legitimacy for law. At a different level, the construct of the legal subject deepened the integrational force of law and government because it separated law's authority from the ancient military class, standing outside the legal system. Through the construct of the individual legal person, the law, in its legitimational origin, was separated from collective actors, and *demilitarized*. This construct expanded the integrational force of law because it created normative premises on which the state could legislate in an independent constitutional form, not dictated by persons with influence derived from the military. At core, the integrational focus of modern society, the individual citizen as uniform legal subject, was crystallized as an expression of deep structural forces in society. It was created as part of a broader impulse to differentiate legal and military functions, to eradicate military violence from society and to subject violence to legal-political control. The legitimational construct that first underpinned the rise of the modern state and the expansion of modern law was configured through the differentiation of the legal system and the military system. This construct underpinned the transformation of society as a whole into its first integrational form. The initial integrational form of modern society was established by the construction of the citizen as a point of normative attribution, a *functional norm*, which detached law from war.

Early Democracy and Social Militarization

The transformation of state, law and society in early modern Europe was conducted around a two-tiered concept of citizenship, in which persons in society were recognized as inhabitants of an increasingly uniform territory and as individual subjects holding some procedural rights and some rights of legal recognition. Notable in these processes, however, is the fact that this thin, legal pattern of citizenship did not ultimately produce a principle of legitimacy for law that was able to translate the law into a universal medium of social integration. As discussed later, the form of early modern society contained a structural paradox which made comprehensive legal-political integration impossible. The legal system in early modern society was founded increasingly in normative principles oriented towards individual integration, serving to place the law on public footing and to attach law's authority directly to the sovereign state. However, the legal construct of the citizen that sustained the legal system was not sufficiently robust – finally – to abstract the law against historical centres of private authority.

The vital stage in the transformation of society into a system of general legal integration occurred as an additional layer of meaning was attached to the concept of the citizen. This took place as a distinct vocabulary of citizenship began to emerge, in which the citizen appeared as a claimant to *political rights*: that is, to rights exercised through participation in governmental decision-making, enabling citizens not only to acquire formal-subjective recognition in law, but also to influence directly the production of law. As discussed, the revolutionary polities founded in America and France between 1776 and 1795 differed from earlier governments in that they cemented the principle that law was legitimated by institutionalized cycles of electoral communication between the people and government. In key respects, this political aspect of citizenship formed the wellspring of modern constitutionalism and modern ideas of political legitimacy more widely. The expectation that laws trace their origin back to the acts of citizens and that the collective will of citizens must be defined as the origin of legitimate law is the principle that separates modern constitutional order from the regulatory patterns of legal codification that occurred in the decades before 1789. Indeed, modern constitutionalism as a whole can be understood as a diction for constructing state legitimacy that results from the fusion of two lines of legitimational reflection, articulated in two concepts of the citizen. One line expresses the principle that legitimate government is framed in a codified judicial and administrative order which recognizes citizens as holders of formal subjective rights. One line expresses the conviction that legitimate government manifests the will of politically active citizens. This fusion of legal codification and popular self-legislation stands at the centre of modern constitutional thinking. These two distinct constructs of citizenship were galvanized in the revolutionary *époque*, especially in America and France.

In most social environments, as discussed, the modern figure of the citizen, possessing shared political rights, took shape as a construct that was deeply shaped by underlying social processes, and it both reflected and intensified the trajectories that had begun to define modern society. This figure appeared, most specifically, as a construct that supported the integrational functions of modern society, enabling society to consolidate normative and administrative structures beyond the local boundaries of pre-modern social order. As discussed, the formation of citizenship on an early democratic design led to the dramatic acceleration of the processes of centralization and integration attached to the legal figure of the citizen that had already shaped early modern society.

Despite this, the projection of the citizen as the active author of legislation cannot be seamlessly aligned to pre-existing patterns of social formation and integration. On the contrary, the political aspect of citizenship expressed in the revolutionary period contradicted, and, in some ways, unsettled the integrational trajectories that had begun to acquire established form in early modern societies. The normative figure of the active political citizen had a number of conflicting, or dialectical, societal outcomes. Over a longer period of time, the projective structuring of law around political citizenship that occurred between 1776 and 1795 created normative conflicts that deeply destabilized the emergent integrational form of society. This figure simultaneously promoted and impeded the formation of modern society as a system of integration, and it both set the foundations for, yet also obdurately eroded, the integrational grammar required to capture the constituencies of national society. This dialectical content of the modern concept of the citizen is strongly connected to the implications of active citizenship for the second system of integration, whose formation had shaped the development of early modern society – the system of military activity.

As examined, up to the late eighteenth century, the progressive construction of the law as an integrational system had depended on the partial separation of the law's authority from actors with constitutional roles anchored in military functions. This separation of law and war was reliant, necessarily, on the construction of an effective fiscal system, in which regents extracted sufficient revenue from society to ensure that military necessities could be met without recurrent political consultation with corporate organizations that represented the aristocracy. As mentioned, the consolidation of the law on individualistic premises was inseparable from the consolidation of a public fiscal system. Both processes created the prerequisites for a system of state authority not determined by the nobility. Consequently, the national fiscal system usually evolved, in parallel to the legal apparatus and the military administration, as a third constitutional domain in the emergence of European polities and societies. The relative separation of civil and military organizations within the early modern state was contingent, centrally, on the capacity of the state to organize fiscal extraction in a viable constitutional order, in order to raise and maintain costly independent standing armies.

As in other social spheres, this process of fiscal ordering remained incipient in the eighteenth century. As mentioned, the rising assertion of fiscal sovereignty by national states was often accompanied by the reinforcement of neo-feudal powers within noble estates. In

Brandenburg-Prussia, indicatively, the fiscal agreements required to finance a standing army had first been sealed in 1653. In effect, however, this arrangement formed a pact between the Hohenzollern dynasty and the Brandenburg estates which was very beneficial for the nobility. In this arrangement, on one side, the estates granted increased fiscal sovereignty to the prince, and, on the other side, the prince heightened the powers of the aristocracy in its domains and guaranteed the fiscal exemptions of the nobility.[41] Similar fiscal exemptions for the nobility were mirrored across much of Europe in the seventeenth and eighteenth centuries.[42] In France, the fact that the aristocracy retained judicial influence meant that it possessed a strong instrument to defend its fiscal privileges. As a result, the extractive force of national governments was always limited, as the nobility was exempt from many taxes. In England, the reinforcement of parliament after 1689 meant that the aristocracy was, in essence, co-opted into a new fiscal constitution, after the crisis caused by enforced monetary extraction in the 1630s.

Despite such variations and qualifications, the period between 1648 and 1789 saw endeavours in most European polities to place the fiscal system on constitutionally independent foundations. As discussed, the motivation for this was that a strong fiscal system allowed the state to weaken its ties to the nobility, to increase the legislative autonomy of the government, and to minimize the impact of military calculations on the legislative constitution of state. Fiscal extraction was promoted, in essence, as a means of concentrating military power in the state and of providing general insurance against the social costs of war. By establishing such insurance, state institutions were able both increasingly to legitimate and to extend their sovereign political force.

By the late eighteenth century, however, national fiscal constitutions in much of Europe were subject to strain. This strain was caused, first, by the essential precondition of the modern state – it arose from the costs incurred by growing standing armies. However, this strain was caused, more specifically, by the fact that, in most polities, regents had only been able to arrogate powers of fiscal sovereignty on condition that they upheld many economic privileges and exemptions of the nobility, allowing members of the aristocracy to control the agricultural economy in their estates. The preservation of serfdom that was guaranteed through this

---

[41] On the privileges reserved for the aristocracy in Prussia, see Isaacsohn (1884: 76–77); Schmoller (1921: 56); Schwennicke (1996: 319).
[42] On France, see Kwass (2000: 23–29).

compromise meant that the largest groups in society shouldered disproportionately high tax burdens, it obstructed increases in agricultural productivity, and it generally curtailed the revenue-generating capacity of productive labour. On each count, the post-1648 state was built around fiscal and constitutional premises, designed to solidify the basic sovereignty of the state, which persistently limited the extent to which the state could obtain revenue from, or in fact legislate against the interests of, noble families. Through the eighteenth century, the cost of standing armies weighed heavily on the fiscal resources of European states. In such situations, states were unable to generate sufficient revenue to cover their costs, and the bargains that they had entered with the nobility in order to maintain standing armies exacerbated their financial weakness. Ultimately, the basic preconditions on which regents established their sovereignty reduced the integrational force of state institutions. In fact, by the late eighteenth century, many states began to alter the constitutional terms of their negotiation with traditional suppliers of taxation, the nobility, such that some regents began to surrender their sovereignty to the corporate bodies from which they had originally taken it, or tried to take it. In many late eighteenth-century polities, the nobility resumed its position as a core constitutional actor, at times with acutely destabilizing results.[43] This was most manifest in pre-revolutionary France. The meeting of the Estates-General that instigated the 1789 Revolution had been prompted by an Assembly of Notables, organized to address the parlous fiscal situation of the monarchy. This Assembly worked in partial alliance with the *parlements*, ancient bastions of noble interest, and the *parlements* used the opportunity opened by the Assembly to strengthen their opposition to royal taxation (Kwass 2000: 274). In most eighteenth-century societies, however, the constitutional arrangements required to stabilize the sovereign state against the aristocracy brought the state towards fiscal crisis. The fiscal systems created in the eighteenth century contained deep structural weaknesses, largely caused by persistent privileging of the aristocracy.

The underlying problem in this constellation was that emergent territorial states organized their interactions with society by recognizing persons in society as legal subjects, with basic shared protections under law. This concept formed the essential lever for the reinforcement of central government. However, early territorial states were unable to impose this

---

[43] In France, the eighteenth century saw a rapid growth in the number of nobles (Blum 1978: 15–16). On the general re-emergence of noble estates in the eighteenth century, see Gehrke (2005: 2).

construction deeply in society, and their failure to establish a uniform legal order was especially evident in the fiscal domain. Contemporary observers of *ancien-régime* states identified these problems very perspicaciously. Many theorists of government and political economy in the eighteenth century claimed that the weak fiscal constitution of their states could only be remedied if governments imposed a system of universal legal integration on their populations, and if this system were enforced, specifically, to limit fiscal privileges. Indeed, knowledge of this potential solution for fiscal crisis was implied in much government policy. The plans designed by early modern governments to stabilize their fiscal constitutions typically contained an attempt to restrict status variations adversely affecting royal revenue, and they were intended to impose uniform legal duties across all society. In France, indicatively, the latter part of the eighteenth century witnessed numerous plans for both agrarian and commercial reform. The same period saw a series of endeavours to improve the individual legal standing of peasants (Root 1987: 193). It also saw the promotion of several far-reaching policies, notably in 1763, to establish the basis for universal taxation (Kwass 2000: 181; Decroix 2006: 183, 228). The demand for uniform taxation was prominent amongst complaints registered against the monarchy before 1789 (see Norberg 1994: 294). At the same time, both Prussia and some Habsburg domains witnessed agrarian reforms, including measures to establish full legal personality for serfs, which were directly driven by fiscal imperatives (see Link 1949: 26; Kaak 1991: 76–77, 411; Reinhard 1996: 307). In each case, the basic construct of the person as legal subject was shaped by the need to imprint a flat taxation regime on society. The construction of the individual person as legal subject again acted as a primary source of effective state sovereignty. Although these problems were commonly identified, however, simple solutions were not implemented. In most eighteenth-century societies, members of the nobility utilized monarchical weakness to reassert their traditional privileges, either by tightening their grip on their domains or by seeking renewed protection for their prerogatives within the state. In key cases, members of the nobility drew profit from processes of legal and economic individualization promoted by regents. They utilized such processes as an opportunity to weaken their obligations towards the peasantry and to reinforce their seigneurial rights in land at the same time.[44] The construction of taxation regimes based in individual legal obligation proved very elusive.

---

[44] For classical analysis of this process in France, see Saint Jacob (1960: 414); Van den Heuvel (1980: 79).

By the late eighteenth century, in short, the three pillars on which the post-1648 state had begun to acquire form, the military constitution, the legal/judicial constitution, and the fiscal constitution, had become haphazardly interlocked. Pressures on the military system produced chronically unsettling pressures within other constitutional dimensions of the polity. In acute cases, such as Poland and France, the incapacity of rulers to construct generalized models of citizenship, linked to general fiscal obligations, led to the collapse of the state, either by occupation in Poland or by revolution in France. The deep constitutional crises that afflicted many European states were caused, at a profound level, by the fact that societies were emerging as systems of integration, legitimated by the construction of laws on public premises: as laws authorized by *legal subjects*. These subjects supported the formation of centralized institutions, with centralized fiscal regimes. They also promoted the consolidation of a legal system able to abstract itself against particular persons. Yet, many polities in the eighteenth century lacked the institutional capacity to enforce recognition of individual legal subjectivity and to consolidate general conditions of integration through society. Where they attempted to impose such integrational conditions, they induced unsettling resistance. This became most apparent in the fiscal domain.

It was in this deep integrational and constitutional crisis that the legitimational figure of the modern political citizen emerged, gaining exemplary form in the French Revolution and the American Revolution. In each setting, the modern construct of the citizen acquired shape within political systems that had been bankrupted, or brought close to bankruptcy, by the cost of standing armies, or in which the financing of standing armies provoked deep hostility.[45] This conjuncture created the social opening in which the construct of the modern political citizen, attached to the sovereign people, became a vital source of legal norms. This construct was established as a new category of legal personhood, which provided normative justification for law that was strong enough to break through conventional resistance to fiscal equality. This construct thus established an integrational norm of legal personality that was able finally to separate the law from the influence of the nobility. One leading historian of the French Revolution explains that political power was transferred to 'the sovereign nation' in Versailles in 1789 as part of a plan for resolving financial crisis (Sonenscher 1997: 70). In its first

---

[45] See general analysis in Neugebauer (2003: 230). On this nexus in Prussia, see Vogel (1981: 40); Schissler (1982: 382). On France, see Kwass (2004: 1).

articulation, the concept of the citizen as sovereign actor impacted on governmental structures by placing the fiscal system on new footing, and eradicating counterweights to the effective authority of the state. At this time, the idea that each person in society should be construed as an equal person, actively linked to government, appeared as a legal solution for the weak integrational force of government, reflected in fiscal problems caused by military financing.

The extent to which the figure of the modern citizen articulated strains in the integrational structure of society can be clearly seen in the terms in which political rights of citizenship were first demanded and exercised.

The modern political citizen acquired a voice, first, in protests over taxation, as a figure demanding greater consideration and representation in the fiscal domain. In most settings, early political citizenship took shape because citizens rejected perceived iniquities in existing taxation regimes, and they claimed the right to participate actively in representative procedures to decide on fiscal policies. Consequently, citizenship was first expressed as a demand for collective influence on the fiscal constitution of society. This was axiomatic for the development of citizenship in all revolutionary settings of the eighteenth century. Accordingly, each revolutionary upheaval of this *époque* created fiscal regimes in which public spending was more strictly controlled by elected bodies and popular representatives (Bosher 1970: 219). In each case, the construction of citizenship enhanced the fiscal security of government.[46] The modern citizen gained voice, second, as a figure that negated formal legal privilege, especially privilege in governmental taxation, and that demanded equality before the law for all. At one level, this aspect of revolutionary citizenship intensified existing plans to consolidate legal uniformity across society. However, this aspect of citizenship acquired particular force in the common fiscal crisis of the late eighteenth century. Revolutionary demands for equality under law were usually reflected in reforms to the legal system that reduced legal status distinctions. In most states shaped by revolutionary citizenship, legal reforms were imposed that promoted greater legal uniformity in fiscal matters, so that taxation was construed as a general obligation which was equally binding (in principle) on all. Through this, all, or at least most, persons, were defined as fiscal subjects who were integrated in an immediate legal-economic

---

[46] On increased taxation in revolutionary France, see Lefebvre (1971: 581) and Norberg (1994: 264). On the creation of a stable system of public finance thereafter, see Bosher (1970: 317–318).

relation to the state.[47] On each count, the emergence of political citizenship was inseparable from the fiscal weakness of early modern states, and its primary outcome was to create a legal/political order that responded to and assuaged fiscal crises. The modern political citizen, in short, created the basis for a new fiscal constitution.

A fact that becomes striking in this analysis is that, in its relevance for the fiscal constitution of society, the construct of the political citizen possessed implications that extended beyond taxation policies. Indeed, owing to its origins in fiscal crisis, the construct of the modern citizen was deeply determined by military pressures. As it created the premise for a new fiscal constitution, this construct also, inevitably, created the premise for a new military constitution. As mentioned, prior to the revolutionary *époque*, the fiscal constitution of most states had served as a partition between the civil and the military spheres. Changes to the fiscal constitution, therefore, necessarily had deep impact on the military system. Indicatively, early proponents of political citizenship reserved particular hostility for standing armies, which they identified as threats to liberty and as the cause of high fiscal burdens.[48] In most states in which rights of political citizenship were expanded in the revolutionary era, the existing military system was dismantled, and the power of standing armies was reduced. On each count, the rise of modern citizenship deeply modified the existing military constitution. The legitimational construct of the citizen reconfigured the basic terms in which states organized both their fiscal and their military exchanges with society.

The transformation of the military constitution that accompanied the rise of political citizenship had the most enduring impact on modern society. Modern principles of citizenship were, to some degree, a continuous product of the military orders that had evolved in parts of pre-1789 Europe. In some areas, the military apparatus had already pierced deep into everyday life in eighteenth-century society, and military organizations were precursors of national citizenship.[49] However, the rise of modern citizenship around 1789 profoundly modified the

---

[47] On the symbolic importance of uniformity in taxation in revolutionary France, see Kwass (2000: 255–231). In Prussia, certain tax exemptions for the nobility were upheld after 1815, but the definition of taxation as a duty of citizens was established at this time (see Mamroth 1890: 776–777).

[48] Robespierre associated military power repeatedly with 'military despotism' and 'cruel tyranny' (1792b: 34). In America, Madison declared before the Constitutional Convention in 1787 that 'A standing military force, with an overgrown Executive will not long be safe companions to liberty' (Farrand 1911: 464–465).

[49] See p. 84.

position of the military in national society. In key respects, modern citizenship created polities marked by deep discontinuities with earlier patterns of constitutional organization and sociopolitical formation. Most importantly, the rise of political citizenship led to a redirection in the integrational structure of society. The basic differentiation of the military and the civil spheres was weakened through the emergence of the sovereign political citizen as legitimational figure, and both normative and institutional processes underlying modern society were re-attached to the military system. In ways discussed later, the deep linkage between law and war became constitutional for modern society from this point on. In the *ancien régime*, states had tended to integrate their citizens through processes of normative and institutional integration that were, as far as possible, severed from the military domain. This was expressed in the basic construct of the citizen as legal subject. After the revolutionary period, both processes of integration were based in the structural reconnection of war and law, and the constitutional figure of the sovereign citizen standing at the centre of post-revolutionary states distilled a deep nexus between the legal system and the military system.

The Soldat-Citoyen

At the end of the eighteenth century, citizenship acquired a distinctive military dimension, and states legitimated by principles of political citizenship were constructed, intrinsically, on military foundations.

As mentioned, the rise of political citizenship occurred in settings in which traditional mechanisms for raising military finance were collapsing. This meant that states based in citizenship were forced, often very rapidly, to design new techniques for mobilizing troops. This in turn meant, inevitably, that practices of citizenship acquired immediate military relevance, as citizens were integrated in new procedures for recruiting and financing armies. This problem appeared in most pressing form in France after 1789. The various governmental orders formed in revolutionary France were defined by the fact that the Revolution destroyed the fiscal foundations of the *ancien régime*. Consequently, the revolutionary period saw the creation both of new fiscal instruments and of new arrangements, depending on popular sanction, for the engaging and financing of military units. The need to establish such mechanisms was especially potent as, by 1792, the revolutionary polity had entered war with seemingly more powerful European monarchies. War was not the goal of all leaders in revolutionary France. Robespierre was unwilling to declare war on other states. He anticipated with horror that war would cause the reinforcement of 'the executive power', allowing military leaders to 'overthrow the constitution' (1792a: 72).[50] Soon, however, the revolutionary regime in France was involved in war on several fronts, and it assumed a strongly militaristic character. In this situation, its leaders were forced to mobilize armies without a fully consolidated fiscal system. To accomplish this, national armies in the French Revolution were transformed, step by step, from standing mercenary armies into armies created through mass recruitment, and eventually through mandatory military service. The basic contract tying soldiers to the state changed profoundly at this time. The ability to enforce obligatory mobilization of troops became a defining constitutional feature of revolutionary government, replacing existing fiscal arrangements for conducting warfare.[51]

The most apt pattern of constitutional organization for the army was discussed in the first months of the French Revolution. Initially, the revolutionaries adopted the principle of voluntary engagement, and a professional army was retained (Wohlfeil 1983: 39). In fact, hostility to mandatory recruitment in the army was salient amongst complaints voiced by opponents of the Bourbon monarchy up to 1789, and aversion to militia service was an important factor in the background to revolution (Grebelon 1882: 259; Corvisier 1964: 118; Crépin 2003: 314). Yet, in the years following 1789, the need to muster large armies became a vital political consideration, and recruitment was eventually conducted through compulsory drafts.[52] This was anticipated as early as December 1789, as Dubois de Crancé, charged with responsibility for military reform, spoke in the National Assembly in favour of a 'truly national' type of military conscription, stating that 'every citizen must be ready at all times to march in defence of his county'.[53] Enrolment in the National Guard, the militias created to defend the Republic, became obligatory for active citizens in 1790. Large-scale voluntary recruitment, focused on active citizens and sons of active citizens, began in 1791, which meant that military engagement and political citizenship became normatively connected (Crépin 1998: 20). Compulsory military obligation

---

[50] One interpreter argues that Robespierre was haunted by military dictatorship (Michon 1920: 301).
[51] On the fiscal origins of military conscription, see Köllner (1982: 37).
[52] This mirrors the third phase in Lynn's typology of military recruitment from high feudalism to early democracy: the shift to the *popular conscript army* (1997: 9).
[53] This speech of 12 December 1789 is printed in *Archives Parlementaires* (1878: 521).

was then prescribed in the Jacobin Constitution of 1793. It was enacted in the first *levée en masse*, also in 1793, which implied a deepened association between national citizenship and military duties.[54] The figure of the soldier and the figure of the citizen entered a strong normative connection at this time, conjoined in the construct of the *soldat-citoyen*. Formal universal conscription was introduced in France in 1798, which transformed military obligations enforced during the Revolution into a more secure legal form and effectively brought the *levée en masse* under sovereign control (see Crépin 2011: 33).

Through these processes, the principles of political citizenship that underpinned the revolutionary polities in France were closely attached to military obligation. At this time, rights of *active citizenship*, entailing entitlement to participate in political elections and, through this, to influence law-making acts, were originally rights allotted to persons who performed military service.[55] Conscription was initially inseparable from active citizenship, and it was through acceptance of military obligation that the citizen first acquired the liberty to exercise political rights (see Hippler 2006: 43, 147). As under feudalism, the military relation became the primary social relation, underpinning and giving rise to core rights and duties. The right to shape the legal order of society was once again construed as a right flowing from the right to bear arms. In these processes, the underlying balance between the societal and the fiscal costs of war, which underpinned the rise of the modern state more broadly, was revised. The creation of armies of conscripted soldiers in the French Revolution meant that blood and tax were reconnected, and conscription served as a military taxation paid in kind.[56] Tellingly, in post-1789 France, military service was often conceived in fiscal terms, and it was expressly intended to offset shortfalls in revenue associated with fiscal crisis. Military service was described, somewhat later, as 'a tax that each family pays in kind to the defence of the country' with 'the character of a personal and local charge for the public interest' (Laferrière 1841: 351–352). In both respects, a concept of citizenship was proposed that specifically rejected

---

[54] Article 109 of the Jacobin Constitution of 1793 declared: 'Tous les Français sont soldats; ils sont tous exercés au maniement des armes.'
[55] As early as 1790, a certain period of unbroken military service was rewarded with full rights of political participation, or active citizenship. See Art. 7 of the *Décret sur la constitution militaire* (28 February 1790).
[56] Military service has often been seen as taxation (Vocke 1903: 1; Lefebvre 1972: 582).

the constitutional terms in which, in early modern societies, the civil and the military spheres had been separated.

Similar linkages between citizenship and military mobilization were visible, with variations, in other polities of the revolutionary era. Clearly, the early American Republic was born in war against Britain, and the recruitment and organization of armies were the first functions of senior figures in the nascent Republic. American society was not militarized to the same degree as some European societies at this time. Legislative frameworks for mandatory recruitment were tested out in the 1790s, but national conscription was not introduced until the Civil War of the 1860s. Even in the Civil War, conscription did not generate large numbers of troops, especially in the armies of the Union.[57] The deep linkage between war and citizenship became fully evident in the United States at a later stage.[58] However, during the revolutionary years, America saw mandatory conscription for state militias and for quotas required by the Continental Army, and military participation formed an important qualification for citizenship.[59] One account argues that the 'armed militia was a civic foundation of the American nation' (Izecksohn 2014: 96). In other parts of revolutionary Europe, French techniques for mass military mobilization became widespread. The popularization of mandatory military service in France was emulated in other countries, especially those defeated by armies created through the *levée en masse* and subsequent conscription. Prussia, for example, did not undergo even partial democratization in the wake of 1789. However, conscription was introduced in Prussia, in various forms, in compulsory recruitment laws passed in 1813-14. In Prussia, conscription was specifically designed to promote ideas of citizenship and national unity, integrating people as soldiers in the state to underpin intensified state construction.[60]

---

[57] Only approximately 5-7 per cent of the Union Army in the Civil War was made up of conscripted recruits (Frank 1998: 7).

[58] See pp. 138-39.

[59] See for comment Kettner (1974); Janowitz (1980: 14); Cress (1982: 51); Duffy (1987: 51); Kestnbaum (2000: 21).

[60] See discussion in Huber (1937b); Händel (1962: 74); Frevert (2001: 36-39). The years 1813-14 witnessed the establishment of the *Landsturm* and the *Landwehr* in Prussia, in which citizenship and mandatory military engagement were closely connected. One analysis claims that the transformation of the subject (*Untertan*) into the citizen (*Staatsbürger*) was the 'basis of the reform' conducted in Prussia after 1806 (Stübig 1971: 193).

Military Legitimacy

For these reasons, the late eighteenth century witnessed a transformation in the essential legitimational fabric of the state. From the revolutionary period onwards, the modern state began to assume form as a type of polity that depended – essentially – on the willingness of citizens to fight for it, and it attached its legitimacy to its capacity to mobilize citizens as combatants. Pre-revolutionary states had construed citizens and soldiers as individual subjects. Revolutionary states demanded military service as part of a collective duty, compensated through the allocation of collective rights of political engagement. Discharge of military service was defined, not as an obligation arising from an individual contract, but as an activity that expressed a deep constitutional bond between government and citizens. Military service was seen as the collective payment of a military debt (blood) to the government, through which soldiers acquired rights formative of citizenship.

In certain respects, again, this construction of the democratic citizen on a military design expressed a certain continuity with the earlier implications of citizenship. In some respects, the conscription laws introduced in revolutionary Europe were influenced by recruitment policies used to fill earlier standing armies. The introduction of conscription was intended, in essence, to create a large-scale military apparatus which was not immediately sensitive to the changing desires and political sentiments of influential families and powerful potential taxpayers. To this degree, conscription intensified the military processes of state building pioneered after 1648, and it accelerated the imposition of a centralized system of fiscal-military control across different parts of society. The idea of the *soldat-citoyen* had existed before the revolutionary period, and the close association of citizenship, political legitimacy and military duties was frequently endorsed by luminaries of the Enlightenment government – notably, Vattel, Rousseau, Justi and Mably.[61] The emergence of mass conscription after 1789 also replicated some previous designs for military reform. As early as the late sixteenth century, influential reformers construed obligatory military service, based in a deep mutual commitment between people and regents, as the premise of good government.[62] The deep linkage between citizenship and military duties had already been expressed in earlier revolutionary

---

[61] See Vattel (1758: 4); Justi (1761: 51); Rousseau (1782); Mably (1783: 199).

[62] The military order (*Landesdefensionsordnung*) of the House of Nassau-Siegen (1590s) reflected distrust of paid soldiers and provided for twice-yearly mustering of troops. This

situations, for example England in the 1640s (Cressy 2006: 68–69).The Militia Ordinance of 1642, which allowed the English parliament to raise troops without royal consent, was in some ways a forerunner of later provisions for revolutionary mobilization.

Nonetheless, the connection between citizenship and military obligation in the revolutionary era placed the polity on legitimational foundations that were clearly distinct from those shaped by earlier lines of citizenship. The growth of extensive military conscription presupposed a more immediate and intense pattern of interaction between the military and society than had existed in earlier states that had maintained standing armies. Mass military conscription after 1789 relied on the willingness of subjects in society to serve the polity in war for personal motivations and obligations – for singularly held loyalties, for sentiments of collective affiliation and for rights and commitments shared with other citizens, often forged in war. As a result, conscription implied that all persons in society were immediately connected to the state, that all persons transferred certain basic liberties to the state and that the force and legitimacy of the state resided, fundamentally, in obligations accepted by all members of society, as a national collective. In this respect, the individual contracts that had sustained military recruitment before 1789 were translated into a collective contract between all society and the state which was binding on all persons. In turn, the expectation of self-sacrifice in combat intensified the lines of immediate dependence between the state and the citizen. In prescribing self-sacrifice, citizenship imposed heightened duties on the state itself, so that the state obtained increased responsibilities for the representation and the welfare of those committed to die for it. In each respect, the relationship between the citizen and the state was tightened, and the citizen brought legitimacy to the state, not simply as the holder of individual legal rights, but as the categorical precondition of the state's authority, or, in effect, as part of the foundation of the state itself. In the revolutionary construct of the citizen, the citizen conferred legitimacy on the state as a collective actor standing within the state, resulting from the state's reliance on citizens as potential combatants. This meant that the citizen and state were brought into unity. The military unity between citizen and state formed the essence of early democracy.

Importantly, the intensity of the link between citizen and state meant that early democratic citizenship was envisaged in *total* categories. On

document is printed in Frauenholz (1939: 47–76). See for comment Hahlweg (1941: 191); Ehlert (1985: 33).

the one hand, possession of rights of national citizenship implied that the citizen formed part of a collective entity, the state, which owned the biological existence of the single person, and rights obtained by persons as citizens arose, in essence, in recognition of a mortal duty of sacrifice.[63] Notably, the obligation to die for the Republic that was instilled in the political souls of soldiers in revolutionary France was defined, not primarily as a duty, but rather, in itself, as a *right*. During the Revolution, military service, historically subject to laws of privilege, was opened to all citizens, so that all men were accorded the liberty – that is, the right – to die in the defence of the nation.[64] Liberty itself, in its most essential form, was articulated as a condition of total self-surrender to the government. On the other hand, the claims and obligations expressed in citizenship were strongly shaped by the fact that, in the revolutionary period, the scale of warfare expanded dramatically. At this time, war assumed annihilating character, distinct from the more tactically defined, elite-led wars of the pre-revolutionary period (Forrest 1989: 4; Holsti 1996: 4). War itself began to appear as a total phenomenon. Clausewitz observed this clearly, noting that revolutionary wars infused with the 'full weight' of 'national force' were qualitatively different from wars waged by standing armies (2008[1832]: 229). In such wars, belligerent states were forced to reach deeper into their societies for military resources, and the full mobilization of society meant that interstate hostilities acquired particular intensity. This was especially manifest in the multi-polar conflicts that defined the French Revolution and in the later Napoleonic wars, which anticipated the total wars of the twentieth century (Bertaud 1979: 230; Leonhard 2004: 88). This transformation of war was reflected in the attachments that connected the citizen and the state, and the obligations of citizenship facilitated the total mobilization of society required for total war. In both respects, the extraction of legitimacy from the citizen involved the total incorporation of the citizen in the state, in which the authority of the state relied on visceral unity with the citizen.

For these reasons, the link between war and citizenship meant that the modern political system acquired a form that, both normatively and institutionally, was far more encompassing than that of pre-revolutionary states. Early democratic polities formed after 1789 placed demands on citizens that possessed much greater authority than those

---

[63] One historian observes that death in combat was the paradigmatic 'act of citizenship' in the revolutionary period (Jeismann 1992: 152).

[64] Danton argued that the revolution put an end to the monopolization of the 'le droit exclusif de sauver la patrie' by privileged social groups (Buchez 1835: 250).

previously articulated by state officials, and the price of active political citizenship was deep obligation to the political order in which citizenship was exercised. The period of revolutionary transformation in France from 1789 to 1815 is often perceived as the origin of modern European democracy. This is of course accurate. However, early democracy reflected a series of experiments in institution building that, with different structural emphases, had strong similarities to military regimes. At each stage in the French Revolution, the constitutional form of the state was driven by the need for intensified military mobilization. The first major democratic experiment in Europe led to the construction of democracy on a model in which democracy and military rule were not easily separable, and in which the construction of legitimacy for the government took place in highly invasive fashion.[65]

The Army and Democratic Expansion

In each of these processes, the political rights that attached citizens to the national polities that emerged in the revolutionary period were built around military activities. Constitutional roles that allowed citizens to shape the law were strongly attached to military functions. As in feudal society, the rights that supported the production of legislation were usually thickened in war or in preparation for war, as the state granted rights in order to legitimate itself to persons that it might need to deploy as soldiers. From the outset, therefore, early democracy was inseparably connected to conscription, and democratic citizenship was consolidated as part of a bargain, in which persons performing military service claimed political reward for their service. Indicatively, later military theorists in France emphasized the connection between conscription and deepening democracy in the revolutionary era (see Jaurès 1932: 148). One analyst argued that the French Revolution 'transformed subjects into citizens and citizens into soldiers', expressing a 'dual evolution', which resulted 'in universal suffrage and universal military service' (Monteilhet 1926: xxi–xxii). In post-revolutionary Europe, similarly, the link between democratic citizenship and conscription was often discussed with alarm by figures attached to the *ancien régime* (Frevert 2001: 19). Prominent Conservatives such as Chateaubriand described conscription as a 'mode

---

[65] One historian stated simply: 'La Révolution française n'a été qu'une longue dictature' (Mathiez 1937: 97). For claims that Napoleon's regime fell short of dictatorship, see Pietri (1955: 8); Kirsch (1999: 212).

of recruitment that leads to democracy because of the principle of equality on which it is founded' (Chas 1819: 105). One historian explains that general military service was surrounded by the 'stench of Jacobinism' for Conservatives after 1815 (Walter 2003: 327). In the longer aftermath of 1789, the correlation between democratic rights and military mobilization instilled a permanent dynamic of integration in the state, and the expansion of democratic rights was almost invariably connected to military pressures. Throughout the nineteenth century, military factors lay at the core of patterns of political institution-building and legal-normative integration in different national societies.[66]

There are two important caveats to note in this respect.

In the decades after 1815, relations between European states were peaceful, as major European polities directed their expansionist proclivities to other continents. The period from 1815 to the 1850s was a period of unprecedented peace in Europe. In parallel, the years that followed the Napoleonic era witnessed a widespread return to an estate-based system of political representation. After 1815, pro-democratic reform movements lost influence until 1848, and arguably until the 1860s. As an exception, the longer aftermath of the Napoleonic wars saw the introduction of a more defined construction of political rights in Britain, in the 1832 Reform Act. However, core European states, including Britain, retained only very small electoral franchises after 1815.[67]

Through the nineteenth century, nonetheless, the promotion of national citizenship and the connected expansion of political institutions in European polities were usually linked, at least in part, to interstate hostility, either in the form of actual war or anxiety about war. Eventually, a renewed push for democratic citizenship began in the period 1850–70. This push was closely linked to the position of different states in international conflicts and power struggles, and the widening of citizenship rights at this time was strongly driven by military pressures. Consequently, by the final third of the nineteenth century, the link between war and democratic enfranchisement that began around 1789 acquired unmistakable force. The last decades of the nineteenth century saw, across a range of European societies, a deepening of both conscription and enfranchisement. Citizenship and conscription usually expanded together, as two parts of the process in which the state became

---

[66] See the broad claim that national recruitment was a precondition for the overcoming of deep divides in national societies in Krebs (2006: 7).
[67] See p. 106.

more reliant on its constituents and individual persons were drawn into a more direct relation to the state.[68]

This bundle of processes was partly connected to Imperialism. The increased enfranchisement that occurred in many European polities after 1860 was widely advocated by Imperialists, who viewed national political integration as a springboard for effective external expansion. Major franchise reforms in European societies coincided with periods of external Imperial enlargement.[69] This bundle of processes was also connected to increasing volatility in the relations between European states. In many polities, the introduction of mass-political representation and electoral participation coincided with European warfare or intensified preparation for war. In Germany, indicatively, full male suffrage was introduced during the earlier part of the wars of unification, in 1867. This coincided with the introduction of conscription in the North German Federation. In the Habsburg monarchy, universal conscription and a liberal constitution were introduced at the same time, after military defeat by Prussia in 1866. The unification of Italy in the 1860s was partly conducted by irregular troops. It resulted in a polity under a representative constitution, with extended conscription laws introduced in the period 1870–75 (see Rovinello 2013: 488).

These connections are most clearly visible in the French Third Republic. The Third Republic was by far the most advanced major democracy in nineteenth-century Europe, and it was based from the outset in full male suffrage and competitive elections. It was founded in 1870–71, after the defeat of the Bonapartist Second Empire by Prussian and other German troops in the Franco-Prussian War.

One direct outcome of the Franco-Prussian war was that it led to the formation of the unified German state in 1871. In fact, soldiers of different German states fought together against France before Germany was unified, so that the German nation possessed an army before it possessed

---

[68] See the broad sociological argument that universal suffrage and military conscription are elements of the 'propédeutique de la citoyenneté' that underpins the emergence of modern society in Gresle (1996: 107). One analysis describes conscription as 'apprenticeship for the nation and citizenship' (Crépin 1998: 13). On the empirical connection between enfranchisement and conscription, see Ingesson, Lindberg, Lindvall and Teorell (2018: 646). For a synthetic account of the ways in which conscription 'significantly extends ... the reach of the state', see Levi (1996: 133). For a broader sociological account, see also Tilly (1999: 57).

[69] This can be seen in Bismarck's electoral reforms in the period 1867–71. It can be seen in reforms introduced by the Tory Party in Britain in 1867, and, above all, in Giolitti's franchise extension in Italy in 1912, following the invasion of Libya in 1911.

a state. Unified Germany took shape as a nation-state in conditions deeply defined by military conscription. In contemporary reflections, observers as distinct as Friedrich Engels and Theodor Fontane claimed that German superiority in the Franco-Prussian war was due to the fact that, owing to more effective conscription, Prussian society was more comprehensively militarized than France (Fontane 1985[1873]: 120). Engels in fact argued that the introduction of full national conscription would be the only way to defeat the Prussian army (1962[1870]: 107).

At the same time, the Franco-Prussian war led to the foundation of the French Third Republic, which, unsurprisingly, was deeply affected by the military basis of the new German state. After the military defeat of the Second Empire, the new Republic was proclaimed in France in September 1870, while France was still at war. France then continued war with Prussia, not as an Empire, but as a Republic. At this point, French soldiers were mobilized and recruited in the army on altered terms, with altered commitments and obligations, and the new Republican government reached more deeply into society to organize military defence. Soldiers were recruited by *levée en masse* in late 1870. In addition, the ranks of the French army were swelled with partisans and guerillas (*francs-tireurs*). The troops arrayed against Prussia by late 1870 were only uncertainly tied to formal acts of sovereignty, illuminating the precarious legitimacy of the Republic itself. Indeed, these informal troops symbolized, exactly, the shift in sovereignty from the Emperor to citizens that occurred at the beginning of the Republic, so that the Republic first constructed its popular foundation in soldiers mobilized as partisans. In numerous cases, French partisans were not recognized as subject to the laws of war by the Prussian army, and many were summarily executed on capture (Kühlich 1995: 316; Wawro 2003: 279, 289). Historians have characterized the last months of the Franco-Prussian War, after the new Republic had been declared, as a period of 'total war', fuelled by the intensified nationalism of conscript armies and partisan units.[70] This condition was rendered more complex by the fact that some factions in Paris embarked on a radical Republican experiment in early 1871, the Paris Commune, which led to a short civil war. The Commune itself resulted from divisions in the military, as it was founded in part by dissident elements of the National Guard.[71] The Commune was brutally

---

[70] See analysis of the Franco-Prussia War as the prototype of the modern war in Howard (1961: 233); Taithe (2001: 23, 73); Walter (2003: 176).
[71] See the account in Tombs (1981: 4–5).

suppressed by the regular army, representing more Conservative factions in the early Republic. After this, the Third Republic was progressively consolidated on the basis of manhood suffrage.

The founding of the Third Republic contained a series of constitutional elements that proved deeply characteristic of modern democratic polities. It resulted from armed resistance to military occupation by Prussia, partly conducted by partisans. Simultaneously, it was born from armed suppression of civil insurgents in the Paris Commune and subsequent repressive measures against dissidents. In these respects, it reflected the paradigmatic origin of modern democracy in the relocation of sovereignty to citizens acting as soldiers. After 1870-71, then, domestic politics in France displayed intensified militarization. On the one hand, the government of the Third Republic was initially marked by precarious control of its own society. It owed its eventual stability in part to the fact that military factions were brought under the jurisdiction of the Republican government, which, after the suppression of the Commune, was consolidated as the focus of political sovereignty. It also owed its stability to the progressive integration of society through democratic elections. On the other hand, up to 1918, the Republic was deeply affected by its birth in Prussian victory, and, under the shadow of the new *Kaiserreich*, it was marked by a frenetic dynamic of militarization and sovereign regimentation. To be sure, the army of the Third Republic was subject to civil command, and the Minister of War was accountable to parliament (Ralston 1967: 65, 161). However, military reform policies assumed an important position in French society, such that the military became a core link between government and society. Laws introduced in 1872-73 in France reformed the army on the basis of mandatory five-year conscription, albeit with variable application and strong presumptions in favour of protecting wealthier young men from service.[72] As the Republican system was consolidated, conscription laws acquired more equal reach. By 1889, the principle of uniform military service was consolidated, albeit with some exemptions (see Challener 1965: 47-48).[73] Leading public lawyers in post-1870 France argued, indicatively, that governmental legitimacy was built upon a system of equal and reciprocal rights between government and individual citizens. These rights included, as public rights of citizens, the right to vote and the

---

[72] On one calculation well over 50 per cent of men were not subject to conscription (Mitchell 1984: 30). One observer explains how these laws failed to satisfy Republican ideals (Crépin 2009: 288-289).

[73] On persistent restrictions and variation in the application of this law, see Geva (2013: 63).

right to be a soldier (Hauriou 1890: 76). By 1905, all male French citizens had legally binding equal military duties, including reserve service.[74] Debate about the extension of conscription, which culminated in new legislation of 1913, proved incendiary in articulating fault lines between parties and factions on left and right (Michon 1935: 175). In each respect, the Third Republic forms an important example of the correlation between citizenship, militarization and deepening democratization. Throughout the Republic, the direct political powers of the military were carefully circumscribed. However, both inwardly and outwardly, the legitimacy and integrational force of the polity resided simultaneously in universal (male) suffrage and universal (male) conscription (see Monteilhet 1926: 118; Crépin 2005: 351).

Military Citizenship and Freed Labour

In many societies, the connection between military functions and early democratic politics was heightened by the fact that the growth of citizenship coincided with the abolition of serfdom or other types of coerced labour. As mentioned, the abolition of serfdom was usually connected to changes in the military domain. Typically, states abolished serfdom in order to consolidate revenue supplies that were not limited by noble privileges. In addition, however, states also abolished serfdom in order to gain access to pools of potential soldiers, and, in many polities, armies formed the integration mechanism in which released serfs first acquired personality as citizens.

The role of the army in the integration of former serfs had been consolidated before the revolutionary era. In many regions in Europe, standing armies had offered a pathway out of the different variants on serfdom that existed in the eighteenth century. In different contexts, military recruitment brought liberation from aristocratic jurisdiction (Frauenholz 1940: 21; Benecke 2006: 29), and, in some case, soldiers could not be returned to their landlords after discharge of military service.[75] One analysis explains how, in some contexts, military service could provide unusual opportunities for social mobility for persons in marginal social positions, offering escape from personalized status

---

[74] One authority claims that, by 1905, French men were normally conscripted for two years of active duty and were potentially obligated to twenty-six years of reserve army service (Becker 1987: 8). Conscription was again extended to three years in 1913. See on this general point Klausen (1998: 233); Tarrow (2015: 241).
[75] See analysis of this in Russia in Jones (1985: 34).

hierarchies (Sikora 2003: 213). In some areas, standing armies had performed extensive welfare and insurance functions for soldiers and their dependents, which made release from serfdom sustainable (see Pröve 1995a: 27–28).

After 1789, however, one key function of the military in many societies was that it integrated persons recently released from serfdom and other types of tied labour. One process that appears across many European polities is that the release of peasants from serfdom was rapidly followed by the introduction of military conscription for former serfs, so that serfs frequently left serfdom, in effect, to become soldiers. In France, the years 1789–93 saw the abolition of the seigneurial rights that allowed landowners to exercise personal control of peasants. Such rights did not imply powers to compare with those enforced by landowners in the neo-feudal regimes of Central Europe. However, the vestiges of feudal laws in pre-1789 France still imposed deep constraints on the peasants bound by them.[76] In France, as mentioned, military conscription began in 1793, and it was formalized in 1798.[77] In different parts of Prussia, the abolition of serfdom had been anticipated in a series of edicts, notably in 1763 and 1777, which were connected to the cantonal system of military conscription. The years after 1806 then saw the implementation of a complex strategy of social and agrarian reform, intended both to eradicate serfdom (defined as 'personal slavery') and to create a 'completely new constitution' for the army.[78] The abolition of serfdom was (notionally) completed in Prussia in 1807, during debates about the introduction of military conscription. The first conscription laws were implemented six years later. In Bavaria, serfdom was abolished in 1808. The introduction of conscription was an incremental process, starting in 1804/5 and consolidated in 1812. In territories under Habsburg rule, this process was less linear. The abolition of serfdom began (inconclusively) in some Habsburg territories between 1781 and 1785, and, still inconclusively, it

---

[76] In debates on the abolition of feudal law in the Revolution, it was argued that feudal law constituted a mass of obligations, directly and indirectly based in fiefs: a *complexum feudale*. This included special taxes, powers to impose mandatory labour and rights of private jurisdiction (this is printed in *Archives Parlementaires* 1875: 574).

[77] On the persistent weight of feudal obligations in pre-1789 France, see Soboul (1968: 983); Lefebvre (1972: 185); Hayhoe (2008: 48). Various historians claim that, before 1789, seigneurial rights in France preserved core elements of feudalism, including noble control of courts, agrarian production, some taxes, local government and aspects of personal bondage (Lefebvre 1972: 109, 117; Lemarchand 1980: 537, 543, 547).

[78] These terms were used in Altenstein's famous *Denkschrift*, which planned reforms for the Prussian state to emulate the results of the French Revolution (1807[1931]: 403, 431).

was reinforced in the Civil Code of 1812. Some form of cantonal conscription was introduced in some areas in the 1770s, and a reinforced method of conscription was imposed in 1808. In the Polish territories added to the Habsburg domains in the 1770s, some military conscription was introduced at the same time as (partial) abolition of serfdom. This conjoined process acquired paradigmatic expression in Russia, where fiscal pressures linked to military disaster in the Crimean War led to the Great Reforms, which included the formal abolition of serfdom in 1861 (see Beyrau 1975: 207–209). The abolition of serfdom was flanked by the extension of mandatory military service, formalized in legislation of 1874, and the early widening of citizenship in Russia was deeply correlated with the construction of the soldier-citizen (Sanborn 2003: 4; Lohr 2006: 177).[79]

These processes were not exclusive to Europe. In Latin America, the linkage between these processes of integration was further accentuated. Generally, war formed a less important determinant of state formation and political integration in Latin American than in Europe. Interstate wars in Latin America were less frequent and deep-reaching, and they placed lighter extractive burdens on government than in Europe. Even the wars of independence were often fought by foreign soldiers (Soifer 2015: 95). As Latin American armies took independent form in the early nineteenth century, however, military conflicts clearly intensified patterns of inner-societal integration and citizenship formation. This occurred in settings that were profoundly defined by slavery and the legacies of African slavery, and military recruitment impacted pervasively on the position of persons bound to involuntary labour regimes.

During the independence era, military service was a path to eventual release from slavery in many parts of Latin America. Chile was the only polity in Latin America that gave full freedom to slaves in the process of liberation (1823). At this time, many governments introduced legislation to abolish slavery that was either not enforced or quickly rescinded. However, many states promoted the recruitment of slaves in anticolonial armies, which in some instances led to their liberation (see Blanchard 2008: 46–47). In the region that eventually became present-day Colombia, for instance, a gradualist approach to the abolition of slavery was adopted during the independence era, and slaves played a limited role in the pro-independence movement (Helg 2004:

---

[79] For an excellent study of the relation between the army and serfdom in Russia, see Wirtschafter (1990).

152–153). However, slaves who took up arms against Spain were liberated, and slaves were again offered freedom in return for armed service in the civil war of 1839–42 (Lohse 2001: 208).[80] The legislation that abolished slavery in Uruguay in 1842 expressly dictated that former slaves must enter military service (Sales de Bohigas 1970: 281). In both cases, military recruitment formed an important, although typically incomplete, framework for integration of persons previously in servitude.[81]

In Brazil, importantly, slavery survived until the late nineteenth century. The persistence of slavery in Brazil may be partly attributable to the fact that Brazil became independent under Portuguese dynastic rule. This meant that national militarization in a war of independence did not occur, and military recruitment remained concentrated around social elites. The evolution of broad-based national citizenship was manifestly decelerated by this fact (see Carvalho 1996: 349). Brazilian slavery was typically centred around sugar plantations and coffee farms. As such, it formed the socio-economic base to support rural administrative hierarchies, and it transferred patterns of oligarchical stratification analogous to those that defined European feudalism into Brazilian society (see Schwartz 1985: 245–251). Generally, after Brazil became an independent Empire, familial oligarchy and modes of patronage attached to family membership were vital both to the political system and to the structure of Brazilian society more broadly (Bieber 1999: 67), and both these patterns of social coordination were sustained by slavery. In the second half of the nineteenth century, opposition to slavery increased. Persons that supported the abolitionist movement were usually hostile to the underlying oligarchical structure of the Empire, and the campaign for abolition brought to articulation a long-standing – often latent – conflict that existed between groups committed to preserving local hierarchies and groups supporting intensified centralization of the Imperial state.[82] Eventually, the abolition of slavery in 1888 weakened the support of landed elites for the Empire. This quickly led to the collapse of the Empire and to the creation of a Republic (1889), based on altered definitions of citizenship (see Castilho 2016: 182).

The abolition of slavery in Brazil was strongly determined by military politics. It resulted from deep-lying rivalry between beneficiaries of the

---

[80] In Colombia, partial liberation was enforced in 1821, but it was not complete until 1851/52. See for analysis of the role of military recruitment in the early years of this process (Castaño 2011: 230).
[81] For this general claim, see Voelz (1993: 456–464).
[82] See analyses of this contradiction in Salles (1990: 132, 148); Carvalho (2018: 232–234).

old oligarchical regime, who were committed to the defence of local interests, and elements in the army that sought both to reinforce military institutions and to expand the national capacity of governmental institutions (Alonso 2015: 318; Carvalho 2019: 138). Above all, the push for more effective military mobilization was an important factor in the abolition process. Traditionally, the national militia (the *Guarda Nacional*) had been deeply enlaced in the familial/clientelistic system that defined the Brazilian Empire, and it often assumed important functions in policing and perpetuating slavery (Kraay 2001: 84–85; Fertig 2010: 21, 152; Carvalho 2019: 40). By the 1860s, however, the need to recruit more military forces in the Paraguayan War (1864–70) created an impetus to modernize the army. This meant that many senior military figures supported abolition, and they viewed abolition as vital in promoting the rise of a more centralized national Republic with an adequately nationalized army (Toplin 1969: 650).[83] On the Paraguayan side, where the war led to unprecedented devastation and social mobilization, slaves were freed to fight in the war (Reber 1999: 31). In Brazil, the army suffered a shortage of combatants during the war, and some military units were formed through recruitment of freed black soldiers, which – to some degree – expedited their social integration.[84] After the war, a law imposing limited lottery-based conscription was introduced, although not enforced, in Brazil (1874). As mentioned, slavery was finally abolished in 1888. War, therefore, did not bring an immediate end to slavery in Brazil, but it hastened its prohibition (Izecksohn 2014: 127). From the 1860s onwards, the military remained at the centre of the process of political nationalization linked to abolitionism, and military leaders generally viewed the army as a motor for national unification and the modernization of Brazilian society (Torres 2018[1943]: 86). Importantly, the conflict between the army and the oligarchical system of the Empire was re-articulated, in new form, by the groups that supported Getúlio Vargas in 1930. At this time, the endeavour to establish fully national citizenship and to consolidate the nation-building process was closely tied to military prerogatives, and even to ideals of the *soldat-citoyen* (Borges 1992: 158; Fausto 2010: 89).

---

[83] On broader grounds for military opposition to the Empire, including complaints about military spending and wage decreases, and increasing military professionalism, see Dudley (1975: 54, 63–64).

[84] For different analyses, see Martin (1933: 174); Graden (2006: 81); Corrêa do Lago (2014: 307); Izecksohn (2014: 91, 140).

In the United States, similarly, military service played a central role in the abolition of slavery. Slavery in the United States was only terminated by military conflict, in the Civil War of the 1860s, and by a series of constitutional amendments resulting from the Civil War. The Civil War brought the erosion of localized power enclaves in the Southern States, which had traditionally opposed the formation of a genuinely national polity in the United States, tied to equal rights of national citizenship. In the Civil War, further, both the Northern and the Southern States enlisted members of the black population in the army, stimulating expectations of further sociopolitical integration (Berry 1977: 92).[85] One historian has identified the Civil War as the context in which, for 'the first time in American history', black citizens and white citizens were 'treated as equals before law' (Foner 1987: 864). Military law acted as a testing ground for national constitutional law, and uniform citizenship norms first acquired substance in the military domain.

Overall, it is fundamental to the development of national polities in different global regions that the construction of the modern citizen was linked to military forces. In most early national societies, citizenship rights were extended to new social groups as states reached into their populations to find soldiers and to organize potential military agents for war. As discussed, only infrequently did this create a condition of full enfranchisement. However, the granting of citizenship rights through military conscription set the foundations for the later expansion of electoral rights, and, as discussed later, full democratic citizenship usually resulted from war. This means, simply, that the basic political subjects in modern society were constructed on military premises, in response to military demands. The core subjects of early democratic institution building – the sovereign people, the national citizen – were extracted from the military domain, and they transposed military pressures into the political system.[86] The basic form of the modern citizen emerged as people were integrated into a corpus of rights that allowed them to gain

---

[85] In the Union, official recruitment of black citizens began in 1863, and by 1865, 10 per cent of Union army recruits were black (Izecksohn 2014: 109, 115).

[86] See the analysis of the close relation between democratization and mass mobilization in revolutionary polities in Skocpol (1988: 151). On the centrality of war in early democratic subject formation, see Ritter (1965: 70); Finer (2002: 227); Gueniffey (2000: 63); Kruse (2003: 10); Planert and Frie (2016: 1). One historian construes the essence of modern citizenship, simply, as 'born of war' (Leonhard 2004: 85). On the deep connection between 'people', 'state' and 'war' in the revolutionary period, see Pröve (2000: 139).

recognition in, and to confer legitimacy on, the law because this was the price that the state was willing to pay for their gift of military violence.

Much sociological research focused on citizenship and social integration in democratic polities contains the optimistic claim that the citizen has propelled the integration of democratic societies by establishing expansive sets of rights that draw individual persons into overarching societal cooperation (Durkheim 1950: 93; Marshall 1992[1950]; Parsons 1965). Durkheim argued, illustratively, that the establishment of citizenship rights finds its greatest obstruction in war (1950: 92). In some sociological inquiry, it is even suggested that democratic citizenship promotes patterns of integration because citizens ensure that law is informed by, and obtains legitimational force through, principles of rational consensus (Habermas 1973: 153). Traced to its sociological origin, however, the form of the citizen that stands at the centre of modern democratic politics is anything but a focus of rational-reflexive legislation. The subject of democracy first appeared as a figure that acquired influence on legislation as part of an arrangement in which states purchased lethal force, and it is inseparable from the war-like conditions that defined and resulted from early democratic revolutions and early processes of nation building. At their origins, national polities began to obtain broad legitimacy for legislative functions by recognizing persons as citizens in a form created by war. The figure of the modern active citizen first appeared as a construct that re-attached the legal system to the military system, and it connected processes of normative integration, institutional integration and military mobilization in one hard nexus. The modern citizen emerged, specifically, as a figure that created the norms that support legal integration by translating military impulses into law. In each respect, it is sociologically more accurate to examine the subjective form of modern society, the society of national citizens, as a *community integrated by violence*. In this community, basic processes of integration and organization were originally defined and propelled by military necessities, and their outcomes were only infrequently liberating for the persons concerned.[87] Tellingly, one historian has claimed that the 'sociable killer' stands at the integrational core of national society (Sanborn 2003: 166).

---

[87] The community of violence (*Gewaltgemeinschaft*) is defined as a social association whose identity is formed through the 'communal exercise of violence' in Speitkamp (2015: 27) and 'for whose evolution and continued existence physical violence possesses an integral function' in Xenakis (2015: 12).

War and the Dialectic of Political Citizenship

In key respects, the fact that early democratic citizenship was connected to military service greatly hardened the processes of institutional integration that underpin modern society. In fact, in many societies, the linkage between citizenship and military recruitment was at the centre of basic patterns of geographical and territorial inclusion, and conscription was instrumental in giving objective form to societies as *nations*.[88] After 1789, conscription was conducted, in many polities, as an almost uniquely national process, in which the lives of citizens were immediately touched by state institutions.[89] In many societies, further, the army played a key role in the integration of peripheral social groups within the framework of the nation state. For instance, it is often argued that French society became politically centralized because of military recruitment (see Weber 1976: 292–302). In Prussia, military recruitment before and after 1789 helped to unify members of disparate territorial regions within the national structure of the polity. Slightly earlier, Britain had seen high levels of military recruitment in Scotland. This played an important role in hardening the territorial basis of the emergent British polity by providing new professional openings for the Highlanders and by removing them from familial ties likely to promote rebellion (Cookson 1997: 35; Conway 2006: 207; Wold 2015: 72). Similar patterns were observable across Latin America throughout the nineteenth century.

Despite such consequences of conscription, the early figure of the active political citizen possessed a range of conflicting implications for

---

[88] One analysis states that conscription was a factor of 'first order in the formation of national identity' in France (Boulanger 2001: 251). Importantly, in the French Revolution, recruitment was partly separated from regional departments, so that soldiers were released from regional allegiances (Birnbaum 1988: 61). A parallel analysis of the USA states that since the late eighteenth century 'participation in the national army has been an integral aspect of the normative definition of citizenship' (Janowitz 1978:178).

[89] This began in the years after the French Revolution (see Schmitt 2007: 39, 87). The nationalizing impact of conscription should not be exaggerated. Recruitment usually remained subject to local variations up to World War I. In both Germany and the United Kingdom, mobilization for war in 1914 was focused on local or regional military units. One analysis argues that mass mobilization in Germany in 1914 intensified the distinction of territorial units within the state, as recruitment was conducted by agencies with regional focus (Daniel 1989: 53). In Britain, regiments were separated from localities in the latter part of the war, but local loyalties remained prominent in individual battalions (Watson 2008: 65). For discussion of France, explaining that conscription was still not geographically universalized by 1914, see Boulanger (2001: 143, 159, 161). This account stresses, however, that in France recruitment was 'par excellence a factor that impelled national mobility and assimilation' (2001: 251).

modern society and the modern state. The figure of the modern citizen projected in the revolutionary era became a construct of global importance which shaped processes of legitimation and integration across the world. The French Revolution formed a global normative event, whose implications profoundly determined integration processes across a broad spectrum of national environments. In tying the legitimacy of integration processes to military functions, the figure of the modern citizen instilled deep instability in many modern societies. Owing to its military origins, the modern citizen always appeared as a dialectically insecure source of legal normativity, at once reinforcing and challenging the state's powers of integration and legitimation. Discernibly, the figure of the citizen articulated legitimational norms that did not provide a firm basis for legal integration and imprinted deep volatility in the integrational structure of society. Across the world, different polities internalized antinomies generated by experiences of revolutionary citizenship at the origins of modern society. Indeed, patterns of normative instability that were first articulated in revolutionary polities resonated through most subsequent expressions of citizenship.

The first dialectical aspect in the figure of the modern citizen resulted from the fact that citizenship, as it was linked to military mobilization, created conflictual conditions in the societies in which citizens were integrated and mobilized. The fact that states granted political rights to citizens to support military actions meant that states relied on, and often gave privileged status to, those social groups that were committed to fight, so that access to rights was partly determined by enthusiasm for war. This meant, inevitably, that states accentuated and militarized divisions within their own societies, and they often reproduced some aspects of international conflict in domestic conflict. From the revolutionary period on, consequently, national politics often moved close to civil war. This began in France in the 1790s. The government of revolutionary France mobilized citizens, at the same time, in external and internal conflicts, and the latter were often connected to and exacerbated by the former (see Soboul 1959: 67; Kruse 2003: 130; Leonhard 2008: 223). As a result, the acquisition of citizenship rights often depended on the willingness of citizens to take up arms against both external and internal adversaries, which meant that citizenship instilled and intensified deep cleavages within national society. Robespierre made this connection quite clear. He stated that, in consolidating the Republic, it was vital to tame 'internal enemies' before taking action against 'foreign enemies' (1954: 47).

From 1789 onwards, the mobilization of citizens for war was typically a factionalizing experience, and it brought the risk of acute domestic instability. Mass mobilization almost inevitably met with internal resistance, increasing the possibility of insurrection and civil war if war proved unsuccessful. In France, famously, the Vendée uprising against the revolution was mainly caused by the imposition of conscription in the countryside (Tilly 1964: 308; Broers 2010: 25). This created a symbolic division in the French nation, and it bred abiding hostility between the rural population and more progressive urban groups (Tombs 1981: 106; Lehning 1995: 25–26; Gaboriaux 2010: 181). In each respect, mass-military mobilization provoked deep-lying antagonisms amongst mobilized populations, and the militarization of the citizen spilled into inner-societal antagonisms between citizenship groups. From 1789, the figure of the citizen appeared, not as a stable centre of norm production, but as a fissured form, defined by antagonism both towards other nations and towards other citizens.

The second dialectical aspect in the figure of the modern citizen arose from the fact that, after 1789, the capacity of governments to assert military supremacy became a key determinant of their inner-societal recognition. As states integrated their populations through war, wars became fundamental to the production of legitimacy for government: legitimacy became inseparable from violence, and governments constructed their legitimacy through their ability to mobilize one people against a different people (Walter 2003: 175; Martin 2006: 16; Sellin 2011: 105). In most cases, by consequence, governments that waged unsuccessful wars were brought to crisis by the people that they had mobilized. Unsuccessful belligerent states were frequently exposed to the threat of revolution or radical reform during or after the war, and military defeat typically led to the assumption of power by oppositional groups. In this respect, the citizen did not form a reliable source of legitimacy for states. States that mobilized citizens as soldiers were always, potentially, involved in a war on two fronts.

The third dialectical aspect in the figure of the modern citizen became evident in the fact that, after 1789, the citizen always threatened the basic institutional form of the state. After 1789, as discussed, the introduction of national military service meant that states attached their legitimacy to persons motivated to fight. However, the motivation of such persons to fight was not solely loyalty to a monarch or to a government. Rather, persons were motivated to fight because they fought for national society, for their status as citizens in this society, and for their liberty to shape the laws of this society. Such persons, once armed, always posed an implicit threat to the states that mobilized them, as, in principle, their loyalty was only coincidentally focused on service for a particular government (Walter 2003: 107–108). From the revolutionary period onwards, soldiers were recruited through appeals to national obligations and sentiments, which could not easily be monopolized by sovereign institutions. As a result, state agents engaged warily with soldiers over whom they exercised mobilizational force, and from which they extracted legitimacy. This was reflected in the French Constitution of 1795, which, in Art. 365, expressly subject all military force to the state. Importantly, the 1791 Constitution specifically defined the army as a force whose duty was, not to deliberate, but to obey. This uncertain relation between the state and the soldier was intensified by the fact, as discussed, that armies usually created foundations for citizenship by releasing persons from serfdom, and they gave arms to many persons previously denied effective personal rights. In some cases, armies of early national polities recruited slaves, who, once armed, posed a palpable threat to existing systems of order and ownership (see Quarles 1961: 13). Across the globe, states first encountered their citizens both as urgently needed conscripts and as potential revolutionaries.

This third dialectic principle was intensified by the fact that, in some European polities, both the institutionalization of military conscription and the abolition of serfdom were connected to the outbreak of wars against Napoleonic occupation, which saw mass mobilization of citizens as militias or as *partisans*. The partisan emerged as a figure that symbolized the precarious reserves of legitimacy provided by modern citizens. To be sure, the phenomenon of the partisan in this context should not be over-dramatized. The common idea that European nations spontaneously erupted in national wars of liberation during the Napoleonic era is – at least in part – the result of later nationalist projections (see Planert 2007: 23). Nonetheless, in the Napoleonic era, soldiers in many occupied states were spontaneously mobilized, and military units were informally constructed around national attachments, which were not subject to conventional laws of sovereignty. In such circumstances, the *soldat* and the *citoyen* were fused on a voluntary basis, and many citizens freely elected to demonstrate virtues of citizenship by taking up arms. This was exemplified in the wars against Napoleon in Spain, where national populations armed themselves in resistance to occupation. This was replicated in other countries, including Austria and some German states. In Prussia, military reforms designed to mobilize and incorporate partisan groups in the regular army were proposed in 1808, although this plan was not implemented.[90] The partisan had in fact already assumed constitutional importance as an agent of national citizenship in revolutionary America (Kwasny 1996: 112).

In these contexts, the figure of the modern citizen distilled a deeply ambiguous set of motivations. Of key significance in the figure of the partisan is the fact that it contradicted the basic principle of eighteenth-century military law, and early public law more widely: namely, that the power to mobilize troops is an exclusive attribute of sovereign power (Wohlfeil 1965: 217; Schmitt 2017: 17). Where partisans were mobilized, persons not strictly subject to state command armed themselves and assumed the right to exercise military violence, in the name of the national polity. Moreover, such persons claimed membership rights in the national polity because of their military actions. Governments were supported by military-political forces which they did not fully control, and, in waging war, their ability to assert formal sovereignty was potentially threatened by the soldiers on which they depended, and to which, to some degree, they owed their legitimacy. Importantly, some European states introduced conscription in a form that was close to partisan mobilization. This occurred, for example, in Austria in 1808 and in Prussia in 1813–14, where conscription was promoted to resist occupation. In such cases, conscription was introduced as part of a strategy intended both to harness the potential of partisan movements for effective national defence, but also to subordinate these movements to state control, avoiding spontaneous or uncontrolled arming of the populace.[91] By 1820, the restoration of monarchical rule across Europe meant that most states had limited conscription, assimilated conscripted units into regular armies, or preserved general conscription in merely superficial fashion (Walter 2003: 108). Over a longer period, conscription became an instrument for disciplining potential partisans and for ensuring that partisan energies were expressed in a form that was fully controlled by the state.

Taken together, these factors mean, simply, that, in many contexts, the people first became a presence within the modern state in circumstances

---

[90] For analysis of ways in which partisans transformed war after 1789, see Wohlfeil (1983: 18–21); Rink (2000); Schmidt (2003: 186); Barth (2005). See discussion of resistance to Napoleon in Spain as the model for later popular uprisings in Wolhlfeil (1965); Rink (1999: 282). Traditional accounts of the role of the partisan in Spain under Napoleon are questioned in Esdaile (2004: 159).

[91] See discussion of the Austrian and Prussian conscription laws of 1808, 1813 and 1814 in Rassow (1943: 311); Wohlfeil (1965: 227); Rink (1999: 373).

in which regular military capacity was insufficient to react to external threats, and governments relied on citizens for military force. In such contexts, the citizen appeared as the legitimational subject of the modern polity, not because the citizen simply demanded political rights of self-legislation, but because traditional sovereign institutions had fractured under military pressure. In some societies, the first direct encounter between the national state and the national people occurred in the mobilization of partisans. In such cases, the citizen appeared as an actor on which the nation state relied, existentially, yet which also required constant domestication: the citizen appeared to public authorities in a form that was both liberating and threatening. Famously, Carl Schmitt argued in the 1920s that states establish their sovereignty by differentiating between friends and foes (1932: 26). What Schmitt omitted to consider in making this observation, however, was that, in their origins, modern states could not easily make this distinction. In their first formation, modern states depended for sovereignty and legitimacy on actors that also, potentially, unsettled their sovereignty and legitimacy. As discussed later, polities legitimated by citizenship were typically defined, at the structural level, by the fact that they devised methods to expand their sovereign powers over their citizens.[92] States began to construct their integrational form by using military means to assert sovereignty over their citizens, and they stabilized their position in society through violent regimentation of the persons from which they extracted legitimacy.

A fourth dialectical aspect in the figure of the citizen was visible, accordingly, in the fact that citizenship appeared as a focus of legal integration in environments where serfs or slaves had been recruited for war, usually for wars of national defence or foundation. As mentioned, the release of persons from coercive labour regimes was an ineradicable aspect of the modern constitutional form, and this form was often imprinted on society by the army. In such processes, however, the figure of the citizen cast a deeply ambivalent light on the legal system in which persons released from coerced labour were incorporated, and the link between military engagement and citizenship created extremely fragile legitimational premises for government. As discussed, for many people the experience of acquiring a legal-political personality as a citizen was a process in which they underwent a rapid transition from a condition of forced labour to a condition of forced military recruitment.

[92] See p. 131.

For many people, therefore, the typical path to citizenship, through the army, led to a condition not far removed from the condition of serfdom from which they had been released. The initial reality of citizenship was frequently a life of forced combat, which was little more than 'a new form of serfdom', imposed by the central state instead of a local lord, and entailing significantly increased exposure to the risk of violent death.[93] Quite generally, military labour formed a mode of employment that was not categorically distinct from serfdom or slavery, or in which, at least, some aspect of involuntary labour persisted.[94] In fact, the army was frequently was not fully distinct from a penitentiary, and military service was used to punish criminals.[95] In acquiring citizenship, therefore, citizens entered a new condition of bodily alienation, which was created by the demand for cheap and easily motivated soldiers in emerging nation states. Naturally, many new citizens immediately rebelled against the military preconditions of their citizenship, and the implications of citizenship were widely seen as undesirable.[96]

In these respects, the army developed after the revolutionary era as a key system of personal integration, in which norms of national obligation were instilled into citizens, and it promulgated principles both of individual citizenship and of national unity and cohesion, from which national society as whole was expected to emanate. Yet, the army also absorbed some of the administrative and disciplining functions originally attached to the institutions that controlled serfs, and military

---

[93] See, for this citation, Hochedlinger (2009: 90). In a number of societies, released slaves or serfs were not entirely free, and they lived in a condition of restricted liberty, deprived of some rights.

[94] See excellent analysis of this point in Beattie (1999: 868) and Kraay (2001: 75). For discussion of the claim that 'army life is similar to the slave condition', see Voelz (1993: 390). On the deep historical connection between military recruitment and prison, see Gird (1921: 137). On the link between the acquisition of citizenship, the abolition of serfdom and military incarceration, see Blessing (1991: 469). For important historical discussion, claiming that slavery and military activity were always connected, see Sellin (1976: 83).

[95] See discussion of the case of Brazil in Meznar (1992: 341); Carvalho (1996: 350). One historian of Brazil argues that impressment in the army in and after the Paraguayan War 'filled an important niche in the twilight world between slavery and the emergence of free labor and a more inclusive ideal of citizenship' (Beattie 2001: 269). This had widely been the case in Europe before 1789 (see Planert 2007: 406–407). For analysis of Russian serfdom in this respect, see Kolchin (1987: 75).

[96] In 1813, the first wave of conscription in Prussia led to almost 25 per cent desertion in some regions. France had a running desertion rate of circa 10 per cent from 1803 to 1814 (Hewitson 2013: 468). On anti-conscription sentiments in different countries, see Frevert (2001: 19).

organizations assumed responsibilities for forcible socialization and repression of former serfs. In many settings, in fact, armies were deployed to ensure that persons released from serfdom could not exercise rights of full citizenship. Almost without exception, release from serfdom through military pressures did not lead to democratic integration – that is, full citizenship – for former serfs. In most polities, a full century passed between the formal abolition of serfdom or slavery and the full enfranchisement of former serfs or slaves.[97] In most post-abolition societies, the army, having played a key role in liberating serfs, was frequently used as an instrument to repress these persons, where they demanded more expansive rights. The army was typically converted into part of an institutional apparatus, in which serfs were again deprived of liberty, or at least prevented from obtaining full political rights.[98]

In these respects, early citizenship reflected a deep and inextricably involved dialectic between liberation and repression. Access to citizenship was always subject, by the organization that granted it, to highly coercive processes of regimentation and selection. After 1789, the army remained a source of liberation and a source of incarceration, and it vacillated between both functions for much of the nineteenth century, and beyond. For many people, the army was both the path to citizenship and the bar that blocked the same path.

On each count, the military definition of the citizen in the revolutionary era always contained a deep dialectical implication for emergent national polities. On the one hand, this definition entailed an extension of state's sovereignty, and it increased the mobilizational force of the state, allowing the state to reach into national society to an unprecedented degree. It also provided an expanded principle of collective

---

[97] In France, the last traces of serfdom were eradicated in the years after 1789, but full political enfranchisement of (male) former serfs only occurred in 1870–75, over eighty years later. In Prussia, serfdom was abolished in 1807. Partial enfranchisement of former serfs occurred in the semi-representative constitutional systems later established in Prussia (1848–50) and Imperial Germany (1871). However, full enfranchisement was only fully cemented in 1918, 111 years after abolition. In the United States, slavery was abolished in 1865, but full enfranchisement of persons formerly held as slaves was only secured in the Civil Rights Act of 1964 and the Voting Rights Act of 1965, exactly one century after abolition. In Brazil, slavery was abolished in 1888. Yet, prior to abolition, stricter literacy qualifications for the exercise of electoral rights were introduced in the *Lei Saraiva* (1881), which meant that few emancipated slaves could vote in elections. The power of local oligarchies survived long after the collapse of the Empire, and the Republic retained much of its existing privatistic power structures (Leal 2012: 235). Full and equal suffrage was not introduced until 1985, ninety-seven years after abolition.

[98] See p. 135.

legitimacy for the state's legal foundations. On the other hand, this definition underlined the limits of state sovereignty, and it instilled an unpredictable popular element in the form of sovereignty. The state entered the modern era in a form in which its essential sovereignty was split, and it was required to stabilize itself against the persons on whom its sovereignty depended. From the revolutionary era onwards, the state was forced to assert its sovereignty in two directions, and it encountered new threats as it faced in each direction. The state was required to mobilize an increasing number of troops for war. Yet, it was also threatened, in different ways, by these troops. The state emerged, thus, under conditions of fractured sovereignty, and its ability to preserve sovereignty usually presupposed military success. This meant that modern states, linked to legitimational constructs of the citizen, were often driven to risk war to preserve sovereign control over their populations.

A fifth, more general, dialectical aspect in the figure of the modern citizen became visible in the fact that, as post-1789 states derived legitimacy from divided populations, the construction of a state's legitimacy was tied to its activities in regulating inner-societal conflicts. In polities based in citizenship, deep-lying social conflicts acquired heightened relevance for the legitimation of the political system, and citizenship led to the politicization of group conflicts as different actors in society competed over the definition of state legitimacy. This meant that the idea of citizenship underpinning the state was envisaged in highly volatile fashion, and the basic terms of legitimacy produced by citizens were open to violent contestation. Within the overarching national community of violence, sub-categories of violent subjectivity also took shape. As a result, the maintenance of sovereignty by the state usually required the promotion of one model of citizenship against alternative, potentially plausible models, and the state was forced to reach into society to manufacture, sometimes by military means, the conditions of citizenship that it presupposed for its legitimacy. From the outset, modern states were required to construct their legitimacy by softening conflicts between different groups, classes and sectors within the population or – where necessary – by suppressing the concepts of citizenship advanced by some elements of the national community.

One expression of this violent construction of the citizen is visible in the fact that, in many polities, the attachment of state legitimacy to citizenship led directly to actual civil war, induced by the orientation of governmental legitimacy around citizenship norms. In such settings, legitimational norms of governance were only established through the political suppression of groups proposing contrary understandings of citizenship. As mentioned, citizenship in the French Revolution was first consolidated through the annihilation of opponents of the Revolution. The American Revolution promulgated a concept of citizenship that triggered deep civil instability, and eventually civil war. The normative-legitimational implications of American citizenship only approached realization through the protracted military imposition of a uniform pattern of citizenship on society. In many Latin American countries, democratic ideals of citizenship generated rival accounts of legitimacy, and most polities experienced either short or intermittent civil war in their founding periods. Few societies did not experience civil war as citizenship was established as the core integrational principle.

A further expression of the violent construction of the citizen is perceptible in the fact that, after 1789, the institutional position of the military became a matter of intense controversy, reflecting different constructions of political sovereignty. Typically, the proximity between people and army after the eighteenth century meant that each political group claiming citizenship rights adopted a distinct approach to the military, and different concepts of citizenship were expressed in rival accounts of how military units should be positioned in the polity. Contestation over the role of the military accompanied the rise of early democracy, and the military was transformed into a focus of constitutional antagonism. This was especially the case in polities that had witnessed popular mobilization and the fracturing of sovereignty during the Napoleonic era, where popular mobilization had opened access to citizenship.

On the one hand, it was common for earlier nineteenth-century constitutionalists in Europe to argue that military force should be exercised by the people, within constitutional constraints.[99] Such theorists usually advocated the creation of a civil militia, claiming that defence of the polity was best guaranteed by voluntary armies, subject to constitutional laws (Höhn 1938: 39; Pröve 2000: 145). This view remained an important aspect of European liberal politics throughout the earlier nineteenth century. The demand – infrequently realized – that the army should swear fidelity to constitutional principles was a pressing preoccupation for many parties that promoted early experiments in representative government.[100] After 1848, the distinctive military

---

[99] See, for instance, Rotteck (1816: 134–135).
[100] For example, German soldiers who fought for the government created in Frankfurt in 1848–49 were expected to swear an oath on the Constitution (Müller 1999: 110). For discussion of Prussia in this regard, see Buschmann (2003: 146). By contrast, Article 64 of

outlook in early Liberalism became weaker. However, democratic militarism did not disappear, and many democrats endorsed the creation of a popular army. This was exemplified in the Paris Commune of 1871, in which irregular troops assumed political control of the city. In the French Third Republic, enthusiasm on the democratic left for an army comprising 'strong national militias' remained strong (Jaurès 1932: 50). This view was echoed in some sections of the Social Democratic Party in Germany (Bebel 1898: 45).

On the other hand, reactionary groups in the nineteenth century were strongly connected to the army. In many societies, Conservative political factions acted in close conjunction with the military establishment to impose a distinct constitutional vision on society. In many nations, the military establishment, whose position remained tied to social standing, saw its authority as vindicated by the threat of civil war, and it committed itself expressly to the protection of reactionary social groups (Messerschmidt 1980: 71). After 1815, Conservative governments frequently used the military to suppress radical movements. This was expressed emblematically at Peterloo in Manchester. But, after 1815, use of the army to quell radicalism was formally endorsed in the German states. In Prussia, an ordinance of 1820 provided for deployment of military units to restore public order (Vollert 2014: 173). In some German states, the failed constitutional uprisings of 1848–49, which were partly supported by popular militias, were suppressed by Prussian troops. After 1848, early German Conservative associations were often attached to military organizations, effectively serving as a permanently institutionalized counter-revolution (see Trox 1990: 157, 283; Gresle 2003: 788). In France, the Second Republic was decisively shaped by Cavaignac's suppression of armed insurgents, and it was brought down by a Bonapartist coup. By this time, different national armies routinely joined forces with the regular police to suppress insurrection and industrial activism.[101] By the late nineteenth century, in short, the linkage between the *citoyen* and the *soldat* that had first promoted democracy had been dissolved in much of Europe. The army turned against its

---

the 1871 Constitution imposed on servicemen an oath of personal loyalty to the *Kaiser*. In his abdication in 1918, the *Kaiser* freed all soldiers from this oath. This created the basis for a Republican army.

[101] On Prussia, the United Kingdom and France, see Lüdtke (1982: 324, 341, 345). One important discussion explains that after 1870, the use of the army against industrial protests was more common in democratic France than in Germany (Johansen 2005: 89, 278).

original position as a path to citizenship, and it acted increasingly as the vanguard of the social bloc that obstructed democratic integration and citizenship rights. In states that maintained conscription, military service frequently functioned as a system for initiating young men in antidemocratic principles.

A further expression of the violent construction of the citizen became observable as societies progressed towards more extensive democratic integration and institutional expansion. As discussed, after 1815, most citizens were excluded from the exercise of rights that permit popular influence on legislative processes, and most trajectories of democratization were either reversed or retarded. In many polities, the army played an important role in this process. However, as constitutional systems in Europe gradually became more democratic, contestation over citizenship split society into counter-posed collective membership groups which challenged each other for access to rights of legislative influence. In most national societies, the early rise of democracy led to the deeply antagonistic fragmentation of citizenship, in which different groups internalized the essential militaristic principle that assumption of citizenship rights entails the negation of the rights of rival groups. Rights of citizenship – that is, rights to form laws recognized as legitimate – became immediate objects of collective military contestation.

This pattern became manifest, in particular, in the party-based systems of political representation that evolved in European states on the path towards democracy. A deep impetus to militarization was instilled in political parties from the time of their first emergence, during the French Revolution. Importantly, before the French Revolution and the Napoleonic period, parties were normally seen as detrimental to legitimate political organization. In fact, much early constitutional theory rejected party-based majoritarianism, which it derided as factionalism.[102] Distinct political parties had existed in Britain and Sweden before the revolutionary era. However, the first categorization of parties as parties of the right and parties of the left, separated by consistent political dichotomies, occurred in the French Revolution. In this context, political parties developed in a setting close to civil war, and they internalized some military functions. A core objective of governing political parties was to solidify regimes formed in conditions of extreme

[102] This is implied throughout Rousseau's theory of the social contract. The classic example is Madison's claim in *Federalist 10* that a party is a body that seeks 'to sacrifice to its ruling passion or interest both the public good and the rights of other citizens' (Madison, Hamilton and Jay (1987[1787–88]): 125).

antagonism, usually through deployment of military force against adversaries. In response, political parties that opposed governing parties were likely, inevitably, to develop highly militarized qualities, as their objective was to overthrow parties attached to existing military regimes. Military organizations with partial affinities to parties also proliferated at this time. In some countries, the French Revolution prompted the creation of voluntary military units which fused characteristics of military and political associations.[103] In many countries, as mentioned, the Napoleonic period saw the growth of partisan movements, so that early national political movements intersected with military organizations. Generally, political parties were consolidated in environments in which the state's sovereignty had been fractured in war or revolution, and different parties emerged as combatants for a share of this sovereignty. In fact, the basic concept of the party originally possessed military implications. In the eighteenth century, indicatively, 'party' was understood both as a political term and as a military term. In the political sense, it referred to small factions at royal courts pursuing 'selfish objectives' and likely to 'cause great damage'. As a 'military term', it referred to small military units, separate from the main part of an army, and led by partisans (Jablonski 1748: 780–781).

Political parties began to develop firm institutional structures through the nineteenth century, as part of the wider process of early democratic polity building and institutional integration. Importantly, political parties assumed dense organizational form at the same time that persons living in similar economic conditions in national societies began to understand themselves as members of a specific social class. Consequently, the construction of class affiliations often fed directly into the formation of political parties, and political parties acquired central importance in articulating interests typical of rival social classes (see Kocka 1990: 3). Early political parties were designed to guarantee and expand rights of citizenship for their memberships, and their primary function was to ensure that their members could not be excluded from the exercise of citizenship rights. Parties thus grew around the contested fault lines of citizenship, and they mobilized sectoral groups of citizens against each other. It is often noted that political parties played a central role in instilling a national form within nineteenth-century societies, especially as they linked sociopolitical movements in different regions to central institutions (Caramani

---

[103] On this phenomenon in Britain in the years after 1789, see Gee (2013: 21).

2003: 436). In doing this, however, parties replicated certain functions of the army, and they ensured that persons in society encountered each other as national citizens in potentially combative roles. In each respect, the political system became a domain of conflict between adversarial collective subjects, tending to converge around class interests.

This linkage between political party and social class coincided historically with the wider militarization of European society, and early political parties often understood themselves as organs of class warfare. As mentioned, Conservative parties in the nineteenth century entertained close links with military milieux. Radical parties commonly projected a role for themselves as collective protagonists in civil war, and the vocabulary of warfare became vital to political parties of the European left. In fact, many theorists of political organization attached to the left were close observers of military politics, and their construction of society was imbued with military reflection. Illustratively, Marx and Engels viewed capitalism as an economic system arising at the end of feudalism, in which individual economic agents (released serfs) were coercively assimilated into 'industrial armies'. They wished to replace capitalism with socialism, a system which they also viewed as based in 'industrial armies', serving freely defined collective commitments (Marx and Engels 1959[1848]: 481). They depicted the Communist Party as the political vanguard in this transition from one militarized economic system to another. The contribution of Engels to the development of political Marxism is especially important in this regard. Like Marx, Engels viewed class conflict as a pattern of social militarization, in which different classes form analogues to armies (1865: 24). In addition, he concluded that military service promotes personal dignity amongst soldiers, meaning that socialist citizenship was likely to thrive in societies with a military emphasis (1865: 32). He described conscription as a distinctive 'democratic institution', and he shared the Republican view that the 'effective implementation of military service' would lead to full national enfranchisement (1865: 7, 38). Later, Karl Kautsky argued that socialist politics entails the waging of 'a long civil war' (1907: 53). Jean Jaurès projected socialist activism in military terms, and he accentuated the direct connection between social militarization and radical democracy (1932: 82, 137). On the far left, the association of political parties with military units was still more emphatic. For Lenin, the basic function of a political party was to act as a vanguard in global revolution (Rabinovitch 2007: 2).

In most polities, in short, the original linkage between the *soldat* and the *citoyen* proved a precarious premise for democratic formation, and it constructed primary norms for the polity in implacably divisive terms. The democratic subject extracted from processes of social militarization scarcely provided stable foundations for reliable normative integration. In most cases, as examined later, the rise of citizenship created legitimational premises for the polity that eventually fractured the institutional resources of the polity itself.

Conclusion

Prior to the revolutionary period in the late eighteenth century, states developed by constructing persons as individual agents and by integrating them in society as such. Primarily, pre-revolutionary states integrated persons as *legal subjects*, and, to some degree, as *fiscal subjects*, and they secured their sovereignty by releasing such subjects from the mesh of private authority attached to aristocratic domains. The individualization of social agents as legal subjects formed a core normative prerequisite for the emergence of the modern state and the construction of the modern legal system. The revolutionary period, however, witnessed a deep transformation in the integrational unit of the nation states: persons were integrated into the polity as *military subjects*, and military subjectivity formed the constitutional source of legitimacy for polities oriented towards democratization. The rise of military citizenship resulted, largely, from the fact that, before 1789, the legal system had promoted processes of inclusion that lacked sufficient robustness to integrate all society. Many governments before 1789 had attempted both to solidify their institutions and to liberate individual persons in society, but these processes only had limited effect. The inability of emergent states to transform persons in society into uniform legal and fiscal subjects led to malfunction in the fiscal system and in the military system, and it undermined the sovereign power of state institutions. It was in this context of integrational crisis that the constitutional figure of the modern citizen emerged, exercising rights of political sovereignty. The modern citizen took form, primarily, not as the expression of factually existing persons, but as the result of integrational pressures in society. This led to a deep fusion of the person as a focus of legal integration with the person as a focus of military integration, and the production of law's normative legitimacy became strongly dependent on the ability of governments to motivate citizens to fight. The citizen acquired two sides – a legal and a military side – which were not easily separable, and both sides of the citizen were integrated, essentially, through the same processes.

The revolutionary linkage of citizenship and military service in the late eighteenth century instilled a complex, dialectical dynamic in national societies, and it proved formative of the modern state. As discussed, the revolutionary construct of the citizen expressed a certain continuity with existing patterns of social and national formation that pre-existed the revolutionary era. In the revolutionary period, modern societies approached an elevated degree of legal and political integration, in which social obligations were defined on increasingly robust, publicly sanctioned principles. This weakened privatistic elements in the state, and it promoted the integration of society in relatively uniform public institutions and a relatively uniform legal order.

Seen in a longer historical perspective, however, the construct of the citizen that emerged in the revolutionary period at the end of the eighteenth century had several results which significantly re-directed the basic integrational processes that underlie modern society. In these respects, the construct of the citizen forfeited its original quality as a functional norm to support social integration, and it tended to erode the preconditions required for its own realization

First, the revolutionary construct of the citizen connected processes of inner-societal integration to external military pressures. As the exercise of political rights by citizens was attached to military recruitment, external warfare or the threat of warfare typically led to the intensified integration of citizens in national polities, and it bound citizens more closely to the state. In its earliest definition, modern democracy was described as a system of government that is averse to war. The revolutionaries in France argued that democracy made war unlikely. Abbé Grégoire's draft for a Declaration of the Rights of Nations suggested that Republican constitutions would commit their polities to peaceful coexistence with others (Grewe 1988: 660–661).[104] Kant argued similarly that Republican constitutionalism would eradicate war from society (Kant 1977b [1795]).[105] However, early democratic citizenship was inseparable from war. Once established, citizenship opened society to military impulses.

---

[104] The reciprocity between national rights and international rights was also central to the thought of Condorcet (1847: 527).
[105] Kant also described military volunteers in revolutionary France as *soldiers of law*, motivated to take up arms by pure thought of the 'law of the people to which they belonged' (1977c[1798]: 359).

From the first advent of modern democracy, the basic organization of society as a system of legal integration, initiated at the end of feudal society, was again placed on premises defined, as in feudal society, by war. Citizens became integrated in democratic legal systems because these systems provided recompense for military mobilization.

Second, the revolutionary construct of the citizen meant that the basic process that underpinned the dissolution of feudalism, the construction of each person as an individual legal person, was partly reversed. The militarization of citizenship meant that legal entitlements and claims to legal recognition and legitimacy were attached to collective subjects, usually linked to class formation. Leading sociologists have identified protracted individualization as the main feature of modern society (Durkheim 1950: 99; Luhmann 1965). Originally, however, individualization only characterized modern society at the level of private interaction. At the level of legitimacy production, modern society was first defined by the termination of earlier patterns of individualization. As analysed later, the collective construction of political subjectivity increased the sensitivity of national political systems to external conflicts, and it meant that groups of citizens mobilized domestically around prerogatives defined at the international level.

Third, the revolutionary construct of the citizen instilled a precarious and unsettling element in the sovereignty of the state. After the revolutionary era, the state's power to wage war depended on its ability to mobilize its population as combatants. However, the military loyalty of citizens proved a perennially fragile legitimational resource. States struggled to institutionalize a grammar in which citizens could be integrated as agents whose own exercise of sovereignty did not fracture the state's own sovereignty. In fact, the assertion of sovereignty by the state usually triggered rival assertions of sovereignty: *state sovereignty was always linked to revolutionary counter-sovereignty*. This instilled a dialectic of emancipation and repression in the core of the modern state. States became reliant on violent citizens. But they were also required to use violence to motivate and pacify these citizens. Their sovereignty and legitimacy hinged on their capacity to ensure that citizens did not acquire military powers sufficient to unsettle the state itself. Most states periodically manufactured the loyalty of the persons on whom their sovereignty depended through the inner-societal deployment of extreme coercion and repression. The revolutionary origin of the modern state meant that the state's internal regulatory functions necessarily assumed a military emphasis.

In each of these points, fourth, one defining result of the modern concept of citizenship is that it created a strong and immediate nexus between the contest over the form of law in national society and the position of the state with regard to international conflicts. From the revolutionary period, the constitutional subject of democracy – the sovereign citizen – evolved as a construct, which made the state's legitimacy contingent on its position in the international arena. First, the state's legitimacy was attached to success in war. Second, the state's legitimacy was attached to the mobilization of soldiers to guarantee such success. Such mobilization depended on the projection of an external risk to the state and its citizens that was sufficient to warrant death in combat. State legitimacy was constructed in an environment in which both the external and the internal sovereignty of the state was placed under strain. Third, the pacification of national citizens was often pursued through interstate war. The integrational focus of national society was determined, in essence, by the articulation of the national citizen, and of the national legal-political system, with processes of interstate conflict, which resonated immediately through antagonisms between groups within national societies. Most people were released into citizenship at times when interstate hostility was acute, and, in different ways, this was directly expressed in citizenship practices.

The figure of the citizen had already taken shape, in rather inchoate form, before the revolutions that set the basic political-legitimational form of modern national society. This figure had served, structurally, to create a constitutional partition between the construction of legitimacy for law and the exercise of military violence. In the revolutionary *époque*, the legal contours of the citizen, which had informed the earlier construction of modern society, were expanded to include distinctive and emphatic political dimensions. Accordingly, the legitimational focus of the law was attached to the citizen as a political actor, incrementally endowed with voting rights and other rights of electoral engagement. This expansion of the construct of the citizen defined, in essence, the constitution of the modern national political system. An initial consequence of the development of the modern political system was that, as in feudal society, the legal system fused with the military system. This meant that the two systems that had been kept separate through the formation of early modern society were, once more, integrally connected.[106] A further consequence of this

---

[106] For parallel analysis of the reconnection of the civil and the military spheres at the core of modern society, see Walter (2003: 319); Spreen (2008: 125); Rink (2010: 70); Poßelt (2013: 5–6).

was that the legal system became deeply attached to external conflicts, and military contestation over law in national society became porous to lines of antagonism in the international domain. This set of relations created the modern political system.

The figure of the modern citizen was constructed through integrational forces in society, and it reflected patterns of national institutional and legal integration. In key respects, however, the modern citizen undermined the material preconditions – that is, the existence of sovereign state institutions, nationally integrated populations and unified legal orders – that citizenship presupposed for its own realization. As examined later, the figure of the citizen cemented a deep rupture between the normative and functional dimensions of society. In its initial formulation, it created conditions in which its own normative essence, democracy, became improbable.

3

Democracy and Global Law

As mentioned earlier in this book, the revolutions of the late eighteenth century did not lead to full democratic citizenship in any polity. Only in the last decades of the nineteenth century did it become common for European polities to adopt constitutions with strong democratic features. It was not until around the end of World War I in 1918 that the core legitimational principle implied in modern citizenship – namely, that mass-political participation in legislative procedures forms the primary source of governmental legitimacy – became, in some locations, a common political reality. Before this time, all but a few European states had restricted democracy either by excluding some groups, typically members of the working class, from equal electoral participation, or by ensuring that elected legislatures only possessed limited powers.[1] Around 1918, a number of polities in Europe and Latin America began, usually temporarily, to meet basic threshold definitions of (male) democracy: that is, they tied their legitimacy to the full enfranchisement of their male populations, and they institutionalized competitive elections for representation in autonomous legislative bodies. In some polities, it was also accepted around 1918 that female members of national populations should be enfranchised as citizens.[2]

The patterns of mass-political inclusion that occurred around 1918 possessed a number of features that reflected the military aspect of modern citizenship. At this time, generally, the deep connection between

---

[1] Before 1918, Germany had full male enfranchisement, but elections were for a weak legislature. The United Kingdom had only roughly 60 per cent male enfranchisement until 1918. Italy had extensive but incomplete male enfranchisement from 1912. The United States had a large male franchise, but it was only universal for white men. Democracy was most consolidated in Scandinavia. Before 1918, Finland, not yet fully independent, and Norway had full male and female enfranchisement. Sweden was fully democratized in 1919–21 and Iceland in 1920.

[2] Women gained the vote in the United States in 1920. In the United Kingdom, some women were allowed to vote in 1918. Women were enfranchised in Germany, Austria, and Poland in 1918.

the legal side and the military side of the citizen was intensified. In fact, the dialectical potential inherent in the process of socio-political formation initiated around 1789 acquired particularly intense expression at the time of World War I.[3] It became clear at this time that the linkage of political rights to military engagement created a construction of legitimacy that obstructed the realization of democracy as a functional-institutional reality. The subjective form of the mass-democratic citizen pulled strongly against the formation of an integrational system in which this subject could become real.

The intersection between military functions and constructs of citizenship in new democracies formed around 1918 became manifest in the following respects.

First, in most European democracies established in and after 1918, many people obtained full democratic citizenship as soldiers, or at least in a legal process immediately determined by war. Citizenship was often defined at this point as a bundle of political rights to be given to soldiers, partly as compensation for hardships suffered during combat,[4] and the concept of the *soldat-citoyen* was again placed at the core of many national polities. In Germany, for example, all men and women first exercised democratic electoral rights in early 1919. In the United Kingdom, the elections of late 1918 were the first elections in which universal male suffrage (and partial female suffrage) was established. In both polities, the expansion of electoral rights was directly linked to the war. In Sweden, which remained neutral in the war but had general conscription from 1901, the campaign for universal suffrage, finalized between 1919 and 1921, was initially backed by the simple slogan: 'One man, one gun, one vote'. In many societies around 1918, further, soldiers obtained privileged citizenship rights. This occurred in the United Kingdom in 1918, as soldiers were allowed to vote at a younger age than other citizens. This occurred in Russia during the revolutionary period, where military mobilization and political citizenship were 'comingled', and soldiers acquired elevated political influence (von Hagen 1990: 35, 329).[5] In some societies, military service led to the extension of citizenship rights to groups

---

[3] One analysis sees 1914 as the 'result of a process which, since 1789, had lasted about 120 years', expressing a deep 'approximation between state and society' (Ingenlath 1998: 16). An alternative view explains that 1914 was the 'outcome of a process at work since the revolutionary wars' (Crépin 2009: 335).

[4] On this connection in Germany, see Llanque (2000: 158).

[5] The expansion of citizenship in revolutionary Russia was inseparable from military mobilization (Holquist 2002: 45; Retish 2008: 1–2; Kotsonis 2014: 292, 301).

previously excluded on ethnic grounds. In the United States, integration of ethnic minorities remained limited after 1918. In fact, World War I instilled a heightened intensity in ethnic conflicts in the United States. Disappointment amongst black American recruits at their protracted lack of integration after 1918 created a deep impetus for activism, which shaped black politics throughout the twentieth century (Williams 2010: 245, 264, 287). However, World War I clearly created expectations of integration amongst black Americans, and, as in Europe, it conjured the promise of full citizenship for persons formerly held in servitude.[6] In post-1918 Germany, many Jewish citizens assumed that military service would lead to greater inclusion. In some polities, the political enfranchisement of women after 1918 was connected to recognition for their service in wartime activities (Schaffer 1991: 94; Ross 2017: 149). In some polities, women acquired increased citizenship rights because their position in national labour markets had changed during the war, and they assumed new professional roles that released them from domestic obligations. In Canada, women were enfranchised step by step during the war. Priority was given to those whose contribution to the war effort was deemed greatest.

In Europe, the process of citizenship formation that began around 1789 approached completion for many people (at least many men) around 1918. For many men and women in Europe, the formal end of serfdom in the revolutionary period after 1789 had, up to 1914, only led to the notional, superficial transformation of their social status. For many Europeans, as mentioned, conditions of life and employment throughout the nineteenth century remained close to serfdom. For most European citizens up to 1914, political rights were not robustly established. Owing to franchise restrictions, political rights that did exist, formally, could not be easily exercised to affect labour and employment relations. In much of Europe, aspects of feudal law remained in force after its formal suspension. Working conditions in the countryside, in particular, perpetuated elements of serfdom.[7] In most of Europe, consequently, it was only

---

[6] See the discussion in Chambers II (1987: 6); Slotkin (2005 153–55); Capozzola (2010: 34).
[7] See discussion of the employment contract in nineteenth-century Germany as a 'relation based, not in law, but in violence' in Führer (1990: 41). Until 1900, rural estate workers and household staff in Germany were subject to direct personal control by landlords, who retained authority to exercise corporal discipline (see Vormbaum 1980: 356). Following the abolition of serfdom, approximately a third of poor workers worked under such conditions, so that the abolition of feudal law was only partial (Pierson 2016: 12). In Britain, the Master and Servant Act (1867) shows the proximity between labour and servitude at this time. This Act construed contractual relations at the workplace in terms close to bondage and it prescribed imprisonment for breach of contract (see Steinfeld

around 1918 that the deep structural transition, initiated in 1789, which led from conditions of limited citizenship and unfree labour towards full legal and political integration, was (temporarily) concluded. Indeed, in much of Europe, it was only in 1918 that the large landed estates originally built on serf labour were (partly) destroyed (see Halperin 2004: 152). The end of this transition from serfdom to citizenship which occurred around 1918 was, like its beginning around 1789, driven by military recruitment. As after 1789, in fact, for many people in Europe the experience of becoming a citizen around 1918 was not strictly distinguishable from the experience of becoming a soldier. In most settings, discernibly, the military pathway to citizenship created citizens by chance, and citizenship was conferred on many persons as an unforeseen outcome of their duties as soldiers. For many such persons, democratic citizenship was not a specifically desired condition. In many settings, the conditions in which full citizenship was attained, purchased through the devastation of World War I, left citizens ill-qualified to exercise rights attached to citizenship. Many early mass democracies were marked by the clear absence of democratic citizens at their legitimational centre, and the fact that citizens obtained democratic rights in war meant that few polities possessed a strong bedrock in democratic commitments.

Second, in many European polities, full citizenship was given to soldiers who, in 1918, were not yet fully demobilized, so that citizenship rights were exercised for the first time by persons who were, in part, still in a state of preparedness for war. This meant that, in different ways, wartime practices were carried over into peacetime, and many post-1918 democracies took shape, initially, in a condition in which irregular or semi-organized military groups prolonged aspects of warfare.

An important example of this interpenetration of war and peace is Germany. After 1918, Germany was temporarily the most advanced major democracy in Europe. The democratization of Germany in 1918–19 showed strong similarities to the foundation of the Third Republic in France, in 1870–71. In 1918–19, the transition to democracy

---

2001: 203). One account calculates that from 1847 to 1875 criminal proceedings were initiated against 10,000 British workers per annum for breaches of contract (Steinfeld 1999: 146). In Russia, former serfs lacked full citizenship and remained subject to separate courts until the Stolypin Land Reforms, initiated after 1905 (Leonard 2011: 257). In Brazil, abolition of slavery was preceded by laws imposing imprisonment for breach of certain contractual obligations (Conrad 1972: 73).

in Germany resulted from military defeat and the abdication of the ruling Emperor. It also occurred in conditions, in some regions, close to civil war. In the winter of 1918–19, the Social Democratic Party, which had been placed at the head of an interim government, consolidated its hold on power by mobilizing partly disbanded military units against its political opponents on the far left. Such interpenetration of war and peace was deepest in the states in Eastern and Central Europe, which emerged from former multi-ethnic Empires in Europe. In such settings, the boundaries of new ethno-political communities were established through war, and new polities were constructed through mobilization of irregular nationalist troops. Most societies in Eastern Europe were not pacified until 1922–23, and the establishment of new institutions coincided with ongoing civil conflict (Gewarth 2016: 248–267). In Hungary, war and civil conflict prevented the full establishment of democracy after 1918, facilitating the eventual formation of an authoritarian government, under Horthy, with strong military support. In Poland, the democratic experiment initiated in 1918 started in the army. In fact, the origins of the modern Polish state have a uniquely military nature. It was only because of World War I that the partition of Poland that began in the 1770s came to an end, and war created otherwise unforeseen opportunities for independent national democratic organization. The early political career of Piłsudski, periodic de facto leader of the Polish Second Republic from 1918, was strongly linked to paramilitary organizations. After 1918, the Polish army, comprising units that had operated in different Imperial forces in World War I, constituted the primary national institution.[8] The Polish Republic was then consolidated in multi-polar hostility, including war with Ukrainian and Russian forces, inter-partisan clashes with German militias and conflicts with different minorities. In this process, the military leadership around Piłsudski was central to the government, but the government struggled to assert full control over different military bodies (Böhler 2018: 176). The foundation in 1918 of the state that eventually became Yugoslavia was deeply marked by guerrilla violence and conflict between irregular soldiers (Gumz 2009: 194; Newman 2015: 41). Even Czechoslovakia, which stabilized more rapidly than other new states in Central Europe, saw widespread paramilitary violence (Kučera 2016: 828). In short, many new nation states created after 1918 had their origins in military bodies, in which regular armies, irregular armies and

---

[8] On the separate formation of Polish units in the Austro-Hungarian army during World War I, see Conze (1958: 39); Szlanta (2006: 154–157).

even armies of private warlords interacted closely. In some cases, the political sovereignty of new nations originated in partisan movements. This provided the raw substance from which interwar polities were created. Unsurprisingly, most new Central European 'democracies' either began life as dictatorships or soon descended into dictatorship.

In these conditions, the exercise of citizenship in early mass democracies retained an overtly military character. In many post-1918 polities, belligerent actions saturated peacetime politics. In particular, many political parties contained elements that were closely attached to military or paramilitary units, or at least to organizations that imprinted military-style discipline on political behaviour. This political model took shape in Italy after 1918, where the Fascist Party emerged from semi-demobilized paramilitary bodies and young volunteers recruited to join them. In interwar Germany, many parties – on left and right – contained associations which used military symbolism to generate party support (Voigt 2009: 42). Militarized groups in the Weimar era were not strongly incorporated in the regular army, as conscription had been abolished. By 1930, most German parties had organizations with partial military features (Reichardt 2002: 383). As a result, political parties were often required to compete for a stake in political decision-making both by participation in normal electoral competition and by engagement in street-level violence. In each respect, the first construction of mass democracies after 1918 involved the integration of citizens in soldierly form, and the processes of social mobilization and party-political formation that typified this period were not fully separable from military regimentation. Important in this regard is the fact that most European states lacked the sovereign authority required to regulate political conflict between mobilized parties. This was clear in Central Europe, where state control of military units was patchy. Even in polities such as the United Kingdom with moderately strong institutional systems, elite politicians recognized that political competition had become volatile through the creation of mass-democratic franchises, and arenas of public political contest were closely monitored and controlled.[9] This situation reproduced, in acutely intensified form, patterns of party formation after the French Revolution, in which militia groups and political factions interacted closely to challenge the sovereignty of state institutions. It was a characteristic of post-1918 polities that the military emphasis of

---

[9] For the United Kingdom, see analysis of rising elite anxiety about social politicization in Lawrence (2006: 213).

political organization increased, but the ability of states to manage such organization decreased.

Third, many democracies created after 1918 were legitimated by reference to aggregates of citizens that had only acquired firm national shape in World War I, and whose affiliation to political institutions with a specifically national character was largely the product of war. In different settings, national populations first assumed citizenship identities in war, and their experience of citizenship was often ill-matched to the roles and expectations essential to peaceful democratization.

For example, in relatively established European states, it was often only in the military environments created after 1914 that individual persons fully understood themselves as members of the same socio-geographical order.[10] This change in popular self-perception was caused by the fact that, in the course of the war, state institutions penetrated more evenly into national societies, and military organizations tended, to some degree, to bring persons from different social and regional backgrounds into proximity. This claim can, of course, be exaggerated. In most belligerent societies, class divisions were strictly reflected in military command structures and personal experience (Sheffield 2000: 72; Mariot 2013: 377). Moreover, military recruitment was marked by regional variations, and conscription was only integrally nationalized in the latter stages of war.[11] This meant that regional hostilities between social groups remained pervasive in national armies. This is well documented in armies, such as those of Great Britain and Germany, which incorporated many soldiers from regions with pronounced aversion to the dominant cultural group in national society (Ziemann 1997: 273). In its basic tendency, however, war did much to imprint increased national uniformity on different European populations. In many cases, wartime communities forged amongst soldiers at the frontlines were transferred back into domestic society after 1918, providing a foundation for constructions of citizenship and political affiliation. This is recorded in states

---

[10] The integrational outcomes of World War I in different societies, leading to reduction of class and ethnic divisions, are widely documented. See for Germany Kocka (1973); Llanque (2000: 42); for the United Kingdom, Leed (1979: 45); Cannadine (1990: 455); Gregory (2008: 205); for the United States Chambers (1987: 6); Slotkin 2005 (153–155); Capozzola (2010: 34). On the reduction of gender and class divisions at the same time, see Roberts (1971: 203); Gullace (2002: 3); Rabinowitch (2007: 65).

[11] In the United Kingdom, forces raised between 1914 and 1916 were often recruited by particular localities, containing an unprecedentedly 'high proportion of units directly linked to individual communities' (Simkins 1988: 186). In France, recruitment was highest in areas directly affected by war.

already formed before the war, such as France, Britain, Germany and Russia (Cabanes 2004: 78; Retish 2008: 264).

In less established states, populations acquired their essential definition as nations in the war. The foundation of national citizenship in war was particularly accentuated in polities created through the dissolution of multinational Empires. In many such environments, national population groups had, before 1918, lacked full legal recognition and representative government.[12] In such settings, the first path to political citizenship appeared in the armies gathered in 1914. In some cases, the citizens of new polities had fought in different Imperial armies until 1918, and they constructed national membership by splitting Imperial armies into particular national groups in the last months of the war. In these settings, new polities arose from the midst of armies, and popular sovereignty was indivisible from military mobilization. As a result, the growth of national citizenship was often propelled by armed forces in which, as under Napoleon, classical distinctions between regular soldiers, partisans and paramilitary units were non-existent (Böhler 2018: 176; Borodzieij and Górny 2018b: 133). In some parts of Eastern Europe, populations lived under direct military rule from 1914 to 1917–18. In some cases, military rule included enforced labour, close to serfdom (Westerhoff 2012: 181). The assumption of national citizenship in these domains occurred in a fully exceptionalist legal environment, in which partisan units accelerated processes of polity building that had traditionally taken a century or more to complete.[13] Unsurprisingly, many national polities were established in an environment marked by extreme social brutality.

Fourth, new democratic polities in Europe were deeply determined by the Bolshevik experiment in Russia, starting in 1917, which was conceived by its initiators as the first step in a global revolution (Rabinowitch 2007: 2). This event subjected the militarization of European society caused by World War I to febrile intensification, and it dramatically augmented existing propensities for volatile citizenship. Carl Schmitt explained, indicatively, that early mass-democratic polity formation around 1918 unfolded *sous l'oeil des Russes* (1932: 79). The basic sovereign form of the state was, in much of interwar Europe, defined by this fact.

---

[12] In the Russian Empire, the representative assemblies that existed before 1917 in majority-Russian areas were not established in all colonized areas (see Weeks 1996: 133).
[13] See analysis of the impact of military law in Russia during World War I in Graf (1974: 395). See similar analysis of borderlands between the Habsburg and Russian Empires in Borodziej and Górny (2018a: 210–211).

On the one hand, the coincidence between mass-democratization in Europe and the Russian Revolution meant that most post-1918 European polities were partly established on a defensive design. Democracy was conceived as a system of social demilitarization, intended to integrate citizens in non-revolutionary fashion.

One essential objective of early mass democracy in Europe was to avert Bolshevik-inspired insurrection. Importantly, the Revolution in Russia had originated in part in industrial unrest, and revolutionary activism had frequently been triggered in contexts created by strikes (Koenker and Rosenberg 1989: 23). High levels of industrial unrest were also widespread in Central and Western Europe in and after 1918, as economies emerging from war experienced labour surpluses and correlated intensification of industrial agitation. Such militancy included large-scale strikes in Spain, the resurgence of syndicalism and the foundation of the Communist Party in France, and protracted agitation in Italy, in the *biennio rosso*. In some parts of Europe, including in Germany and Hungary, industry was temporarily organized in 1918–19 by councils of soldiers and workers, borrowed from the Bolshevik model. In such settings, industrial activism assumed military dimensions, and strikes were not strictly separable from military action. In response to this, the years after 1918 saw a common shift towards state-directed welfarism, and some degree of welfare provision was institutionalized in much of Europe.[14] Early welfare states in Europe were partly designed to weaken any popular enthusiasm for the Russian Revolution, and their purpose was to ensure that material frictions between social groups were subject to state supervision and control. Welfarism played a vital role in the consolidation of the sovereignty of national state institutions in the aftermath of war.

The creation of early welfare states after 1918 was not solely driven by the need to mollify conflicts between citizens. In most post-1918 societies, the growth in welfare provision was linked to compensation for war veterans and for the dependants of soldiers fallen in war. As mentioned, as early as the eighteenth century, armies had assumed some welfare functions for combatants, keeping soldiers fit to fight and insulating them against poverty in case of injury.[15] In the nineteenth century, national

---

[14] For accounts of this process in different settings, see Preller (1949: 85); Reidegelt (1989: 480, 524); Weber (2010: 378). On the link between public welfarism and fear of the 'radicalizing consequences of unemployment' after 1918, see Führer (1990: 154).

[15] Many accounts exist that stress the importance of provision for veterans in state-building processes in the early modern period. See for example Becker (2016: 386).

increases in welfare provision were often linked to the expansion of military recruitment, and the dispensation of welfare was frequently enlarged under states marked by intensification in their military dimension.[16] The period before 1914, notably, had seen a substantial increase in welfare provision in many European societies. Democracies created in the wake of World War I usually established welfare institutions to avert extreme material hardship amongst ex-combatants. In fact, welfare provisions at this time were based on the assumption, to use a contemporary formulation, that 'general conscription and a general duty to provide care are inseparable concepts' (Marchet 1915: 27).[17] In most societies, it was only through war that the basic institutional apparatus able to integrate populations in welfare care structures developed. Notably, World War I generally gave rise to states with strengthened executive bodies, armed with enhanced powers of fiscal extraction and social coordination. Such powers typically became the basis for the later development of welfare systems.[18] One account has even claimed that the 'roots of modern welfare policies' are to be found in the 'provisions for war victims in World War I' (Pawlowsky and Wendelin 2015: 18).

Nonetheless, the early form of the welfare state which evolved after 1918 was discernibly designed to obviate political radicalization, to pacify industrial unrest, and to position state institutions as guarantors of social stability. The increasing commitment to welfarism at this time meant that democracy was ordered as a palliative system, acting to defuse inter-

---

[16] This is not a universal rule, but it clearly applies to many major polities, for example, post-1865 USA, post-1870 Germany, and pre-1914 Britain. See analysis of such provision in the post-1865 United States in Katz (1986: 207); Skocpol (1992: 59, 65, 531; 1993: 115); Orloff (1993: 138, 151). One author claims that, in the earlier twentieth century, 'a substantial portion of the American welfare effort was devoted to veterans' – after 1918, nearly 50 per cent of non-military non-debt spending was for veterans (Campbell 2004: 264–65, 253). See also Janowitz (1978: 12, 216).

[17] On the importance of care for veterans in the early Weimar Republic, perhaps the most advanced major welfare system of interwar Europe, see Sachße and Tennstedt (1988: 88–92). See comparative analysis of the relation between welfarism and care for veterans in post-1918 Europe in Meyer (1983); Pironti (2015); Cohen (2000: 78).

[18] See claims that in the United States the institutional preconditions of the New Deal were set in World War I in Eisner (2000: 19); Sparrow (2011: 25–6). On the general link between war and welfare in the United States, see further Adler (2017: 194). On post-1918 France, see Smith (2003: 75). See for general analysis Wilensky (1975 72). One account states on this point simply: 'The strong historical connection between warfare and welfare is uncontested' (Obinger and Schmitt 2011: 247).

group conflicts and to mediate antagonisms between different classes of citizens.

On the other hand, the coincidence between mass-democratization in Europe and the Russian Revolution meant that attitudes towards Russian Communism were deeply internalized in the domestic politics of different states. It also meant that anxiety about the geo-political expansion of Russian power conditioned loyalties and motivations of citizens across Europe.

One way in which anxieties about Communist revolution impacted on mass democracy after 1918 was visible in the fact that, in different European societies, already highly conflictual patterns of political interaction were exacerbated by the fact that some political groups aligned themselves to Bolshevism.[19] Most interwar European polities, based in newly extended franchises, were defined, structurally, by conflict between collective organizations closely attached to distinct social classes. The strong attachment between party and class that began in the middle of the nineteenth century was greatly reinforced at this juncture. Naturally, this polarization took different form in different polities, and class divisions were expressed with varying degrees of intensity. In some polities, such as Sweden, it became possible to establish cross-class governmental coalitions. However, most newly enfranchised electorates were divided into political organizations representing sharply antagonistic class interests. As a result, new democratic polities were required to integrate a number of highly organized and highly adversarial social factions, and different citizenship groups encountered each other in democratic procedures as actors linked to acutely counter-posed class prerogatives. Through the 1920s, such conflicts were articulated against a background shaped by the Russian Revolution, and all parties, expressly or implicitly, explained their commitments through reference to ideological positions resulting from the Russian Revolution. The Revolution in Russia generated an environment of global ideological adversity which intensified existing sociopolitical conflicts in national societies. In this environment, domestic patterns of political interaction tended to reproduce aspects of global conflict, so that the exercise of citizenship typically acquired violent form: this proved the defining characteristic of interwar democracy.

[19] For excellent historical analysis of this, see Wirsching (1999: 15). See analysis of Weimar Germany, claiming that fear of Bolshevik insurrection led to the emergence of 'a consensus about defence that crossed all political camps' (Bergien 2012: 387). See the related claim that military prerogatives pervaded all 'areas of civil life and order' in Geyer (1978: 43). For excellent comparative analysis of Germany and France, see Weber (2010: 378).

In Russia, the Revolution and its aftermath were shaped by intrinsically militarized forms of political citizenship and contestation. Bolshevism developed in Russia as the expression of a society that was deeply oriented towards warfare, in which realities usually associated with war penetrated into everyday social exchange.[20] During World War I, military and civilian institutions in Russia had already become closely connected, and military organizations acted as suppliers and extractors of goods, fixers of prices and providers of welfare in society at large (Sanborn 2005: 308). This background was reflected in the growth of Bolshevism. Key early revolutionary measures were introduced in the military.[21] The first attempts to institutionalize Bolshevik rule were experiments in war communism, in which state control over trade and industrial production was patterned on wartime economic policies to supply the army (Sakwa 1988: 57, 216; Smele 2015: 183). The Bolshevik party itself had some features of a radical partisan unit; it conducted irregular warfare, and it strategically linked citizenship and military service. During the civil war connected to the Revolution, the Red Army, founded in 1918, grew rapidly into an army formed through proletarian conscription, and it became an important cultural and organizational centre of the emerging Russian state (Figes 1990: 169). In areas close to the civil-war front, ultimately, Russian society entered a state of total, multi-polar and often diffusely focused violence, in which partisan units played important military roles, and 'the distinctiveness between civil and military spaces was suspended, both geographically and mentally' (Plaggenborg 1996: 417). The civil war brought far greater loss of life in Russia than World War I itself. Moreover, the militarization of political practice in Bolshevism was sustained by political outlooks based in irreducibly class-based analyses of politics, which defined representatives of the bourgeoisie as objects of implacable class enmity. The Revolution in Russia entailed a quite profound militarization of political citizenship and social class at the same time (see Brovkin 1994: 189).

Aspects of this militarization were transferred into other European polities after 1918. At this time, parties of the radical left frequently internalized practices and attitudes typical of Bolshevism. In most parts

---

[20] See discussions in Holquist (2002: 142); Lohr (2003); Rabinowitch (2007: 355); Kruse (2009: 206).

[21] On the centrality of violence to the early Soviet system, see Sanborn (2003: 5). On the military beginnings of the Russian Revolution, see analysis in Sanborn (2014: 196–97) of Order Nr. 1 of the Petrograd Soviet (March 1917), which abolished Tsarist command structures in the army.

of Europe, as discussed, left-oriented political constituencies were only fully enfranchised around 1918. In many settings, the enfranchisement of the left occurred in conditions in which many groups attached to the far right had not disbanded after the war. This meant that parties of the left operated in settings that conditioned them for intense violence, shaped by recent examples in Moscow and St Petersburg. Given the recollection of recent mass slaughter in the war, in fact, many left-wing voters and activists after 1918 articulated their hostility to capitalism as a civil-war ideology, in which, not unreasonably, they observed capitalism as a mode of production that threatened their physical existence (Wirsching 1999: 113; Bergien 2012: 389). From the outset, therefore, some parties of the left acquired a propensity for violence, against even moderate advocates of democracy.[22] Naturally, this propensity was mirrored, in heightened form, amongst the adversaries of the radical left. On both sides, the years after 1918 witnessed the formation of deeply hostile collective political subjects, linked to global ideological polarities. Consequently, many European democracies were born, after 1918, in circumstances not easily distinguishable from inter-ideological partisan warfare.

For these reasons, many European societies after 1918 quickly collapsed into armed or at least semi-militarized conflicts between groups defined by different attitudes to Bolshevism. Such ideological adversity was typically expressed, as mentioned, in societies in which formal institutions were weak, and governments did not possess sovereign control of the military dimension of society. It was in this conjuncture, then, that Fascist movements were able to take root in some European societies. Fascism originally emerged as a pattern of violent citizenship, expressed as a counter-revolutionary response to Bolshevism, driven by militarized parties with armed paramilitary wings. Fascism gained impetus through a process in which external ideological polarization was translated into domestic citizenship practices, and political violence was deployed, within national societies, as part of a global ideological war. Fascism was frequently fostered by military units whose positions had been reinforced, in different societies, because of the prevalence of conditions close to civil war. In fact, many members of Fascist movements had first-hand experience of fighting against Bolsheviks in the civil wars and border conflicts that erupted in and after 1918. Once established, Fascist parties were often supported by traditional elite actors, especially those with high-ranking military offices, who used them to

---

[22] See on Germany Schumann (2001: 11, 306).

combat Bolshevik ideals. Not surprisingly, once installed into government, Fascist parties created regimes with striking similarities to the systems of command that typify armies, and they imposed wartime conditions on their societies. Both Bolshevism and Fascism promoted models of citizenship in which military techniques of integration and regimentation prevailed, and structures of socio-economic control pioneered in World War I assumed permanence.[23] Under Fascism, political institutions were deployed, in essence, as instruments of military repression, reward and reprisal, and government was constructed as a solidified civil war against all groups that stood accused of Bolshevik sympathies. After 1918, it was a common experience that both military units and political parties escaped the sovereign control of national states. Fascism developed as a mode of governance in which the state radically re-asserted its sovereignty by mobilizing existing military forces to stabilize an anti-Bolshevik bloc.

Two rival models of state formation became visible in Europe after 1918. These models were starkly opposed: *Welfare democracy or Fascism*. Both models of statehood reflected a reaction to the end of the long process of citizenship formation that began around 1789. Both models reflected distinct strategies to establish the sovereignty of the state over its population in a highly militarized environment, caused by World War I and the rise of Bolshevism. Both models in fact took shape as alternative responses to the essential sociological feature of modern democracy: namely, that democracy usually took shape in societies in which the state struggled to exercise sovereignty over its own citizens, and citizens tended to form collective patterns of political subjectivity along lines defined by class prerogatives. In this stark counter-position, it was Fascism that prevailed in interwar Europe. Fascism formed a regime type in which rights of citizenship obtained in 1918 through the army were retracted with the assistance of the army, and the sovereign power of the state was re-consolidated by military means. Most European populations were placed in a position of military servitude by Fascist governments. In most societies, Fascist governments imposed either partial or comprehensive forced-labour regimes, so that the threat, palpable since 1789, that released serfs would be re-converted into conscripted workers became a brutal reality.

---

[23] The two pillars of European Fascism – centralized and authoritarian command structures and economic corporatism – simply extended into peacetime the system of social control created in World War I. For an important sociological analysis of Communism and Fascism as 'war economies', perpetuating military adversity into economic relations, see Kruse (2009: 205–206).

Fascist governments formed an emblematic expression of the contradictions resulting from the military aspects of citizenship.

Fifth, the legal orders of post-1918 democracies were frequently rooted in military laws, in which exceptional prerogative powers were accorded to governmental leaders. In each belligerent polity between 1914 and 1918, government was conducted under special provisions, usually based in emergency powers, which heightened the authority of the executive branch, especially in matters essential for military supply and industrial production. There were of course variations in this process, as some polities retained relatively strong checks on executive power.[24] Nonetheless, the tendency towards executive reinforcement was widespread. After 1918, most constitutions reproduced such tendencies by establishing systems of government with strong executives. In addition, several post-1918 constitutions contained either formal or informal provisions for the deployment of military force to impose order in situations in which the polity was threatened by unrest. Typically, such provisions indicated that, in moments of crisis, supreme political authority should be withdrawn from representative organs, attached to citizens through controlled lines of electoral communication, and the ultimate power to make law should be vested in figures possessing legitimacy of an exceptionalist nature. In constitutional provisions of this type, the essential legitimacy of the state was constructed in analogy to military legitimacy. In many polities after 1918, such provisions were used with greater frequency than had originally been foreseen. The category of political challenges classifiable as examples of emergency situations was sometimes interpreted broadly, to incorporate economic problems and problems caused by inter-party discord. This was evident in Germany, where extensive and very destabilizing use was made of emergency laws after 1919. This was prominent in Austria, where laws of military origin formed the basis for authoritarian constitutional reform in the late 1920s. In the supposedly more liberal context of the United Kingdom, exceptional governmental powers were established in the Emergency Powers Act (1920), and military diction was used to justify the establishment of semi-dictatorial government in 1931 (see Kent 2009: 192). Through the 1920s, many day-to-day political problems were addressed under laws of a military nature, and in much of Europe the legitimacy of government was presented in categories with a strong

---

[24] In France, strong parliamentary controls on the executive remained in place in World War I (Renouvin 1925: 92–93; Bock 2002: 246–249).

military inflection: democracy assumed the form of a war society. This in turn lent legitimacy to political movements that were willing to use violence to destabilize the architecture of democracy. Emergency provisions in national constitutions often opened a doorway through which military leaderships, or political parties supported by military leaders, were able to take hold of the instruments of government. This happened in Germany and Austria in the early 1930s.

In each of these respects, in the first creation of mass democracy as a common system of political order, the primary subject of democratic government – the sovereign political citizen – was configured in terms that prevented the formation of political systems likely to preserve legitimacy. The citizen was configured in a violent form, articulating political agency as military solidarity, and showing a strong proclivity to acquire divisive collective expression, linked to binary global oppositions. Most early mass democracies were marked by high levels of social polarization, and few democracies consolidated a model of citizenship able to appeal to and to integrate persons beyond fissures resulting from social rivalry. Few states were able to establish a sovereign order to integrate their citizens, and both their institutional and their normative functions of integration approached crisis. By consequence, mass democracy did not originally take shape, as implied in standard accounts of democratization, as a system of collective emancipation or popular self-legislation. On the contrary, democracy first emerged as a system of interaction between organized groups of citizens which sought to secure control of political institutions for the violent monopolization of power and the structural defence of select social interests. In such settings, democratic rules of government were incapable of organizing hostilities between different political groups, and democracy retained – at least latently – its original quality as de facto civil war. In most instances, post-1918 democracies were soon replaced by dictatorships. This usually created a societal reality in which one or more of the groups that had originally contested the sovereignty of the state acquired sufficient power to take full control of the state apparatus, deploying its resources to ensure that opposing interests were excluded from the system of political representation. This often occurred with the help of military elites. Early mass-democratic polities thus brought the underlying antinomies of political citizenship to the sharpest articulation.

Modern democracy, based in full (male) citizenship, was brought into life after 1918 by political forces linked to military recruitment. Democratic polities created after 1918 were rapidly plunged into crisis by the transposition of principles of global warfare into domestic political conflict. In its first incarnation, national democracy was, almost universally, a failed experiment. Most national polities that underwent democratic transformation around 1918 arrived, at best, at a condition of *intermittent democracy*. This term can be used to describe most democracies established in Central and Eastern Europe around 1918, in which short-lived periods of full political integration stimulated a brutal backlash amongst elites, who used a mixture of democratic organization and military force to gain control of the means of social coercion in their societies. Those few polities that did not subside into complete authoritarianism in the 1920s and 1930s also struggled to preserve a condition of full democracy. Indeed, polities such as the United States and the United Kingdom that avoided extreme authoritarianism at this time only institutionalized a system of selective enfranchisement or *partial democracy*: that is, they weakened procedures for democratic representation, and they ensured that full democratic citizenship remained a privilege for designated social groups. In virtually all states legitimated by concepts of national citizenship, therefore, the formation of democratic institutions came to a halt some way short of comprehensive democratic integration and legitimation, and civil conflict or civil exclusion remained core features of the polity. Across the range of national societies, democratic citizenship rarely formed more than a partial, unstable foundation for the law. Very few national societies were able to extract a generalized integrational form from the construct of the sovereign political citizen. Although conventionally observed as a political system based in collective liberty and self-determination, national democracy almost invariably developed as a system of selective repression.

What this means, in essence, is that, in its first full expression, democratic citizenship did not act as a political form that facilitated the positive construction of the law, or that translated social relations into an inclusive system of integration. As discussed, the basic structure of modern society was determined by overlapping processes of normative integration and institutional integration. However, these processes were, from the outset, undermined by the normative constructions of legitimacy on which they relied. The construct of the political citizen eventually instilled a pathologically unsettling paradox into these processes of integration. The modern citizen created political systems in which the two core processes of integration – institutional integration and normative integration – were fused together by a shared military emphasis. This meant that the basic normative subject of democracy, the sovereign citizen, spelled out a principle of legitimacy which fractured the institutional structure presupposed by citizenship, and which impeded the integration of national society. *The more social interactions were translated into norms constructed and authorized by citizens, the more the processes of integration promoted and presupposed by citizenship approached crisis.*

At the core of this pathology was the fact that the modern construct of the citizen tied the legitimation of law to the mobilization of military force. This fact placed a deep contradiction between the normative subject and the functional-integrational reality of democracy at the nervous centre of most modern polities. This fact meant that citizenship internalized in national political practices the conflicts articulated in the international arena, and it often reconstructed these conflicts as elements of inner-societal interaction. It also meant that the citizen tended to assume the shape of a collective subject, articulating collective prerogatives in national societies in form that reflected external military and ideological polarities. At the most fundamental level, this fact meant that the production of law, shaping the integrational structure of society as a whole, resulted from contests between mobilized, often armed groups of citizens, which were deeply sensitive to international adversities. In each respect, the development and eventual crisis of mass democracy after 1918 gave expression to one deep-lying antinomy in modern democracy: democracy was invariably unsettled by its own basic normative definition, and the endeavour to consolidate the norm of the sovereign citizen as the premise of democracy consistently conflicted with the functional dimension of democracy, as a system of effective institutional integration. This was caused by the fact that, after 1789 and then more intensely after 1918, democracy was driven by the fusion of two key integration systems in modern society – the legal system and the military system. Democracy proved incapable of developing on this foundation. This deep constitutional antinomy of modern democracy was reflected, paradigmatically, in the forms of extreme authoritarianism initiated in the 1920s and 1930s, in which the military was used to re-establish the state's sovereignty in society. In such regimes, military actors reinstituted serfdom or conditions of private dominion close to serfdom in much of Europe, and the essential integrational dynamic that underpins national society was reversed. In this process, polities legitimated by citizenship lost their distinction as centres of public integration and the societies which they governed lost their basic character as nations.

Militarized Citizenship After 1945

In the decades after 1945, the normative substance of national democracy gradually became a reality. In this period, the political systems of an increasing number of societies were centred around national citizenship as legitimational norm. From the 1940s to the 1960s, as mentioned, democracy was little more than a tentative, localized experiment, primarily concentrated in Northern Europe. Even in the polities of post-1945 Northern Europe, democracy was not secured overnight, and its period of consolidation lasted into the 1960s. Over a longer period, however, democracy evolved into a global political form. From the mid-1960s to the mid-1970s, an international consensus was established that polities that fell short of democracy lacked legitimacy. This was expressed in the International Covenant on Civil and Political Rights adopted by the United Nations (UN) in 1966, which declared a presumption in favour of a global right to democracy. This was also expressed in the Helsinki Accords of 1975. To reflect this, polities such as the United States that had already possessed a partial democratic character before 1945 approached complete democratization in the 1960s, ensuring electoral enfranchisement of all citizens. In the 1970s and 1980s, foundations for democracy were set in many authoritarian polities in Southern Europe, Latin America and, later, Eastern Europe. By the late 1990s, many African polities had embarked on democratic transitions, and some degree of democracy had spread to most polities in the world. After 1945, therefore, most polities became *democratizing polities*: that is, most polities acquired a form in which – as a minimum – some democratic features became the norm, and commitment to democracy could not easily be eliminated from formal projections of governmental legitimacy. Vital in this respect is the fact that, unlike after 1918, the widening of citizenship led, gradually, to the formation of national polities as reasonably stable systems of legal and institutional integration, in which a large number of citizens were able to exercise electoral functions without inducing systemic collapse.

The progressive globalization of democracy after 1945 appears, at first glance, as a process that contradicts the main assertion in the analysis above – namely, that crisis potentials in mass democracy are connected to the internalization of international conflicts in the normative figure of the national citizen. After 1945, the global political environment was marked by persistently intense inter-ideological rivalry, and global hostilities had a profound universal impact on societal construction and national polity building. This hostility was reflected, most obviously, in the onset of the Cold War between the United States and the Soviet Union in the 1940s. This was accompanied by the background threat of global nuclear war, and, frequently, by the increased determination of national policymaking by global military pressures. Indicatively, one leading commentator expressed the view before 1945 that a system of militarized statehood was about to become commonplace (Lasswell 1941: 461). The same theorist observed seven years later that politics had frozen into a 'bipolar world', in which 'policies in every sphere of human activity are affected by calculations of the relative strength of America and Russia' (Lasswell 1948: 877). In addition, outside Europe and the United States, warfare after 1945 was not usually very *cold*. Interstate conflict continued in large regions of the globe, typically in a form intensified by the position of belligerent states in the system of international alliances created by the Cold War. The decades after 1945 saw a high number of military coups, and armies frequently acquired a leading role in processes of state formation, especially in decolonizing polities. Even in Europe, democratic polity building after 1945 remained partly linked to military mobilization. Both the 1958 Constitution of France and the 1976 Constitution of Portugal were created in military conflicts arising from decolonization. The constitution of the Fifth Republic in France was established to stabilize the governmental executive amidst instability caused by the Algerian War, and the Portuguese constitution had its origins in military insurgency. France saw two major wars in the years after 1945. The United Kingdom imposed peacetime conscription for the first time after 1945. Quite persuasively, therefore, some sociologists and historians have described universal militarization as a distinct hallmark of post-1945 societies (Enloe 1993: 5; Saull 2001: 70).

This background meant that the deep historical linkage between citizenship and militarism persisted in many societies after 1945. Many societies experienced patterns of institutional integration that strongly reflected this linkage.

This persistent link between citizenship and militarism was expressed, first, in the fact that many democratizing states saw an expansion of citizenship that was driven by war. As in earlier post-bellum contexts, one legacy of World War II was that, in many settings, it led to the reinforcement of citizenship rights. As in 1918, widened legal-political integration of citizens was promoted after 1918 as recompense for military labour.

In a number of democratizing polities, this reinforcement of rights was demonstrated in the extension of core political rights. In many polities that had fought for the allied forces, franchise extensions were implemented immediately after the war. In the United Kingdom, the inherited unequal franchise was abolished in legislation of 1948, taking effect in 1950. In France, women were enfranchised in 1944–45. However, this reinforcement of rights was more strongly demonstrated in the field of social rights. This was clear in the early design of the post-1945 welfare state in the United Kingdom, which was intended to extend wartime solidarities into a permanent integrational system. Comparable tendencies appeared in Canada, where the expansion of welfare rights grew from military responsibilities (Cowen 2005: 660). Important early welfare provisions in the Federal Republic of Germany (FRG), notably the *Bundesversorgungsgesetz* (1950), were focused on persons adversely affected by military service or military internment. In the Soviet Union, claims to social rights were also justified on grounds of military sacrifice (Dale 2015: 163).

Exemplary of the post-1945 expansion of citizenship rights is the United States. After 1945, Truman's presidency was shaped by a new conception of national citizenship, designed to link citizens to the national government though a thickened body of rights. As discussed below, this new conception of citizenship was partly intended to extend political rights to minority groups. Distinctively, however, Truman promoted the widening of citizenship to place emphasis on social rights. In his famous speech to representatives of the Civil Rights Movement in 1947, Truman committed himself to securing both political and social rights for all citizens – the right to a 'decent home', 'to an education', to 'adequate medical care', to 'a worthwhile job' and to 'an equal share in making public decisions through the ballot' (McCoy and Ruetten 1973: 74–75). Building on earlier principles of the New Deal, these policies meant that the language of social rights permeated into government agencies, becoming a 'staple of federal-state communication' (Tani 2016: 81). Overall, although hardly marked by concerted welfarism, this period saw a wider configuration of citizenship, in which political rights and social rights played a leading role in integrating national society.

Truman's policies had a clear military background. First, central agencies with the force to give effect to civil and social rights policies in the United States had only been created in World War II, so that the hard infrastructure of citizenship resulted from war (Reed 1991: 345). Further, Truman was an advocate of the draft, and he introduced a series of provisions to improve national security.[25] At this time, moreover, protections for social rights were allotted preferentially to soldiers and combatants, who derived privileges from social-welfare policies, introduced to facilitate the integration of ex-military personnel. For example, the end of the war saw the implementation of the G.I. Bill of Rights (Servicemen's Readjustment Act of 1944), which opened professional opportunities to servicemen and recognized military service as a distinguished form of citizenship (Mettler 2005: 361). The need to provide care for veterans also acquired increased social impact at this time (Segal 1989: 87). By the 1970s, it is estimated that roughly 15 per cent of Americans were military veterans, with some potential entitlement to welfare on these grounds (see Levitan and Cleary 1973: 4). In these respects, post-1945 statehood in the United States corresponded, in part, to the classical model of the militarized democracy. As in earlier settings, the thickening of citizenship rights served both to integrate communities mobilized by war in an extended corpus of rights and to solidify the foundations of government in society, in an environment still pervasively marked by conflict.

This persistent linkage of citizenship and militarism after 1945 was expressed, second, in the fact that, in states with central positions in the Cold War, international tensions had far-reaching implications for the citizenship of marginalized groups. Global military pressures frequently promoted full democratic inclusion.

In the United States, for example, the broad redefinition of national citizenship that characterized the postwar period meant that citizenship rights for historically marginalized ethnic minorities, especially black citizens in the Southern States, were reinforced (see Parker 2009: 12). Arguably, it was only at this time that federal civil rights law took shape in the United States as a body of constitutional norms with binding effect for all citizens (Lovell 2012: 43). In fact, it was only in the decades after 1945 that the Bill of Rights was applied, relatively uniformly, in different states.[26] These processes were reflected in important pieces of legislation, especially the Civil Rights Act (1964) and the Voting Rights Act (1965), which extended rights of electoral participation to all citizens. These

---

[25] See p. 147.
[26] See the contrast between positions regarding the incorporation of the Bill of Rights between *Adamson* v. *California*, 332 US 46 (1947) and *Duncan* v. *Louisiana*, 391 US 145 (1968). One observer claims, with regard to the implementation of constitutional rights at state level, that the 1960s eventually saw an 'incorporation explosion' (Yarbrough 1976: 258).

processes were also reflected in a series of landmark legal rulings that promoted minority rights.[27]

Such widening of constitutional rights in the United States also had a strong military dimension. In fact, the extension of citizenship was partly stimulated by actors in the army. First, experiences in the army during the war, including formal and overt discrimination, led to increased protest amongst many black soldiers, which paved the way for later civil rights activism (Sitkoff 1971: 661). Second, the army played a leading role in reducing ethnic segregation, in allocating social roles in ethnically neutral procedures (Sherry 1995: 145; Moskos and Butler 1996: 2) and even in promoting activist attitudes amongst disadvantaged minorities (Moskos 1966: 146). Systematic desegregation after 1945 began in the military domain, with Executive Order 9981 (1948). In some respects, third, the enforcement of civil rights for black citizens was similar to a process of territorial administration, in which military units were deployed to impose uniform terms of citizenship across American society.[28]

In addition, civil rights policies in the United States were strongly determined by global conflicts in the Cold War context. Such policies formed a reaction to attempts in the Soviet Union to undermine the legitimacy of the United States both globally and – in particular – in decolonizing societies in Africa, by drawing attention to apartheid conditions in the south of the United States.[29] Truman's civil rights policies were strongly shaped by the view that racial discrimination in the United States adversely affected the international interests of the United States, so that civil rights policies and national security concerns were closely connected (Rosenberg 2006: 183; Berg 2007: 81). Even legal judgements that expanded civil rights were expressly coloured by the global military conjuncture. Leading judges at this time explained that their rulings against racial discrimination were part of a strategy to uphold the moral supremacy of the United States in the Cold War.[30] For example,

---

[27] See by way of example *Shelley* v. *Kraemer*, 334 US 1 (1948); *Brown* v. *Board of Education of Topeka*, 347 US 483 (1954).

[28] Eisenhower used military justifications for his actions at Little Rock in 1957, insisting that 'the force we send there is strong enough that it will not be challenged' (Sherry 1995: 211).

[29] See extensive analysis in Berman (1970: 77); McCoy and Ruetten (1973: 66); Lauren (1983); Lockwood (1984); Layton (2000); Skrentny (2002); Rosenberg (2006: 175); Borstelmann (2009); Westad (2007: 134); Jensen (2016).

[30] The Department of Justice provided amicus curiae briefs in *Brown* v. *Board of Education of Topeka*, 347 US 483 (1954). It stated that *Brown* possessed particular significance because of the international context, in which United States was 'trying to prove to the

Chief Justice Earl Warren justified his civil rights jurisprudence as follows: 'Our American system like all others is on trial both at home and abroad ... the extent to which we maintain the spirit of our Constitution with its Bill of Rights, will in the long run do more to make it secure and the object of adulation than the number of hydrogen bombs we stockpile' (cited in Dudziak 2004: 37). Indicatively, judicial recognition of human rights in national politics was strongly promoted by the executive branch, which, under Truman, provided amicus curiae briefs endorsing international human rights law in cases concerning racial equality (see Elliff 1987: 254; Dudziac 2000: 90–91, 102; Cleveland 2006).

This persistent linkage of citizenship and militarism after 1945 was expressed, third, in the fact that, in many polities, the role of domestic military organizations was influenced by the global polarization between the Soviet Union and the United States. The Cold War had the result that most states were required to assume a strategic position within the global partition of military and economic influence. In most polities, global military calculations formed an important aspect of domestic policy-making and institutional formation, and national citizenship practices mirrored global military constellations.

After 1945, states that were centrally impacted by the Cold War experienced close interaction between military elites and political office-holders, military spending increased and military actors often reached deep into civil politics. This was most palpably evident in the United States and the Soviet Union, in which politicians with military backgrounds assumed strong influence, and investment in the military reached unprecedented heights. In the United States, the architecture of government was altered by the National Security Act (1947), which meant that the military apparatus was more closely attached to governmental offices (Leffler 1992: 176; Hogan 1998: 66). From 1945, many traditionally restrictive maxims of spending policy in the United States were suspended because of budgetary demands arising from global polarization.[31] Indeed, for the first time in American history, the period after 1945 did not see full military demobilization and the perceived threat of war acquired acute state-building force within national society (Friedberg 2000: 40; Thorpe 2014: 15). In each respect, military politics

people of the world, of every nationality, race and color, that a free democracy is the most civilized and most secure form of government yet devised by man' (Dudziak 1988: 65).

[31] Important analyses have argued that budgetary expansion should not be exaggerated, and that the fiscal impact of the Cold War was always countervailed by a culture of anti-statism (Friedberg 2000: 81).

had an unprecedented impact on domestic institutions. After 1945, the Soviet Union had extremely high levels of defence spending, up to about 13 per cent of GDP by the 1960s. The military formed the second pillar of the state in the Soviet Union, although it clearly retained a subordinate position in relation to the Communist Party leadership.

In states more marginally positioned in the Cold War, the political role of military personnel acquired greater salience than in earlier historical periods. In Latin America, for example, military engagement in politics became widespread. This tendency was especially pronounced after the successful revolution in Cuba culminating in 1959, and it was strongly shaped by global tensions. Notable in the Cuban Revolution was the fact that Fidel Castro utilized militias to promote regime change, mobilizing sectors of the population in intensely politicized fashion and blurring divisions between military and civilian functions (Stepan 1971: 155; Enloe 1980a: 160). This renewed emergence of the partisan was replicated in other countries, for example in Colombia, and polities in Central America (Goodwin 2001: 162). This gave rise to a fear of partisan mobilization across Latin America, which in turn led to a distinctive pattern of official security politics, in which armies turned their security prerogatives inward and military units were deployed mainly as bulwarks against revolutionary groups within national societies (Morley 1987: 133; Skidmore 1988: 4). Such environments saw a steep rise in the violence used by state agencies. After this time, further, the military apparatus in many Latin American states was closely correlated with economic groups whose prerogatives were influenced by the security policies of the United States. In Brazil in 1964, in Chile in 1973 and in Argentina in 1976, for example, military regimes were established whose main purpose was to ensure that economic groups affiliated to the United States were stabilized across the continent (Westad 2007: 151). In such settings, opponents of democratically elected left-leaning governments deployed a diction that was closely modelled on global ideological polarities, and domestic conflict immediately reflected wider political-economic antagonisms. This was illustrated by the mobilization of reactionary forces against President Goulart in Brazil around 1964, where the paramilitary groups that sabotaged Goulart's government extracted legitimacy directly from the Cold War scenario (Bandeira 2010: 353).

In many instances, military engagement in civil politics in post-1945 Latin America occurred in social contexts similar to those that characterized post-1918 Europe. In most cases, military regimes were installed as national societies experienced polarization into deeply hostile and strongly mobilized citizenship groups which endeavoured to monopolize the instruments of government. These groups were typically linked to counter-posed economic blocs, and they articulated their positions in relation to global ideological distinctions, defined in the circumstances of the Cold War. This polarization was particularly unsettling in the Latin American context, where, historically, interstate war had only played a limited role in institution building and inner-societal integration. As discussed, external conflict had shaped socio-institutional integration in some societies in Latin America in the 1860s, during the Paraguayan War. Typically, however, Latin American states were not supported by deeply embedded citizenship norms, and they did not establish close institutional linkage with their citizens. One reason for this, importantly, was that they had not originally been formed through large-scale wars, their military and fiscal capacities were low and their armies were not fully nationalized and did not impose solid integrational form on national society (Centeno 2002: 37; Holden 2004: 107).[32] Weak states, weak citizenship, weak institutional structure and weak capacity for national military mobilization were common features of Latin American societies: this of itself underlines the formative connection, observed in other parts of the globe, between legal integration, shared citizenship, solid fiscal obligations and military engagement. As a result, historically, Latin American governments were less strongly linked than European polities to external conflicts. Although Latin American societies saw frequent internal conflict between rival militias and military factions, governments were relatively insulated against external pressures (Centeno 2002: 16; Soifer 2015: 205). However, the Cold War created an unusual geopolitical constellation in Latin America, in which external military plans and economic prerogatives led to heightened intervention of national armies in civilian politics, and the armed forces assumed new directive roles in defining the contours of citizenship.[33]

This persistent linkage of citizenship and militarism after 1945 was expressed, fourth, in processes of decolonization that took place in many parts of the globe. Not all decolonization involved open war or revolution. In many cases, colonized societies assumed independence in compacted, negotiated agreements between metropolitan and colonial

---

[32] In Brazil, for example, by the late nineteenth century the army was the only genuinely national institution, and by 1930 it was a core bulwark of government. Yet, its capacities were limited and its national societal penetration restricted (see McCann 2004: 10, 176).

[33] See analysis of how, before 1964, the Brazilian army acquired the position of a political '*director*' in Stepan (1971: 134).

powers. Generally, however, even the more peaceful processes of decolonization contained military and revolutionary components. Some mobilization against the colonial power or actors close to colonial interests was an essential aspect of citizenship formation in new nations. In societies that underwent decolonization, the army usually pre-existed the formation of the state, and it acted as a central agent in nation building. In such cases, the integrational foundations of new nations were created by military elites and within military institutions.[34] This usually occurred in states governed by single political parties, which were often linked to dominant ethnic groups, and in which military units and political factions were closely linked. In many such settings, the military promoted specific group interests, and it did not solidify a state structure able to overarch diverse communities in society (Enloe 1980b: 23). This frequently led to unmanageable polarization and competition for military control between ethnically self-identified factions. Military processes of integration and citizenship formation often led to military coups or to civil war, in which the premises of citizenship remained objects of extremely violent contest.

On balance, the initial trajectory of post-1945 institutional formation was defined by the recurrence of a sharp intersection between the international political domain and domestic integrational processes. The militarization of citizenship became, in many respects, a global phenomenon, and societies that previously showed limited susceptibility to such tendencies refracted global political divisions within domestic political institutions. Discernibly, the fact that the years after 1945 saw the emergence of many new states meant that the violent intensification of citizenship as domestic civil war, common in Europe after 1789, was globalized. The decades after 1945 saw many more revolutions than the decades after 1789 (see Gurr 1988: 53; Goodwin 2001: 3).

Demilitarized Citizenship: Institutional Integration

In the years after 1945, nonetheless, global conflicts were not invariably refracted in national polities. At this time, domestic patterns of citizenship began to develop in a form that was less immediately articulated with global military positions, and less focused on inner-societal mobilization. In fact, after 1945, a slow process occurred in many democratic polities

---

[34] For discussion of this process in Rwanda, see Adenumobi (2001: 162). See general analysis in Janowitz (1964: 53).

that can be characterized as the *demilitarization* of citizenship. This proved to be the vital premise for effective democratization. In this process, polities found constitutional designs that allowed them to separate the primary legal relations in society from military practices, and legal obligations became less dependent on integration processes determined by war. After 1918, the close constitutional thread tying democratic citizenship and societal integration to war had relentlessly unstitched the fabric of new democratic institutions. After 1945, by contrast, the basic constitutional unit of the democratic citizen was progressively cast in terms which, although still conditioned by global conflicts, attached the law to modes of norm construction less strongly shaped by military conflict. Such demilitarization of citizenship had the result that modes of institutional integration and legal integration required for the consolidation of democracies could be conducted in a fashion that was not unsettled by external antagonisms. It became possible, in principle, to stabilize the full inclusion of national citizens without releasing unmanageable conflicts, of a type that had historically led to conditions close either to civil war or to dictatorship.

The gradual reorientation of citizenship at this time became evident, first, in the institutional processes of integration that hold together national societies. The relative demilitarization of core aspects of citizenship after 1945 can be seen in certain characteristics of polities formed at this point, in which institutional interactions between government and society were placed on new premises. In this process, states devised new techniques for integrating citizens into political institutions, and they learned to establish sovereign power in society without fragmenting society into violently opposed constituencies. Most of these institutional characteristics were connected to processes of legal-political individualization, in which the tendency for individual citizens to interact with government in highly mobilized roles was reduced.

First, the partial demilitarization of citizenship after 1945 can be observed in changes in the status and function of political parties in many democratizing polities. The transformation in the position of political parties after 1945 is evident in some obvious attributes. Compared with the period before 1945, political parties in democratizing polities after 1945 usually weakened their ties to the military, they were less likely to deploy military force to secure political prerogatives and they were less likely to foster paramilitary wings. Further, the connection between national political parties and hostile global positions became weaker, at least to the extent that, in democratizing polities, fewer parties were willing overtly to mobilize military force to impose globally defined political or economic interests. Such pacification of political parties is always a precarious accomplishment. This condition is currently only weakly institutionalized in some countries, especially in Africa. As a result of this tendency, however, it became possible for an increased number of polities to presuppose that different social groups recognized the political system as a set of institutions endowed with some perennial constitutional identity. Accordingly, the willingness of parties to accept the presence of opposition parties, and to construe the relation between government and opposition as something other than a zero-sum conflict for full monopoly of state offices, also increased. In the European context, tellingly, this development was originally connected to the fact that, in the decades after 1945, political parties of the far left gradually dissociated themselves from Moscow, and, in so doing, they abandoned constructions of their roles as actors in a global civil war. In some Latin American polities, where such pacification occurred later, the separation of party agendas from global polarities played an important role in the demilitarization of political rivalries. In Colombia, for example, one prerequisite for the gradual cessation of civil conflict that began in the 1990s was that, in the 1980s, parties on the far left watered down their Marxist commitments and began to accept orienting norms separate from the ideology of global civil war.[35]

The transformation in the position of political parties is also visible in less obvious respects. In most democracies consolidated after 1945, political parties became clearly distinct, not only from military units but from other structured associations in society. For instance, organizations with a religious function (churches) or an economic function (trade unions) are generally less strongly attached to political parties than before 1945. This statement requires some qualification. Manifestly, many post-1945 European states witnessed the emergence of cross-confessional Christian parties, so that mainstream democratic parties recruited religious communities for their support. Typically, however, such parties were less integrally linked to ecclesiastical institutions than interwar religious parties, and the religious content of their programmes served, not as means to realize institutional strategies of religious organizations, but as broad declarations of religious values. After 1945, further, socialist parties and trade unions often pursued convergent prerogatives.

[35] See the excellent analysis in González-Jácome (2018), explaining the contested framework in which this occurred.

Nonetheless, the relation between trade unions and left-leaning parties was usually modified after 1945.

In many pre-1945 societies, trade unions and parties had been integrally connected, as conjoined organs of class mobilization.[36] This had often led to repressive government measures against trade unions. After 1945, parties and trade unions usually became focused on separate functions and on the aggregation of interests in different social domains. There are clear exceptions to this tendency. One notable exception is the United Kingdom in the 1970s.[37] Student movements and trade unions also formed broad political fronts in some countries in the late 1960s. Indicatively, however, the frequency of strikes with broad political objectives declined in most polities after 1945 (see Lipset 1964: 282; Ross 1982: 314). One account explains simply that after 1945 most unions no longer viewed their goal as to 'overthrow the government of the state through a political strike' (Streeck and Hassell 2003: 335). After 1945, further, democratizing polities specifically protected rights of free collective bargaining for trade unions. This created, in essence, a system of democratic representation in the economy, which meant that industrial conflicts involving trade unions could usually be resolved outside core political institutions (Clegg 1976: 97). On this basis, many trade unions redefined their primary functions, and they focused on regulating labour markets, setting conditions for industrial interaction and intercepting social conflicts at the local level. In this respect, trade unions assumed only limited political functions, and they worked with national governments to stabilize the sphere of industrial interaction outside the state. In many ways, trade unions actually promoted the individualization of citizenship rights, and they created preconditions for the exercise of individual autonomy in economic practices. They protected individuals from the collective power of employers, but they also released citizens from traditional 'sites of solidarity' such as familial, religious and party-political organizations, which had historically assumed expansive political roles (Streeck and Hassell 2003: 354). In consequence, situations in which Socialist parties and trade unions mobilized together in parallel political and economic actions became infrequent. Indicatively, in the years after 1945, membership in parties of the left declined and trade union membership increased in much of Europe. This suggests that trade union membership was partly detached from political roles, and unions

---

[36] On variations in this relation, see Ebbinghaus (1995); Bartolini (2000: 245–246).
[37] For a typology of state–union relations in Europe, see Kitschelt (1994: 225).

were used to pursue economic goals in a more functionally specialized manner (Bartolini 2000: 279–280). At the same time, political parties tended to lose their character as milieu-specific organizations. For example, most Social Democratic parties, even those with a long history of militarism, progressively redefined themselves as cross-class parties.[38]

On balance, after 1945, political parties tended to assume a more differentiated position in democratizing polities. They became less likely to articulate comprehensive political outlooks, and the extent to which they mobilized entire social blocs decreased. In some cases, this transformation occurred through relatively contingent social processes, in which the efficacy of political organizations was optimized by the fact that they weakened their ties to parallel associations. This can be seen in the rise of Christian Democratic parties in post-1945 Europe, in which parties supporting Christian values expanded their electoral appeal by reducing their direct attachment to particular religious groups. In some cases, this transformation occurred through more strategic designs, as governments and their constitutions specifically segregated political parties both from the army and from economic organizations, especially trade unions.[39] Generally, however, membership in a political party was less frequently defined as a totalizing organizational position, in which affiliation entailed religious commitment or hard obligations outside the party in question. Instead, party membership was increasingly able to sit alongside other affiliations, so that party members were able to adopt multiple group affiliations, in different functional segments of society.[40] The reduction of the conflictual aspect of party formation was closely linked to the individualization of party membership, and both processes depended on the positioning of political parties as functionally differentiated organizations.

Second, the partial demilitarization of citizenship after 1945 can be seen in changes in the political importance attached to social class.

Democracy began to become a common reality after 1945, primarily, because democratizing states reduced the intensity attached to conflicts

---

[38] For discussion of Germany, see Mooser (1983: 305).
[39] This occurred in western parts of Germany after 1945 and in Argentina after 1983.
[40] Leading sociologists of the post-1945 decades noted how, while party membership declined amongst the European working class, participation in other associations increased sharply. This reflects the transformation of the working-class citizen into a 'segmentalized individual involved in many roles' (Lipset 1964: 281). One key recent account explains that after 1945 political roles were increasingly divided between a 'differentiated number of voluntary associations' reflecting 'new modalities of political participation' (Bartolini 2000: 275–276).

between members of different social classes. In so doing, democratizing polities found ways to diminish the articulation between national citizenship and international conflict, and they softened the echo given to global hostilities in patterns of national citizenship and subject formation. This process can be attributed – primarily – to the fact that, in virtually all polities that assumed a democratic orientation after 1945, citizenship was extended to incorporate a strong social-welfare emphasis. At this time, democracy usually took shape as welfare democracy.

The social-welfare element in national citizenship was established in very diverse fashion after 1945, and generalizations regarding welfare-state construction should be avoided.[41] In only a few states, notably in the United Kingdom and Scandinavia, was a universal right to welfare entitlement immediately enshrined. It is sometimes argued that only such states can truly be classified as welfare states (Briggs 1961: 228). In other states, the right to welfare was established more gradually and more unevenly. Despite great variations, nonetheless, a broad reorientation in state formation towards recognition of welfare rights occurred after 1945. The creation of state institutions to facilitate social provision and to bolster income security became a common political goal. Even in polities that lacked the infrastructure to create a full welfare system, increased welfare provision became the norm. Some Latin American countries saw a growth in welfare provision.[42] This tendency was also reflected in newly founded post-colonial states with weak capacity and limited access to resources (Lindert 2004: 218). The Indian Constitution of 1950 signalled a commitment to social rights, and it was supported by additional welfare legislation, notably the Employees' State Insurance Act (1948). Although it did not see the full formation of a welfare state, the United States formed one distinct variant on the global welfare revolution that took place after 1945 (Baldwin 2009: 213). Beginning under Truman and gaining pace in the 1960s, the decades after 1945 saw a remarkable expansion of social transfers in the United States, so that by 1965 welfare spending amounted to over 10 per cent of GNP (Patterson

---

[41] For key distinctions see the classical typology in Esping-Andersen (1990: 1–2).
[42] Before 1945, some societies, notably Chile and Brazil, saw the historical incorporation of trade unions to create authoritarian-paternalistic welfare regimes (Collier and Collier 1991: 185–195). After 1945, welfare states were not necessarily expressions of democracy. Post-1964 Brazil saw increased welfare coverage (see Malloy 1979: 134; Haggard and Kaufman 2008: 102). Argentina retained a comparatively high level of social-insurance coverage despite repeated military intervention. Even authoritarian Chile did not see a constant decline in welfare spending. See on these points Segura-Ubiergo (2007: 30, 183).

1986: 164). From 1960 to 1980, the proportion of Americans living in poverty declined by 60 per cent.[43] Historians of American welfare regimes have explained that welfare increased 'dramatically' and that it showed a 'stunning enlargement' after 1960 (Grønbjerg 1977: 152; Patterson 1986: 157). On balance, the period 1945–80 witnessed a rapid rise in social spending across almost all polity types.

As a general point, after 1789, states had exercised integrational force in society by referring to the citizen, in distilled essence, as the soldier. From 1789 onwards, states had integrated citizens in their institutions primarily in their quality as soldiers. As discussed, other exchanges between governments and citizens, for example, in the fiscal domain, were determined by military pressures. Of course, states interacted with their citizens in other ways, notably through national administration of school-level education. Yet, by the late nineteenth century, the military formed, in most polities, the most expansive channel of articulation between government and society. This nexus between state and soldier was dramatically intensified, in contested form, after 1918. At this time, military membership often became fundamental to the state, and citizens acquired political roles because of military conflict. At this time, however, many states struggled to assert a monopoly of power over the militarized organizations in which citizens presented themselves. As examined, many states eventually re-established this nexus in brutal fashion, integrating their populations through acts of military violence. After 1945, by contrast, states developed by engaging with the citizen, primarily, as the object of institutions responsible for providing welfare. Indicatively, it was only after 1945 that welfare provision began to surpass military spending as the primary governmental expenditure, so that interaction between citizens and government agencies was more strongly linked to welfare than to conscription. Before 1914, in many European countries, defence accounted for well over a quarter of all public expenditure (see Eloranta 2007: 260). After 1945, some polities continued to spend more on defence than on welfare. However, with a few exceptions, such polities were military regimes. In democratizing polities, there was a strong tendency towards higher welfare than military budgets (Kennedy 1974: 162). Even in democratizing polities with high defence budgets, such as the United Kingdom, military investment was rapidly eclipsed by social spending.[44] Even in the United States, which saw

---

[43] For these claims, see Katz (1986: 255, 278).

[44] By 1950, British defence spending was equal to less than 50 per cent of social spending (Gould and Roweth 1980: 349).

a long-term rise in defence expenditure against pre-1945 levels, military investment declined in the decades after 1950 as a proportion of overall public spending. In some welfare states, such interaction between citizens and government was focused on the simple extraction and allocation of resources, in the form of social transfers. More universally, however, such interaction was focused on the enhancement of longer-term opportunities, especially via access to education. While all social transfers increased sharply after 1945, the most generalized increase was visible in educational provision. This became a distinctively universal function of states, and even states with depleted infrastructures promoted mass schooling. In the period 1950–70, the mean school enrolment ratio rose from 60 per cent to 84 per cent globally. Especially important in this statistic is the fact that mean enrolment rose from 27 to 54 per cent in Africa, showing the universality of this policy feature (Ramirez and Ventresca 1992: 55).

Taken together, this means that, after 1945, the basic relation between citizens and the state changed. From this point on, citizens paid money to governments, not primarily for war, but for welfare. They also encountered agents of their governments, not as military administrators, but as providers of welfare services. From this point on, citizens increasingly engaged with state institutions not primarily as soldiers or as contributors to military budgets, but as recipients of resources, amenities and knowledge, and as contributors to the financing of resources, amenities and knowledge. Most communications between citizen and state became attached, not to military recruitment, but to claims to welfare provision and to enhanced personal opportunities. This rise of the resource-allocating state dramatically redirected the lines of obligation connecting citizens and state, and bargains between state and citizens were elaborated on new premises.

Of particular importance in this respect is the fact that the reorientation of institutional integration from the military to welfare functions after 1945 meant that states were increasingly able to integrate citizens in relatively pacified form. Integration in the state tended to occur without volatile expressions of class formation. State institutions began to integrate populations in procedures that were less likely to induce dramatic reactions in society, or to break society into overtly hostile factions. The reduction of the military aspect of institutional integration coincided with, and was in fact causally linked to, a reduction in the importance of social class in national integration processes. The separation of the citizen from the soldier that occurred through the growth of welfare states also entailed a separation of the citizen from particular class milieux.

Self-evidently, the growth of the welfare state did not mean that class-determined conflict disappeared from interactions between government and society. There is clear evidence to indicate that welfare states institutionalized class-based collective subject formation in a series of new ways.[45] First, for example, it is often claimed that strong welfare states evolved in polities with successful histories of labour mobilization. As a result, it is frequently assumed that welfare policies directly internalize class interests, and that strong welfare states express the capacity of political organizations to cement working-class prerogatives in the state.[46] This claim may be questioned, as many welfare states were designed without strong input from national labour movements. The British welfare state can be partly traced to the Beveridge Report, which was submitted to and (selectively) endorsed by a predominantly Conservative government in 1942. In fact, Britain developed a strong welfare state after 1945 despite the fact that, historically, the Labour movement had only been either fleetingly or marginally involved in government. The post-war welfare system of France was planned by exiled Gaullists in London (Dutton 2002: 202–203).[47] Nonetheless, there appears to be some correlation between the strength of organized labour and the robustness of welfare provision. The very limited welfare state of the United States, for example, is frequently attributed to the weak tradition of labour mobilization (Piven and Cloward 1993: 427). Second, welfare states created after 1945 tended to establish semi-formal systems of mediation to organize exchanges with professional associations in society and to negotiate the apportionment of national resources. Influential observers have argued that this led to the division of society into collective negotiating organs, linked to different sectors and classes, in which organized interest groups established powerful positions in the margins of government (Offe 1972: 25; Habermas 1990 [1962]: 336). In many polities, this led to the creation of neo-corporatist welfare systems, in which interest groups became deeply articulated with the state. Indeed, some welfare states have a clearly corporatist character,

---

[45] For outstanding analysis of variable patterns of citizenship in different welfare regimes, see Janoski (1998: 136–138).
[46] See Rimlinger (1971: 8); Korpi (1983: 25); Swank (1983); Hicks and Swank (1984: 105); Therborn (1984: 25); Huber, Ragin and Stephens (1993: 729); Hicks (1999: 19); Huber and Stephens (2001: 17). Silver (2003: 17).
[47] These facts call into question the common claim that 'the political organization of the working class was the crucial foundation of most welfare states' (Gingrich and Häusermann 2015: 56).

and they selectively protect particular professions and interest groups (Mesa-Lago 1978: 3; Esping-Andersen 1990: 2; Janoski 1998: 109–110; Korpi and Palme 2003: 432). Third, governing parties in welfare states remain susceptible to influence by activist groups with specific economic prerogatives (Piven and Cloward 1993: 220; Swank 1983: 296, 305; Zarate Tenorio 2014: 1947). In these respects, welfare states can be viewed as systems of balanced class conflict, which actively promoted the aggregation of conflictual actors around the state. Importantly, fourth, political mobilization linked to welfare often intensified in the 1980s, when many social spending regimes were exposed to political retrenchment and structures of protective individualism were eroded.

These qualifications notwithstanding, the increasing formation of national states on a welfarist model reduced the intensity of class-defined political organization in a number of ways. On the one hand, states with a welfarist emphasis acquired increased capacity to mediate inter-class conflict through administrative techniques and expenditure, and so to reduce open mobilization around class interests. Even theorists who stress the class origins of welfare states claim that welfare states created a procedural framework, in which organizations representing class interests could be incorporated in relatively pacified manner into an institutionally robust system of political-economic bargaining (Korpi 1983: 21; Edlund and Lindh 2015: 312). Most importantly, states that promoted relatively uniform welfare coverage tended to weaken the attachments of individual persons to social groups defined by class. As discussed later, although partly based in inter-group bargains, welfare states developed a range of mechanisms to incorporate persons immediately within the state, and to construct the single citizen as the primary integrational unit. Whatever their foundations, further, the primary societal effect of welfare states was that political institutions increasingly addressed persons immediately and individually, and they linked single persons directly to public agencies: the primary unit of the welfare state became the single person, outside structures of collective antagonism. In doing this, welfare states began to separate social agents from potentially violent communities, and they weakened propensities for conflict both in society and in the state itself.

In analysing post-1945 welfare states as systems promoting pacified patterns of citizenship, some further nuance is necessary.

Like other polity types, welfare states created after 1945 were products of war, and they reflected constructions of the relation between polity and citizen configured by war. World War II created a wide social consensus that endorsed the material integration of the population, and this supported welfare-state construction (Segal 1989: 7; Klausen 1998: 128). Indeed, in many post-1945 polities, welfare-state formation was once again driven by provisions for veterans.[48] Like electoral rights, welfare provision can be observed as one side of a constitutional contract offered by governments to soldiers who accepted conscription in the army. Both elements of the deep constitutional wiring of modern democratic states – universal suffrage and welfare systems – can be traced to implied military bargains and acts of public recompense to combatants. After 1945, further, welfare states relied on institutional structures resulting from war. As in World War I, patterns of institutional formation promoted in World War II created a distinct form of statehood, in which business and unions were galvanized to support production for war and increased coordinating powers were transferred to the governmental executive. This again facilitated the construction of states with strong administrative capacities, able to promote social intervention, increased fiscal extraction, increased public spending and autonomous redistribution of resources across society.[49] In each respect, the basic form of the post-1945 welfare state was partly established through wartime institution building.

Importantly, moreover, the rise of welfare states after 1945 can be viewed as the result of normative expectations that gained expression through war, and which, owing to the war, obtained influence at the transnational level. In most polities, early plans for the creation of welfare states were drafted in the course of World War II, and such plans often acquired far-reaching transnational impact. As mentioned, the British welfare state was partly based on the Beveridge Report, published in 1942. This report rapidly acquired normative force across national boundaries, and it shaped proposals and policies relating to welfare-state design in many other countries, before and after 1945.[50] Knowledge of the Atlantic Charter (1941) also penetrated deep into national societies, forming a core point of reference for the establishment of different welfare

---

[48] After 1945, one author estimates that belligerent countries spent between 10 and 35 per cent of total social expenditure on persons affected by war (Obinger and Schmitt 2018: 497).

[49] See examination of this in Klausen (1998: 2); Edgerton (2006: 145).

[50] On reception of the Beveridge Report in Sweden, see Heclo (1974: 229); in France, see Kerschen (1995); Dutton (2002: 202–208); in Germany, see Abelshauser (1996: 377); in Japan, see Estévez-Abe (2008: 138); in Czechoslovakia, see Inglot (2008: 75); in Canada, see Cowen (2008: 50).

systems (Sparrow 2011: 44). The Atlantic Charter expressed a strong transnational commitment to 'improved labor standards, economic advancement and social security'. In fact, the Atlantic Charter and the Beveridge Report were closely connected. The Beveridge Report declared that it was intended to put the provisions for general social security set out in the Atlantic Charter into deeds (Beveridge 1943: 305). Similarly, objectives established by the International Labour Organization in Philadelphia in 1944 provided transnational premises for welfare-state development.

Welfare states are often viewed as singularly national achievements, expressing reserves of solidarity resulting from strong national bonds and affiliations.[51] One eminent commentator has stated, simply, that the 'Welfare State is nationalistic', and it forms a mechanism to 'defend the national community' by promoting economic autarky (Myrdal 1960: 117–118). It is also frequently observed that, after 1945, welfare systems galvanized national societies into collectively integrated form, such that the territorial order of modern nations actually resulted from processes of welfare-state formation (Keating 1988: 126). In fact, however, post-1945 welfare systems originated – in part – in inter- or transnational norms. Of course, international norms reflecting presumptions in favour of welfare were guided by principles already established in different national polities. The New Deal in the United States had expressed a general commitment to protection of social rights. Social rights had been elevated to constitutional rank in the Weimar Constitution (1919) and spelled out as norms of public law in the Nehru Report (1928), envisioning a new constitutional order for India. Only in a few pre-1945 national societies, however, did there exist a sufficient quantity of inner-societal solidarity to bind together different social groups in an even moderately stable cross-class community of distribution. In the period after 1945, by contrast, the welfare state became a phenomenon with general reach. This was strongly linked to global norms established in the course of World War II. After 1945, some pattern of welfare statehood became part of an international political culture which most states, in varying ways, tended to emulate.[52] One analysis describes this as an example of 'international cultural modelling' (Skocpol and Amenta

---

[51] See variations on this claim in Seymour (1999: 230); Dutton (2002: 210); McEwen (2002: 66); Cowen (2008: 8).

[52] For views close to this argument, see Collier and Messnick (1975: 1305); Thomas and Meyer (1984: 476); Baldwin (1990: 108); Abbott and DeViney (1992: 266). See discussions of the transnational diffusion of the Beveridge plan at note 52. One analysis stresses how

1986: 144). One sociologist has argued that states recognized 'the principle of inclusion' linked to welfare provision as one core part of the process in which, after 1945, states were integrated into 'world society' (Stichweh 2000: 59).

Equally importantly, the rise of the welfare state was strongly marked by the Cold War, and the growing commitment to welfare provision was partly the result of the fact that democratizing polities were exposed to global conflicts. In some accounts of post-1945 society, the Cold War is seen as a factor that inhibited the growth of national welfare states (Russett 1970: 170; Wilensky 1975: 71; Katz 1986: 266). In key respects, however, the expansion of welfare provisions in democratizing polities after 1945 was inseparable from the Cold War. One primary objective of the welfare state in many societies was that it was intended to lessen the ideological appeal of radical alternatives to capitalism.[53] Governments on different sides of the global ideological division in the Cold War showed high commitment to welfare spending, and states with opposed ideological dispositions promoted welfare investment for purposes of ideological competition and domestic legitimation.

Overall, in short, post-1945 welfare states originated – largely – in war. Welfarism became part of a transnational polity design in a global environment created by war. Despite its military origins, nonetheless, one tangible result of the global spread of the welfare-state model after 1945 was that states rapidly reduced the militarization of conflicts between citizenship groups in the domestic societies in which they exercised sovereignty.[54] Moreover, this model tended to create social conditions in which global ideological pressures were less likely to ignite unmanageable antagonisms in the domestic political arena. Although brought into being by interstate hostility, the welfare-state systems created after 1945 tended to promote equipoise between inner-societal factions, to insulate

---

social security developed in different societies from a mixture of national and international sources (Perrin 1969).

[53] The Cold War is often seen as a period marked by conflict between investment in defence and investment in welfare. But see Peterson's account of welfare-state promotion as part of an 'anti-communist strategy' (2013: 233). See also the claim that regime competition between East and West triggered welfare investment on both sides in Obinger and Schmitt (2011: 265). This is also implied in Ritter (1991: 201). See the argument in Domke, Eichenberg and Kelleher that military investment and heightened welfare provision are often compatible (1983: 33).

[54] Before 1933, German governments had been unsettled by extremely acute class conflicts. On the rapid 'defusing of social conflicts' and 'spread of consensus' in the FRG after 1949, see Hockerts (1988: 55).

national citizenship against global conflicts and – in each respect – to solidify the position of the state as a whole within national societies.

The pacifying impact of welfare states is primarily linked to the fact that in democratizing polities after 1945, the provision of welfare was attached to an essentially individualistic construction of welfare rights. Indicatively, Beveridge first defined social security as 'security for the individual, organized or assisted by the State' (1943: 306). At the centre of the welfare state was the assumption, implied or explicit, that persons possess certain protective rights outside the collective groups that mobilize for rights, and these rights place the individual person in an immediate relation to the state. This principle was of course very variably expressed, and it was only fully articulated in welfare states with universal coverage. However, this construct of the individual subject as the primary link between state and society underscored the global welfare revolution more widely. This aspect of the welfare state weakened the role of collective subject formation as a pathway to the rights associated with citizenship, and it played a vital role in the pacification of national patterns of citizenship.

There are – clearly – many arguments that contradict this association of the welfare state with subjective individualization. It is often critically declared that welfare systems protect rights of a collective nature, reaching beyond, and even potentially eroding, individual principles of entitlement and freedom enshrined in classical personal and private/monetary rights.[55] It is also self-evident that welfare arrangements originate in patterns of inter-group accommodation in particular nations. They reflect balanced constructions of societal interest, framing expectations that the resolution of problems of scarcity and security is a public responsibility. On each account, welfare states can clearly be seen, in some features, as entities based in the weakening of individualism.

Nonetheless, post-1945 welfare systems possessed strong individualist dimensions, and they secured welfare provisions in a form not neatly correlated with collective patterns of subject formation. The more

[55] This view is expressed both affirmatively and critically, at different points on the spectrum of political opinion. See, as examples, Hayek (1960: 273); Ewald (1986: 367); Kosotieti (1987: 286–287). For a rejection of such critiques see Rothstein (1998: 30). A more positive link between welfare and individualism is posited in Beck (1986: 133). My analysis of individualization shows some parallels to Beck's theory. Unlike Beck, however, my account emphasizes the legal-subjective aspect of individualization, it links individualization to global legal form, and it observes individualization as the expression of deep-lying structural forces. For one analysis that, like mine, argues emphatically that the welfare state is 'essentially a source of modern individualism', see Leisering (1997: 147).

advanced welfare states created after 1945 allotted social resources to persons as single agents, in a form that was legally distinct from the collectively structured organizations to which these persons had been historically attached. Across a spectrum of variations, the rise of the welfare state meant that the allocation of material goods was distinctively linked to the definition of the single citizen, with shared common rights, as the primary bearer of entitlements in society.[56]

As indicated, some polities in the interwar period had already created expansive systems of public welfare provision. In the years 1913–29, for instance, Germany saw a 500 per cent increase in public welfare spending (Sachße and Tennstedt 1988: 211). The Weimar Constitution of 1919 provided for the creation of a welfare state offering protection from loss of earnings caused by illness or unemployment (Art. 161), and it projected welfarism as the integrational axis of the new democratic polity. By 1927, Germany had legislation providing for full unemployment insurance. Some polities in Scandinavia had developed extensive welfare systems before 1945. Poland saw the growth of a welfare system under Piłsudski. The United States developed a rudimentary welfare state through Roosevelt's New Deal, although this did not cover health insurance or a minimum income (Patterson 1986: 75–76). Britain also saw marked centralization of welfare provision in the 1920s and 1930s, so that, before 1945, the British government was amongst those that spent most on social transfers (Boyer 2019: 307). In such polities, however, welfare coverage was usually limited in volume. It was also uneven and subject to high regional variations, and it was provided by a wide array of associations – some public, some private, some charitable, some local, some national, some rooted in religious organizations. In some polities, claims to welfare were often attached to military affiliation, and organizations that provided welfare were frequently focused on persons who had suffered either physical or monetary loss through World War I.[57] Notably, such systems were not very effective in promoting political loyalty, and many groups that received welfare were only weakly integrated into the polity. The selective focus on groups of veterans in early welfare policies often left the targeted groups isolated, and such groups

---

[56] For this view, see Rimlinger (1971: 152); Kaim-Chaudle (1979: 22); Christiansen and Petersen (2001: 182).

[57] In Germany, early social welfare programmes created after 1918 were intended to protect injured ex-servicemen – a group defined as the 'new poor'. Subsequent legislation (1923) extended welfare protection to retired persons with low incomes adversely affected by the consequences of the war (Hong 1998: 92, 109).

emerged within the polity as resentful oppositional factions.[58] Even in the more advanced interwar welfare systems, welfare was a precarious form of institutional integration. Welfare remained deeply linked to organized class mobilization, it intensified collective patterns of conflict, and protection of welfare rights largely presupposed membership in political-economic organizations. In consequence, welfare policies became the main focus of political contest, and inter-group fault lines were often hardened by controversy about the material responsibilities of government. In Germany, for example, the establishment of reactionary government after 1930 was reflected, first, in deep cuts to public spending, imposed under the Chancellorships of Brüning and Papen, from 1930 to 1932. Welfare provisions were then radically reduced after 1933, under a regime that replaced welfare with forced labour.

The design of the welfare state after 1945, by contrast, tended to isolate the individual citizen as the unit recipient of welfare. To an increasing degree, some claim to welfare was, in principle, open to all citizens. This individualistic emphasis of welfare systems after 1945 was reflected in the fact that persons acquired increased autonomy with regard to the social groups that had traditionally supported welfare arrangements. For instance, citizens became able to access rights without relying on unions, parties, churches, guilds, religious associations or military organizations.[59] In many cases, the fact that the path to welfare led directly from the state to the citizen meant that ties attaching citizens to social clusters outside the state were partly softened, and obligations linked to such clusters lost some force.

To illustrate this, the construction of welfare states typically meant that individual persons experienced a weakening of traditional forms of collective dependency. Importantly, it is often noted that strong welfare systems promoted a range of individual liberties, and that, over time, welfare regimes established normative structures that modified common gender roles, separating persons from coercive familial obligations (Lundberg and Åmark 2001: 170). In some polities, early welfare states saw the projection and tentative introduction of legislation to improve the financial position and to reduce the material dependency of women.[60]

---

[58] See brilliant historical-anthropological inquiry on this question in Kienitz (2008: 306).
[59] One important observer has noted how welfare states liberated persons from immediate collective obligations towards families and informal associations, promoting a 'very extreme degree' of individualism (Trägårdh 1990: 579).
[60] In the United Kingdom, the otherwise very restrictive report of the Royal Commission on Marriage and Divorce (1956) led to some legislation of this nature.

In most welfare states, gradually, legislation was implemented that weakened the force of familial and religious solidarities, ultimately leading to the liberalization of laws regarding divorce, reproduction and sexual preference. In such instances, the direct link between citizens and the state gradually cut through bonds created by more traditional associations, and it meant that groups with authority not resulting from the state lost power. Most importantly, however, the construction of welfare states meant that access to welfare was not fully determined by class affiliation or acquired through class-defined organizations.[61] As mentioned, trade union membership did not decline because of the growth of welfare states. On the contrary, early welfare states usually saw, and presupposed, high levels of unionization, and the bargaining power of unions generally increased. Yet, trade union activity was increasingly focused on labour-market regulation and co-determination of conditions of contract, which generally served to protect the status of individual workers in the economy.[62] Class-based subject formation lost its status as a structural precondition for access to material goods, and some material entitlements were separated from collective mobilization.

What occurred through these processes, in effect, was that states developed some mechanisms in which collective material interests could, to some degree, be transformed into interests that could be articulated at an individual level. Historically, persons bound by class affiliations had tended to mobilize collectively against the state to secure material rights to protect their employment status and income security. After 1945, the state began to construct welfare rights as general norms, and the state itself became the primary protector of such rights for individual people.[63] As a result, agents in the economic sphere assumed a more immediate relation to the state through the institutionalization of individual rights and individual entitlements, and they transferred some of their agency to the state. Of course, this was not an invariable phenomenon, and it was less pronounced where welfare states provided coverage that varied greatly from class to class (Swank 1983: 295). Through the rise of the welfare state, however,

---

[61] In early welfare states that reflected Christian values, welfare was strictly separated from class. On the FRG, see Hilpert (2012: 71, 82). In more social-democratic systems, such as the United Kingdom and the Scandinavian countries, welfare provision was supported by the assumption that 'all citizens command an identical status and entitlement to any given benefit' (see Esping-Andersen 1985: 176–177).
[62] See p. 147.
[63] For a parallel argument, see Stichweh (2000: 68).

exchanges regarding personal security were increasingly conducted through individual channels between citizens and government. In this respect, importantly, individual persons engaged with the state as a collective organization in which they retained a position defined by legal individuality. Once welfare was established as a right, much of the responsibility for delivering welfare was transferred to administrative office-holders, and citizens organized their public interactions with particular members of the civil service, which expanded accordingly. This meant, inevitably, that much controversy conventionally attached to material security was absorbed by judicial and administrative tribunals (see Volkmann 1978: 168).

Underlying these processes, it is possible to observe a development of vital importance in modern society. As, after 1945, they began to structure their communications with citizens in a system of protective individualism, states developed an interactional grammar in which citizens turned to the state for an expanded range of services, and in which the number of exchanges in which citizens and government agencies encountered each other in immediate form was dramatically increased. Through this, states solidified their position as the primary membership group, or the primary collective organization, in society, and many exchanges were redirected from other collective organizations towards the state. In consequence, the welfare state emerged as a political form in which the state expanded its integrational force deep into society. Unlike previous exercises in state construction, however, welfare states increased their societal sovereignty on a design that, simultaneously, promoted individualized articulations with members of society and relegated class-based mobilization to a position of secondary importance. The transformation of citizens into holders of protected individual rights meant that states could simultaneously incorporate citizens in their own functions, yet also limit the extent to which they were unsettled by conflicts between citizens. Such individualization provided a foundation on which states were able to reach a high level of societal integration without extreme destabilization. On this basis, states, for the first time, acquired the capacity to exercise sovereignty in stable integrational procedures in their own societies. The translation of the social costs of war into fiscal costs, which originally underpinned the modern sovereign state, was greatly intensified through this process. In fact, welfare states can be viewed as a new iteration of this original state-building bargain. The price for the ultimate pacification of society was the translation of fiscal expenditure required for war into fiscal expenditure required for welfare, which meant that states interacted with citizens, primarily, not through armies, but through welfare arrangements. This provided the premise for the consolidation of the state as an institution with sovereign integrational force in society.

As explained, there were great polity-to-polity variations in welfare-state construction. However, the individualistic bias in welfare states became almost universally manifest in the fact that welfare states introduced policies designed to expand equality in education and to promote educational opportunities for citizens. Even states such as the United States that did not establish comprehensive welfare systems substantially broadened their role as educational providers. The years 1950–70 saw a 'universal expansion of education', such that, regardless of global position, each state extended access to schools and other pedagogic institutions (Meyer, Ramirez, Rubinson and Boli-Bennett 1977: 251). In this respect, the transnational pro-welfare bias after 1945 tended to promote enhanced professional opportunities for individual agents, and, as a result, it stimulated increased labour mobility, especially for persons with enlarged access to educational resources.

The expansion of education rights also had a clear impact on patterns of political organization and mobilization in society. In the decades after 1945, increased educational opportunities were widely seen as leading to increased political activity amongst recipients of educational benefits (Lipset 1960: 112; Meyer and Rubinson 1975: 157; Almond and Verba 1989[1963]: 176). However, such opportunities altered the typical form of political agency, again helping to separate individual agents from collective class-based organizations. By definition, the expansion of access to education meant, at least, that, at an everyday level, individual agents were distanced from familiar organizational structures. Increases in educational options enabled citizens to structure political life trajectories for themselves that were not fully defined by class association. Moreover, such increases typically led to the construction of new patterns of political motivation, as rising education levels were closely correlated with the proliferation of new political identities amongst students. This was strongly reflected in the rise of alternative and more individualistic expressions of radical political agency in the 1960s.[64] Indicatively, some sociologists have identified a decline in

---

[64] For brilliant analysis of the impact of educational opportunities on the transformation of left-wing political attitudes in Britain, see Rose (2001: 144).

class-determined electoral behaviour as a primary outcome of these processes, at least in some countries.[65]

For these reasons, the welfare-oriented polities that developed after 1945 saw a partial mitigation of the inter-class conflicts over material resources that had, historically, proved destabilizing for national governments. The rise of the welfare state had a deep impact on patterns of political subject formation in society. Vitally, the welfare state concretized a deep immediate nexus between the individual person and the state. As stated, this varied from society to society and this nexus cannot be observed as an absolutely generalized social feature. However, individual persons became more immediately dependent on state agencies, and they were strongly incorporated in political communities centred around states. Through these processes, membership in the state became the primary membership in society, and it became the primary route to effective rights and the primary guarantee of effective integration. As a result, citizens were partly liberated in their other affiliations, and they were less likely to rely upon structured organizations in other spheres of life. The new nexus between polity and citizen weakened the force of other associations, especially those articulated with class interests, and it reduced the necessity for citizens to form collective subjects in society. The immediate integration of citizens in the state was a deeply individualizing process, in which reliance on large organized collectives was reduced.

Viewed in this way, the welfare state emerged after 1945 as a continuation of the state-building patterns that appeared in the eighteenth century, as the state first assumed contours as a system of institutional integration defined by the individualization of social agents, and the reduction in force of intermediary associations. The allocation of material goods to individual persons after 1945 re-articulated the same logic of individual immediacy in the relation between polity and citizen that first characterized the modern state. Above all, the welfare state re-articulated the strong connection between state sovereignty and legal individualization that had first appeared in the eighteenth century, and it

---

[65] For analysis of these processes in the United States, see Wright (2013: 126–135, 151). On the United Kingdom see Kelley, McAllister and Mughan (1985: 726). On this process more generally, see Meyer (1977: 70); Kitschelt (1994: 30); Clark and Lipset (1991: 403). For one authoritative analysis of twenty countries, concluding that in the period 1945–90 there were, in many but not all cases, 'substantial declines in levels of class voting', see Nieuwbeerta (1996: 370). Some sociologists have rejected or added nuance to these claims (Korpi 1983; Brooks and Manza 1997: 397; Weakliem and Heath 1999: 132).

constructed an institutional order in which states were able both to integrate individual persons in society and to preserve their essential sovereign structure. To achieve this, the welfare state partly erased one deep structural feature of post-1789 society: namely, the strong convergence between political subject formation and social class formation. In so doing, the welfare state partly erased a further structural feature of post-1789 society: that is, the loss of sovereignty by state institutions in face of collectively mobilized organizations. At the centre of these achievements was the fact that, for the first time, states interacted with their citizens, not as members of military communities, but as recipients of individual welfare rights and opportunities.

This analysis contains no claim that class distinctions disappeared in emergent welfare states after 1945. Indeed, this analysis accepts the claim that weaker welfare states tend to induce class tension (Piven and Cloward 1993: 449). Yet, this analysis implies that the formation of welfare states promoted more individualistic patterns of interaction between citizens and government bodies, partly splitting individual agency from class-based and segmentary organizations. Above all, states were able to form articulations with citizens separate from collective memberships. Central to this process was a basic reorientation in the assertion of governmental sovereignty, in which processes of institutional integration were more strongly focused on single rights-holding persons. As a result, inter-class conflict over material security lost some of its power to destabilize state institutions.

Third, the demilitarization of citizenship after 1945 can be seen as the result of changes in the political importance attached to ethnicity.

Democratizing polities after 1945 were, initially at least, less effective in reducing the intensity of political conflicts caused by ethnicity than was the case in relation to class conflict. In fact, violent ethnic conflicts appeared as a distinctive phenomenon in late twentieth-century politics. Typically, these conflicts were caused, first, by the legacies of European Empires in former colonies, and, second, by the processes of nation building that accompanied decolonization in Africa and Asia, and later in post-Soviet states.[66] In many such contexts, democratic political

---

[66] The Soviet Union was not a classic Empire as it promoted equality between regions and Republics and it did not institutionalize the primacy of Russian identity. However, historians hostile to the Soviet Union and historians relatively sympathetic to it have noted its similarity to an Empire and the resemblance of post-Soviet nation building to post-colonial nation building (see Northrop 2004: 22; Markowitz 2013: 30; Newton 2015: 217).

organization, focused on central state institutions, led to the sharpened articulation of ethnic prerogatives. However, conflict between dominant groups and ethnic minorities also persisted in other settings. Such conflict restricted democratization in the United States until 1964/65. In different locations, the attachment of citizenship expectations to ethnic affiliations imprinted, to varying degrees, highly antagonistic mobilizational structures on democratizing polities. In many settings, ethnicity replaced class affiliation as the main determinant of citizenship practices.

Despite this, democratizing polities after 1945 also developed ways of promoting national integration without acute politicization of ethnic variations. Democracies confronted with conflicts between ethnically defined citizenship groups have at times sought to overcome such conflicts by designating ethnic groups as distinctively entitled collective subjects. In some societies marked by ethnic antagonism, democratic polities have been established in constitution-making processes, in which groups representing non-dominant ethnic affiliations have acquired separate rights and representation. Some polities seeking to overcome acute inter-ethnic conflict have adopted legislation or constitutions that grant collective rights to ethnic or indigenous groups, at times reinforcing the separate identity and constitutional positions of such memberships (see Lijphart 1969; Andeweg 2000; Lerner 2011). More generally, however, in societies with complex ethnic structures, inter-ethnic conflict has been softened and the integration of different groups has been promoted through a process of normative assimilation, in which the strict attachment of rights to collective affiliations has been weakened. In most such cases, rights attributed to distinct ethnic groups have been constructed as components of a wider range of rights which are accorded to all citizens as individual agents. In most democratizing polities, rights ascribed to ethnically categorized collectives have been defined in terms that do not specifically reinforce the uniqueness of ethnic identity, but which, at most, establish ethnic identity as grounds for facilitated access to rights that are open to all individual persons. In such circumstances, the exercise of rights allows ethnic collectives both to cleave to traditional group solidarities and to accept integration into a more general system of normative expectations. In the United States, as discussed, ethnic minority rights were consolidated in the 1950s and 1960s in conjunction with other rights, and the political enfranchisement of minorities was accompanied by the expansion of individual rights more widely (Epp 1998: 27–30). Recently, important examples of this phenomenon are found in societies in Latin America with multi-centric populations. In Colombia, some distinct protection has been provided for ethnically defined cultural groups. But, under Colombian constitutional law, the interests of ethnically marginal groups are more strongly protected by guarantees for rights of a more universal nature. The Constitutional Court has established the principle that all Colombians are entitled to a 'universal minimum' enjoyment of basic rights, which can be enforced to protect rights of minority groups.[67] In Bolivia, analogously, rights of ethnic groups have been secured to the extent that they are commensurate with a universal system of rights.[68] As a result, the reduction of conflict between ethnic groups has been promoted through the generalization of individualized rights, and, through this, ethnicity itself, as a collective-subjective characteristic, has been structurally deprioritized. The establishment of a solid corpus of individual subjective rights has typically formed a precondition for the softening of social conflicts in ethnically divided societies. In most cases, this process segregated citizenship from structurally ingrained solidarities.

At a more general level, a fourth striking feature of the demilitarization of citizenship after 1945 is that political agency itself became, in part, a mode of interaction that impacted less disruptively on society as a whole. Most notably, political agency was increasingly patterned on more general propensities for individual subject formation in society, and political engagement tended to detach itself from goals whose realization necessarily presupposed the mobilized agency of collective actors.

As discussed, the period after 1945 was marked by the fact that political agency was gradually separated from class milieux and class-determined motivations, so that individual agents were able to construct political positions in terms less uniformly dependent on class prerogatives. Increasingly, further, political agency became attached to questions that were not necessarily addressed through party-based mobilization. Political participation frequently assumed less structured form, often acquiring expression in impermanent membership groups, established around particular interests and unlikely to acquire enduring organizational order. Evidence of these processes can be found, for example, in the fact that, in the decades after 1945, protest movements, informal political groupings and radical libertarian movements, with relatively eclectic ideological premises, gained importance. The landscape of oppositional politics was increasingly defined by the political weakening

---

[67] See discussion in Constitutional Court T-485/11.
[68] Plurinational Constitutional Court of Bolivia, Decision 1422/2012.

of class-determined organizations, and by the emergence of cross-class movements and of groups designed to entrench new political identities, linked – for example – to sexual, to medical, to ethnic or to educational prerogatives. This typically meant that interests asserted politically were less likely to induce overarching conflicts or to strain the integrational capacities of society.

Lastly, fifth, the demilitarization of citizenship after 1945 can be seen in the fact that social conflict was increasingly articulated through multiple institutional channels. After 1945, democratizing polities tended to create new channels of communication with their citizens. In particular, many states greatly reinforced their judicial institutions, so that judiciaries came to sit alongside legislative bodies as core channels of interaction between polity and society. This occurred, most strikingly, in polities that had converted to authoritarianism in the 1920s and 1930s. For example, the re-formed democratizing polities in Italy, Japan and the FRG created after 1945 developed strong judiciaries, with, eventually, powerful protections for individual rights, in both public and private law. However, this also occurred in states that had preserved some democratic structures during the 1930s. In the United States, as discussed, the willingness of courts to apply federal civil rights in constitutional cases expanded exponentially after 1945. In the United States, moreover, judicial reinforcement was reflected in the sphere of administrative law. For example, the Administrative Procedure Act (1946) broadened the supervisory scope of the judiciary in administrative matters. This Act is described by one observer as a 'constitution for the bureaucracy' (Cane 2016: 90). In the United Kingdom, similarly, public accountability under administrative law was strengthened through the widening of judicial review as a common-law power.[69] Eventually, administrative law assumed particular constitutional significance in the United Kingdom, as it was in administrative law that a consistent public-law principle of citizenship was first elaborated. The hardening of constitutional norms in the United Kingdom since the 1960s resulted mainly from litigation regarding administrative acts.[70]

These changes in the position of judiciaries had the consequence that conflicts between citizens and the state could be conducted through an expanded array of channels. As judiciaries grew in power, many conflicts

---

[69] See the seminal case *Ridge* v. *Baldwin* [1964] AC 40.
[70] The concept of constitutional rights in UK public law appeared in administrative law. See *Morris* v. *Beardmore* – [1980] 2 All ER 753; *Bugdaycay* v. *Secretary of State for the Home Department and Related Appeals* [1987] 1 All ER 940.

could be attached to claims over rights, and addressed in relatively individualized form. As provision for individual remedies increased, in turn, grievances of single agents were less likely to trigger large-scale political mobilization around collective prerogatives or encompassing social interests. In many polities, this meant that pursuit of common interests was increasingly conducted through legal actions: that is, through class actions or strategic litigation.[71] One result of this was that conflicts over collective interests in national societies did not converge in unsettling manner around single institutions, and conflicts in society could be directed towards different points in the organizational order of state. A further result of this was that societies were able to sustain multiple patterns of political subject formation, focused on ethnic or environmental or sexuality-related prerogatives, in which new political groups took shape around the pursuit of particular rights. This again imprinted a poly-centric individualized political form on society, tending to segregate political agency from overarching class interests.

At the core of the increase in democratic stability that occurred throughout the latter half of the twentieth century, we can identify three ways in which the institutional grammar through which states interacted with and integrated their citizens was revised. Each of these changes was connected to a broader pattern of legal individualization. First, most democratizing polities found ways to diminish motivations for collective political mobilization linked to material security. The capacity of individual citizens to obtain material goods to sustain their security was partly separated from collective subjects, especially from subjects articulating strong class prerogatives. Second, democratizing polities usually stimulated the multiplication of individual integration opportunities, such that classical political roles appeared as one source of integration amongst others. Third, such polities tended to promote the individualization of organizational affiliation, so that membership in many social associations, with varying functional emphases and varying levels of formality, became the norm. In each respect, the emergence of relatively stable democracies after 1945 presupposed a high degree of

---

[71] Public interest litigation formed a new pattern of political agency in the United States, where litigation was strongly linked to the construction of ethnic and health rights. One influential account has explained how individualized legal actions assumed a key role in the 'generalization of rights' concerning health care and welfare in the United States (Starr 1982: 388). The focusing of political agency around public-interest litigation reached a peak in India in the 1980s and 1990s, where such litigation led to the construction of welfare rights and justiciable rights to education (Ruparelia 2013: 574).

individualized subject formation. The core political consequence of this was that members of society could be integrated, both politically and at a wider level, without intensified articulation of their core structural polarities. In these processes, neither class nor ethnicity, traditional obstructions to democratic integration, vanished. Yet, the formation of more individualized, often multi-focal, forms of political agency meant that societies could preserve some degree of cohesion, without obdurate thematization of these sources of conflict.

One central outcome of this transformation was that, through its increasingly individual construction, the citizen was uncoupled from its quintessentially modern-democratic linkage with international antagonisms. As discussed, the period after 1945 hardly witnessed any de-intensification of global conflict. However, democratizing polities after 1945 were able, to some degree, to insulate domestic processes of institutional integration against patterns of mobilization that allowed international wars and hostilities to reverberate, in simply duplicated form, through national citizenship. Most importantly, new democracies gradually managed to disarticulate class identities at the domestic level from ideological antagonisms at the global level, which meant that global polarities were not simply re-enacted in inner-societal contests between hostile citizenship groups.

On the one hand, this disarticulation became visible in the practices of political organization amongst institutionalized oppositional factions. For example, one salient characteristic of post-1945 European politics is that political parties of the left developed increasingly individualized political programmes. As a result, left-oriented parties refused, progressively, to attach their stance to the ideological orthodoxy of the Soviet Union, and they campaigned on platforms outside global dichotomies (see Weiler 1988: 279; Brogi 2011: 356). This meant that even acutely divisive domestic conflicts could be addressed without reference to global ideological polarities. On the other hand, this disarticulation was reflected in the increasing proliferation of informal political groups. Even in settings in which national political interactions were sharply determined by external pressures, the influence of global conflicts on national politics did not occur as a process in which global faultlines were immediately mirrored in national societies. In fact, even in domestic contexts that were defined by extreme political ferment caused by international conflicts, political agency tended to reflect a disalignment between global and national contestation. An illuminating example of this is the Vietnam War in the United States, in which domestic political exchanges were acutely affected by international antagonism, such that American society at this time entered a condition close to cultural civil war. At one level, this triggered a typical societal response to external conflict, and it led to the deep polarization of domestic political constituencies. In this context, however, it is striking that, despite the externally determined politicization of American society, socio-political conflicts were not primarily expressed in binary oppositional struggles. On the contrary, the exposure of American society to external conflict triggered a proliferation of political movements, often with a highly individualistic emphasis. Mobilization caused by war was typically expressed in demands for distinct sectoral rights, linked to a plurality of oppositional identities and motivations, which gave rise to informally organized aesthetic, generational, ethnic or moral political communities.[72] Even in conditions of palpable social militarization, the form of political citizenship did not immediately reproduce global military affiliations, and it tended not to gravitate around simple collective subjects. As a result, the exercise of citizenship became less likely to unsettle political institutions.

It was on premises created by the demilitarization of citizenship and the rupture between international and national politics that, after 1945, national societies acquired a distinctively integrated institutional form. National democratic societies were originally formed by war, as war constructed the core pattern of national citizenship and the essential premise for national integration. The collective expression of such citizenship, however, usually impeded the emergence of genuinely democratic nationalized societies. The deepening individualization of citizenship after 1945 placed national societies on integrational foundations that softened the direct impact of global conflicts and enabled states to integrate social conflicts and participants in such conflicts in more stable fashion.

Demilitarized Citizenship: Normative Integration

As discussed, the underlying demilitarization of citizenship after 1945 was not due to any reduction in the political relevance of warfare, and war continued to affect states in different ways. Moreover, national welfare states did not reflect a uniform model of state construction. Consequently, a multi-focal framework is required to account for the gradual stabilization of democratizing polities after 1945. In some

---

[72] One observer has explained how oppositional groups in the United States in the 1960s were specifically 'not united by class, ethnicity, or national origin' (Suri 2005: 93).

democratizing polities, the reinforcement of democracy was eventually linked to the fact that these polities converged in normatively prescriptive external communities, such as human rights systems or international organizations with a primary economic focus, such as the EU. In such settings, economic integration was sometimes tied to the implementation of certain democratic procedures. Additionally, after 1945, national societies generally approached a higher level of structural unity, and states secured their monopoly of power more fully and acquired deeper purchase in society. This was itself partly a product of war, as many states had intensified their administrative penetration into national society through mobilization for war, at different junctures. This meant that states were less frequently undermined by extreme inter-group rivalry, and they were increasingly able to protect democratic institutions from minority monopolization.[73] This process was deeply reinforced by the growth of welfare states. The high levels of violence that persisted in some societies were caused by the fact that many new states came into being after 1945, and many of these did not possess sufficiently robust institutions to exercise a stable monopoly of power.[74]

At the same time, reasons for the increasing stabilization of democracy after 1945 can be identified in the basic normative order of democracy, as the essential legitimational focus of the democratic political system was transformed at this time. As discussed, it was only after 1945 that welfare replaced war as the primary channel of *institutional interaction* between states and citizens, such that citizens assumed roles vis-à-vis their governments in a form that was functionally separate from war. Only at that point did it become possible for states to integrate sovereign populations in stable fashion, and to preserve their own sovereignty in so doing. At the same time, the typical channel of *normative integration* between state and citizen was revised, and states constructed the legitimacy of law on new constitutional premises which were also detached from military functions. As explained, the evolution of democratic polities in national societies had typically been interrupted, initially, by the fact that the core

---

[73] On the causal connection between early-stage democratization, weak statehood and political instability, see Mansfield and Snyder (1995: 88).

[74] Evidence for this theory is found in Holden's brilliant analysis (2004: 117–118). Holden argues that many post-1945 states were strengthened because they took control of the range of violent groups in society. This meant that they could weaken factions traditionally able to shake the authority of the state. However, their strength remained limited and they remained reliant on violent suppression. This theory is also supported by Goodwin's claim that post-1945 states marked by high levels of violence were 'weak authoritarian regimes' (2001: 180).

source of constitutional legitimacy – the citizen – was defined in terms affected by international politics. The figure of the modern national citizen first acquired form as a construct that was positioned, simultaneously, in the domestic domain and in the international domain. After 1945, however, the figure of the citizen assumed new normative contours. In its domestic implications, as discussed, the citizen began to appear as an individual holder of multiple rights, whose integration within the democratic polity did not presuppose comprehensive or acutely conflictual social mobilization. At the same time, the citizen was transformed in its external articulations, as it began to assimilate aspects of international law. After 1945, the citizen was affected by a reorientation in patterns of legitimation and norm construction in the international arena, in which norms of citizenship acquired high prominence. After 1945, a new international diction of citizenship was promoted in the global domain, which coincided with the reorientation of citizenship in domestic integration processes. This diction separated the production and legitimation of law from ideas of political subjectivity attached to war, and it created a normative basis for law that strongly promoted inner-societal processes of democratic integration.

The reorientation in global patterns of norm production after 1945 was expressed, primarily, in the rising importance of human rights as global norms. The period beginning in 1945 saw the promulgation of a number of human rights declarations and conventions, both at the global and at the regional international level, which acquired varying impact in different national societies. Distinctive in this emergent corpus of human rights law is the fact that human rights were conceived, in essence, as rights held by particular individual subjects, so that each human subject appeared, however abstractly, as the holder of entitlements established in international law. To be sure, the emergent system of international law sanctioned rights to be exercised collectively, such as labour rights and rights of political participation. Given the background of the industrial-scale ethnic violence perpetrated in pre-1945 Europe, international law attached particular weight to rights providing protection for ethnic groups. In principle, however, each set of rights created in international law after 1945 was established in a form that gave recognition to individual subjects as the primary addressees of rights. This meant that, even within sovereign polities, individual subjects could, notionally if not practically, lay claim to such rights. Importantly, the corpus of human rights that appeared after 1945 was not enforceable in individual cases until much later. Such rights usually only became justiciable after the creation of regional human rights systems in some parts of the globe. The European Court of Human Rights began to decide cases to protect individual persons in the 1960s; the Inter-American Court of Human Rights started to hear contentious cases in the 1980s; the African human rights system acquired greater judicial force after 2000. However, even before such rights acquired international judicial protection, guarantees for individual rights became a core part of domestic constitutions. In most democratizing polities after 1945, constitutions were written in, or adapted to, a form that gave recognition to global human rights law. Even in polities such as the United States, in which national jurisprudence retained a superficial hostility to the reception of international law, domestic judges found ways of aligning domestic constitutional law to international human rights law. Major changes in American constitutional law in the decades after 1945 closely matched developments in international law.[75] With variations, single human rights became more prominent in domestic jurisprudence and domestic legislation. Rights-based constitutionalism became the dominant model for ordering and legitimating the claims of national citizens.

This new individualist emphasis in international law had clear origins in World War II. The drafting of the UN Charter, which initiated the global commitment to human rights law, was planned during the war, in a period in which the boundaries of sovereign statehood were globally precarious. Moreover, human rights norms acquired legal form in a global environment marked by wartime legal experiences. The war clearly demonstrated the vulnerability of refugees and minority groups under potentially hostile states. This manifestly shaped the individual focus of international human rights law. International norms promulgated after 1945 also reflected the fact that in World War II much fighting was conducted by persons with indeterminate positions under military

---

[75] See p. 140. The Civil Rights Act and the Voting Rights Act were passed in the United States at a point in time immediately after President Johnson had declared commitment to the global promotion of human rights in the UN General Assembly. The Voting Rights Act was passed in the same year that the Convention on the Elimination of All Forms of Racial Discrimination was adopted in the UN. These are inextricably connected historical events. In 1964, the American Supreme Court declared commitment to the 'achievement of fair and effective representation for all citizens' (*Reynolds* v. *Sims*, 377 US 533 (1964)). This case was not centrally concerned with anti-minority politics. However, it made clear the Court's insistence on its political role in promoting equal access to the electoral franchise. It also implicitly attached domestic constitutional law to norms set out in the global arena in the mid-1960s, especially to the International Covenant on Civil and Political Rights.

law. This was especially the case in Eastern and Southern Europe, for example, in Russia, Poland, Greece and Yugoslavia, where resistance to German occupation was organized by partisans. The Geneva Conventions of 1949 acknowledged members of informal armed groups as actors with protected rights, even in occupied territories. The individualization of international law was strongly shaped by changes to legal personhood wrought by war.

Despite its military origins, human rights law had a deep pacifying impact on national democracy. This occurred in divergent processes, with great polity-to-polity variations. However, it is difficult to find democratizing polities in the later twentieth century that were not strongly marked by international human rights law. It is possible to identify a range of ways in which the formalization of individual rights in the international arena stimulated patterns of subject construction that came to define, and helped to consolidate, democratizing polities. In each case, this was linked to the fact that the individualistic aspect of human rights law allowed states to generate legitimacy for their functions without deep collective mobilization of citizens. Indeed, human rights law created a construct of the citizen to support normative integration that could easily be reflected in processes of institutional integration. Historically, the national construct of the citizen had undermined domestic integration by attaching citizenship to global conflicts. After 1945, this process was reversed. A construct of the citizen was established in global society that promoted domestic integration by weakening the link between national citizenship and global conflicts.

First, the construction of individual rights in the international domain had the result in national polities that the substance of legal-political subjectivity was partly established outside national society, and international human rights predefined expressions of political agency at the national level. Political mobilization in national societies is now frequently conducted in the name of subjectivities whose normative origins lie outside national patterns of association, and the outcomes of such mobilization are partly determined by external norm setters. For example, in the 1970s, authoritarian regimes in Latin America were criticized in the international domain for their violations of human rights. On this basis, domestic protest against these regimes was frequently organized by human rights organizations with links to international bodies, and it was focused on human rights abuse. Similarly, from the 1970s onwards, authoritarian regimes in Eastern Europe were often criticized because of their weak protection of human rights, and mobilization within these societies was strongly connected to such criticisms (Thomas 2001: 160–194). As a result, in both settings, human rights norms provided a sanctioned framework for the de-legitimation of national governments, and they projected a simplified path towards democratization in these polities. It became possible for polities in these regions to oversee democratic transitions in which recognition of human rights law was the defining emphasis in constitutional consolidation, such that, in recognizing human rights, states could signal democratic legitimacy without deep engagement with factual communities in society. This is exemplified – primarily – by transitions in Argentina and Chile, where the recognition of international human rights law formed a key step in processes of democratic transition, in 1983 and 1988–90, respectively. The transition in Brazil in 1985 also entailed recognition of international human rights laws before the approval of the 1988 Constitution. In fact, this phenomenon was already exemplified in the transition in what became the FRG after 1945, where an individualized construction of the rights-holding citizen, borrowed from international law, was projected as a source of legitimacy before the new democracy had been created. In such instances, human rights law provided a template for political subject construction that meant that democratic polities could be legitimated on individualized premises, in processes that obviated the need for the encompassing mobilization of citizens. As a result, human rights law created a construct of the citizen that allowed governments to explain and to demonstrate their legitimacy without exposure to deep-lying conflicts, simplifying their integrational functions.

Second, the construction of individual rights in the international domain has transformed national polities because it has consistently supported the individualistic design of democratic government. In particular, it has projected a global *meta-constitution* to support welfare democracy as a dominant institutional order.

As discussed, welfare states were partly constructed through global normative expectations, strongly backed by human rights law. The reformulation of the state–citizen nexus realized through welfare democracies was frequently underpinned by the self-comprehension of the citizen as a holder of transnationally defined social rights.[76] In addition, welfare democracies have been sustained by the fact that parties of the political left have adopted more individualistic approaches to welfare rights. In most democratic polities, such parties learned to negotiate for their

---

[76] See analysis of this intersection in the United States in Abramowitz (2011: 61).

memberships, increasingly, on foundations pre-defined by international human rights. This began after 1945, as Social Democratic parties in Europe campaigned for welfare rights on a human rights foundation. Ultimately, Communist parties in Europe followed a similar path in the 1970s. The integration of Communist parties in European polities increased as the Helsinki Final Act was agreed in 1975, which discredited the Soviet Union internationally (see Lomellini 2012: 97–98). The integration of left-wing parties in democratic political systems became even more pronounced after the wave of democratization in Latin America in the 1980s. By 2000, many parties of the left in Latin America defined themselves, broadly, as Social Democratic parties, with a strong focus on human rights protection. As such, they frequently proved very effective in creating protective welfare systems for citizens of their polities.[77] In each respect, global human rights law provided a multi-level constitutional framework for welfare states. It allowed polities to focus their integrational functions on welfare provision instead of inter-group conflict management.

Third, the construction of individual rights in the international domain shaped national polities because elements of international law tended to affect patterns of subject construction in national societies. Since 1945, the international domain has been occupied by normative declarations and conventions providing protection for rights of particular subjects and groups of subjects.[78] The importance of individual rights at the international level has tended to promote, within national societies, lines of political subject formation with a strong individual emphasis, consolidated around clusters of individual rights, such as ethnic, gender-related, medical, educational, religious and economic rights. In this regard, it is difficult to observe a simple and immediate process of global translation, through which international norms have entered national society and established premises for political agency at the national level. Discernibly, however, the decades after 1945 witnessed the emergence of a transnational political culture, traversing positions on the political

---

[77] Between 2000 and 2010, Argentina, Chile, Uruguay and Brazil moved, in select policies, towards universalist welfare states (Pribble 2013: 1–2; Hunter 2014: 28–29). On the decline in inequality at this time, see Huber and Stephens (2012: 9).

[78] This began with protections for minorities in UN instruments after 1945 and with recognition of education rights in the Universal Declaration of Human Rights. Protection of specific rights increased through the 1960s and 1970s, notably in the International Convention on the Elimination of All Forms of Racial Discrimination (1965), the two Covenants of 1966, and the Convention on the Elimination of all Forms of Discrimination Against Women (1979).

spectrum, which was shaped by individualistic principles of citizenship and marked by deep intersection between national citizenship and global constitutional principles.

On the one hand, this tendency can be seen in the fact that political subjects in national societies were increasingly constructed around claims to rights of a partial or functionally selective nature, for the realization of which the mobilization of all society was not a precondition. In recent contexts, actors in society have been able to claim particular rights and even to shape the legal form of society without exercising any manifest political agency, simply through legal actions referring to international normative standards. In many polities, basic rights have been generated and strengthened by litigation, and litigants have often been able to find support for their claims in international human rights law. This is visible across a range of cases, from the consolidation of rights regarding sexual preference in the United Kingdom,[79] to education rights in Colombia,[80] to welfare rights in Germany.[81] The fact that rights can be constructed through single legal actions inevitably reinforces tendencies towards the individualization of political agency. In many cases, rights secured through individual legal actions relate specifically to the interests of relatively differentiated groups within society. The initiation of legal action based in international human rights gradually became a vital strategy for many groups with distinct – for instance – sexual, ethnic or environmental interests.[82]

On the other hand, this tendency can be seen in the patterns of radical political subjectivity that characterized world society in the longer wake of 1945. For example, in some polities, the 1960s saw manifestations of social activism close to civil war, incubated by international conflicts. Yet, it was distinctive for the political environment of this period that political identities and motivations were partly separated from conventional political organizations, and participants in conflict tended to organize political agency in loosely configured movements. Moreover, oppositional agency in the late 1960s took remarkably similar form in different national contexts, so that political radicalism assumed a clear transnational

---

[79] See the famous decision in the European Court of Human Rights expanding sexual rights in the United Kingdom, *Smith and Grady* v. *UK* (1999) 29 EHRR 493.
[80] The Colombian Constitutional Court created a constitutional right to education. This right was implied in decision T-406/92 and hardened in T-329/93.
[81] BVerfG, 05.11.2019 – 1 BvL 7/16
[82] Consideration of international human rights law has supported claims to freedom in sexual decisions in unlikely locations. See *Lawrence* v. *Texas*, 539 US 558 (2003).

dimension, which further detached it from common patterns of solidarity (Wallerstein and Zukin 1989: 431; della Porta 1998: 132). One observer argues that the transnational aspect of political activism in the 1960s forms the 'crucial paradigm' in which this period is to be examined (Sanders 2013: 76). On both counts, citizenship tended to assume expression in individualistic form, and traditional collectivities lost some force as the premise for political motivations and commitments.

This transnational linkage was partly driven by the centrality of universities in the political world of the 1960s. At this time, students emerged as key political actors, and they found themselves at the epicentre of far-reaching processes of transnational integration, even conceiving themselves as members of a new transnational political class. To this degree, political mobilization in the 1960s was deeply determined by pre-existing processes of class dissolution and resultant individualization. However, this transnational linkage was also driven by the fact that sites of political agency in different societies were increasingly connected by universal normative parameters, with a strong focus on human rights.[83] At this time, as discussed, the diction of human rights had become established as part of a global legal horizon, which was centrally embodied in the UN, but which penetrated diffusely into different national societies. In many countries, activists in the 1960s openly campaigned on human rights platforms, and human rights norms overarched different national political spaces. Anti-Soviet protests in Czechoslovakia were expressed in part as protests against human rights abuses. African-American protests against the Olympic Games in Mexico were shaped by human rights initiatives. Although of limited significance, in fact, 1968 was the International Year for Human Rights. At this time, more importantly, political agents often identified with transnational communities asserting claims to rights, so that political agents articulated normative solidarities that positioned them outside inherited organizational structures. The Civil Rights Movement in the United States in the 1950s and 1960s expressly associated itself with anti-discrimination protests in decolonizing countries which were also shaped by global pressures for human rights protection. Less obviously, mobilization for gender rights after 1968 had a distinct transnational basis, and mobilized groups in different societies were linked by declarations of cross-border solidarity. Reproductive rights, a core object of subsequent gender-related

---

[83] My reflections on these points are influenced by conversations with Hauke Brunkhorst and by his publications.

mobilization, were first formally recognized in the Tehran Conference on Human Rights of 1968. Later, mobilization for indigenous rights acquired an explicit transnational dimension, and it was flanked by processes of legal codification at the international level.

In these respects, political activity itself was often separated from the classical emphases of national solidarity and popular sovereignty, and political agents increasingly explained their citizenship as the expression of an elective, individual affiliation to different transnational communities. One important outcome of this was that periods of shared political protest after 1945 tended to connect single transnational groups, promoting greater individualization and further disaggregation of common class identities. The defining legacy of political radicalization in the late 1960s was that it led to the increased institutionalization of protest for particular rights, which in turn established stronger legal protections for individual freedoms. One further result of this was that radical agency was often, gradually, translated into legal agency, and, in the years after 1968, political action was increasingly attached to specific causes and the extension of specific rights. Owing to its promotion of single rights, in fact, 1960s activism created a setting in which politically liberalized elite factions often committed to inner-institutional activism and strategies for human rights expansion.[84] The implications of 1968 were frequently expressed, nationally, in increased legal mobilization, and in the growth of public interest litigation and cause lawyering.[85] In Eastern Europe, many activists of 1968 soon re-emerged as members of human rights groups. The implications of 1968 became visible, transnationally, in the rise of non-governmental organizations, environmental bodies and human rights groups whose origins can be traced to domestic patterns of mobilization (Della Porta 1998: 144, 148; Cmiel 1999: 1233; Cummings and Trubek 2008: 13). The short-lived moment of radicalization around 1968 was followed by a period in which many liberalized recipients of educational rights adopted a strong orientation to institutional transformation, both inside and outside their national polities. Changes to

---

[84] On the link between human rights activism, educational opportunities and transnational openness, see Tsutsui and Wotipka (2004: 596). This study shows the causal connection between the rise of human rights activism in the 1970s and 1980s and civil rights activism in the late 1960s (602).

[85] As mentioned, public-interest litigation accompanied the civil rights movement in the United States. It became more widespread in the United States and across the world in the longer aftermath of 1968. By the 1980s, public-interest lawyers in many countries made broad use of international law (see Thornhill 2018: 466–486).

legal practice and patterns of litigation were amongst the most notable results of the 1960s, and these changes were strongly driven by the rising prominence of human rights law.

Overall, the period after 1968 witnessed the distillation of radical claims to popular sovereignty into a process in which the integrational structure of national democracies was diversified, and patterns of protective individualism generated after 1945 were extended to new social groups and affiliations. The patterning of citizenship on constructions of transnational rights meant that persons engaging in political mobilization were not exclusively tied to conventional lines of solidarity. This in turn meant that they were able to promote transnational commitments in complex, multi-focal processes of inclusion in different national contexts. Despite the revolutionary impulse behind this period of political activism, it managed to create a normative form for citizenship that clearly solidified processes of integration in national polities. The period culminating in 1968 appeared, like the years around 1945, as one part of a long global constitutional moment, in which the articulation between national agency and transnational norms led to the incorporation of new groups within democratic polities, the increased inclusivity of national legal systems and the reinforced protection of individual rights. From this point, transformative expressions of political subjectivity were defined in a global normative form, and inner-societal democracy was firmly attached to transnational dispositions. After this point, in fact, democratization processes almost invariably depended on transnational convergence.

In each respect, since 1945, principles expressed in the international domain have generated new models of political subject construction which are now fundamental to more stable democracies. In such democracies, the national citizen has acquired a pronounced normative connection to citizens in other polities which is strongly expressed through human rights law. In such democracies, further, the citizen is defined as a person holding a plurality of individual rights which are in essence attributed to the citizen, in simple form, as a single human subject. This meant, over a longer period, that governments explained their legitimacy as the result of interactions with single rights-holding subjects. This also meant that the nexus between citizen and government became increasingly individualized, and institutions extracted legitimacy from normative constructs of citizenship that did not entail unsettling exposure to social conflicts. In each respect, state institutions acquired the capacity to perform integrational functions in relatively pacified fashion.

None of this implies that individual rights do not have origins in global political strategies. In the United States, as mentioned, the increasing importance of civil rights law was driven by anti-American propaganda in the Soviet Union. In Europe, the rise of human rights law, and most obviously the ratification of the European Convention on Human Rights (ECHR), can easily be explained as an ideological shift. The ECHR was designed to project legitimational principles for new democracies in Western Europe, and to distinguish European polities allied to Washington from those allied to Moscow (Duranti 2017: 149, 233). Yet, whatever intentions brought it into being, the global corpus of human rights law that emerged after 1945 led to a refocusing of the sources of normative integration within national societies. The fact that the unit citizen became defined in globally individualized form altered the traditional alignment between national and domestic politics. The rise of international human rights law meant that the rights claimed by citizens existed, under global legal preconditions, before any particular demand for such rights was expressed. This meant that such rights could be claimed by subjects without any affiliation to structured organizational forms, and mobilization of collective subjects was not essential for the elaboration of laws supported by such rights. Historically, the national citizen had connected the national polity to the international domain by promoting patterns of integration that strongly attached national political movements to global conflicts. This had resonated deeply into national political procedures, dividing societies into intensely opposed collective factions. After 1945, however, the international domain was increasingly populated by a new normative order – human rights law – and the articulation between national and international law was coloured by an alternative form of citizenship: by the construct of the citizen as a single holder of particular rights. The legitimational intersection between the national and the international political spheres switched from military citizenship to citizenship as a condition of individual rights holding, and the norm of citizenship that entered national society from the global domain was focused, not on the mobilized citizen, but on the citizen as single rights holder. Through this switch, law's legitimacy could be secured through reference to a formal definition of the citizen, and this meant that institutional integration within national polities could be conducted in simplified fashion.

Conclusion: Democracy and the Hyper-Differentiation of the Law

Modern democracy tended to develop on three conjoined premises, which, for embedded sociological reasons, acted as its core foundations. It tended to presuppose strong welfare systems. It entailed strong protection of individual rights. It also usually emerged in societies shaped, however diversely, by interpenetration between national constitutional law and global human rights law. This tripartite constitutional model is merely an ideal type. These three elements of polity building are only variably represented in different democratic states. However, few polities have acquired democratic status without some consolidation of each of these premises. These premises had the distinctive result that, first, they acted to redefine the articulation between national citizenship and the interstate domain, and, second, they promoted individualized patterns of political subject formation. In both respects, this meant that the two processes of integration that underlie national societies – institutional integration and normative integration – were separated from military constructions and pressures. On these foundations, democracy began to take shape as a system of reasonably comprehensive integration, and it began to solidify the processes of legal and institutional formation that can be traced back to the origins of modern European society. In fact, the global model of rights-based welfare democracy can be interpreted as a political regime type in which, finally, the basic socio-political contradictions arising from the end of feudalism were softened. This model created national political systems able to stabilize both an administrative regime and a normative legal order for individual citizens that did not hinge on the intense militarization of citizenship. Even in periods where experiences of citizenship were radicalized, citizens tended to express claims to solidarity of a pluralistic nature, not tied to the idea of the simple sovereign people, and radicalized citizens could easily be re-integrated through the consolidation of particular rights. In this process, uniquely, population groups released from unfree labour at different junctures since 1789 were integrated in political institutions by mechanisms in which the direct deployment of violence was not required. The separation of war and law at the origin of the modern sovereign state, obstructed by revolutionary constructs of citizenship, approached temporary realization.

In these respects, the modern democratic polity need not be seen as the result of normative choices by actual citizens. Instead, it can be seen as the outcome of a process of normative and institutional evolution that was able to capture and balance in a *protective system of individualized legal integration* the diverse social processes initiated in the eighteenth century. To achieve this equilibrium, modern democratic polities constructed legitimacy for law in a form of legal subjectivity very different from that which underpinned democracy in the revolutionary era in the late eighteenth century. Indeed, democratic polities acquired contours that had little in common with original democratic constitutional designs. As a general rule, democratic polities were defined by the fact that *individual legal integration superseded collective norm construction as the core prerequisite of democracy*. Democracy was stabilized as the primary constitutional source of democratic legitimacy – the citizen – was patterned on a transnational normative form, which meant that the integrational processes that underpin democracy could be promoted through reference to individualized socio-political subjects. The formation of national democracy had historically been unsettled by the fact that the construct of the national citizen allowed international conflicts to reverberate in domestic politics. The rise of the global human rights system, however, created a normative diction in which the international definition of the citizen had the converse effect, checking the replication of international conflicts in national polities and stabilizing national political institutions against uncontrollable organizational mobilization. This depended on the composition of a global model of individual legal subjectivity, abstracted against the factual conditions of collective social conflict. On this basis, classical functions of democratic institutions, especially legislatures, could be conducted without extreme volatility. Both elements in this process of individualization – the welfare state and human rights law – meant that state institutions were able exponentially to augment their sovereign force. Paradoxically, the determination of national sovereignty by global human rights law created a condition in which, finally, national citizens were able to exercise popular sovereignty and national states were able to preserve institutional sovereignty in their interactions with citizens.

The construct of the citizen first came into being around 1789 as a constitutional figure that articulated deep-lying integration processes in society. However, this construct, in its initial form, usually blocked the integration processes that it articulated. After 1945, a new construct of citizenship emerged. The second construct of the citizen was based in welfare provision and individual human rights, which served as principles to support institutional integration and normative integration, respectively. This construct insulated society against antinomies inherent in the earlier construct. Like the first figure of the citizen, this construct did not describe a real existing person or aggregate of persons. As discussed, core elements of this construct were created during World War II, through the contingent, transnational rise of a welfare consensus and a human rights consensus. The welfare aspect of this consensus reflected the fact that, in World War II, governments acquired increasing fiscal power and increasing national penetration and infrastructure (see Klausen 1998: 165). The human rights aspect of this consensus resulted from massive experience of individual vulnerability in the war and from a broad endeavour to protect persons from societal militarization. In both respects, this construct internalized transnational processes of institution building and norm formation. Crucially, this construct took shape as an adaptive norm – or as a *functional norm* – that facilitated the core processes of integration on which a democratic society depends. It achieved this by separating the normative basis of democratic integration from real political subjects. Up to World War II, democratic formation had been driven by the subjective norm of democracy. From this point onwards, democratic formation increasingly focused on the integrational dimension of democracy, and the original subjective-normative dimension of democracy lost relative importance.

The growth of democracy has shown that national political integration presupposes a process of global legal integration which preforms constructions of national sovereignty and national citizenship. As discussed, the national political system originally evolved through the interlocking of the legal system and the military system. After 1945, however, the national political system was partly reintegrated in the legal system, as the legal system was consolidated at the global level. The emergence of a system of legal norms in global society, able partly to predefine the legitimacy of national political processes and to separate the national political system from its attachment to militarized forms of agency, became the foundation for the production of democratic legitimacy in national society. There are many definitions of global law. Some of these definitions see global law as a set of internationally binding legal standards applied to all persons (Peters 2014: 469); some observe global law as the mass of pluralistic legal norms that exist in different spheres of global society (Teubner 1997). In the sphere of constitutional law, however, it is possible to define a series of globally convergent processes that have created the legal basis for sustainable constitutional-democratic order. Taken together, these processes form global constitutional law. In fact, it is possible to propose a broad global-legal framework to explain the trajectories that give rise to constitutional democracy, to identify primary challenges to it, and to determine constitutional preconditions for its survival.

In most societies, constitutional democracy was originally created by armies, reflecting a deep fusion between the roles of soldiers and the roles of voters, which were amalgamated to produce the modern form of the citizen. The modern figure of the sovereign citizen expressed a deep connection between the legal system and the military system. Democracy only became stable when these roles and these systems were constitutionally separated. This occurred through the creation of welfare states, to support the state's functions of institutional integration, and through the global rise of human rights law, to support the state's functions of normative integration. This does not imply that all democratizing polities locked themselves equally into a global constitutional system. Nonetheless, with variations in each component, this formed a global polity model for democratizing states. Based on this dual foundation, modern states learned to establish articulations with their citizens through a grammar of legal-subjective individualization. On this basis, democratic polities were able to ensure that the collective subjects, which they incorporated through mass enfranchisement, were integrated in a form that reduced their propensity for full mobilization. As a result, they were able to communicate with citizens without forfeiting their sovereignty.

A general model of global constitutional law likely to sustain democracy can be extracted from this analysis. It is reasonable to propose that national democracy is most likely to survive if, in broad definition, it is inserted into a global constitutional system. This sense of a global constitution does not necessarily imply the existence of a fully binding supranational constitutional order, to which national constitutions are fully subordinate. In fact, this sense of a global constitution does not imply that recognition of global principles, such as welfare rights or international human rights law, needs to be expressly protected in the formal provisions of national constitutional law. Many polities have constructed patterns of citizenship defined by welfare and human rights without spelling this out in the literal texts of their constitutions. However, this implies that that core processes of subject formation in national societies are deeply shaped by transnational normative models. Both the normative and the functional processes of integration required by national democracy are reinforced where they are supported by global constitutional norms. The incorporation of the democratic polity in the global constitutional order has the particular legitimational function that it separates citizens from soldiers, it separates the legal system from the military system and it allows state institutions to legitimate laws for citizens without integrational crisis. Crucially, this global-constitutional model can be traced to antinomies lying deep in the structure of modern society, and it has its remote origins in the original emergence of the modern legal order at the end of feudalism. This global constitutional model is based, not in a real condition of citizenship, but in the construction of a figure of the citizen able to balance society's deep integrational trajectory towards sovereign state formation and its trajectory towards legal individualization.

4

Populism as Misunderstood Democracy

Populism and Democracy

As stated in previous chapters the modern democratic state is currently afflicted by crisis in many parts of the globe. In many cases, such crisis is reflected in the rise of populist movements or parties that gain support by denouncing the form that democracy has assumed in their polities. The rise of populism has interrupted, or at least added complexity to, the global turn towards constitutional democracy that was initiated in the 1980s. The spread of populism means that the distinctions that once separated democratic from authoritarian states have become blurred, and many polities now possess both democratic and authoritarian elements. As discussed later, populism is not categorically outside the family of democratic political movements. Yet, by most measures, populist government leads to democratic deterioration, and it promotes authoritarian tendencies in democratic states.

As a global phenomenon of first-order importance, the recent proliferation of populism has attracted much analytical attention. There have been many theoretical attempts both to explain it, and to buttress democracy against the threats posed by it. Increasingly, two lines of analysis have become pronounced in current inquiries into populism. These lines of analysis address both the causes of populism and the relation between populism and democratic decline. Despite differences in emphasis and method, these analyses contain a number of similar observations and arrive at convergent conclusions. Both lines of analysis indicate that liberal democracy depends on selective procedures for determining which social interests should be represented in legislation, which means that some social groups are less fully integrated in the political system than others. Both lines of analysis imply that, because of this, populism gains support in circumstances in which democratic institutions struggle to capture and articulate all societal interests, and these interests find new forms of expression, in populism. In consequence, both lines of analysis indicate that populism is part of democratic life. Both lines of analysis observe populism as a generic side effect of democracy, and they share the view that democratic polities are always likely to generate populist movements.

On the one hand, there exists a body of research with a political-science or sociological emphasis that explains populism from a behavioural or motivational perspective. In political science, it has long been conventional to observe populism as a type of movement that depends on particular politicians who appeal most strongly to social groups with weaker attachments to democracy.[1] Contemporary research expands such analysis by attributing the current success of populist movements to the personal impact of certain politicians, implying that some social groups are more likely to respond positively to populist politicians than others, and such groups are frequently marked by limited commitment to democratic values (Norris and Inglehart 2019: 65, 247). Such research typically explains that populism finds support among social groups whose motivations are determined by specific social experiences, such as limited access to education.[2] The motivations of such groups are often viewed as disproportionately linked to single issues, such as immigration (Mudde 2002: 173; Muis and Immerzeel 2017: 912; Shehaj, Shin and Inglehart 2019: 2). Populist politicians are thus presented as figures who can appeal to groups that are marginally positioned vis-à-vis mainstream politics, and whose engagement in political debate is very selective. On each point, such research indicates that populism thrives in contexts in which some voters are not fully adapted to democratic roles, and its success is due to the fact that it mobilizes groups and sectors whose interests challenge the democratic balance of society as a whole. At the same time, some observers argue that the expansion of the spectrum of openly politicized themes in populist politics is not in itself detrimental to democracy. Increasingly, some political scientists are inclined to advance the view that populism may enrich democracy and it may entail a 'push for the democratization of democracy' (Kaltwasser and Hauwaert 2020: 15).

On the other hand, a more normative body of research has emerged that addresses populism as reflective of deep legitimational problems in contemporary democracy. Crossing the boundaries between legal analysis and political theory, this research has become increasingly

---

[1] See expressions of this view in Ignazi (2002: 34); Mudde (2002: 15); de Lange (2007: 430).
[2] See p. 201, note 11.

concerned with the constitutional aspects of populism, which it examines as a specifically constitutional phenomenon (see Corrias 2016: 8; Blokker 2019). Some observers in this field are unreservedly hostile to populism (Landau 2018). Broadly, however, populism is described in this research as a type of politics that is naturally parasitic on constitutional government (Fournier 2018: 1). The persistent threat of populism in democratic polities is attributed to the fact that liberal democratic government is excessively organized around formal patterns of procedural representation and constitutional balancing.[3] Common constitutional models of representation tend, thus, to alienate governmental functions from the people themselves, and they attenuate expressions of popular agency in government. As a result, constitutional democracy inevitably creates spaces in which populism can take root: populism arises as a reflection of democracy's weak legitimation by the demos. In this perspective, the constitutional organization of democracy stimulates populism, and populism critically highlights the excessive formalism of liberal-democratic patterns of representation.[4] In some cases, political and constitutional theorists claim that high-quality democracy relies on the presence of some populist elements in the system of electoral representation, as these provide a corrective reminder of its foundation in the will of the people (Laclau 1977: 196–197; Tännsjö 1992: 61; Canovan 1999: 14; Möller 2017: 247). Such approaches in fact build on stock positions in constitutional theory that oppose constitutional orders that contain strong anti-majoritarian counterweights (see Tushnet 1999). Some accounts emphasize the 'emancipatory' aspect of populist anti-formalism (Bugaric 2019: 42). One recurrent claim in the constitutionalist analysis of populism is that the excessive constitutionalization of government is a primary cause of populism.[5]

Both these lines of engagement with populism overlap with claims set out in the previous chapters of this book. Notably, both lines imply that democracy invariably contains certain dialectical potentials which form important background for explaining populism. Both lines touch on ways in which democratic polities generate expectations of inclusion among citizens that can easily stretch the integrational capacities of representative institutions. At the same time, existing explanations of populism reflect a certain hesitancy and contain clear shortcomings in

---

[3] See expressions of this claim in Arditi (2005: 93); Panizza (2005: 29); Cannon (2009: 77); Müller (2017: 101); Issacharoff (2018: 453).
[4] As a survey, see Landau (2016). See also Corrias (2016); Blokker (2018); Zaccaria (2018).
[5] This is the implicit suggestion in Blokker (2019: 338).

key points of analysis, and some factors in the resurgence of populism in recent years have not come fully into view. At a specific level, existing research does not yet offer a clear explanation of the reasons why populism has become a global phenomenon, affecting, at the same time, a number of polities with very different traditions and positioned in different global locations. Related to this, existing research has not provided an explanation of the reasons why populism tends to adopt such hostility to global legal principles and to global governance arrangements, and why its emergence appears to be linked to patterns of global norm construction. At a more general level, further, the existing body of research does not explain the exact features of democracy that induce populism. As discussed, critical analyses of populism draw attention to the fact that populism gains resonance in situations where frequently marginalized social groups are able to place their interests in the political arena or where the constitutional order is perceived as obstructing representation of concerns that preoccupy weakly integrated social groups. However, such analyses do little to isolate the specific causes of populism within democracy, and they do not identify the wider conjunctures in which the more dialectical aspects of democracy become unsettling. In fact, in describing populism as a parasitical growth within constitutional democracy, existing analyses lack criteria to show why democracy does not always have a populist tone, to determine why populism usually leads to democratic deterioration or even to explain why populism is a less than ideal form of democracy. Most importantly, it is a feature of these different approaches that, although they view populism as an outgrowth of democracy, they do not submit democracy itself to internal critique, and they do not subject the propensities in democracy for stimulating populism to specific critical examination. As mentioned, influential exponents of both political-scientific and constitutionalist approaches to populism are inclined to underline the salutary effects of populist impulses in democratic polities.

This chapter aims to propose an examination of populism that is more robust, both in explanatory and normative terms, than those offered in other lines of analysis. It attempts to explain why populism has become such a salient feature of contemporary society, and to illuminate the distinctive global reasons for the spread of populism. At the same time, it aims to reconstruct, in specific terms, the dialectical features within democratic polities that recurrently give rise to populist politics. In pursuing these ends, this chapter builds on the second line of analysis outlined earlier. It accepts the insight that populism has emerged as a distinct constitutional phenomenon, caused in part by constitutional constructions, and that constitutional inquiry has a particular qualification to explain it. However, it argues that theorists that examine populism as a constitutional form have struggled to provide a full explanation because they have often obscured the ways in which constitutional norms promote democracy. This chapter proposes a distinctive analysis of populism by arguing that populism thrives because of constitutional weaknesses in the terms in which democracy is usually comprehended. In this respect, it proposes claims that run parallel to Nadia Urbinati's outstanding analysis, which explains how populism reflects a misinterpretation of the essentially representative nature of democracy (2019: 71). Yet, the claims advanced in this chapter extend beyond this position, arguing that the fundamental constitutional vocabulary in which democracy is interpreted contains antinomies that lead to and often legitimate populism.

As discussed, in most definitions, democracy is viewed as a political order that depends on the exercise of sovereignty by concrete political subjects: *citizens*. As examined, this construct formed the first legitimational principle in classical democratic thinking. This construct now forms the first legitimational principle in democratic constitutionalism, which has established itself as the primary conceptual framework for promoting and organizing democracy. Self-evidently, constitutionalism is a theory of procedurally ordered democracy. In its different forms, constitutionalism establishes organizational principles to ensure that a political system is reinforced against momentary expressions of popular interest, and it is clearly distinct from theories of pure democracy. Moreover, the most essential implication in constitutional theory is that, in adopting a constitution, members of a people become different from their organic or pre-constitutional identities. As a result, citizenship is separated from simple personhood, and attached to a series of moral and legal obligations. In key respects, however, constitutionalism proposes an account of governmental legitimacy that is reducible to normative claims about the subjective origins of political power, and it predicates political legitimacy on a construct of the citizen as sovereign political subject. Different positions in constitutional thinking can be viewed as designs for engineering government so that the citizen remains at the subjective fulcrum of the state, and the state as a whole contains a deep vision of political life proposed originally by citizens.

In origin, first, constitutionalism developed as a theory of constituent power, which argues that a political order obtains legitimacy if it is willed into being by the citizens that are to be subject to it, such that the primary constituent acts of the citizens stand prior to and at the origin of the political system. On this principle, the political system demonstrates its legitimacy by legislating in accordance with the collective will originally declared by the constituent power. This view is expressed in classical theories of constitutional legitimacy.[6] In contemporary debate, this view is expressed in more conventional volitional theories of constitutional sovereignty (Böckenförde 1991: 294–295; Grimm 2012: 223). However, in different form, this idea underpins a range of current constitutional outlooks which insist that constitutional law must be interpreted in a fashion to give expression to the changing experiences and collective expectations of citizens.[7] Even the most discerning reflections on this question construe constitutional law as authorized by a 'constitutional subject' with an 'evolving identity' (Rosenfeld 1995: 1069). The idea of an originating constitutional subject even informs theories that argue that constitutional democracy can be separated from specifically national acts of popular sovereignty (Habermas 2014). Across this spectrum of opinions, the view is shared that the sovereign citizen forms the deep subject of the legitimate constitutional state, and the legitimating force of the citizen qua sovereign subject is never fully extinguished from the constitution. In most cases, the legitimational force imputed to the citizen is associated with the citizen of a specific place, with legally guaranteed rights of national affiliation. Alongside this, second, constitutionalism implies that, in a legitimate polity, citizens must be organically implicated in government, and the exercise of governmental power depends on the existence of a deep line of communication between sovereign citizens and the government (see Böckenförde 1991: 299). In each respect, constitutionalism indicates that the shared will of citizens must remain the normative standard by which the legitimacy of governmental acts is determined, so that a construction of the sovereign citizen must be co-implied in, and act as the measure of, all governmental acts. At the core of constitutional thinking is the legitimational claim, first, that the citizen is

---

[6] The main constitutionalist of revolutionary France, Emmanuel-Joseph Sieyès, defined the nation (people) as 'the origin of everything [...] the law itself' (1789: 79). This idea was later replicated in Carl Schmitt's classic distinction between constituent power as decision and constituted power as norm (1928: 76).

[7] See the leading expression of this view in Ackerman (1991: 19–21). In some respects, this view was anticipated by John Marshall, who argued that a 'provision is made in a Constitution intended to endure for ages to come, and consequently to be adapted to the various crises of human affairs': *McCulloch v. Maryland*, 117 US 316 (1819).

originally external to procedures used for democratic legislation and representation, such that the citizen retains a submerged yet primary subjective role within the polity. Also at the core of constitutionalism, second, is the claim that citizens must be constantly present as norm suppliers within the political system. In each respect, constitutionalism is a particular type of democratic theory, designed to construct roles within the polity in which the original subjective link between the citizen and the polity can be rearticulated.

In many ways, in contemporary societies, constitutionalism brings the deep antinomies of democracy to heightened articulation. As a grammar for organizing democracy, constitutional thought endlessly declares that the source of governmental legitimacy resides in original acts of popular will formation. This claim cannot easily be eradicated from modern constitutionalism. In recent years, in fact, increasing emphasis has been given to this assertion. Many recent constitutionalists have accentuated the popular-subjective elements in constitutionalism, stating that the exercise of power must be more fully attached to acts of sovereign will formation.[8] In making this claim, however, constitutionalism provides an account of democratic legitimacy in which the tensions between the subjective principles and the integrational processes that underlie democracy are sharply and visibly expressed. Indeed, in promoting this account of political legitimacy, constitutionalism specifically denies its own functions, and it conjures constructs of legitimacy that contradict the actual role of constitutional norms in bringing legitimacy to the political system.

The historical-sociological analyses set out in the previous chapters present an alternative constitutional theory, explaining that the basic constitutional subjects of democracy – sovereign citizens, sovereign institutions – acquired reality on premises that were not envisaged in classical constructions of these subjects. In fact, democratic subjects became real through integration processes that could only occur when classical models of democratic subjectivity had been abandoned. As a result, democracy was not created in enduring form by sovereign citizens. At the most basic level, democracy is a system of integration which, where successful, constructs legitimational norms that facilitate the establishment of integrational conditions, in which these norms gain real form. As such, however, democracy

---

[8] See examples in Tushnet (1999); Bellamy (2007: 154); Webber (2009: 27); Loughlin (2014); Ackerman (2019: 400).

is marked by an incessant conflict between the normative subjects in reference to which it constructs legitimacy and the societal preconditions required to give expression to these subjects. In most societies, this deep dialectic of democracy was reflected in the fact that the citizen first entered the constitution through integrational forces linked to military mobilization, and it was strongly patterned on the figure of the soldier. Partly because of this, classical explanations of democratic citizenship did not effectively support the integrational processes around which they crystallized, and the creation of democracies centred around factual citizens eroded the integrational foundations of democracy itself. Only after 1945 did a sustainable form of sovereign citizenship emerge, and this was linked to processes of integration based in protected subjective individualization and global-constitutional norm construction. The construct of the citizen developed at this time as a normative constitutional form, in which societies gradually evolved a vocabulary for separating citizenship from its original attachment to military patterns of agency, and in which state institutions stabilized their own political sovereignty in society. To assume that the citizen of modern democracy is a real person, to which real appeals can be made, is always profoundly to simplify the complex nature of democracy. The construct of the citizen that appeared after 1945 allowed democracy to come into existence because, quite specifically, it abstracted processes of institutional and normative integration from real citizens.

The basic claim in this chapter, consequently, is that there is always a disjuncture between the subjective construction of democracy and the integrational reality in which democratic practices are put into effect. In many respects, this disjuncture is intensified by literal constitutional accounts of democracy. Democracy has evolved under contemporary constitutional orders as a pattern of state building through complex integration. As a system of integration, constitutional democracy depends on multiple sets of individual rights, and it is typically sustained by a deep linkage with the global legal order. As such, it is based in a highly abstracted and multi-focal pattern of legal subjectivity. At the same time, democracy is accounted for and defined by constitutionalist outlooks that place the subjectivist dimension of democracy at the centre of the legitimational self-comprehension of citizens. In so doing, such outlooks are forgetful of the deep constitutional experiences that have shaped modern society, and they look for simplified modes of legitimating agency to explain democratic government. To propose such accounts of democracy, constitutionalism is forced, in effect, to avoid reflection on its own conceptual construction, to simplify and deny its own global form, to mobilize fictitious constructs of citizenship and to project principles of governmental legitimacy that erode its own foundations. In such respects, constitutionalism appears as the circular expression of democracy's deeply troubled conscience. It promotes processes of integration at the institutional level by attaching these processes to highly individualized principles and to globally constructed norms. Yet, it claims to sustain governmental legitimacy through reference to sovereign constitutional subjects that do not exist, and whose normative content disrupts the institutional integration processes that it stimulates. This means that democracy is centred on the basic paradox that the constitutional diction that is used to describe it does not appreciate the processes by which democracy is brought into being, and it only provides a self-subverting foundation to support democracy. Under certain conditions, by consequence, there is a heightened risk that the legitimational disjuncture that is expressed by constitutionalism will become manifest, and that the literal subjective construction of democracy will be adopted by citizens to undermine the integrational preconditions of democracy. The constitutional diction of democracy always contains the potential that, in the name of legitimacy, it encourages citizens to transpose themselves into legitimational roles that do not produce legitimacy.

It is in the context of these deep tensions that we can propose an explanation of populism. Populism tends to appear in environments where such tensions become tangible, and it flourishes where the basic paradoxes in democratic legitimacy are publicly visible. In such conditions, populism gains traction by offering simplified constitutional roles to persons in society, and it allows these persons to imagine themselves in the legitimational positions originally allotted to them in the construct of the democratic constitution. On this basis, populism can be understood as a constitutional reaction caused by the constitutional antinomies of democracy.

If populism is viewed in this way, it becomes possible to understand the conditions in which populism typically appears in contemporary society and to outline a relatively constant causal model for explaining it. Populism usually acquires influence in conditions in which the paradoxical disjuncture between democracy's functional-integrational reality and its original normative-subjective description becomes perceptible. Typically, populism assumes reality in circumstances in which political actors can use the primary subjective vocabulary of constitutionalism to challenge, plausibly, the global-constitutional subjective form around which democratic systems of integration were actually consolidated. The disjuncture between the normative and the institutional aspect of democracy is likely to become most palpable in situations in which – for whatever reason – the integration processes that cement democracy become unstable. This often occurs in conditions in which large segments of society experience weakness or volatility in institutional integration processes. This also occurs, frequently, in locations where global norms that support integration processes lose legitimating force, and where, because of this, the ability of these norms to sustain integration processes is reduced. Such circumstances bring to light the paradoxical legitimacy of democracy. Populist movements exploit this paradox to motivate political agents to assume very reductive accounts of their democratic subjectivity.

If populism is viewed in this way, it also becomes possible to understand why populism leads to democratic deterioration. As discussed, the rise of democracy from the eighteenth century onwards was marked by the deep paradox that the constructs of citizenship used to legitimate democracy militated against the realization of citizenship as an objective set of practices. In many cases, these subjects actually reversed the sociological processes that they presupposed for their own reality. As examined later, this antinomy in democracy now re-appears in populism, whose strong assertion of sovereign citizenship roles habitually impedes the basic societal trajectories that are required for the exercise of citizenship by sovereign peoples. In giving simple articulation to democratic subjectivity, populism frequently destroys the foundations of democracy. Populism always underlines the deep dependence of democracy on global norms, and it reflects the paradoxical incapacity of national constitutional subjects to create democracy.

This chapter argues that populism is created by deep-lying antinomies in constitutional democracy which are strongly linked to global conjunctures. It claims, accordingly, that populism can only be fully understood and averted if its deep conceptual relation to democracy is clarified, and if observers of democracy reflect on ways in which their descriptions of constitutional agency and legitimacy create a terrain that intrinsically legitimates populist movements.

Populism as Integrational Crisis

The origins of populism in the constitutional antinomies of democracy are evident in the normative stance endorsed by populist movements. Populist outlooks are defined by the fact that they project the legitimational subjects of democracy in simple, literal terms, and they acquire force by measuring existing democratic systems by standards derived from classical constitutional expectations (see Pinelli 2011: 15; Möller 2017: 247; Zaccaria 2018: 44).

First, populist outlooks promote a version of democracy that links the legitimacy of government to the immediate exercise of the popular will. For the populist outlook, democracy necessitates the expression of a popular will that is independent of, or in some way radically prior to, the institutions in which the people gain representative form. For the populist outlook, consequently, a polity can only claim legitimacy if members of the people imagine themselves as actors engaged in the continuous exercise of *sovereign constituent power* (see Blokker 2019: 333–334). On this basis, the constituted institutions of liberal democracy which possess a primarily procedural nature, constraining the direct translation of the popular will into a governmental mandate, are dismissed as anti-democratic. This erosion of the classical distinction between constituent and constituted power was pioneered by some progressive populist movements in Latin America, exemplified in constitution-making processes in Colombia and Venezuela, which attempted to incorporate the people as a live constituent power in the state. The Colombian Constitution of 1991 was created in part because protest movements, mainly connected to universities, insisted on the convocation of a Constituent Assembly to create a new political order. The Venezuelan Constitution of 1999 contains articles, especially Arts 6, 62, 70 and 184, that aim to create spaces in which the people can act as an unending constituent power. The weakening of this distinction is now widely replicated amongst populist political groups. Such emphasis on the exercise of constituent power by the people means that populist government commonly acquires a plebiscitary emphasis. In proclaiming to extract legitimacy directly from the people, moreover, populist politicians are easily able to assume authoritarian or at least weakly counterbalanced positions in government, and they usually create governmental systems with strong executives.

Second, populist outlooks tend to view legitimate government in identitarian terms. In presupposing that the people exist as a body of subjects outside the political system, they imagine that persons exercising sovereignty are aggregated as more than a group of individuals, and that some political substance connects the different actors forming the constituent power. In this respect, the populist outlook usually posits the existence of the people as a collective subject, whose will is directed by unifying interests and common prerogatives. Quite manifestly, populism invites individual members of society to coalesce around new political collectivities, defined, not by balanced representation, but by their commitment to shared sovereign action. The focus on the exercise of sovereignty has often allowed populist parties to break particular societal constituencies out of national systems of inclusion, and to mobilize them in emphatically solidaristic fashion, often by accentuating opposition to other political groups. It is for this reason that populism frequently constructs the will of the people in nationalist terms, as opposed to minority groups and as vindicating rejection of individual rights-based protection for minorities. As mentioned, the nationalist tendency is not universal amongst populists, and there is no necessary convergence of populism and nationalism (see Brubaker 2020). In some cases, governments that can be characterized as populist are supported by minority communities, and they have projected a construct of the sovereign people that embraces multiple ethnic groups. An important example of this is found in recent Bolivian history, under Evo Morales. In most cases, however, populist support is partly sustained by the ability of political parties to project national identities linked to anti-minority sentiments. This is clear in the discriminatory rhetoric used against migrants and minorities in Brazil, the United States, Poland, the United Kingdom and Hungary. It is especially clear in the anti-Muslim bias of Narendra Modi's Hindu nationalism in India, reflected in the reduced protection for minority religious rights (Kim 2017: 360–363).

Third, populist outlooks normally oppose the power of courts, and they view the judicial restriction of popular legislative acts as a singularly illegitimate institutional function. This anti-judicial attitude is closely linked, rhetorically, to the anti-proceduralist and to the anti-elitist aspects of populism. However, it is also caused by the fact that populist outlooks express a deep rejection of the more strictly constitutionalized components of the political system, which they see as forming static blocks on the dynamic manifestation of the popular will – the constituent power. This attitude was reflected at an early stage in the populist experiment conducted by Chávez in Venezuela, which involved a direct attack on the autonomy of the courts (Brewer-Carías 2007: 440). This attitude was also reflected in early populist experiments in Italy (see Dallara 2015: 59). This attitude is now replicated across the spectrum of populist governments, in each of which settings political capital has been gained from anti-judicial policies and attitudes. Many populist governments have seen the imposition of hard restrictions on judicial autonomy. This ranges from strategic judicial restructuring in Poland and Hungary, to persecution of judges in Bolivia, to hand-picked judicial appointments in the United States, Poland and Brazil.[9] Such policies are supported by the general populist antipathy towards global human rights law. In protecting individuals from majority will formation and placing certain prior limits on the exercise of the popular will, human rights law appears to the populist mentality as a body of legal norms that has little justification in a democratic polity.

Fourth, owing to their cult of sovereignty, populist outlooks usually relativize the constitutional importance of international law. Populist movements usually stress the importance of the robust exercise of national sovereignty in the international arena, and they oppose the constraining of sovereign institutions by international norms. This can be seen in the rejection of binding treaties and rules of international organizations by the Trump administration, in the hostility towards international treaties in the post-Brexit United Kingdom, in opposition to EU directives in Poland and Hungary and in Venezuela's withdrawal from the jurisdiction of the Inter-American Court of Human Rights. In addition, such movements denounce international norms for weakening the constituent force of the popular will in domestic institutions. This attitude is linked to the fact that international norms are frequently enforced in the domestic arena by judicial bodies. In most democratic constitutions, international norms are used to confer hyper-constitutional force on certain legal norms and guarantees for individual persons, placing the protection of such norms under the authority of high-level judicial institutions. In some cases, as discussed, international conventions directly establish constitutional norms in national societies. The populist belief that the people must act as constituent power necessarily conflicts with the constitutional claim condensed in international law that certain norms are constructed outside the scope of popular will formation. In many cases, hostility to international law coincides with

---

[9] After 2010, legislation was introduced in Hungary to facilitate the appointment of politically compliant judges. On judicial reform in Poland, see Grzeszczak and Karolewski (2018). On dubious judicial appointments in Poland, see Sadurski (2019: 67–71) and in Brazil see Benvindo (2018).

hostility to judicial institutions. This has been very clear in recent British history where populist politicians and their media outlets have been able to mobilize voters against human rights conventions and against senior judges.

In each respect, populist outlooks are defined by the fact that they envision the production of legitimacy for government as the activity of a subject, expressed as the sovereign people or the sovereign citizen, which possesses a decisively collective quality. This subject is authorized to overrule constitutional protections that are provided for abstractly individualized persons. In addition, populist outlooks view this subject as a subject that possesses a categorically political, or *pre-legal* emphasis, which means that it can legitimately reject formal-legal or constitutional principles that stand in the way of its full and immediate material expression. In each respect, the legitimacy of such subjectivity is not easy to separate from the constitutional imagination of democracy. In fact, this subject replicates core elements of the vocabulary of classical constitutionalism, proposing the people as a group of subjects standing prior to, and giving authority to, the constitutional order under which they live.[10]

As mentioned, populism is typically consolidated in situations in which the latent tension between democracy as subjective norm and democracy as integrational reality has, mainly for quite contingent reasons, become acute. That is, populism usually gains influence by persuading people to adopt simplified constitutional roles in contexts in which the functional balance between transnational subject formation and domestic individual integration has become weak, such that both the subjective and the functional sources of legitimacy appear precarious. In such settings, populist politics obtains purchase as the subjects of democracy (citizens) find specific reasons to view themselves as political role players outside the functional parameters in which democratic citizenship is exercised. In such circumstances, the success of populism depends on its ability to persuade populations to revert, literally, to political self-constructions offered to them in classical constitutional outlooks.

On the one hand, the literal pattern of sovereign subject construction promoted by populism often assumes plausibility in settings in which the institutional foundations of democratic integration, linked to welfare, to educational opportunities and to protected societal individualization, have become unstable. In many societies, this has been a common

---

[10] See p. 192, note 6.

phenomenon in recent decades. This is partly due to the fact that many democratic transitions that occurred in the 1980s and 1990s were not framed by adequate welfare regimes. In many cases, this is also due to changes in national welfare regimes and educational funding that occurred after 2008.

To illustrate this, populist movements frequently appeal to citizens by launching campaigns with a focus on national welfare systems and by constructing political subjects around experiences of weak welfare or educational integration. Such movements recruit support amongst people who are, or can be made to observe themselves as, marginalized from welfare regimes, whose educational chances appear sub-optimal, and for whom the integrational path through individual choice making, usually enhanced by education, has been partly obstructed.[11] Until recently, populist movements were generally hostile to welfare states. Anti-welfarist attitudes are still prominent amongst populists. Populist movements often claim the loyalty of citizens by persuading them that they are the victims of welfare systems, either because welfare regimes are based in unjust monetary transfers or because they appear to privilege particular social groups, often migrants.[12] However, welfare-supportive populism has recently appeared as a distinct phenomenon in many countries, even amongst political parties notionally on the right of the spectrum. Such populism tends to attract voters by promising exclusionary welfare policies: that is, it supports strong welfare regimes, but primarily for members of defined national groups (Schumacher and van Kersbergen 2014: 309). Populist outlooks in the United Kingdom have recently moved away from traditional opposition to welfare, and they are increasingly linked to notional protection of welfare regimes. Polish populism fuses a strong welfare component with hostility to migrants. Populist governments in Italy have introduced new welfare packages, using executive legislation to do so.[13] In India, selective welfarism is used as a source of electoral support for populist policies. Whether hostile or favourable to welfare states, however, populist movements identify welfare as a primary focus of populist subject construction. In

---

[11] On the impact of limited access to education as a source of electoral support for populist parties, see Swank and Betz (2003: 255); Elchardus and Spruyt (2016: 115); Spruyt, Keppens and Van Droogenbroeck (2016: 338); Anduiza, Guinjoan and Rico (2019: 109). The connection between educational exclusion and populist voting is much less pronounced in Latina America than in Europe.

[12] See p. 210.

[13] Decree-Law 28 January 2019, nr. 4.

deploying this focus, populists are able to identify spheres of society in which the preconditions for democratic citizenship formation are weakly consolidated, and they promote new patterns of political agency to match experiences of low integration and low protected individualization. In cases of this kind, the legitimational force of populism resides in the fact that it mobilizes collective patterns of subject construction in settings where state-mediated individualism is relatively weak.

On the other hand, the simplified pattern of subject construction promoted by populism commonly gains influence in settings in which the normative foundations of integration are destabilized. Populist movements often establish their appeal in conditions where citizens are, or can be made to identify themselves as, alienated from global norms, and where global norms appear to weaken the premises of domestic citizenship. Recent years have seen a number of occurrences in the global domain, including recessions caused by global financial regimes and crises in international trading systems, which adversely affect experiences of personal stability in national societies. In such contexts, as discussed, populist movements gain capital by campaigning against international norms and discrediting global patterns of political subjectivity. In many such cases, populist movements project an imaginary space in which people observe themselves as new political subjects, able to detach themselves from global norms and to assert control over global processes.

As one example, first, populist movements often alienate citizens from global norms by utilizing anti-immigrant rhetoric. Although this is not invariably the case, populists widely assert that immigration reflects a condition in which sovereign citizens lose control of their national societies. This view is frequently expressed in the Trump administration, and it figured prominently in debates in the United Kingdom about Brexit.

Second, populist movements alienate citizens from global norms by promoting the assumption that such norms undermine national welfare systems. This idea often appears in trivial form, as media organs promote the belief that migrant communities sap the welfare resources of national institutions. However, the conviction has become widespread that the promotion of binding norms in the global domain leads to the reduction in material security for agents within national societies. This view, of course, is not exclusive to right-wing advocates of populism. In populist outlooks of all stripes, national population groups with insecure rights to welfare provision are encouraged to believe that their precarious position is caused by the fact that they live in polities that are integrated in international normative systems. In many populist outlooks, the conviction is fostered that the reclaiming of national sovereignty by the people will stimulate an increase in inner-societal solidarity, expressed in reinforced welfare provision. This was clear in the period around the Brexit referendum in the United Kingdom. At the opposite end of the spectrum, it is reflected in Bolivia and Venezuela, where domestic solidarity is, or has been, projected in inherently anti-globalist terms. The constitutions of both Venezuela and Bolivia contain provisions to restrict foreign investment regimes and extractive activities.[14] Such claims have acquired particular purchase in polities in which domestic spending policies have been adversely affected by the global financial crisis whose consequences have remained palpable since 2008. Under conditions in which many national governments have reacted to global economic contraction by imposing deep cuts on domestic welfare systems, populist movements have been to able deliver an anti-globalist message that focuses on unstable welfare regimes.

Third, perhaps most commonly, populist movements alienate citizens from global norms by using arguments connected to questions of national security. In most contemporary polities with a populist emphasis, international security threats, often linked to global terrorism, are utilized to provide a justification to limit the jurisdiction of international courts and to solidify national legal orders on premises separate from international legal preconditions. President Trump has of course repeatedly tried to restrict the jurisdiction of the International Criminal Court by indicating that cases against American military personnel weaken national security interests. In the United Kingdom, judicial rulings in human rights cases have provoked media outcry, and Conservative media organs have repeatedly denounced the European Court of Human Rights as a threat to national security. One newspaper described the United Kingdom as: 'A nation imperilled by the Human Rights Act'.[15] In Hungary, courts have been pressured in terrorism-related cases against foreign nationals. In such cases, national governments have frequently projected legitimacy by claiming to protect national populations from threats of violence, often of a transnational character, to which they are – allegedly – left exposed by global norms.

---

[14] See especially Art. 320(1) of the Bolivian Constitution of 2009.
[15] This was printed in the *Daily Mail* (August 2015).

In each respect, populist movements tend to consolidate their influence in contemporary societies by separating political subjectivity from global norms. In this form, populism expresses the claim that phenomena in the transnational arena pose a risk to elemental forms of citizenship, and it uses this claim to alienate people from all norms of international provenance. The appeal of this message usually depends upon a societal condition in which citizens can be persuaded that democratic subjectivity exists outside the deep integrational constitution of society. Typically, this occurs where international norms lose force in framing subject formation at the inner-societal level, and, in particular, where weak normative integration coincides with strained institutional integration. This occurs, in turn, because weak integration makes visible the constitutional paradox that democracy is legitimated on foundations not supported by actual democratic subjects. Populism gains support by mobilizing new social collectives to occupy normative locations left open by this paradox.

The Paradoxes of Populism

Populism can be seen, in essence, as a political movement that emerges as the fragile attachments between the processes of institutional integration and the processes of normative integration that sustain democracy are dissolved. Populism is created by democracy, not because of excessive constitutional formalism, but because of the weak alignment between the norm and the reality of democratic government. Populism grows in spaces where this weak alignment becomes manifest, or can be made to appear manifest. As mentioned, the emergence of such spaces is welcomed by some democratic constitutionalists who perceive populism as an internal corrective to constitutionalism. It is vital in observing this phenomenon, however, that, in capitalizing on the constitutional paradox of democracy, populism does not create real democratic subjects and it does not release real democratic agency. On the contrary, populist government expresses the deep antinomies of democracy most emphatically in the fact that, in claiming to extract legitimacy from pure subjects of democracy, such government typically destroys the integrational conditions on which democracy relies. In reacting against global constitutional form, populism destroys constitutional form per se. Populist governments usually attach governmental legitimacy immediately to the classical subjects of constitutional democracy, *sovereign citizens*, *sovereign peoples*, and *sovereign institutions*. In so doing, however, populism creates political environments in which these concepts cannot find purchase in society, and it almost invariably dismantles the material preconditions for the real expression and solidification of these subjects. In separating sovereignty from transnational norms, populist governments destroy the actual structures of integration and solidarity in which sovereignty becomes possible. Indeed, at the core of populism is an at least partial negation of the sociological processes that have made democracy sustainable. In key respects, populist government allows us to see clearly how, stripped of their complex and transnational mediated form, classical principles of democratic subjectivity do not provide a *functional norm* for society and do not uphold democratic government, and the basic constitutional vocabulary of democracy subverts the sociological preconditions for its realization.

Populism and Integrational Crisis 1: Weak Citizenship

As mentioned, populism typically arises in contexts where global norms appear to weaken national reserves of sovereignty. In such contexts, populist governments and movements usually claim legitimacy by arguing that national citizens should reclaim political agency, and government should be emphatically centred around the collective commitments of citizens.

In its societal impact, however, populism almost invariably weakens the basic preconditions of political life founded in national sovereignty and national citizenship. Indeed, where established at the governmental level, populism usually impedes the institutionalization of those subjects to which, projectively, it attaches its legitimacy. Each current example of populist government creates a societal reality in which the simplification of political agency in the form of sovereign subjects impacts corrosively on democracy: it does this because it fractures the integrational structures in which the powers of sovereign citizens can be exercised, and it destroys the institutional grammar in which governments structure their exchanges with citizens. In populist government, the re-assertion of the citizen as the subjective source of democratic legitimacy usually leads to the political neutralization of this subject itself.

To illustrate this, first, it is an almost uniform feature of populist regimes that, despite their claim to refocus government around immediate manifestations of national citizenship, they reduce the capacity of citizens to influence the form of government and the content of legislation. Such weakening of effective citizenship is apparent, most obviously, in the fact, discussed earlier, that populist movements create governments that transfer power to executive institutions, so that governmental authority becomes tenuously linked to actual constitutional subjects (citizens). Although this tendency varies from polity to polity, this is a common outcome of the institutional politics of populism. Causally, this is largely determined by the weak regard for human rights law shown by populist politicians and parties. Hostility to human rights law is frequently reflected in lax approaches to governmental procedure and in the loosening of constraints on legislative process. This creates enhanced scope for executive legislation and reduces the factual exercise of political citizenship rights.

One example of such privileging of the executive is evident in the United States, where the reliance of the Trump presidency on legislation introduced through executive orders is well researched. The use of executive ordinances is widespread in India under Modi (Ruparelia 2015: 267–268). Periods of populist or semi-populist rule in Italy have seen frequent executive legislation. A very acute example of this phenomenon is found in Brazil, where President Bolsonaro relies extensively on executive legislation, often attempting to use prerogative acts to change already existing legal provisions (see Cerdeira 2018: 20–21). In other polities in Latin America, populist mandates have resulted in the transfer of authority from legislative to executive actors, and the ability of politicians to introduce laws by using executive powers has exponentially increased. Evidently, the populist experiment in Venezuela initiated by Chávez contained the ambiguity that it established mechanisms for greater popular participation, but it also created an executive system in which the president was able to legislate, with limited accountability, at a high level of autonomy (Garcia-Serra 2001: 285).

A very illuminating example of this phenomenon is perceptible in the United Kingdom. In the United Kingdom, a referendum was held in 2016 to determine whether or not the United Kingdom should leave the EU. This referendum was organized because it was widely claimed that the sovereign power of the parliamentary government of the United Kingdom had been limited because the United Kingdom had been integrated in an external normative system, primarily based in European law but also including the human rights law applied by the European Court of Human Rights. The resumption of full parliamentary sovereignty through withdrawal from this transnational normative system was presented, by its populist advocates, as an opportunity for the United Kingdom as a nation and for UK citizens as individual persons to reacquire the original democratic sovereignty that had been forfeited through the passing of the European Communities Act (1972). Indeed, Boris Johnson, later Prime Minister of the United Kingdom, made this position clear. Johnson declared that British democracy had been established through historical processes that preceded the development of the EU, and it had been sacrificed through the incorporation of the United Kingdom as sovereign nation in the European legal order. He stated that democracy is the 'most precious thing' offered by Britain to the world, implying that this gift of democracy needed to be rescued.[16] In this rhetoric, the national sovereignty of the British state and the popular sovereignty of British citizens were closely associated. The key to the re-assertion of both was linked to the full resumption of sovereign powers by the UK parliament in Westminster.

Despite these intentions, the choice of a plebiscitary mechanism for releasing the UK parliament from its position in the European legal system produced a decision that could not be easily incorporated in typical parliamentary procedures for expressing the commitments of sovereign citizens in the United Kingdom. The referendum created a dual construction of sovereignty, in which a plebiscitary definition of popular sovereignty came to sit alongside and rival the conventional definition of sovereignty as the attribute of parliament. The outcome of this dual construction of sovereignty was, first, that the sovereignty of parliament was eroded, and it lost its original status as an institution in which citizens could be politically integrated. In fact, after the referendum, political campaigning often assumed a form in which groups of citizens were openly mobilized against parliament itself, the traditional repository of sovereignty. The outcome of this, second, was that, as parliament renounced much of its sovereign power, the locus of decision-making authority was primarily transferred to the executive: that is, to office holders in the governmental cabinet.[17] In both respects, the construction of sovereignty as the property of citizens was weakened, and the actual extent to which citizens were able to exercise sovereignty was dramatically reduced.

In these cases, hostility to the restriction of national sovereignty and national citizenship by external norms helped to create governmental orders that curtailed the role of citizens in government. In each case, the

---

[16] www.telegraph.co.uk/news/2016/06/24/the-european-elite-forgot-that-democracy-is-the-one-thing-britai/(last accessed 7 April 2020).

[17] On use of executive laws to implement Brexit, see Sinclair and Tomlinson (2019).

principle that the sovereign people could be made to reappear in a classical constitutional role proved illusory. The attempt to overcome the contradiction between the subjective norm and the integrated form of democracy through the simple reassertion of national sovereignty substantially limited the political agency and the political rights of national citizens.

Populism and Integrational Crisis 2: Depleted Sovereignty

Most governments based in populist constructions of legitimacy stress the need to build and to consolidate strong sovereign institutions, which they see as threatened by global norms. However, in different ways, populist movements undermine the sovereign force of the institutions that they purport to reinforce.

One notable phenomenon in populist governments, for example, is that public institutions become porous to the private influence of elite actors. This can be observed in many contexts, and there are many reasons for this. First, the weakening of robust legal procedures that accompanies populism usually means, of necessity, that public institutions are opened to influence by actors whose access to the political system is not subject to full constitutional control.[18] Further, the plebiscitary aspect of populism often means that populist groups rely on improvised sources of mobilizational support when campaigning for election. Then, once installed in office, they retain obligations to actors who assisted their rise to power. For both reasons, populist movements often depend on informal support. This in turn has the frequent consequence that persons with informal authority obtain positions of political influence as reward for their support. This phenomenon tends to become salient in settings that are geographically distant from political centres, where private actors often form points of articulation between regional and national political institutions. In such situations, national governments frequently cede sovereignty to actors outside the state. This is especially visible in Brazil, where the reliance of the government on regional elites has visibly cemented private power structures in society, such that pre-national oligarchical structures are in the process of being re-consolidated.[19]

---

[18] On this process in Venezuela, see Maya (2014: 73). On the general link between populism and patronage, see Pappas (2019: 73–74).

[19] The debate about the re-emergence of oligarchical power in Brazil pre-dates the present government, and it is often argued that radio and television stations are owned by actors

At a more fundamental level, the tendency of populist governments to weaken sovereign state institutions is caused by the fact that they erode the basic premises on which modern states are built. In crucial respects, populist movements inflict deep damage on the fundamental integrational foundations of modern statehood.

First, the tendency of populist governments to reduce the sovereignty of state institutions is linked to the fact that they dissolve the individualized lines of interaction that support sovereign states and sustain the integrational primacy of state institutions in contemporary societies. As examined previously, most democratic states have acquired sovereign form by, as far as possible, translating the articulations between government and society into individualized points of contact, such that persons are integrated in the political system as single agents. Quite generally, modern democratic states have established their integrational force in a process in which collective patterns of interest aggregation have been weakened through the consolidation of multiple individual bonds between citizens and public institutions.

This basic precondition of modern democracy is frequently unsettled by populist governments. This can be observed in the hostility to human rights law amongst populist governments, which weakens individual protection, and tends to impose an uneven legal fabric on society. This can also be observed in the welfare policies adopted by populist parties. As discussed, populist governments increasingly adopt a policy of selective anti-globalism, which condemns the depletion of social welfare arrangements as the result of forces emanating from the international domain. Despite this, however, few populist movements are prepared to rebuild national welfare systems, supposedly damaged by global forces. Where populist governments support welfare provision, they frequently do this on very selective grounds, so that welfare is bound to collective group privileges. This can be seen in Poland, where key pieces of welfare legislation specifically benefit groups with strong familial attachments.[20] In most cases,

---

that reproduce long-standing patterns of oligarchical dominance and electoral control (Martins, Moura and Imasato 2011: 393). It is also noted that the old oligarchical class represents its commercial interests in concerted form in national government assemblies (Bruno 2017). Minority and environmental policies implemented by the current government are closely linked to such interests.

Brazil has seen an increasingly uneven distribution of resources from the national government to the states, in which states that supported Bolsonaro, and elite leaders in these states, have received reward for political loyalty. For similar processes in Venezuela, see Albertus (2015: 1705).

[20] See Act on State Assistance in Childcare, Official Journal No. 2016 item 195 (with amendments).

however, populist governments organize the domestic public economy in ways that reduce welfare commitments. Despite their overt anti-globalism, they usually weaken welfare regimes by heightening the openness of the national economy to global capital flows. This attitude to welfare is clearly exemplified by the United States. This is partly and ambiguously reflected in India. Modi's party has a strong basis in groups that historically expressed strong ideological opposition to welfarism (Chhibber and Verma 2018: 41). Under Modi, some well-publicized welfare programmes have been implemented, targeting particular electoral groups, and welfare provision appears as a core part of governmental legitimacy (Aiyar 2019: 83). However welfare investment has been cut in core areas (Ruparelia 2015: 772). Moreover, the introduction of personalized welfare benefits has been flanked by legislative proposals to limit labour protection, notably in the Labour Code on Industrial Relations Bill (2015). This attitude to welfare is also reflected in Hungary (Vidra 2018: 74). The most important example of this is Brazil. In Brazil, the rise of populism has been flanked by vicious attacks on welfare provisions and protective labour-law arrangements, designed to attract investment from global monetary elites. Restrictions to social spending and labour protection were introduced by President Temer before the rise of Bolsonaro, and they have subsequently been reinforced. Indicatively, many populist parties have gained support by discrediting welfare policies introduced by previous governments, breaking out new political subjects around such controversies. India before Modi saw the broad implementation of a human rights agenda, originating in progressive actions of the Supreme Court (Ruparelia 2013: 573). Prior to 2015, Brazil witnessed unprecedented human rights activism and rights-based labour protection. President Obama implemented an expansion of healthcare insurance in the United States.

In weakening the individual articulation between state and society, populist governments force groups in society into new collectivities, often mobilized against each other. It is characteristic of populism that it undermines tendencies to universal membership in society, which is dependent on the state, and it breaks society into segmentary form. This can be seen, as a general phenomenon, in the fact that populist movements deliberately provoke a strategic polarization between their supporters and other groups. In mild cases, as discussed, this is expressed in the fact that populist movements seek particular material benefits for their affiliates, frequently attached to the reconstruction or re-alignment of welfare systems. In moderate cases, this is reflected in the fact that populism imprints oppositional identities on different social groups, often loosely underpinned by class-related or ethnic distinctions, so that society becomes partitioned around repoliticized group attachments (Kaltwasser and Hauwaert 2020: 4). Examples of this are found in the United Kingdom, the United States and Brazil, where attachment to populist causes, partly linked to class or educational position, has become an emphatic affiliation, likely to instil powerful antipathies in exchanges between political groups. What occurs in such processes is that states attach their sovereignty to partial constituencies in society, and the state relies on specific solidarities to consolidate integrational force. In extreme cases, class or ethnic relations are politicized in volatile fashion, and the state becomes an agent in inter-group conflict. This in turn creates the risk that state institutions revert to assertions of sovereignty by exceptional means. This is evident in Brazil, where ethnic groups have been exposed to coordinated violence, and normal legal regimes are suspended in areas with strong minority populations. This is evident in India, where the status of a region, Kashmir, has been altered through exceptionalist constitutional provisions. As discussed earlier, use of emergency legislation is a common symptom of weak integration.[21] In each regard, the weakening of individual articulations between state and citizens typically diminishes the integrational force of the state itself.

In parallel, second, the tendency of populist government to diminish the sovereignty of state institutions is linked to the fact that such governments often re-assimilate military diction in national politics, usually doing so as part of their strategic re-assertion of national sovereignty. Populist movements typically acquire mobilizational power by connecting domestic policy conflicts to global conflicts, and they often generate legitimacy through reference to antagonisms extending beyond national society. In some cases, for example, Poland and Brazil, populist parties and politicians have revived the diction of global polarization that defined the era of the Cold War, suggesting that their legitimacy is due to their ability to hold in check, respectively, a persistent Russian or a persistent Communist threat. In Brazil, Bolsonaro has frequently proposed himself as a leading adversary of global Communism. In more absurd examples, typified by the British Conservative Party, the supranational political order of the EU has been compared to a hostile foreign power, threatening the territorial security of the nation. Furthermore, the projection of a Russian threat to national security has been used by the British Prime Minister to discredit political rivals. At a more general level,

---

[21] See pp. 132–33.

as mentioned, most populist parties attach symbolic importance to border security, which often creates a space in which military constructs enter political diction. In many instances, such use of military imagery is connected to the hostility to human rights law in populist thinking. As mentioned, populist governments diminish their compliance with human rights agreements because human rights law can be presented as a corpus of norms that undermines the capacity of national state institutions to defend themselves and their populations from military threats.

The populist promotion of national sovereignty through reference to external conflict has far-reaching implications for domestic politics, and it usually configures democratic political systems around intensified expressions of inter-group conflict. At one level, first, the fact that populist parties link domestic political diction to (perceived or projected) global polarities means that, in their domestic positions, they harden exclusionary attitudes between opposing political groups, and they cement domestic cleavages around global fault lines. In addition, second, use of such political rhetoric means that some populist parties promote the remilitarization of national polities in more concrete, institutional fashion. In more extreme cases of populism, the military acquires an engaged role in government, or government supports its power by threatening to use military force against adversaries. The most obvious example of this is Venezuela. But this can also be seen in Brazil, where military figures hold leading governmental offices and the government attaches part of its legitimacy to a fully exceptionalist construction of national politics (Goldstein 2019: 251). In milder cases, populist government triggers less visible mobilization processes, and the populist emphasis on national sovereignty generates new models of military activism. This is exemplified by Poland, where the projection of a threat from Russia has stimulated new forms of militia recruitment.

The re-emergence of military rhetoric in populist polities obstructs the consolidation of sovereign institutions which populism claims to intensify. The remilitarization of political life – even where this is conducted at a solely rhetorical level – usually weakens the integrational force of national institutions across society as a whole. Such remilitarization has the obvious result that generalized patterns of citizenship become less consolidated, and different citizenship groups are segregated into hostile camps. It also has the frequent result that polities revert, in part, to patterns of institutional construction seen in times of external conflict, and they reduce the restrictive force of judicial institutions and cement power in executive bodies. The military aspect of populism provides strong legitimation for executive-led government, in which executive bodies are able to obtain selective support from highly mobilized constituencies. The intensification of political authority held in executive institutions normally has the result that levels of legal and political compliance in society fall, as free-standing executives usually show reduced ability to exercise effective sovereignty across society. This is expressed most emphatically in the process of regime collapse in Venezuela. In other cases, for example Brazil, the formal sovereignty of state institutions is also diminished. The militarization of government in Brazil has been accompanied by a process in which the government's control of violence in society has discernibly weakened. Military force is deployed by many units, including private militias, which perform protection and security functions in parts of some cities. In fact, government bodies at times rely on militias to muster political support in the areas that they control, and militias then expect patrimonial recompense. In such cases, the focus of sovereign force in society is divided between a range of actors. In each respect, the linkage of national political practices to global ideological fissures tends, not to strengthen, but to erode both the actual integrity of national society and the factual sovereignty of public institutions.

Populism and Integrational Crisis 3: Weak National Integration

Populist governments often promote a rhetoric of national unity, and they invigorate national identity as the source of constitutional legitimacy. However, such governments typically debilitate the integrational structure of national society, and, in extreme examples, they undermine the basic territorial dimensions of the nation itself.

The weakening of national integration under populist regimes is visible in the main processes described earlier. For example, the weakening of national integration under populism is visible in the rising power of private elites, which means that uniformity in the application of law across society is undermined and persons in society are subject to variable legal/political regimes. The weakening of national integration under populism is also visible in the fact that populist politicians normally introduce legislation that reduces legal protection for non-majority population groups. This is not invariably the case, and some populist governments in Latin America specifically deviate from this pattern. Usually, however, populist governments are inclined to weaken legal protection for minorities, consolidating diverse legal orders in society. This can be seen in India and Brazil, where thresholds of legal protection for minorities have been diminished. In extreme cases, the relaxation of legal uniformity means that persons strongly attached to the core pillars of the populist movement are able to assume privileged legal positions. This can be seen in the dispensing of favours under the Trump administration, and, more alarmingly, in the re-appearance of regional oligarchies in Brazil. Where these phenomena become apparent, the essential core of nation building, which relies on the translation of personal power relations into relatively consistent legal orders, is undermined.

Observable in some populist polities, further, is the fact that the mobilizational emphasis of government places the hard territorial fabric of the nation under strain. This is visible, in mild form, in the United States, where variations in support for the government between states are reflected in variations in the distribution of federal resources, meaning that some parts of the national territory assume a privileged position. This is seen in Brazil, particularly in the fact that some sub-national regions receive premiums for political support for the government.[22] This is visible in the United Kingdom, where the focus on nationhood and the correlated emphasis on plebiscitary legitimacy as foundations for government have eroded the patterns of integration that held together the territorial corpus of national society. In fact, the rise of populist nationalism in the United Kingdom has been marked by the emergence of multiple regional nationalisms, the probable outcome of which will be the end of territorial unity.

Conclusion

In most variations, populism can be viewed as a political movement that reacts against experiences of integrational crisis in a form that intensifies these experiences. The populist reaction is particularly focused on the global elements of contemporary democracy, and it attacks the normative constructs formed in the global arena that underpin national democracies. It typically emerges in contexts in which the global subjective forms that support democracy are susceptible to being discredited. In claiming to ensure more direct democracy, however, populism typically weakens the basic institutional preconditions of democracy. On this basis, analysis of populism allows us to gain a deepened sociological understanding of

---

[22] See p. 208, note 19.

democracy and its underlying antinomies. Observation of populist government shows that political movements that emphatically attach their legitimacy to the classical constructs of constitutional democracy – national citizenship, popular sovereignty, and strong sovereign institutions – usually bring these same constructs towards crisis. By tendency, populist government reduces the integrational cohesion of the basic unit that it proposes as the subjective source of its legitimacy: the sovereign people, comprising active citizens and solid central institutions. In so doing, populist governments illustrate the fact that these basic subjects are not fully real, they only exist in conceptual form, and they cannot be simply materialized as realities to underpin democracy. Most populist governmental orders that claim to materialize these subjects as actual living realities are marked by the fragmentation of the people as a sovereign actor, and by the erosion of publicly constructed institutions. In some cases, such government leads to experiences of *structural denationalization*. In claiming to extract legitimacy from sovereign subjects, populism reverses the most deep-lying integrational processes that underlie modern society. Populism countervails the construction of society as a relatively uniform system of legal integration, and it entrenches societal features of variable inclusion and territorial localism, which had been gradually eradicated by the processes of de-feudalization, protected individualization and institutional integration outlined earlier. In each respect, populist governments serve to underline, albeit in unintended fashion, the deep reliance of both democracy and nationhood on a normative system that is not emphatically focused on national sovereignty.

These aspects of populism can obviously be examined from a perspective that stresses the role of ideology in politics. It can simply be claimed that populism obstructs the realization of its core subjects because it uses these subjects as part of an ideological strategy, serving select interests in society. In certain respects, however, populism discloses deep antinomies that are inherent in the fabric of democracy itself, and which are brought into view by the fact that populism accentuates the collective-subjective aspect of democratic legitimation. As discussed, democracy evolved after 1945 as a system of integration, largely based in processes of individual subjectivization conducted through the articulation between national polities and norms set out within the global legal system. In its primary emphases, populism opposes this construction of democracy, and it motivates persons to assume collective roles outside individualistic structures of legal integration and outside patterns of subjectivity projected in the corpus of global constitutional law. It tends to appear in circumstances where the integrational force of global law has become weak, and it proposes a vocabulary of democracy that exacerbates this process. In this respect, populism shows up the essential antinomies of modern democratic constitutionalism. It highlights the basic antinomy of a political system in which legitimacy factually arises from processes of individual legal integration, attached to global normative expectations, which are always contradicted by the collective political subjects from which legitimacy is expected to flow. Populism thus indicates the deep reliance of democracy on processes of global-legal integration and global-constitutional norm construction.

In each respect, populism evolves as the result of a broader constitutional misunderstanding of democracy, which posits a simple reflexive subject at the core of democratic government. The propensity for contemporary democracy to degenerate into authoritarianism is not simply attributable to politicians or political movements who exploit institutional weaknesses and it is not explicable through analysis of social groups that blindly follow charismatic appeals. On the contrary, this authoritarian propensity is inscribed in the basic constitutional terms in which democracy is envisaged and normatively justified. Contemporary society is always exposed to the risk that the disparity between the conceptual subjects in which democratic legitimacy is normatively imagined and the complex integrational form in which democracy has assumed reality will engender systemic crisis. As discussed, this can easily occur when large sectors of the population can be alienated from the integrational dimensions of democracy and persuaded to propose themselves as immediate embodiments of democratic normativity. Constitutional explanations of democracy provide an immediate vocabulary for this experience, and they create a legitimational space in which democracy itself can be undermined. This propensity for democratic sabotage is partly caused by the conceptual simplification of democracy amongst people who defend it.

Conclusion

One underlying claim in this book is that we can identify a deep political paradox at the core of modern society. Since the 1980s, democracy has become a global political form, and adherence to norms of democratic representation is now almost universally defined as a precondition of political legitimacy. However, democracy is described and promoted in constitutional terms that do not fully capture its substance. The progressive consolidation of democracy across the globe has hinged on the assertion that democracy is constitutionally legitimated by acts of popular sovereignty and sovereign citizenship. Yet, this construction does not provide an adequate description of democracy. In most cases, democracy has been created through procedures in which acts of popular sovereignty only play a marginal role in defining the political order of state. Moreover, this construction establishes a diction of legitimacy, in which democracy can easily be, and frequently is, discredited and undermined. This is exemplified most commonly in the emergence of populist governments. Populist governments usually take shape by mobilizing political subjects around the constitutional disjuncture between the normative self-explanation and the functional reality of democracy that characterizes most polities.

On the account offered here, it is sociologically reductive to project democracy as the constitutional result of voluntary actions of, or interactions between, the subjects (sovereign citizens) that were posited as the authors of democracy in the later decades of the eighteenth century. Democracy has developed, not as a system of free collective self-legislation, but as a balanced system of normative and institutional integration. That is, democracy has gradually evolved as a globally prevalent polity type because it is capable of promoting processes of normative and institutional integration adequate to, and able to absorb, the processes of individualization, institutional centralization and spatial convergence that have accompanied the formation of modern society. Observed as an integrational system, democracy affords many benefits to citizens, and democracy can be justified on many normative grounds. Four of the most obvious grounds that justify democracy are that, in its current form, it tends to mitigate extreme social violence; it tends to promote equal personal liberties; it tends to reduce the force of involuntary affiliations or memberships; it tends, at least formally, to avert conditions in which personal ownership of one person by a different person is legally sanctioned. However, it is erroneous to assume that people gain benefits from democracy because it is created or legitimated by citizens in the exercise of popular sovereignty, or that the constitutional order of democracy reflects some deep subjective definition of political life that is projected by citizens.

In modern democracies, naturally, citizens exercise some form of sovereignty through engagement in elections and through accession to acts of legislation. Yet, they do this, typically, in a constitutional order in which the original production of legitimacy does not depend on the exercise of popular sovereignty by citizens. Modern democracy is usually contingent on a process in which the citizen is globally reconfigured: the citizen brings legitimacy to the polity, not by establishing a link between the national political system and sovereign actors in society but by establishing a link between the national political system and the global legal system. As discussed, this moment of constitutional reorientation usually formed the centre of modern democracy, and it created a manageable integrational focus for society in its entirety. Observed in a broad historical perspective, we can observe that the basic legitimational construct of the modern citizen first came into view as part of the integrational reorganization of society in the eighteenth century, and it formed the centre of defining social processes at this time. However, this construct did not originally act as the stable fulcrum for democratic politics, and in many ways it undermined the integrational processes to which it was structurally attached. Democracy only became real as national societies insulated their core processes against this construct. The form of contemporary democracy was established through a constitutional construct of the citizen that specifically removed the actual existing citizen from the legitimational centre of democracy. Most importantly, modern democracy is sustained by the fact that the construction of citizenship around military impulses, which first defined the legitimational essence of democracy in and beyond the eighteenth century, is weakened.

If we approach democracy as a system of reasonably balanced normative and institutional integration, we can see that democracy has two broad and closely interwoven preconditions. The integrational processes that underscore democracy are likely to be consolidated in a polity based, externally, in a deep articulation with the global system of human rights law, and sustaining, internally, a high degree of protective individualization. These processes are very variably expressed in different polities, but they are likely to form strong premises for democracy. These processes have become cemented in society through a long-standing adaptive trajectory, in which the legitimational core of the polity – the citizen – has been detached from classical understandings of democracy and classical understandings of constitutional authority.

Very few theoretical accounts of democracy question the basic premise that democracy is a political system legitimated by the free exercise of sovereignty by citizens. As mentioned, this view is inscribed at the core of classical and neo-classical democratic theory. It is also inscribed at the core of constitutional theory, which has guided the globalization of democracy in recent decades, and which argues that the sovereign citizen is the primary and immovable foundation of the democratic polity. Such theories bring into sharp relief the basic antinomy of modern democracy. In many cases, in fact, the theoretical framework in which democracy is imagined actually brings democracy to crisis, as it attaches the legitimacy of democratic government to fictitious constructs of constituent subjectivity, and it exposes democracy to normative expectations that undermine its institutional-integrational preconditions. As discussed, if directly articulated, the basic concepts of democratic legitimacy usually unsettle the institutional preconditions required to make democracy real. Paradoxically, in fact, the vocabulary of popular sovereignty often contains the risk that it induces attempts to construct legitimacy for a democratic polity in terms that threaten the actual benefits of democracy (i.e. reduction of violence, individual security, release from coercive solidarities and promotion of shared liberties). This antinomy becomes acutely visible in the threats currently posed to democracy by populist parties and governments.

A further underlying claim in this book is that it is now essential to develop a constitutional perspective for examining democracy that acknowledges the material and functional essence of democracy, and which explains democratic legitimacy by observing, in sociologically reflexive terms, what democracy actually is and does. In other words, a perspective is required that understands democracy, primarily, as a system of integration, whose basic theoretical constructs have evolved as reflections of ingrained integrational pressures and processes in society. Accordingly, a perspective is required that interprets the concepts of democracy, not as static entities, but as constructs that articulate and refract social process, and which analyses the preconditions of democratic legitimacy accordingly. A perspective of this kind, indicatively, might proceed from the recognition that the legitimacy of a democratic polity emanates from multiple sites and multiple processes, some normative and some functional, and the production of legitimacy cannot be imputed to simple acts of sovereign subjects. This means that a democracy is likely to contain multiple patterns of citizenship, in which agents engage in political will formation in many different roles, which are typically detached from embedded solidarities. Naturally, this does not mean that democracies contain no space for protest or collective mobilization. Typically, however, political movements capable of enhancing democratic integration at the national level connect people to subjects constructed at the international level. This is not inevitably the case, but patterns of protest or constitutional agency that can be generalized across national boundaries, and are attached to subjects in many countries, are normally more likely to promote non-exclusive interests at the national level. Attachment to transnationally defined rights is likely to be a precondition for expressions of constitutional agency able to increase the factual sovereignty of national citizens. On this basis, a perspective of this kind might look closely at the articulations between global and national patterns of norm construction, and it might observe the interactions between these levels as vital sources of democratic subjectivity and meaningful sovereignty.

A more sociologically informed analysis of constitutional democracy need not promote a restrictive or uncritical approach to debate about democracy. A sociologically reflexive analysis of democratic legitimacy will clearly draw critical attention to questions regarding individual protection, the preconditions of social solidarity, the terms of articulation between global and national norms and the precariousness of the legitimational exchanges between the global and the national arena. An analysis of this kind will be likely to show how constitutional systems can be formed that avert crisis by promoting integration processes through strong protection of welfare regimes and entrenchment of international human rights law, and, accordingly, such analysis may be used to rebuild constitutional orders in contexts in which integrational crisis occurs. Although globalist in outlook, importantly, a sociologically reflexive analysis of democratic legitimacy is likely to provide grounds for strong and robust criticism of global norms. It is self-evident that not all norms that enter national societies from the international domain share equal legitimacy or promote domestic democracy in equal measure. This is not a fact that can be ignored by sociologically reflexive analysis of democracy, however much it stresses the reliance of democratic institutions on global norms. Yet, a sociologically reflexive analysis of democratic legitimacy may well avoid criticizing global norms on the simple grounds that they undermine popular sovereignty or weaken procedures for collective will formation, and it may be unlikely to propose alternative patterns of sovereign subjectivity to counter the force of such norms. A sociological outlook may proceed from the position that, generally, global norms are not limits on, but functional preconditions of sovereign citizenship. In recognition of this, sociologically reflexive analysis of democratic legitimacy will be likely to criticize global norms if they fail to provide constructions that sustain complex democracy within national societies, and if they fail to support inner-societal processes of integration required for democracy. In this regard, a critique of global norms is likely to focus, not on questions of sovereignty or self-legislation, but on questions regarding the ability of global norms to uphold processes of individualized integration. Approached in this way, it would be possible to interrogate the legitimacy of global norms without providing a legitimational space for populism.

Overall, at the centre of a sociologically reflexive analysis of democratic legitimacy there may be the expectation that observers of democracy show some recollection of the ways in which their basic concepts have been formed and what their social effects are. It appears reasonable to expect that observers of democracy might appreciate the intricate interweaving of national and global norms and the multi-centric articulations between national and global subjectivities that democracy presupposes. It also appears reasonable to expect that such observers might show awareness of the deep encouragement given to movements opposed to democracy by the constitutional vocabulary in which democracy is usually discussed and defended.

BIBLIOGRAPHY

Abbott, Andrew and Stanley DeViney (1992), 'The Welfare State as Transnational Event: Evidence from Sequences of Policy Adoption'. *Social Science History* 16 (2): 245-274.

Abelshauser, Werner (1996), 'Erhard oder Bismarck? Die Richtungsentscheidung der deutschen Sozialpolitik am Beispiel der Reform der Sozialversicherung in den Fünfziger Jahren'. *Geschichte und Gesellschaft* 22(3): 376-392.

Abramovitz, Mimi (2011), 'The US Welfare State: A Battleground for Human Rights' in Shareen Hertel and Kathryn Libal (eds.), *Human Rights in the United States: Beyond Exceptionalism*. Cambridge University Press, pp. 46-67.

Ackerman, Bruce (1991), *We the People, I: Foundations*. Cambridge, MA: Harvard University Press.

Ackerman, Bruce (2019), *Revolutionary Constitutionalism. Charismatic Leadership and the Rule of Law*. Cambridge, MA: Harvard University Press.

Adejumobi, Said (2001), 'Citizenship, Rights, and the Problem of Conflicts and Civil Wars in Africa'. *Human Rights Quarterly* 23: 148-170.

Adler, Jessica L. (2017), *Burdens of War. Creating the United States Veterans Health System*. Baltimore: Johns Hopkins University Press.

Aiyar, Yamini (2019), 'Modi Consolidates Power: Leveraging Welfare Politics'. *Journal of Democracy* 30(4): 78-88.

Albertus, Michael (2015), 'The Role of Subnational Politicians in Distributive Politics: Political Bias in Venezuela's Land Reform under Chávez'. *Comparative Political Studies* 48(13): 1667-1710.

Almond, Gabriel A. and Sidney Verba (1989[1963]), *The Civic Culture. Political Attitudes and Democracy in Five Nations*. Newbury Park, CA: Sage.

Alonso, Angela (2015), *Flores, votos e balas. O movimento abolicionista brasileiro (1868-88)*. São Paulo: Editora Schwarcz.

Altenstein, Karl vom Stein zum (1807[1931]), 'Denkschrift (1807)' in Georg Winter (ed.) (1931), *Die Reorganisation des Preussischen Staates unter Stein und Hardenberg. Erster Teil. Allgemeine Verwaltungs- und Behördenreform, I: Vom Beginn des Kampfes gegen die Kabinettsregierung bis zum Wiedereintritt des Mninisters von Stein*. Leipzig: Hirzel, pp. 364-566.

Andeweg, Rudy B. (2000), 'Consociational Democracy'. *Annual Review of Political Science* 3: 509–536.
Anduiza, Eva, Marc Guinjoan and Guillem Rico (2019), 'Populism, Participation, and Political Equality'. *European Political Science Review* 11(1): 109–124.
Antoine, Michel (1970), *Le conseil du roi sous le règne de Louis XV*. Geneva: Droz.
Antoine, Michel (2003), *Le coeur de l'État. Surintendance, contrôle général et intendances des finances 1552–1791*. Paris: Fayard.
Archives Parlementaires de 1787 à 1860, series 1, vol. VIII (1875), Paris: Librairie Administrative P. Dupont.
Archives Parlementaires de 1787 à 1860, series 1, vol. X (1878), Paris: Librairie Administrative P. Dupont.
Arditi, Benjamin (2005), 'Populism as an Internal Periphery' in Francisco Panizza (ed.), *Populism and the Mirror of Democracy*. London: Verso, pp. 72–98.
Asch, Ronald G. (1999), 'Kriegsfinanzierung, Staatsbildung und ständische Ordnung im 17. und 18. Jahrhundert'. *Historische Zeitschrift* 268: 635–671.
Aubert, Félix (1977), *Le Parlement de Paris. De Philippe le Bel a Charles VII (1314–1422). Sa compétence, ses attributions*. Geneva: Slatkine Reprints.
Baldwin, James Fosdick (1913), *The King's Council in England during the Middle Ages*. Oxford: Clarendon.
Baldwin, Peter (1990), *The Politics of Social Solidarity. Class Bases of the European Welfare State 1875–1975*. Cambridge University Press.
Baldwin, Peter (2009), *The Narcissism of Small Differences. How America and Europe are Alike*. Oxford University Press.
Bandeira, Luiz Alberto de Vianna Moniz (2010), *O Governo João Goulart. As lutas sociais no Brasil (1961–1964)*. 8th edition. São Paulo: UNESP.
Barth, Boris (2005), '"Partisan" und "Partisanenkrieg" in Theorie und Geschichte. Zur historischen Dimension der Entstaatlichung von Kriegen'. *Militärgeschichtliche Zeitschrift* 64: 69–100.
Bartolini, Stefano (2000), *The Political Mobilization of the European Left 1860–1980. The Class Cleavage*. Cambridge University Press.
Baumann, Reinhard (1994), *Landsknechte. Ihre Geschichte und Kultur vom späten Mittelalter bis zum Dreißigjährigen Kreg*. Munich: Beck.
Baxter, Douglas Clark (1976), *Servants of the Sword. French Intendants of the Army 1630–70*. Urbana: University of Illinois Press.
Beattie, Peter M. (1999), 'Conscription versus Penal Servitude: Army Reform's Influence on the Brazilian State's Management of Social Control, 1870–1930'. *Journal of Social History* 32(4): 847–878.
Beattie, Peter M. (2001), *The Tribute of Blood. Army, Honor, Race, and Nation in Brazil, 1864–1945*. Durham, NC: Duke University Press.
Bebel, August (1898), *Nicht stehendes Heer sondern Volkswehr*. Stuttgart: Dietz.
Beck, Ulrich (1986), *Risikogesellschaft. Auf dem Wege in eine andere Moderne*. Frankfurt am Main: Suhrkamp.

Becker, Jean-Jacques (1987), 'Les "Trois Ans" et les débuts de la première guerre mondiale'. *Guerres mondiales et conflits contemporains* (145): 7–26.

Beckett, J. V. and Michael Turner, 'Taxation and Economic Growth in Eighteenth-Century England'. *The Economic History Review* 43(3): 377–403.

Bellamy, Richard (2007), *Political Constitutionalism. A Republican Defence of the Constitutionality of Democracy*. Cambridge University Press.

Benecke, Werner (2006), *Militär, Reform und Gesellschaft im Zarenreich. Die Wehrpflicht in Russland 1874–1914*. Paderborn: Ferdinand Schöningh.

Benvindo, Juliano Zaiden (2018), 'The Rule of Law in Brazil: A Conceptual Challenge' at: www.iconnectblog.com/2018/05/the-rule-of-law-in-brazil-a-conceptual-challenge/ (Last accessed 3 May 2020).

Berg, Manfred (2007), 'Black Civil Rights and Liberal Anticommunism: The NAACP in the Early Cold War'. *The Journal of American History* 94(1): 75–96.

Bergien, Rüdiger (2012), *Die bellizistische Republik. Wehrkonsens und "Wehrhaftmachung" in Deutschland 1918–1933*. Munich: Oldenbourg.

Berman, William C. (1970), *The Politics of Civil Rights in the Truman Administration*. Columbus, OH: Ohio State University Press.

Berry, Mary Frances (1977), *Military Necessity and Civil Rights Policy. Black Citizenship and the Constitution, 1861–1868*. Port Washington, NY: Kennikat Press.

Bertaud, Jean-Paul (1979), *La Révolution armée. Les soldats-citoyens et la Révolution française*. Paris: Robert Laffont.

Beust, Joachim Ernst von (1747), *Observationes militares*, vol. IV. Gotha: Christian Mevius.

Beveridge, William (1943), 'Social Security: Some Trans-Atlantic Comparisons'. *Journal of the Royal Statistical Society* 106(4): 305–332.

Beyrau, Dietrich (1975), 'Von der Niederlage zur Agrarreform: Leibeigenschaft und Militärverfassung in Rußland nach 1855'. *Jahrbücher für Geschichte Osteuropas* 23(2): 191–212.

Bieber, Judy (1999), *Power, Patronage and Political Violence. State Building on a Brazilian Frontier, 1822–1889*. Lincoln: University of Nebraska Press.

Bigot, Grégoire (1999), *L'autorité judiciaire et le contentieux de l'administration. Vicissitudes d'une ambition 1800–1872*. Paris: Librairie générale de droit et de jurisprudence.

Birnbaum, Pierre (1988), *States and Collective Action: The European Experience*. Cambridge University Press.

Bisson, Thomas N. (1966), 'The Military Origins of Medieval Representation'. *The American Historical Review* 71(4): 1199–1218.

Bisson, Thomas N. (2009), *The Crisis of the Twelfth Century. Power, Lordship, and the Origins of European Government*. Princeton University Press.

Blackstone, William (1979[1765–69], *Commentaries on the Laws of England*, in 4 vols. University of Chicago Press, vol. I.

Blanchard, Peter (2008), *Under the Flags of Freedom. Slave Soldiers and the Wars of Independence in Spanish South America*. University of Pittsburgh Press.

Blanton, Harold D. (2009), 'Conscription in France during the Era of Napoleon' in Donald Stoker, Frederick C. Schneid and Harold D. Blanton (eds.), *Conscription in the Napoleonic Era. A Revolution in Military Affairs?* Abingdon: Routledge, pp. 6–23.

Blaufarb, Rafe (2002), *The French Army 1750–1820. Careers, Talent, Merit*. Manchester University Press.

Blessing, Werner K. (1991), 'Disziplinierung und Qualifizierung. Zur kulturellen Bedeutung des Militärs im Bayern des 19. Jahrhunderts'. *Geschichte und Gesellschaft* 17(4): 459–479.

Blokker, Paul (2018), 'Populist Constitutionalism' in Carlos de la Torre (ed.), *Routledge Handbook of Global Populism*. Abingdon: Routledge, pp. 113–127.

Blokker, Paul (2019), 'Varieties of Populist Constitutionalism: The Transnational Dimension'. *German Law Journal* 20: 333–350.

Blum, Jerome (1957), 'The Rise of Serfdom in Eastern Europe'. *The American Historical Review* 62(4): 807–836.

Blum, Jerome (1978), *The End of the Old Order in Rural Europe*. Princeton University Press.

Bock, Fabienne (2002), *Un parlementarisme de guerre 1914–1919*. Paris: Belin.

Böckenförde, Ernst-Wolfgang (1991), *Staat, Verfassung, Demokratie. Studien zur Verfassungstheorie und zum Verfassungsstaat*. Frankfurt am Main: Suhrkamp.

Böhler, Jochen (2018), *Civil War in Central Europe, 1918–1921. The Reconstruction of Poland*. Oxford University Press.

Böhme, Hans-Georg (1954), *Die Wehrverfassung in Hessen-Kassel im 18. Jahrhundert bis zum Siebenjährigen Kriege*. Kassel: Bärenreiter.

Bonney, Richard and W.M. Ormrod (1999), 'Introduction: Crises, Revolutions and Self-Sustained Growth: Towards a Conceptual Model of Change in Fiscal History' in W. M. Ormrod, Margaret Bonney and Richard Bonney (eds.), *Crises, Revolutions and Self-Sustained Growth. Essays in European Fiscal History, 1130–1830*. Shaun Tyas, pp. 1–21.

Borges, Vavy Pacheco (1992), *Tenentismo e revolução brasileira*. São Paulo: Brasiliense.

Bornhak, Conrad (1884), *Geschichte des Preußischen Verwaltungsrechts, I: Bis zum Regierungsantritt Friedrich Wilhelms I*. Berlin: Springer.

Bornhak, Conrad (1885), *Geschichte des Preußischen Verwaltungsrechts, II: Bis zum Frieden von Tilsit*. Berlin: Springer.

Borodziej, Włodzimierz and Maciej Górny (2018a), *Der vergessene Weltkrieg. Imperien 1912–1916*. Darmstadt: Wissenschaftliche Buchgesellschaft.

Borodziej, Włodzimierz and Maciej Górny (2018b), *Der vergessene Weltkrieg. Nationen 1917–1923*. Darmstadt: Wissenschaftliche Buchgesellschaft.

Borstelmann, Thomas (2009), *The Cold War and the Color Line. American Race Relations in the Global Arena*. Cambridge, MA: Harvard University Press.

Bosher, J. F (1970), *French Finances 1770–1795*. Cambridge University Press.

Boulanger, Philippe (2001), *La France devant la conscription. Géographie historique d'une institution républicaine 1914–1922*. Paris: Economica et Institut de Stratégie comparée.

Boyer, George R. (2019), *The Winding Road to the Welfare State. Economic Insecurity and Social Welfare Policy in Britain*. Princeton University Press.

Breuer, Stefan (1983), *Sozialgeschichte des Naturrechts*. Opladen: Westdeutscher Verlag.

Brewer, John (1989), *The Sinews of Power. War, Money and the English State 1688–1783*. London: Routledge.

Brewer-Carías, Allan R. (2007), 'Judicial Review in Venezuela'. *Duquesne Law Review* 45(3): 439–465.

Briggs, Asa (1961), 'The Welfare State in Historical Perspective'. *European Journal of Sociology* 2(2): 221–258.

Broers, Michael (2010), *Napoleon's Other War. Bandits, Rebels and their Pursuers in the Age of Revolution*. Oxford: Lang.

Brogi, Alessandro (2011), *Confronting America. The Cold War between the United States and the Communists in France and Italy*. Chapel Hill: University of North Carolina Press.

Brooks, Clem and Jeff Manza (1997), 'Class Politics and Political Change in the United States, 1952–1992'. *Social Forces* 76(2): 379–408.

Brovkin, Vladimir N. (1994), *Behind the Front Lines of the Civil War. Political Parties and Social Movements in Russia, 1918–1922*. Princeton University Press.

Brown, Howard G. (1995), *War, Revolution, and the Bureaucratic State. Politics and Army Administration in France, 1791–1799*. Oxford: Clarendon.

Brubaker, Rogers (1994), 'Nationhood and the National Question in the Soviet Union and post-Soviet Russia: An Institutionalist Account'. *Theory and Society* 23: 47–78.

Brubaker, Rogers (2020), 'Populism and Nationalism'. *Nations and Nationalism* 26 (1): 44–66.

Brunner, Heinrich (1887), 'Der Reiterdienst und die Anfänge des Lehnwesens'. *Zeitschrift für Rechtsgeschichte* 8: 1–38.

Bruno, Regina (2017), 'Bancada ruralista, conservadorismo e representação de intereses no Brasil contemporâneo' in Renato S. Maluf and Georges Flexor (eds.), *Questões agrárias, agrícolas e rurais Conjunturas e políticas públicas*. Rio de Janeiro: E-Papers, pp. 155–168.

Brysk, Alison and Carol Wise (1997), 'Liberalization and Ethnic Conflict in Latin America'. *Studies in Comparative International Development* 32(2): 76–104.

Buchez, Philippe-Joseph-Benjamin (1835), *Histoire parlementaire de la Révolution Française*. Paris: Paulin, vol. XVI.

Bugaric, Bojan (2019), 'Could Populism Be Good for Constitutional Democracy?' *Annual Review of Law and Social Science* 15: 41–58.

Burkhardt, Johannes (1995), 'Die Friedlosigkeit der Frühen Neuzeit: Grundlegung einer Theorie der Bellizität'. *Zeitschrift für Historische Forschung* 24(4): 509–574.

Burschel, Peter (1994), *Söldner im Nordwestdeutschland des 16. und 17. Jahrhunderts. Sozialgeschichtliche Studien.* Göttingen: Vandenhoeck und Ruprecht.

Büsch, Otto (1962), *Militärsystem und Sozialleben im Alten Preußen 1713–1807. Die Anfänge der sozialen Militarisierung der preußisch-deutschen Gesellschaft.* Berlin: de Gruyter.

Buschmann, Nikolaus (2003), *Einkreisung und Waffenbruderschaft. Die öffentliche Deutung von Krieg und Nation in Deutschland 1850–1871.* Göttingen: Vandenhoeck und Ruprecht.

Cabanes, Bruno (2004), *La victoire endeuillée. La sortie de guerre des soldats français.* Paris: Seuil.

Campbell, Alec (2004), 'The Invisible Welfare State: Establishing the Phenomenon of Twentieth Century Veteran's Benefits'. *Journal of Political and Military Sociology* 32(2): 249–267.

Cancik, Pascale (2007), *Verwaltung und Öffentlichkeit in Preußen.* Tübingen: Mohr.

Cane, Peter (2016), *Controlling Administrative Power. A Historical Comparison.* Cambridge University Press.

Cannadine, David (1990), *The Decline and Fall of the British Aristocracy.* New Haven: Yale University Press.

Cannon, Barry (2009), *Hugo Chávez and the Bolivarian Revolution. Populism and Democracy in the Globalized Age.* Manchester University Press.

Canovan, Margaret (1999), 'Trust the People! Populism and the Two Faces of Democracy'. *Political Studies* XVVII: 2–16.

Carey, John A. (1981), *Judicial Reform in France before the Revolution of 1789.* Cambridge, MA: Harvard University Press.

Carothers, Thomas (2002), 'The End of the Transition Paradigm'. *Journal of Democracy* 13(1): 5–21.

Carvalho, José Murilo de (1996), 'Cidadania: Tipos e Precursos'. *Revista Estudos Históricos* 18: 337–359.

Carvalho, José Murilo de (2018), *A Construcão da Ordem/Teatro de Sombras.* 11th edition. Rio de Janeiro: Civilizaçao Brasileira.

Carvalho, José Murilo de (2019), *Forças armadas e política no Brasil.* New edition. São Paulo: todavía.

Capozzola, Christopher (2010), *Uncle Sam Wants You. World War I and the Making of the Modern American Citizen.* Oxford University Press.

Caramani, Daniele (2003), 'The End of Silent Elections: The Birth of Electoral Competition, 1832–1915'. *Party Politics* 9(4): 411–443.

Caramani, Daniel (2004), *The Nationalization of Politics. The Formation of National Electorates*. Cambridge University Press.
Carruthers, Bruce G. (1996), *City of Capital. Politics and Markets in the English Financial Revolution*. Princeton University Press.
Castaño, Luis Ociel Zuluaga (2011), 'Modernidad ius-politica y esclavitud en Colombia: el proceso de abrogación de una institución jurídica'. *Revista de la facultad de derecho y ciencias políticas* 41(114): 181–238.
Castilho, Celso Thomas (2016), *Slave Emancipation and Transformations in Brazilian Political Citizenship*. University of Pittsburgh Press.
Centeno, Miguel Angel (2002), *Blood and Debt. War and the Nation State in Latin America*. University Park, PA: Pennsylvania State University Press.
Cerdeira, Pablo de Camargo et al. (2018), *Congresso em números: a produção legislativa do Brasil de 1988 a 2017*, http://bibliotecadigital.fgv.br/dspace/bitstream/handle/10438/24019/Congresso%20em%20n%C3%BAmeros%202017%20-%20a%20produ%C3%A7%C3%A3o%20legislativa%20do%20Brasil.pdf?sequence=1&isAllowed=y.
Challener, Richard D. (1965), *The French Theory of the Nation in Arms 1866–1939*. New York: Russell & Russell.
Chambers II, John Whiteclay (1987), *To Raise an Army. The Draft Comes to Modern America*. London: Macmillan.
Chas, Jean (1819), *Biographie spéciale des pairs et des députés du royaume: Session de 1818–1819*. Paris: Beaucé.
Chhibber, Pradeep K. and Rahul Verma (2018), *Ideology and Identity. The Changing Party Systems of India*. Oxford University Press.
Christiansen, Niels Finn and Klaus Petersen (2001), 'The Dynamics of Social Solidarity: The Danish Welfare State, 1900–2000'. *Scandinavian Journal of History* 26(3): 177–196.
Clark, Nichols Terry and Seymour Marin Lipset (1991), 'Are Social Classes Dying?' *International Sociology* 6(4): 397–410.
Clausewitz, Claus von (2008 [1832]), *Vom Kriege*. Hamburg: Nikol.
Clayton, James L. (1976), 'The Fiscal Limits of the Warfare-Welfare State: Defense and Welfare Spending in the United States since 1900'. *Western Political Quarterly* 29(3): 364–383.
Clegg, Hugh Armstrong (1976), *Trade Unionism and Collective Bargaining. A Theory Based on Comparisons of Six Countries*. Oxford: Blackwell.
Cleveland, Sarah H. (2006), 'Our International Constitution'. *Yale Journal of International Law* 31: 1–125.
Cmiel, Kenneth (1999), 'The Emergence of Human Rights Politics in the United States'. *The Journal of American History*, 86(3): 1231–1250.
Cohen, Deborah (2000), *The War Comes Home. Disabled Veterans in Britain and Germany, 1914–1939*. Berkeley: University of California Press.

Collier, David and Richard E. Messnick (1975), 'Prerequisites versus Diffusion: Testing Alternative Explanations of Social Security'. *The American Political Science Review* 69(4): 1299–1315.

Collier, Ruth Berins and David Collier (1991), *Shaping the Political Arena. Critical Junctures, The Labor Movement, and Regime Dynamics in Latin America*. Princeton University Press.

Condorcet, Marquis de (1847), 'La nation française à tous les peuples' in Condorcet, *Oeuvres* in 12 vols. Paris: Firmin Didot frères, vol. XII: pp. 507–527.

Conway, Stephen (2006), *War, State, and Society in Mid-Eighteenth-Century Britain and Ireland*. Oxford University Press.

Conze, Werner (1958), *Polnische Nation und deutsche Politik im Ersten Weltkrieg*. Cologne: Böhlau.

Cookson, J.E. (1997), *The British Armed Nation 1793–1815*. Oxford: Clarendon.

Corrias, Luigi (2016), 'Populism in a Constitutional Key: Constituent Power, Popular Sovereignty and Constitutional Identity'. *European Constitutional Law Review* (12(1): 6–26.

Corrêa do Lago, Luiz Aranha (2014), *Da escravidão ao trabalho libre. Brasil, 1550–1900*. São Paulo: Companha das letras.

Corvisier, André (1964), *L'armée française de la fin du XVII siècle au ministère de Choiseul: Le soldat*. Paris: PUF.

Cowen, Deborah (2005), 'Welfare Warriors: Towards a Genealogy of the Soldier Citizen in Canada'. *Antipode* 374: 654–678.

Cowen, Deborah (2008), *Military Workfare. The Soldier and Social Citizenship in Canada*. Toronto University Press.

Crépin, Annie (1998), *La conscription en débat. Ou le triple apprentissage de la nation, de la citoyenneté, de la République (1798–1889)*. Arras: Artois Presses Université.

Crépin, Annie (2003), 'Armée, conscription et garde nationale dans l'opinion publique et le discours politique en France septentrionale (1789–1870)'. *Association Revue du Nord* 350(2): 313–332.

Crépin, Annie (2005), *Défendre la France. Les français, la guerre et le service militaire, de la guerre de Sept Ans à Verdun*. Rennes: Presses universitaires de Rennes.

Crépin, Annie (2009), *Histoire de la conscription*. Paris: Gallimard.

Crépin, Annie (2011), *Vers l'armée nationale. Les débuts de la conscription en Seine-et-Marne 1795–1815*. Rennes: Presses universitaires de Rennes.

Cress, Lawrence Delbert (1982), *Citizens in Arms. The Army and the Militia in American Society to the War of 1812*. Chapel Hill: University of North Carolina Press.

Cummings Scott L. and Louise G. Trubeck (2008), 'Globalizing Public Interest Law'. *UCLA Journal of International Law and Foreign Affairs* 13:1–53.

Dahrendorf, Ralf (1965), *Gesellschaft und Demokratie in Deutschland*. Munich: Piper.

Dale, Robert (2015), *Demobilized Veterans in Late Stalinist Leningrad. Soldiers to Civilians*. London: Bloomsbury.

Daniel, Ute (1989), *Arbeiterfrauen in der Kriegsgesellschaft*. Göttingen: Vandenhoeck und Ruprecht.

D'Aguesseau, Henri François (1819), 'Essai d'une Institution au droit public' in D'Aguesseau, *Oeuvres complètes* edited by M. Pardessus, in 16 vols. Paris: Fantins et compagnie, vol. XV: 164–272.

Dallara, Cristina (2015), 'Powerful Resistance against a Long-Running Personal Crusade: The Impact of Silvio Berlusconi on the Italian Judicial System'. *Modern Italy* 920(1): 59–76.

Dareste, Rodolphe (1855a), 'Études sur les origines du contentieux administratif en France, I. Les Intendants et commissaires départis'. *Revue historique de droit français et étranger* 1: 24–68.

Dareste, Rodolphe (1855b), 'Études sur les origines du contentieux administratif en France, II. Le Conseil d'État'. *Revue historique de droit français et étranger* 1: 239–271.

Decroix, Arnaud (2006), *Question fiscale et réforme financière en France (1749–1789). Logique de la transparence et recherche de la confiance publique*. Marseille: Presses universitaires de'Aix-Marseilles.

de Lange, Sarah L. (2007), 'A New Winning Formula? The Programmatic Appeal of the Far Right'. *Party Politics* 13(4): 411–435.

Della Porta, Donatella (1998), '"1968": Zwischennationale Diffusion und Transnationale Strukturen. Eine Forschungsagenda'. *Geschichte und Gesellschaft* Sonderheft 17: 131–150.

Demeter, Karl (1933), *Das deutsche Heer und seine Offiziere*. Berlin: Hobbing.

Dennison, Tracy (2011), *The Institutional Framework of Russian Serfdom*. Cambridge University Press.

Diamond, Larry (2002), 'Thinking about Hybrid Regimes'. *Journal of Democracy* 13(2): 21–35.

Dickson, P.G.M (1987), *Finance and Government under Maria Theresia, 1740-1780, I: Society and Government*. Oxford: Clarendon.

Domat, Jean (1705a), *Les lois civiles dans leur ordre naturel*, vol. I. Revised edition. Paris: Cavelier.

Domat, Jean (1705b), *Les lois civiles dans leur ordre naturel*, vol. II. Revised edition. Paris: Cavelier.

Domke, William K., Richard C. Eichenberg and Catherine M. Kelleher (1983), 'The Illusion of Choice: Defense and Welfare in Advanced Industrial Democracies'. *The American Political Science Review* 77(1): 19–35.

Downing, Brian (1992), *The Military Revolution and Political Change. Origins of Democracy and Autocracy in Early Modern Europe*. Princeton University Press.

Droege, Georg (1969), *Landrecht und Lehnrecht im hohen Mittelalter*. Bonn: Röhrscheid.

Drolet, Jean-François and Michael C. Williams (2018), 'Radical Conservatism and Global Order: International Theory and the New Right'. *International Theory* 10(3): 285–313.
Dudley, William S. (1975), 'Institutional Sources of Officer Discontent in the Brazilian Army, 1870–1889'. *The Hispanic American Historical Review* 55(1): 44–65.
Dudziak, Mary L. (1988), 'Desegregation as a Cold War Imperative'. *Stanford Law Review* 41(1): 61–120.
Dudziac, Mary L. (2000), *Cold War Civil Rights. Race and the Image of American Democracy*. Princeton University Press.
Dudziak, Mary L. (2004), '*Brown* as a Cold War Case'. *The Journal of American History* 91(1): 32–42.
Duffy, Christopher (1987), *The Military Experience in the Age of Reason*. London: Routledge.
Duranti, Marco (2017), *The Conservative Human Rights Revolution. European Identity, Transnational Politics and the Origins of the European Convention*. Oxford University Press.
Durkheim, Émile (1928), *Le Socialisme*. Paris: PUF.
Durkheim, Émile (1950), *Leçons de sociologie*. Paris: PUF.
Duruy, Albert (1887), 'L'Armée royale en 1789: I - L'effectif, La composition et la formation, Le commandement'. *Revue des deux mondes* 81(2): 372–411.
Dutton, Paul V. (2002), *Origins of the French Welfare State. The Struggle for Social Reform in France, 1914–1947*. Cambridge University Press.
Ebbinghaus, Bernhard (1995), 'The Siamese Twins: Citizenship Rights, Cleavage Formation, and Party-Union Relations in Western Europe'. *International Review of Social History* 40(3): 51–89.
Edgerton, David (2006), *Warfare State: Britain 1920–1970*. Oxford University Press.
Edlund, Jonas and Arvid Lindh (2015), 'The Democratic Class Struggle Revisited: The Welfare State, Social Cohesion and Political Conflict'. *Acta Sociologica* 58 (4): 311–328.
Ehlert, Hans (1985), 'Ursprünge des modernen Militärwesens. Die nassau-oranischen Heeresreformen'. *Militärgeschichtliche Mitteilungen* 38: 27–56.
Eisner, Marc Allen (2000), *From Warfare State to Welfare State. World War I, Compensatory State Building and the Limits of Modern Order*. University Park, PA: Pennsylvania State University Press.
Elchardus, Mark and Bram Spruyt (2016), 'Populism, Persistent Republicanism and Declinism: An Empirical Analysis of Populism as a Thin Ideology'. *Government and Opposition* 51(1): 111–133.
Elliff, John T. (1987), *The United States Department of Justice and Individual Rights 1937–1962*. New York: Garland.
Eloranta, Jari (2007), 'From the Great Illusion to the Great War: Military Spending Behaviour of the Great Powers, 1870–1913'. *European Review of Economic History* 11: 255–283.

Engels, Friedrich (1865), *Die Preußische Militärfrage und die Deutsche Arbeiterpartei*. Hamburg: Meißner.

Engels, Friedrich (1962), *Wie die Preußen zu schlagen sind*, in Karl Marx and Friedrich Engels, *Werke*. Berlin: Dietz, vol. XVII, pp. 105–108.

Enloe, Cynthia H. (1980a), *Ethnic Soldiers. State Security in Divided Societies*. Athens: The University of Georgia Press.

Enloe, Cynthia H. (1980b), *Police, Military and Ethnicity. Foundations of State Power*. New Brunswick: Transaction.

Enloe, Cynthia H. (1993), *The Morning After. Sexual Politics at the End of the Cold War*. Berkeley: University of California Press.

Epp, Charles R. (1998), *The Rights Revolution. Lawyers, Activists, and Supreme Courts in Comparative Perspective*. Chicago: University of Chicago Press.

Esdaile, Charles J. (2004), *Fighting Napoleon. Guerillas, Bandits and Adventurers in Spain 1808–1814*. New Haven: Yale University Press.

Esping-Andersen, Gøsta (1985), *Politics against Markets. The Social Democratic Road to Power*. Princeton University Press.

Esping-Andersen, Gøsta (1990), *The Three Worlds of Welfare Capitalism*. Cambridge: Polity.

Estévez-Abe, Margarita (2008), *Welfare and Capitalism in Postwar Japan*. Cambridge University Press.

Ewald, François (1986), *L'état providence*. Paris: Grasset.

Farrand, Max (ed.) (1911), *The Records of the Federal Convention of 1787*, 3 vols. New Haven, vol. I.

Fausto, Boris (2010), *A revoluçao de 1930*. 16th edition. São Paulo: Companhia das Lettras.

Fehr, Hans (1914), 'Das Waffenrecht der Bauern im Mittelalter'. *Zeitschrift für Rechtsgeschichte* 35: 111–211.

Feigl, Helmut (1964), *Die niederösterreichische Grundherrschaft vom ausgehenden Mittelalter bis zu den theresianisch-josephinischen Reformen*. Vienna: Verein für Landeskunde von Niederösterreich und Wien.

Feld, Maury D. (1977), *The Structure of Violence. Armed Forces as Social Systems*. Beverly Hills: Sage.

Fertig, André (2012), *Clientelismo político em tempos belicosos. A guarda nacional da província de São Pedro do Rio Grande do Sul na defesa do império no Brasil (1850–1873)*. Santa Maria: Editor aufsm.

Fichte, Robby (2010), *Die Begründung des Militärdienstverhältnisses (1648–1806). Ein Beitrag zur Frühgeschichte des öffentlich-rechtlichen Vertrages*. Baden-Baden: Nomos.

Figes, Orlando (1990), 'The Red Army and Mass Mobilization during the Russian Civil War 1918–1920'. *Past & Present* 129: 168–211.

Finer, Samuel E. (2002), *The Man on Horseback. The Role of the Military in Politics*, new edition introduced by J. Stanley. New Brunswick: Transaction.

Foner, Eric (1987), 'Rights and the Constitution in Black Life during the Civil War and Reconstruction'. *The Journal of American History* 74(3): 863–883.

Fontane, Theodor (1985[1873]), *Der Krieg gegen Frankreich 1870–1871, 1: Der Krieg gegen das Kaiserreich*. Zurich: Manesse.

Forrest, Alan (1989), *Conscripts and Deserters. The Army and French Society during the Revolution and Empire*. Oxford University Press.

Fournier, Théo (2018), *From Rhetoric to Action – A Constitutional Analysis of Populism*. EUI Department of Law Research Paper No. 2018/08, at: http://cadmus.eui.eu/bitstream/handle/1814/51725/LAW_2018_08.pdf?sequence=1&isAllowed=y.

Frank, Joseph Allan (1998), *With Ballot and Bayonet. The Political Socialization of American Civil War Soldiers*. Athens: University of Georgia Press.

Frauenholz, Eugen von (1939), *Das Heerwesen in der Zeit des dreißigjährigen Krieges*. Munich: Beck.

Frauenholz, Eugen von (1940), *Das Heerwesen in der Zeit des Absolutismus*. Munich: Beck.

Frevert, Ute (2001), *Die Kasernierte Nation. Militärdienst und Zivilgesellschaft in Deutschland*. Munich: Beck.

Friedberg, Aaron L. (2000), *In the Shadow of the Garrison State. America's Anti-Statism and its Cold War Grand Strategy*. Princeton University Press.

Führer, Karl Christian (1990), *Arbeitslosigkeit und die Enstehung der Arbitslosenversicherung in Deutschland 1902–1927*. Berlin: Colloquium.

Gaboriaux, Chloé (2010), *La République en quête de citoyens. Les républicains français face au bonapartisme rural (1848–1880)*. Paris: Presses de Sciences Po.

Garcia-Sierra, Mario J. (2001), 'The "Enabling Law": The Demise of the Separation of Powers in Hugo Chavez's Venezuela'. *University of Miami Inter-American Law Review* 32(2): 265–293.

Gebelin, Jacques (1882), *Histoire des milices provinciales (1688–1791). Le tirage au sort sous l'ancien régime*. Paris: Hachette.

Gee, Austin (2013), *The British Volunteer Movement 1794–1814*. Oxford: Clarendon.

Gehrke, Roland (2005), 'Zwischen altständischer Ordnung und monarchischem Konstitutionalismus. Begriffserklärungen und Fragestellungen' in Roland Gehrke (ed.), *Aufbrüche in die Moderne. Frühparlamentarismus zwischen altständischer Ordnung und monarchischem Konstitutionalismus. Schlesien–Deutschland–Mitteleuropa*. Cologne: Böhlau, pp. 1–13.

Geva, Dorit (2013), *Conscription, Family, and the Modern State. A Comparative Study of France and the United States*. Cambridge University Press.

Gewarth, Robert (2016), *The Vanquished. Why the First World War Failed to End, 1917–1923*. London: Penguin.

Geyer, Michael (1978), 'Der zur Organisation erhobene Burgfrieden' in Klaus-Jürgen Müller and Eckardt Opitz (eds.), *Militär und Militarismus in der Weimarer Republik*. Düsseldorf: Droste, pp. 15–100.

Geyer, Michael (1983), 'Ein Vorbote des Wohlfahrtsstaates. Die Kriegsopferversorgung in Frankreich, Deutschland und Großbritannien nach dem Ersten Weltkrieg'. *Geschichte und Gesellschaft* 9(2): 230–277.

Gingrich, Jane and Silja Häusermann (2015), 'The Decline of the Working-Class Vote, the Reconfiguration of the Welfare Support Coalition and the Consequences for the Welfare State'. *European Journal of Social Policy* 25(1): 50–75.

Ginsburg, Tom and Aziz Z. Huq (2018), *How to Save a Constitutional Democracy*. Chicago University Press.

Girard, Georges (1921), *Racolage et milice (1701–1715). Le service militaire en France à la fin du règne de Louis XIV*. Paris: Plon.

Gneist, Rudolf (1966[1879]), *Der Rechtsstaat und die Verwaltungsgerichte in Deutschland*. Darmstadt: Wissenschaftliche Buchgesellschaft.

Gnügen, Friedrich Andreas Gottlieb (1750), *Gründliche Anleitung zum Kriegs-Recht*. Jena: Christian Friedrich Gollner.

Goldstein, Ariel Alejandro (2019), 'The New Far Right in Brazil and the Construction of a Right-Wing Order'. *Latin American Perspectives* 46(4): 245–262.

González-Jácome, Jorge (2018), 'The Emergence of Revolutionary and Democratic Human Rights Activism in Colombia between 1974 and 1980'. *Human Rights Quarterly* 40(1): 91–118.

Goodwin, Jeff (2001), *No Other Way Out. States and Revolutionary Movements, 1945–1991*. Cambridge University Press.

Gould, Frank and Barbara Roweth (1980), 'Public Spending and Social Policy: The United Kingdom 1950–1977'. *Journal of Social Policy* 9(3): 337–357.

Graden, Dale Torston (2006), *From Slavery to Freedom in Brazil. Bahia, 1835–1900*. Albuquerque: University of New Mexico Press.

Graf, Daniel W. (1974), 'Military Rule behind the Russian Front, 1914–1917: The Political Ramifications'. *Jahrbücher für Geschichte Osteuropas* 22(3): 390–411.

Gregory, Adrian (2008), *The Last Great War. British Society and the First World War*. Cambridge University Press.

Gresle, François (1996), 'Le Citoyen-Soldat garant du pacte républicain'. *L'Année sociologique* 46: 105–125.

Gresle, François (2003), 'La "Société Militaire". Son devenir à la lumière de la professionnalisation'. *Revue française de sociologie* 44: 777–798.

Grewe, William (ed.) (1988), *Fontes Historiae Iuris Gentium*. Berlin: de Gruyter. vol. II.

Grimm, Dieter (2012), *Die Zukunft der Verfassung II. Auswirkungen von Europäisierung und Globalisierung*. Frankfurt am Main: Suhrkamp.

Grønbjerg, Kirsten A. (1977), *Mass Society and the Extension of Welfare, 1960–1970.* Chicago University Press.

Grünbjerg, Karl (1894), *Die Bauernbefreiung und die Auflösung des gutsherrlich-bäuerlichen Verhältnisses in Böhmen, Mähren und Schlesien, I: Überblick der Entwicklung.* Leipzig: Duncker und Humblot.

Grzeszczak, Robert and Ireneusz Pawel Karolewski (2018), 'The Rule of Law Crisis in Poland: A New Chapter.' *VerfBlog*, 2018/8/08, https://verfassungsblog.de/the-rule-of-law-crisis-in-poland-a-new-chapter/, DOI:https://doi.org/10.17176/20180809-090230-0.

Gueniffey, Patrice (2000), *La politique de la terreur. Essai sur la violence révolutionnaire 1789–1794.* Paris: Fayard.

Guinier, Arnaud (2014), 'De l'autorité paternelle au despotisme légal: Pour une réévaluation des origines de l'idéal du soldat-citoyen dans la France des lumières'. *Revue d'histoire moderne & contemporaine* 61-2:150–175.

Gullace, Nicoletta R. (2002) *'The Blood of Our Sons'. Men, Women and the Renegotiation of British Citizenship during the Great War.* Basingstoke: Macmillan.

Gumz, Jonathan E. (2009), *The Resurrection and Collapse of Empire in Habsburg Serbia, 1914–1918.* Cambridge University Press.

Gunn, Steven (2018), *The English People at War in the Age of Henry VIII.* Oxford University Press.

Gurr, Ted R. (1988), 'War, Revolution, and the Growth of the Coercive State'. *Comparative Political Studies* 21(1): 45–65.

Habermas, Jürgen (1973), *Legitimationsprobleme im Spätkapitalismus.* Frankfurt am Main: Suhrkamp.

Habermas, Jürgen (1990[1962]), *Strukturwandel der Öffentlichkeit. Untersuchungen zu einer Kategorie der bürgerlichen Gesellschaft*, new edition. Frankfurt am Main: Suhrkamp.

Habermas, Jürgen (2014), 'Zur Prinzipienkonkurrenz von Bürgergleichheit und Staatengleichheit im supranationalen Gemeinwesen: Eine Notiz aus Anlass der Frage nach der Legitimität der ungleichen Repräsentation der Bürger im Europäischen Parlament'. *Der Staat* 53 (2): 167–192.

Hagen, Mark von (1990), *Soldiers in the Proletarian Revolution. The Red Army and the Soviet Socialist State, 1917–1930.* Ithaca: Cornell University Press.

Hagen, William W. (2002), *Ordinary Prussians. Brandenburg Junkers and Villagers, 1500–1840.* Cambridge University Press.

Haggard, Stephan and Robert R. Kaufman (2008), *Development, Democracy and Welfare States. Latin America, East Asia and Eastern Europe.* Princeton University Press.

Hahlweg, Werner (1941), *Die Heeresreform der Oranier und die Antike.* Berlin: Juncker und Dünnhaupt.

Hahn, Jeffrey W. (1988), *Soviet Grassroots. Citizen Participation in Local Soviet Government*. London: Tauris.

Hale, Henry E. (2015), *Patronal Politics. Eurasian Regime Dynamics in Comparative Perspective*. Cambridge University Press.

Halperin, Sandra (2004), *War and Social Change in Modern Europe. The Great Transformation Revisited*. Cambridge: Cambridge University Press.

Händel, Heribert (1962), *Der Gedanke der allgemeinen Wehrpflicht in der Wehrverfassung des Königreiches Preußen bis 1819*. Frankfurt am Main: Mittler.

Hanisch, Hartmut (1996), 'Preußisches Kantonsystem und ländliche Gesellschaft. Das Beispiel der mittleren Kammerdepartments' in Bernhard R. Kroener and Ralf Pröve (eds.), *Krieg und Frieden. Militär und Gesellschaft in der Frühen Neuzeit*. Paderborn: Schöningh, pp. 137–165.

Hansen, Ernst Willi (1979), 'Zur Problematik einer Sozialgeschichte des deutschen Militärs im 17. und 18. Jahrhundert'. *Zeitschrift für Historische Forschung* 6: 425–460.

Harriss, Gerald L. (1977), 'War and the Emergence of the English Parliament, 1297–1360'. *Journal of Medieval History* 2(1): 35–56.

Harste, Gorm (2016), *Kritik af Krigens Fornuft. Et perspektiv på selvreferentielle systemer fra 11. – 21. Århundrede*. Aarhus: Aarhus University Press.

Hauriou, Maurice (1892), *Précis de droit administratif, contenant le droit public et le droit administratif*. Paris: Larose & Forcel.

Hayek, F.A. (1960), *The Constitution of Liberty*. London: Routledge.

Hayhoe, Jeremy (2008), *Enlightened Feudalism. Seigneurial Justice and Village Society in Eighteenth-Century France*. Rochester, NY: University of Rochester Press.

Heclo, Hugh (1974), *Modern Social Politics in Britain and Sweden. From Relief to Income Maintenance*. New Haven: Yale University Press.

Helg, Aline (2004), *Liberty and Equality in Caribbean Colombia 1770–1835*. Chapel Hill: University of North Carolina Press.

Hellie, Richard (1971), *Enserfment and Military Change in Muscovy*. University of Chicago Press.

Hellmuth, Eckhart (1985), *Naturrechtsphilosophie und bürokratischer Werthorizont. Studien zur preußischen Geistes- und Sozialgeschichte des 18. Jahrhunderts*. Göttingen: Vandenhoeck und Ruprecht.

Henneman, John Bell (1978), 'The Military Class and the French Monarchy in the Late Middle Ages.' *The American Historical Review* 83(4): 946–965.

Heuser, Beatrice (2010), 'Small Wars in the Age of Clausewitz: The Watershed between Partisan War and People's War'. *Journal of Strategic Studies* 33(1): 139–162.

Hewitson, Mark (2013), 'Princes' Wars, Wars of the People, or Total War? Mass Armies and the Question of a Military Revolution in Germany, 1792–1815'. *War in History* 20(4): 452–490.

Hewitson, Mark (2017), *Absolute War. Violence and Mass Warfare in the German Lands, 1792–1820*. Oxford University Press.

Hewitt, H.J. (1966), *The Organization of War under Edward III*. Manchester University Press.

Hicks, Alexander (1999), *Social Democracy and Welfare Capitalism. A Century of Income Security Politics*. Ithaca: Cornell University Press.

Hicks, Alexander and Duane Swank (1984), 'On the Political Economy of Welfare Expansion. A Comparative Analysis of 18 Advanced Democracies, 1960–71'. *Comparative Political Studies* 17(1): 81–119.

Hilpert, Dagmar (2012), *Wohlfahrtsstaat der Mittelschichten? Sozialpolitik und gesellschaftlicher Wandel in der Bundesrepublik Deutschland (1949–1975)*. Göttingen: Vandenhoeck und Ruprecht.

Hintze, Otto (1962), *Staat und Verfassung. Gesammelte Abhandlungen zur allgemeinen Verfassungsgeschichte*, edited by Gerhard Oestreich, 2nd edition. Göttingen: Vandenhoeck & Ruprecht.

Hippler, Thomas (2006), *Soldats et citoyens. Naissance du service militaire en France et en Prusse*. Paris: PUF.

Hochedlinger, Michael (2003), *Austria's Wars of Emergence. War, State and Society in the Habsburg Monarchy 1683–1797*. London: Pearson.

Hochedlinger, Michael (2009), 'The Habsburg Monarchy: From "Military-Fiscal State" to "Militarization"' in Christopher Storrs (ed.), *The Fiscal-Military State in Eighteenth-Century Europe. Essays in Honour of P.G.M. Dickson*. Farnham: Ashgate, pp. 55–94.

Hockerts, Hans Günter (1988), 'Integration der Gesellschaft – Gründungskrise und Sozialpolitik in der frühen Bundesrepublik' in Manfred Funke (ed.), *Entscheidung für den Westen. Vom Besatzungsstatut zur Souveränität der Bundesrepublik 1949–1955*. Bonn: Bouvier, 39–58.

Hoeres, Peter (2004), 'Das Militär der Gesellschaft: Zu Verhältnis von Militär und Politik im deutschen Kaiserreich' in Franz Becker (ed.), *Geschichte und Systemtheorie. Exemplarische Fallstudien*. Frankfurt am Main: Campus, pp. 330–354.

Hofbauer, Martin (2015), *Vom Krieger zum Ritter. Die Professionalisierung der bewaffneten Kämpfer im Mittelalter*. Freiburg: Rombach.

Hogan, Michael J. (1998), *A Cross of Iron. Harry S. Truman and the Origins of the National Security State, 1945–1954*. Cambridge University Press.

Höhn, Reinhard (1938), *Verfassungskampf und Heereseid. Der Kampf des Bürgertums um das Heer (1815–1850)*. Leipzig: Hirzel.

Holbach, Paul Henri Thiry (1776), *Éthocratie ou le gouvernement fondé sur la morale*. Amsterdam: Marc-Michel Rey.

Holden, Robert H. (2004), *Armies without Nations. Public Violence and State Formation in Central America, 1821–1960*. Oxford University Press.

Holquist, Peter (2002), *Making War, Forging Revolution. Russia's Continuum of Crisis, 1914–1922*. Cambridge, MA: Harvard University Press.

Holsti, K.J. (1996), *The State, War, and the State of War*. Cambridge University Press.

Hong, Young-Sun (1998), *Welfare, Modernity, and the Weimar State, 1919–1933*. Princeton University Press.

Howard, Michael (1961), *The Franco-Prussian War*. London: Routledge.

Huber, Ernst Rudolf (1937a), 'Deutsche Wehrordnung und Verfassung bis zum Ende des Absolutismus'. *Zeitschrift für die gesamte Staatswissenschaft* 97(1): 29–70.

Huber, Ernst Rudolf (1937b), 'Volksheer und Verfassung: Ein Beitrag zu der Kernfrage der Scharnhorst-Boyenschen Reform'. *Zeitschrift für die gesamte Staatswissenschaft* 97(2): 213–257.

Huber, Evelyne and John D. Stephens (2001), *Development and Crisis of the Welfare State. Politics and Policies in Global Markets*. Chicago University Press.

Huber, Evelyne and John D. Stephens (2012), *Democracy and the Left. Social Policy and Inequality in Latin America*. Chicago University Press.

Huber, Evelyne, Charles Ragin and John D. Stephens (1993), 'Social Democracy, Christian Democracy, Constitutional Structure, and the Welfare State'. *American Journal of Sociology* 99(3): 711–749.

Huber, Robert A. and Christian H. Schimpf (2016), 'Friend or Foe? Testing the Influence of Populism on Democratic Quality in Latin America'. *Political Studies* 64(4): 872–889.

Huber, Ulrich (1684) *De Jure Civitatis*, 3 vols. Franeker: J. Gyselaar, vol. I.

Hülle, Werner (1971), *Das Auditoriat in Brandenburg-Preußen. Ein rechtshistorischer Beitrag zur Geschichte seines Heerwesens mit einem Exkurs über Österreich*. Göttingen: Otto Schwartz.

Huntebrinker, Jan Willem (2010), *'Fromme Knechte' und 'Garteteufel'. Söldner als soziale Gruppe im 16. und 17. Jahrhundert*. Konstanz: UVK.

Hunter, Wendy (2014), 'Making Citizens: Brazilian Social Policy from Getúlio to Lula'. *Journal of Politics in Latin America* 6(3): 15–37.

Ignazi, Piero (2002), *Extreme Right Parties in Western Europe*. Oxford University Press.

Inama-Sternegg, Karl Theodor von (1865), 'Der Accisenstreit deutscher Finanztheoretiker im 17. und 18. Jahrhundert'. *Zeitschrift für die gesamte Staatswissenschaft* 21(4): 515–545.

Ingenlath, Markus (1998), *Mentale Aufrüstung. Militarisierungstendenzen in Frankreich und Deutschland vor dem Ersten Weltkrieg*. Frankfurt: Campus.

Ingesson, Tony, Mårten Lindberg, Johannes Lindvall and Jan Teorell (2018), 'The Military Origins of Democracy: A Global Study of Military Conscription and

Suffrage Extensions sine the Napoleonic Wars'. *Democratization* 25(4): 633–651.
Inglot, Tomasz (2008), *Welfare States in East Central Europe, 1919–2004*. Cambridge University Press.
Inikori, Joseph E. (2002), *Africans and the Industrial Revolution in England. A Study in International Trade and Economic Development*. Cambridge University Press.
Isaacsohn, Siegfried (1878), *Geschichte des Preußischen Beamtenthums vom Anfang des 15. Jahrhunderts bis auf die Gegenwart, II: Das Beamtenthum im 17. Jahrhundert*. Berlin: Puttkammer & Mühlbrecht.
Issacsohn, Siegfried (1884), *Geschichte des Preußischen Beamtenthums vom Anfang des 15. Jahrhunderts bis auf die Gegenwart, III: Das Beamtenthum unter Friedrich Wilhelm I und während der Anfänge Friedrichs des Großen*. Berlin: Puttkammer & Mühlbrecht.
Issacharoff, Samuel (2018), 'Populism versus Democratic Governance' in Mark A. Graber, Sanford Levinson and Mark Tushnet (eds.), *Constitutional Democracy in Crisis?* Oxford University Press, pp. 445–458.
Izecksohn, Vitor (2014), *Slavery and War in the Americas. Race, Citizenship and State Building in the United States and Brazil, 1861–1870*. Charlottesville: University of Virginia Press.
Jablonski, Johann Theodor (1748), *Lexicon der Künste und Wissenschaften*. Königsberg: Hartung.
Janoski, Thomas (1998), *Citizenship and Civil Society. A Framework of Rights and Obligations in Liberal, Traditional, and Social Democratic Regimes*. Cambridge University Press.
Jansen, Robert S. (2011), 'Populist Mobilization: A New Theoretical Approach to Populism'. *Sociological Theory* 29(2): 75–96.
Janowitz, Morris (1964), *The Military in the Political Development of New Nations. An Essay in Comparative Analysis*. University of Chicago Press.
Janowitz, Morris (1978), *The Last Half Century. Societal Change and Politics in America*. University of Chicago Press.
Janowitz, Morris (1980), 'Observations on the Sociology of Citizenship: Obligations and Rights'. *Social Forces* 59(1): 1–24.
Jany, Curt (1928), *Geschichte der königlich Preußischen Armee bis zum Jahre 1802, I: Von den Anfängen bis 1740*. Berlin: Karl Siegismund.
Jaurès, Jean (1932), *L'Armée nouvelle*, in Jean Jaurès, *Oeuvres*, collected by Max Bonnafous, in 9 vols. Paris: Rieder, vol. IV.
Jeismann, Michael (1992), *Das Vaterland der Feinde. Studien zum nationalen Feindbegriff und Selbstverständnis in Deutschland und Frankreich 1792–1918*. Stuttgart: Klett-Cotta.

Jensen, Steven L.B. (2016), *The Making of International Human Rights. The 1960s, Decolonization and the Reconstruction of Global Values*. Cambridge University Press.

Johansen, Anja (2005), *Soldiers as Police. The French and Prussian Armies and the Policy of Popular Protest, 1889-1914*. Aldershot: Ashgate.

Jones, Ellen (1985), *Red Army and Society. A Sociology of the Soviet Military*. Boston: Allen & Unwin.

Justi, Johann Heinrich Gottlob von (1761), *Gesammelte politische und Finanz-Schriften über wichtige Gegenstände der Staatskunst, der Kriegswissenschaften und des Kameral- und Finanzwesens*, 3 vols. Copenhagen: Rothensche Buchhandlung, vol. I.

Kaak, Heinrich (1991), *Die Gutsherrschaft. Theoriegeschichtliche Untersuchungen zum Agrarwesen im ostelbischen Raum*. Berlin: de Gruyter.

Kaeuper, Richard (1988). *War, Justice, and Public Order. England and France in the later Middle Ages*. Oxford: Clarendon.

Kaim-Chaudle, Peter (1979), 'Moving on From Beveridge' in Hans F. Zacher (ed.), *Bedingungen für die Entstehung und Entwicklung von Sozialversicherung*. Berlin: Duncker und Humblot, pp. 223-248.

Kaltwasser Rovira, Cristóbal and Steven M. Van Hauwaert (2020), 'The Populist Citizen: Empirical Evidence from Europe and Latin America'. *European Political Science Review* 12(1): 1-18.

Kant, Immanuel (1977a[1797]), *Metaphysik der Sitten*, in Kant, *Werkausgabe*, edited by W. Weischedel, 12 vols. Frankfurt am Main: Suhrkamp, vol. VIII.

Kant, Immanuel (1977b[1795]), *Zum Ewigen Frieden*, in Kant, *Werkausgabe*, edited by W. Weischedel, 12 vols. Frankfurt am Main: Suhrkamp, vol. XI, pp. 195-251.

Kant, Immanuel (1977c[1798]), *Der Streit der Fakultäten*, in Kant, *Werkausgabe*, edited by Wilhelm Weischedel, 12 vols. Frankfurt am Main: Suhrkamp, vol. XI, pp. 265-393.

Katz, Michael B. (1986), *In the Shadow of the Poorhouse. A Social History of Welfare in America*. New York: Basic Books.

Kautsky, Karl (1907), *Die soziale Revolution*. Berlin: Buchhandlung Vorwärts.

Keating, Michael (1988), *State and Regional Nationalism. Territorial Politics and the European State*. New York: Harvester.

Keen, M.H. (1965), *The Laws of War in the Late Middle Ages*. London: Routledge.

Keitel, Christian (2000), *Herrschaft über Land und Leute. Leibherrschaft und Territorialisierung in Würtemberg 1246-1593*. Leinfelden-Echterdingen: DRW-Verlag.

Kelley, Joanathan, Ian McAllister and Anthony Mughan (1985), 'The Decline of Class Revisited: Class and Party in England, 1964-1979'. *The American Political Science Review* 79(3): 719-737.

Kennedy, Gavin (1974), *The Military in the Third World*. London: Duckworth.
Kent, Susan Kingsley (2009), *Aftershocks. Politics and Trauma in Britain, 1918-1931*. Basingstoke: Macmillan.
Kerschen, Nicole (1995), 'L'Influence du rapport Beveridge sur le plan français de sécurité sociale de 1945'. *Revue française de science politique* 45(4): 570-595.
Kestnbaum, Meyer (2000), 'Citizenship and Compulsory Military Service: The Revolutionary Origins of Conscription in the United States'. *Armed Forces & Society* 27(1): 7-36.
Kettner, James H. (1974), 'The Development of American Citizenship in the Revolutionary Era: The Idea of Volitional Allegiance'. *The American Journal of Legal History* 18(3): 208-242.
Kieniewicz, Stefan (1969), *The Emancipation of the Polish Peasants*. Chicago University Press.
Kienitz, Sabine (2008), *Beschädigte Helden. Kriegsinvalidität und Körperbilder 1914-1923*. Paderborn: Schöningh.
Kim, Heewon (2017), 'Understanding Modi and Minorities: The BJP-led Government in India and Religious Minorities'. *India Review* 14(6): 357-376.
Kirsch, Martin (1999), *Monarch und Parlament im 19. Jahrhundert. Der monarchische Konstitutionalismus als europäischer Verfassungstyp - Frankreich im Vergleich*. Göttingen: Vandenhoeck und Ruprecht.
Kitschelt, Herbert (1994), *The Transformation of European Social Democracy*. Cambridge University Press.
Klausen, Jytte (1998), *War and Welfare. Europe and the United States, 1945 to the Present*. Basingstoke: Macmillan.
Knapp, Georg Friedrich (1927), *Die Bauernbefreiung und der Ursprung der Landarbeiter in den ältern Theilen Preußens*, 2 vols. Second Edition. Munich: Duncker und Humblot, vol. II.
Kocka, Jürgen (1973), *Klassengesellschaft im Krieg. Deutsche Sozialgeschichte 1914-1918*. Göttingen: Vandenhoeck & Ruprecht.
Kocka, Jürgen (1990), *Arbeitsverhältnisse und Arbeiterexistenzen. Grundlagen der Klassenbildung im 19. Jahrhundert*. Bonn: Dietz.
Koenker, Diane and William G. Rosenberg (1989), *Strikes and Revolution in Russia, 1917*. Princeton University Press.
Kolchin, Peter (1987), *Unfree Labor. American Slavery and Russian Serfdom*. Cambridge, MA: Harvard University Press.
Köllner, Lutz (1982), *Militär und Finanzen. Zur Finanzgeschichte und Finanzsoziologie von Militärausgaben in Deutschland*. Munich: Berhard & Graefe Verlag.
Korpi, Walter (1983), *The Democratic Class Struggle*. London: Routledge.
Korpi, Walter and Joakim Palme (2003), 'New Politics and Class Politics in the Context of Austerity and Globalization: Welfare State Regress in 18 Countries, 1975-95'. *American Political Science Review* 97(3): 425-446.

Koselleck, Reinhart (1977), *Preußen zwischen Reform und Revolution. Allgemeines Landrecht, Verwaltung und soziale Bewegung von 1791 bis 1848*, second edition. Stuttgart: Klett-Cotta.

Koselleck, Reinhart (1979), *Vergangene Zukunft. Zur Semantik geschichtlicher Zeiten*. Frankfurt: Suhrkamp.

Kosotieti, Pekka (1987), 'From Collectivity to Individualism in the Welfare State?' *Acta Sociologica*, 30(3/4): 281–293.

Kotsonis, Yanni (2014), *States of Obligation. Taxes and Citizenship in the Russian Empire and Early Soviet Republic*. University of Toronto Press.

Kraay, Hendrik (2001), *Race, State, and Armed Forces in Independence Era Brazil. Bahia, 1790s-1840s*. Stanford University Press.

Krebs, Ronald R. (2006), *Fighting for Rights. Military Service and the Politics of Citizenship*. Ithaca: Cornell University Press.

Kruse, Volker (2009), 'Mobilisierung und kriegsgesellschaftliches Dilemma. Beobachtungen zur kriegsgesellschaftlichen Moderne'. *Zeitschrift für Soziologie* 38(3): 198–214.

Kruse, Wolfgang (2003), *Die Erfindung des modernen Militarismus. Krieg, Militär und bürgerliche Gesellschaft im politischen Diskurs der Französischen Revolution 1789-1799*. Munich: Oldenbourg.

Krüssmann, Walter (2010), *Ernst von Mansfeld (158-1626). Grafensohn, Söldnerführer, Kriegsunternehmer gegen Habsburg im Dreißigjährigen Krieg*. Berlin: Duncker und Humblot.

Kučera, Rudolf (2016), 'Exploiting Victory, Sinking into Defeat: Uniformed Violence in the Creation of the New Order in Czechoslovakia and Austria'. *The Journal of Modern History* 88: 827–855.

Kuchler, Barbara (2013), 'Krieg und gesellschaftliche Differenzierung'. *Zeitschrift für Soziologie* 42(6): 502–520.

Kühlich, Frank (1995), *Die deutschen Soldaten im Krieg von 1870/71*. Frankfurt am Main: Lang.

Kunisch, Johannes (1973), *Der kleine Krieg. Studien zum Heerwesen des Absolutismus*. Wiesbaden: Steiner.

Kwasny, Mark V. (1996), *Washington's Partisan War 1775-1783*. Kent, OH: Kent State University Press.

Kwass, Michael (2000), *Privilege and the Politics of Taxation in Eighteenth-Century France: Liberté, Egalité, Fiscalité*. Cambridge University Press.

Laclau, Ernesto (1977), *Politics and Ideology. Marxist Theory. Capitalism – Fascism – Populism*. London: NLB.

Laferrière, A.G.D. (1841), *Cours de droit public et administratif*. Paris: Joubert.

Laferrière, Édouard (1896), *Traité de la jurisdiction administrative et des recours contentieux*, second edition. Paris: Bergher-Levrault, vol. II.

Lampe, Albrecht (1951), *Der Milizgedanke und seine Durchführung in Brandenburg-Preussen vom Ausgang des 16. Jahrhunderts bis zur Heeresreform nach 1807*. Dissertation, FU-Berlin.

Landau, David (2018), 'Populist Constitutions'. *University of Chicago Law Review* 85 (2016): 521–543.

Lasswell, Harold D. (1941), 'The Garrison State'. *American Journal of Sociology* 46 (4): 455–468.

Lasswell, Harold D. (1948), 'The Prospects of Cooperation in a Bipolar World'. *University of Chicago Law Review* 15: 877–901.

Lauren, Paul Gordon (1983), 'First Principles of Racial Equality: History and the Politics and Diplomacy of Human Rights Provisions in the United Nations Charter'. *Human Rights Quarterly* 5(1): 1–26.

Laurentius, Johann Gottlieb (1757), *Abhandlung von den Kriegsgerichten zu unsern Zeiten*. Altenburg: Richterische Buchhandlung.

Law, David and Mila Versteeg (2013), 'Sham Constitutions'. *California Law Review* 101(4): 863–952.

Lawrence, Jon (2006), 'The Transformation of British Political Life after the First World War'. *Past & Present* 190: 185–216.

Layton, Azza S. (2000), *International Politics and Civil Rights Policies in the United States, 1941–1960*. Cambridge: Cambridge University Press.

Leal, Victor Nunes (2012), *Coronelismo, enxada e voto. O município e o regime representativo no Brasil*. 7th edition. São Paulo: Editor Schwartz.

Leed, Eric J. (1979), *No Man's Land. Combat and Identity in World War I*. Cambridge University Press.

Lefebvre, Georges (1972), *Les paysans du nord pendant la révolution française*. Paris: Colin.

Leffler, Melvyn (1992), *A Preponderance of Power. National Security, the Truman Administration and the Cold War*. Stanford University Press.

Lehning, James R. (1995), *Peasant and French. Cultural Contact in Rural France during the Nineteenth Century*. Cambridge University Press.

Leibniz, Gottfried Wilhelm (1885), 'De Justicia' in Georg Mollat (ed.), *Rechtsphilosophisches aus Leibnizens ungedruckten Schriften*. Leipzig: Robolsky, pp. 36–42.

Leisering, Lutz (1997), 'Individualisierung und "sekundäre Institutionen" – Der Sozialstaat als Voraussetzung des modernen Individuums' in Ulrich Beck and Peter Sopp (eds.), *Individualisierung und Integration. Neue Konfliktlinien und neuer Integrationsmodus?* Opladen: Leske and Budrich, pp. 143–160.

Lemarchand, Guy (1980), 'La féodalité et la Révolution française: Seigneurie et communauté paysanne (1780–1799)'. *Annales historiques de la Révolution française* 52: 536–558.

Lemarchand, Guy (2011), *Paysans et seigneurs en Europe. Une histoire comparée. XVI-XIX siècle*. Rennes: Presses universitaires de Rennes.

Leonard, Carol S. (2011), *Agrarian Reform in Russia. The Road from Serfdom*. Oxford University Press.

Leonhard, Jörn (2004), 'Die Nationalisierung des Krieges und der Bellizismus der Nation' in Christian Jansen (ed.), *Der Bürger als Soldat. Die Militarisierung europäischer Gesellschaften im langen 19. Jahrhundert: Ein internationaler Vergleich*. Essen: Klartext, pp. 83-105.

Leonhard, Jörn (2008), *Bellizismus und Nation. Kriegsdeutung und Nationsbestimmung in Europa und den Vereinigten Staaten 1750-1914*. Munich: Oldenbourg.

Lerner, Hanna (2011), *Making Constitutions in Deeply Divided Societies*. Cambridge University Press.

Le Roux, Nicolas (2015), *Le créspucule de la chevalerie. Noblesse et guerre au siècle de la Renaissance*. Ceyzétieu: Champ Vallon.

Levi, Margaret (1996), 'The Institution of Conscription'. *Social Science History* 20 (1): 133-167.

Levitan, Sar A. and Karen A. Cleary (1973), *Old Wars Remain Unfinished. The Veteran Benefits System*. Baltimore: The Johns Hopkins University Press.

Lijphart, Arend (1969), 'Consociational Democracy'. *World Politics* 21(2): 207-225.

Limnaeus, Johannes (1699), *Jus publicus imperii romano-germanici*, 3 vols. Strasburg: Spoor, vol. I.

Lindert, Peter H. (2004), *Growing Public. Social Spending and Economic Growth since the Eighteenth Century, I: The Story*. Cambridge University Press.

Link, Edith Murr (1949), *The Emancipation of the Austrian Peasant 1740-1798*. New York: Columbia University Press.

Lipset, Seymour Martin (1960), *Political Man*. London: Heinemann.

Lipset, Seymour Martin (1964), 'The Changing Class Structure and Contemporary European Politics'. *Daedalus* 93(1): 271-303.

Llanque, Marcus (2000), *Demokratisches Denken im Krieg. Die deutsche Debatte im Ersten Weltkrieg*. Berlin: Akademie Verlag.

Locke, John (1960[1689/1690]), *Two Treatises of Government*. Cambridge University Press.

Lockwood, Bert B. (1984), 'The United Nations Charter and United States Civil Rights Litigation: 1946-1955'. *Iowa Law Review* 69: 901-956.

Loening, Edgar (1914), *Gerichte und Verwaltungsbehörden in Brnadenburg-Preußen. Ein Beitrag zur Preußischen Rechts- und Verfassungsgeschichte*. Halle: Verlag der Buchhandlung des Waisenhauses.

Logette, Aline (1964), *Le comité contentieux des finances près le conseil du roi (1777-1791)*. Nancy: Société d'impressions typographiques.

Lohr, Eric (2003), *Nationalizing the Russian Empire. The Campaign against Enemy Aliens during World War I*. Cambridge, MA: Harvard University Press.

Lohr, Eric (2006), 'The Ideal Citizen and the Real Subject in Late Imperial Russia'. *Kritika* 7(2): 173–194.
Lohse, Russell (2001), 'Reconciling Freedom with the Rights of Property: Slave Emancipation in Colombia, 1821–1852, with Special Reference to La Plata'. *Journal of Negro History* 86(3): 203–227.
Lomellini, Valentine (2012), *Les liaisons dangereuses. French Socialists, Communists and the Human Rights Issues in the Soviet Bloc*. Brussels: Lang.
Lorenz, Maren (2007), *Das Rad der Gewalt. Militär und Zivilbevölkerung in Norddeutschland nach dem Dreißjährigen Krieg (1650–1700)*. Cologne: Böhlau.
Loughlin, Martin (2014), 'The Concept of Constituent Power'. *European Journal of Political Theory* 13(2): 218–237.
Lovell, George I. (2012), *This Is Not Civil Rights. Discovering Rights Talk in 1939 America*. Chicago University Press.
Lüdtke, Alf (1982), *'Gemeinwohl', Polizei und 'Festungspraxis': Staatliche Gewaltsamkeit und innere Verwaltung in Preußen, 1815–1850*. Göttingen: Vandenhoeck & Ruprecht.
Luhmann, Niklas (1965), *Grundrechte als Institution. Ein Beitrag zur politischen Soziologie*. Berlin: Duncker und Humblot.
Luhmann, Niklas (1980), *Gesellschaftsstruktur und Semantik. Studien zur Wissenssoziologie der modernen Gesellschaft*, 4 vols. Frankfurt am Main: Suhrkamp, vol. I.
Lundberg, Urban and Klas Åmark (2001), 'Social Rights and Social Security: The Swedish Welfare State, 1900–2000'. *Scandinavian Journal of History* 26(3): 157–176.
Lynn, John A. (1997), *Giant of the Grand Siècle. The French Army, 1610–1725*. Cambridge University Press.
Lyon, Bryce D. (1954), 'The Feudal Antecedent of the Indenture System'. *Speculum* 29(3): 503–511.
Lyon, Bryce D. (1957), *From Fief to Indenture. The Transition from Feudal to Non-Feudal Contract in Western Europe*. Cambridge, MA: Harvard University Press.
Mably, Gabriel Bonot de (1793), *Collection complète des Oeuvres de l'abbé de Mably*, 15 vols. Paris: Desbriere, vol. VIII.
Madison, James, Alexander Hamilton, and John Jay (1987 [1787–88]), *The Federalist Papers*. London: Penguin.
Maldoner, Johan Franz (1724), *Synopsis militaris oder kurtzer Begriff über die Kayserliche Kriegs-Articul*. Nuremberg: Lochner.
Malloy, James M. (1979), *The Politics of Social Security in Brazil*. University of Pittsburgh Press.
Mamroth, Karl (1890), *Geschichte der Preußischen Staats-Besteuerung 1808–1816*. Leipzig: Duncker und Humblot.
Mansfield, Edward D. and Jack Snyder (1995), 'Democratization and War'. *Foreign Affairs* 74(3): 79–97.

Marchadier, André (1904), *Les états généraux sous Charles VII*. Bordeaux: Cadoret.
Marchet, Gustav (1915), *Versorgung der Kriegs-invaliden und ihrer Hinterbliebenen*. Warnsdorf: Strache.
Mariot, Nicolas (2013), *Tous unis dans la tranchée? 1914–1918, les intellectuels recontrent le peuple*. Paris: Seuil.
Markowitz, Lawrence P. (2013), *State Erosion. Unlootable Resources and Unruly Elites in Central Asia*. Ithaca: Cornell University Press.
Marshall, T.H. (1992 [1950]), *Citizenship and Social Class*, introduced by Tom Bottomore. London: Pluto.
Martin, Jean-Clément (2006), *Violence et Révolution. Essai sur la naissance d'un mythe national*. Paris: Seuil.
Martin, Perry Alvin (1933), 'Slavery and Abolition in Brazil'. *The Hispanic American Historical Review* 13(2): 151–196.
Marwitz, Ulrich (1984), *Staatsräson und Landesdefension. Untersuchungen zum Kriegswesen des Herzogtums Preußen 1640–1655*. Boppard am Rhein: Harald Boldt.
Marx, Karl and Friedrich Engels (1962[1848]), 'Manifest der Kommunistischen Partei' in Karl Marx and Friedrich Engels (eds.), *Werke*. Berlin: Dietz, vol. IV, pp. 459–493.
Mathiez, Albert (1937), 'Le gouvernement révolutionnaire'. *Annales historiques de la Révolution française* 80: 97–126.
Mauclair, Fabrice (2008), *La justice au village. Justice seigneuriale et société rurale dans le duché-pairie de la Vallière (1667–1790)*. Rennes: Presses universitaires de Rennes.
Maya, Margarita López (2014), 'Venezuela: The Political Crisis of Post-Chavismo'. *Social Justice* 40(4): 68–87.
McCann, Frank D. (2004), *Soldiers of the Pátria. A History of the Brazilian Army, 1889–1937*. Stanford, CA: Stanford University Press.
McCoy, Donald R. and Richard T. Ruetten (1973), *Quest and Response. Minority Rights and the Truman Administration*. Lawrence: University Press of Kansas.
McEwen, Nicola (2002), 'State Welfare Nationalism: The Territorial Impact of Welfare State Development in Scotland'. *Regional & Federal Studies* 12(1): 66–90.
Mesa-Lago, Carmelo (1978), *Social Security in Latin America. Pressure Groups, Stratification and Inequality*. University of Pittsburgh Press.
Messerschmidt, Manfred (1980), 'Preußens Militär in seinem gesellschaftlichen Umfeld'. *Geschichte und Gesellschaft, Sonderheft* 6: 43–88.
Mestre, Jean-Louis (1976), *Un droit administratif à la fin de l'ancien régime. Le contentieux des communautés de Provence*. Paris: Librairie générale de droit et de jurisprudence.
Mestre, Jean-Louis (1999), 'Le traitement du contentieux administratif au XVIIIe siècle'. *La Revue administratif* 52(3): 83–97.

Mettler, Suzanne (2005), 'The Creation of the G.I. Bill of Rights of 1944: Melding Social and Participatory Citizenship Ideas'. *The Journal of Policy History* 17(4): 345-374.
Meyer, Jean (1983), *Le poids de l'état*. Paris: PUF.
Meyer, John W. (1977), 'The Effects of Education as an Institution'. *American Journal of Sociology* 83(1): 55-77.
Meyer, John (1980), 'The World Polity and the Authority of the Nation-State' in Albert Bergesen (ed.), *Studies of the Modern World-System*. New York: Academic Press, pp. 109-137.
Meyer, John W., John Boli, George M. Thomas and Francisco Ramirez (1997), 'World Society and the Nation-State'. *American Journal of Sociology* 103(1): 144-181.
Meyer, John W., Francisco O. Ramirez, Richard Rubinson and John Boli-Bennett (1977), 'The World Educational Revolution'. *Sociology of Education* 50(4): 242-258.
Meyer, John W. and Richard Rubinson (1975), 'Education and Political Development'. *Review of Research in Education* 3: 134-162.
Meznar, Joan E. (1992), 'The Ranks of the Poor: Military Service and Social Differentiation in Northeast Brazil, 1830-1875'. *The Hispanic American Historical Review* 72(3): 335-351.
Michon, Georges (1920), 'Robespierre et la Guerre'. *Annales révolutionnaires* 12 (4): 265-311.
Michon, Georges (1935), *La preparation à la guerre. La loi de trois ans (1910-1914)*. Paris: Marcel Rivière.
Milot, Jean (1968), 'Evolution du corps des intendants militaires (des origines à 1882)'. *Revue du Nord* 50: 381-410.
Mitchell, Allan (1984), *Victors and Vanquished. The German Influence on Army and Church in France after 1870*. Chapel Hill: The University of North Carolina Press.
Möller, Hans-Michael (1976), *Das Regiment der Landesknechte. Untersuchungen zu Verfassung, Recht und Selbstverständnis in Deutschen Söldnerheeren des 16. Jahrhunderts*. Wiesbaden: Franz Steiner.
Möller, Kolja (2017), 'Invocatio Populi. Autoritärer und demokratischer Populismus'. *Leviathan*, Sonderband 34: 246-267.
Monaghan, Henry P. (1983), 'Marbury and the Administrative State'. *Columbia Law Review* 83(1): 1-34.
Monteilhet, Joseph (1926), *Les institutions militaires de la France (1814-1924). De l'armée permanente à la nation armée*. Paris: Alcan.
Morley, Morris H. (1987), *Imperial State and Revolution. The United States and Cuba, 1952-1986*. Cambridge University Press.
Mooser, Josef (1983), 'Auflösung der proletarischen Milieus: Klassenbindung und Individualisierung in der Arbeiterschaft vom Kaiserreich bis in die Bundesrepublik Deutschland'. *Soziale Welt* 34(3): 270-306.

Moskos, Charles C. (1966), 'Racial Integration in the Armed Forces'. *American Journal of Sociology* 72(2): 132-148.
Moskos, Charles C. and John Sibley Butler (1996), *All that We Can Be. Black Leadership and Racial Integration in the Army*. New York: Basic Books.
Martins, Paulo Emílio Matos, Leandro Souza Moura and Takeyoshi Imasato (2011), 'Coronelismo: um referente anacrônico no espaço organizacional brasileiro contemporâneo?' *Organizações & sociedade* 18(58): 389-402.
Mousnier, Roland (1979), 'La fonction publique en France du début du siezième siècle à la fin du dix-huitième siècle'. *Revue Historique* 261(2): 321-335.
Mudde, Cas (2002), *The Ideology of The Extreme Right*. Manchester University Press.
Muis, Jasper and Tim Immerzeel (2017), 'Causes and Consequences of the Rise of Populist Radical Right Parties and Movements in Europe'. *Current Sociology Review* 65(6): 909-930.
Müller, George Friedrich (1760), *Koniglich-Preußisches Krieges-Recht*. Berlin: Verlag der Haude- und Spenerschen Buchhandlung.
Müller, Jan-Werner (2017), *What is Populism?* London: Penguin.
Müller, Sabrina (1999), *Soldaten in der deutschen Revolution von 1848/49*. Paderborn: Schöningh.
Murphy, Paul L. (1979), *World War I and the Origin of Civil Liberties in the United States*. New York: Norton.
Myrdal, Gunnar (1960), *Beyond the Welfare State. Economic Planning in the Welfare States and its International Implications*. London: Duckworth.
Neugebauer, Wolfgang (2003), 'Staat-Krieg-Korporation. Zur Genese politischer Strukturen im 17. und 18. Jahrhundert'. *Historisches Jahrbuch* 123: 197-233.
Newman, John Paul (2015), *Yugoslavia in the Shadow of War. Veterans and the Limits of State-Building, 1903-1945*. Cambridge University Press.
Newton, Scott (2015), *Law and the Making of the Soviet World*. Abingdon: Routledge.
Nieuwbeerta, Paul (1996), 'The Democratic Class Struggle in Postwar Societies: Class Voting in Twenty Countries, 1945-1990'. *Acta Sociologica* 39: 345-383.
Norberg, Kathryn (1994), 'The French Fiscal Crisis of 1788 and the Financial Origins of the French Revolution of 1789' in Philip T. Hoffmann and Kathryn Norberg (eds.), *Fiscal Crises, Liberty and Representative Government*. Stanford University Press, pp. 252-298.
Norris, Pippa and Ronald Inglehart (2019), *Cultural Backlash. Trump, Brexit and Authoritarian Populism*. Cambridge University Press.
Northrop, Douglas (2004), *Veiled Empire. Gender and Power in Stalinist Central Asia*. Ithaca: Cornell University Press.

Nowosadtko, Jutta (2011), *Stehendes Heer im Ständestaat. Das Zusammenleben von Militär- und Zivilbevölkerung im Fürstentum Münster 1650-1803*. Paderborn: Schöningh.

Obinger, Herbert and Carina Schmitt (2011), 'Guns and Butter? Regime Competition and the Welfare State during the Cold War'. *World Politics* 63 (2): 246-270.

Obinger, Herbert and Carina Schmitt (2018), 'The Impact of the Second World War on Postwar Social Spending'. *European Journal of Political Research* 57: 496-517.

O'Callaghan, Joseph F. (1989), *The Cortes of Castile Leon 1188-1350*. Philadelphia: University of Pennsylvania Press.

Offe, Claus (1972), *Strukturprobleme des kapitalistischen Staates*. Frankfurt am Main: Suhrkamp.

Orloff, Ana Shola (1993), *The Politics of Pensions. A Comparative Analysis of Britain, Canada and the United States 1880-1940*. Madison: University of Wisconsin Press.

Panizza, Francisco (2005), 'Introduction: Populism and the Mirror of Democracy' in Francisco Panizza (ed.), *Populism and the Mirror of Democracy*. London: Verso, pp. 1-31.

Papke, Gerhard (1979), *Von der Miliz zum stehenden Heer. Wehrwesen im Absolutismus*. Munich: Bernard & Graefe.

Pappas, Takis (2019), 'Populists in Power'. *Journal of Democracy* 30(2): 70-84.

Pappus, Petrus (1674), *Corpus juris militaris*. Frankfurt: Hermsdorff.

Paret, Peter (2009), *The Cognitive Challenge of War. Prussia 1806*. Princeton University Press.

Parker, Christopher S. (2009), *Fighting for Democracy. Black Veterans and the Struggle against White Supremacy in the Postwar South*. Princeton University Press.

Parrott, David (2001), *Richelieu's Army. War, Government and Society in France, 1624-1642*. Cambridge University Press.

Parrott, David (2012), *The Business of War. Military Enterprise and Military Revolution in Early Modern Europe*. Cambridge University Press.

Parsons, Talcott (1965), 'Full Citizenship for the Negro American? A Sociological Problem'. *Daedalus* 94(4): 1009-1054.

Patterson, James T. (1986), *America's Struggle against Poverty 1900-1985*. Cambridge, MA: Harvard University Press.

Pawlowsky, Verena and Harald Wendelin (2015), *Die Wunden des Staates: Kriegsopfer und Sozialstaat in Österreich 1914-1938*. Cologne: Böhlau.

Perrin, Guy (1969), 'Reflections on Fifty Years of Social Security'. *International Labour Review* 99(3): 249-292.

Peters, Anne (2014), *Jenseits der Menschenrechte. Die Rechtsstellung des Individuums im Völkerrecht*. Tübingen: Mohr.

Peterson, Klaus (2013), 'The Early Cold War and the Western Welfare State'. *Journal of International and Comparative Social Policy* 29(3): 226–240.

Pierson, Thomas (2016), *Das Gesinde und die Herausbildung moderner Privatrechtsprinzipien*. Frankfurt am Main: Klostermann.

Pietri, François (1955), *Napoléon et le parlement, ou la dictature enchainée*. Paris: Fayard.

Pigeon, Jérôme (2011), *L'intendant de Rouen juge du contentieux au XVIII siècle*. Rouen: Publications des universités de Rouen.

Pinelli, Cesare (2011), 'The Populist Challenge to Constitutional Democracy'. *European Constitutional Law Review* 7(1): 5–16.

Pironti, Pierluigi (2015), *Kriegsopfer und Staat. Sozialpolitik für Invaliden, Witwen und Waisen des Ersten Weltkriegs in Deutschland und Italien (1914–1924)*. Cologne: Böhlau.

Piven, Francis Fox and Richard Cloward (1993), *Regulating the Poor. The Functions of Public Welfare*, revised edition. New York: Vintage.

Plaggenborg, Stefan (1996), 'Gewalt und Militanz in Sowjetrußland 1917–1930'. *Jahrbücher für Geschichte Osteuropas* 44(3): 409–430.

Planert, Ute (2007), *Der Mythos vom Befreiungskrieg. Frankreichs Kriege und der deutsche Süden. Alltag – Wahrnehmung – Deutung. 1792–1841*. Paderborn: Schöningh.

Planert, Ute and Ewald Frie (2016), 'Revolution, Krieg, Nation – ein universelles Muster der Staatsbildung in der Moderne?' in Ewald Frie and Ute Planert (eds.), *Revolution, Krieg und die Geburt von Staat und Nation*. Tübingen: Mohr Siebeck, pp. 1–20.

Poppitz, Johannes (1943), 'Die Anfänge der Verwaltungsgerichtsbarkeit'. *Archiv des öffentlichen Rechts* 72(2/3): 158–221.

Poßelt, Stephanie (2013), *Die Grande Armée in Deutschland 1805 bis 1814. Wahrnehmungen und Erfahrungen von Militärpersonen nd Zivilbevölkerung*. Frankfurt am Main: Lang.

Powicke, Michael (1962), *Military Obligation in Medieval England. A Study in Liberty and Duty*. Oxford: Clarendon.

Pravilova, Ekaterina (2014), *A Public Empire. Property and the Quest for the Common Good in Imperial Russia*. Princeton University Press.

Preller, Ludwig (1949), *Sozialpolitik in der Weimarer Republik*. Kronberg: Athenäum.

Pribble, Jennifer (2013), *Welfare and Party Politics in Latin America*. Cambridge University Press.

Pröve, Ralf (1995a), *Stehendes Heer und städtische Gesellschaft im 18. Jahrhundert. Göttingen und seine Militärbevölkerung 1713–1756*. Munich: Oldenbourg.

Pröve, Ralf (1995b), 'Zum Verhältnis von Militär und Gesellschaft im Spiegel gewaltsamer Rekrutierungen (1648–1789)'. *Zeitschrift für Historische Forschung* 22(2): 191–223.

Pröve, Ralf (2000), *Stadtgemeindlicher Republikanismus und die 'Macht des Volkes'. Civile Ordnungsformationen und kommunale Leitbilder politischer Partizipation in den deutschen Staaten vom Ende des 18. bis zur Mitte des 19. Jahrhunderts*. Göttingen: Vandenhoeck & Ruprecht.

Pröve, Ralf (2016), 'Systematische Herrschaftskonkurrenz durch Instanzenzüge und Patronatsbeziehungen. Probleme im Verwaltungshandeln des 18. Jahrhunderts' in Jutta Nowosadtko, Diethelm Klippel and Kai Lohstäter (eds.), *Militär und Recht vom 16. bis 19. Jahrhundert. Gelehrter Diskurs – Praxis – Transformation*. Göttingen: V & R unipress, pp. 251–268.

Quarles, Benjamin (1961), *The Negro in the American Revolution*. Chapel Hill: University of North Carolina Press.

Rabinowitch, Alexander (2007), *The Bolsheviks in Power. The First Year of Soviet Rule in Petrograd*. Bloomington: Indiana University Press.

Ralston, David B. (1967), *The Army of the Republic. The Place of the Military in the Political Evolution of France, 1871–1914*. Cambridge, MA: MIT Press.

Ramirez, Francisco O. and Marc J. Ventresca (1992), 'Building the Institution of Mass Education: Isomorphism in the Modern World' in Bruce Fuller and Richard Rubinson (eds.), *The Political Construction of Education. The State, School Expansion and Economic Change*. New York: Praeger, pp. 47–59.

Rassow, Peter (1943), 'Die Wirkung der Erhebung Spaniens auf die deutsche Erhebung gegen Napoleon I'. *Historische Zeitschrift* 167(2): 310–335.

Reber, Vera Blinn (1999), 'A Case of Total War: Paraguay, 1864–1870'. *Journal of Iberian and Latin American Research* 5(1): 15–40.

Reed, Merl E. (1991), *Seedtime for the Modern Civil Rights Movement. The President's Committee on Fair Employment Practice 1941–1946*. Baton Rouge: Louisiana State University Press.

Redlich, Fritz (1956), *De Praeda Militari. Looting and Booty 1500–1815*. Wiesbaden: Steiner.

Redlich, Fritz (1964a), *The German Military Enterpriser and his Work Force. A Study in European Economic and Social Policy*. Wiesbaden: Franz Steiner, vol. I.

Redlich, Fritz (1964b), *The German Military Enterpriser and his Work Force. A Study in European Economic and Social Policy*. Wiesbaden: Franz Steiner, vol. II.

Reichardt, Sven (2002), *Faschistische Kampfbünde. Gewalt und Gemeinschaft im italienischen Squadrismus und in der deutschen SA*. Cologne: Böhlau.

Reidegeld, Eckart (1989), 'Krieg und staatliche Sozialpolitik'. *Leviathan* 17(4): 479–526.

Reinhard, Wolfgang (1996), 'Kriegsstaat – Steuerstaat – Machtstaat' in Roland G. Asch and Heinz Duchhardt (eds.), *Der Absolutismus – ein Mythos? Strukturwandel monarchischer Herrschaft in West- und Mitteleuropa (ca.1550–1700)*. Cologne: Böhlau, pp. 277–310.

Renouvin, Pierre (1925), *Les formes du gouvernment de guerre*. Paris: PUF.
Retish, Aaron B. (2008), *Russia's Peasants in Revolution and Civil War. Citizenship, Identity, and the Creation of the Soviet State, 1914–1922*. Cambridge University Press.
Rimlinger, Gaston (1971), *Welfare Policy and Industrialization in Eurupe, America and Russia*. New York: Wiley.
Rink, Martin (1999), *Vom 'Partheygänger' zum Partisanen. Die Konzeption des kleinen Krieges in Preußen 1740–1813*. Frankfurt am Main: Lang.
Rink, Martin (2000), 'Partisanen und Landvolk 1730 bis 1830. Eine militär- und sozialgeschichtliche Beziehung zwischen Schrecken und Schutz, zwischen Kampf und Kollaboration'. *Militärgeschichtliche Zeitschrift* 59: 23–59.
Rink, Martin (2010), 'Preußisch-deutsche Konzeptionen zum "Volkskrieg" im Zeitalter Napoleons' in Karl-Heinz Lutz, Martin Rink and Marcus von Salisch (eds.), *Reform-Reorganisation-Transformation. Zum Wandel in deutschen Streitkräften von der preußischen Heeresreform bis zur Transformation der Bundeswehr*. Munich: Oldenbourg, pp. 65–87.
Ritter, Gerhard (1965), *Staatskunst und Kriegshandwerk. Das Problem des Militarismus in Deutschland, I: Die altpreußische Tradition (1740–1890)*, 3rd edition. Munich: Oldenbourg.
Ritter, Gerhard A. (1991), *Der Sozialstaat. Entstehung und Entwicklung im internationalen Vergleich*. Second edition. Munich: Oldenbourg.
Roberts, Robert (1971), *The Classic Slum. Salford Life in the First Quarter of the Century*. London: Penguin.
Robespierre, Maximilien (1792a), *Discours sur la guerre*. Paris
Robespierre, Maximilien (1792b), *Le Défenseur de la Constitution*. Paris.
Robespierre, Maximilien (1954), *Œuvres complètes*, i 11 vols. Paris: PUF, vol. VIII.
Root, Hilton L. (1987), *Peasants and King in Burgundy. Agrarian Foundations of French Absolutism*. Berkeley: University of California Press.
Rose, Jonathan (2001), *The Intellectual Life of the British Working Classes*. New Haven: Yale University Press.
Rosenberg, Jonathan (2006), *How Far the Promised Land? World Affairs and the American Civil Rights Movement from the First World War to Vietnam*. Princeton University Press.
Rosenfeld, Michel (1995), 'The Identity of the Constitutional Subject'. *Cardozo Law Review* 16(3–4): 1049–1110.
Ross, George (1982), *Workers and Communists in France. From Popular Front to Eurocommunism*. Berkeley: University of California Press.
Ross, William G. (2017), *World War I and the American Constitution*. Cambridge University Press.
Rothstein, Bo (1998), *Just Institutions Matter. The Moral and Political Logic of the Universal Welfare State*. Cambridge University Press.

Rotteck, Carl von (1816), *Ueber stehende Heere und Nationalmiliz*. Freyburg: Herdersche Universitäts-Buchhandlung.
Rousseau, Jean-Jacques (1782), *Considérations sur le gouvernement de Pologne*. Paris: Cazin.
Rovinello, Marco (2013), 'The Draft and Draftees in Italy, 1861–1914' in Erik-Jan Zürcher (ed.), *Fighting for a Living. A Comparative Study of Military Labour 1500–2000*. Amsterdam University Press, pp. 479–517.
Rowlands, Guy (2002), *The Dynastic State and the Army under Louis XIV. Royal Service and Private Interests, 1671–1701*. Cambridge University Press.
Ruparelia, Sanjay (2013), 'India's New Rights Agenda: Genesis, Promises, Risks'. *Pacific Affairs* 86(3): 569–590.
Ruparelia, Sanjay (2015), 'Minimum Government, Maximum Governance: The Restructuring of Power in Modi's India'. *South Asia: Journal of South Asian Studies* 38(4): 755–775.
Russett, Bruce M. (1970), *What Price Vigilance? The Burdens of National Defense*. New Haven: Yale University Press.
Sachße, Christoph and Florian Tennstedt (1988), *Geschichte der Armenfürsorge in Deutschland, 2: Fürsorge und Wohlfahrtspflege 1871–1929*. Stuttgart: Kohlhammer.
Sadurski, Wojciech (2019), 'Polish Constitutional Tribunal under PiS: From an Activist Court, to a Paralysed Tribunal, to a Governmental Enabler'. *Hague Journal on the Rule of Law* 11:63–84.
Sahm, Rainer (2019), *Theorie und Ideengeschichte der Steuergerechtigkeit*. Berlin: Springer.
Saint-Jacob, Pierre de (1960), *Les paysans de la Bourgogne du Nord au dernier siècle de l'Ancien Régime*. Paris: Société les Belles Lettres.
Sakwa, Richard (1988), *Soviet Communists in Power. A Study of Moscow during the Civil War, 1918–21*. Basingstoke: Macmillan.
Sales de Bohigas, Nuria (1970), 'Esclavos y Reclutas en Sudamerica, 1816–1826'. *Revista de Historia de América* 70: 279–337.
Salles, Ricardo (1990), *Guerra do Paraguai: escravidão e cidadania na formaçao do exéercito*. Rio de Janeiro: Paz e Terra.
Sanborn, Joshua A. (2003), *Drafting the Russian Nation. Military Conscription, Total War, 1905–1925*. Dekalb: Northern Illinois University Press.
Sanborn, Joshua A. (2005), 'Unsettling the Empire: Violent Migrations and Social Disaster in Russia During World War I'. *The Journal of Modern History* 77(2): 290–324.
Sanborn, Joshua A. (2014), *Imperial Apocalypse. The Great War and the Destruction of the Russian Empire*. Oxford University Press.
Sanders, Sara Katherine (2013), 'The Mexican Student Movement of 1968' in Jessica Stiles Mor (ed.), *Human Rights and Transnational Solidarity in Cold War Latin America*. Madison: University of Wisconsin Press, pp. 73–98.

Saull, Richard (2001), *Rethinking Theory and History in the Cold War. The State, Military Power and Social Revolution*. London: Cass.

Schaffer, Ronald (1991), *America in the Great War. The Rise of the War Welfare State*. New York: Oxford University Press.

Schissler, Hanna (1982), 'Preußische Finanzpolitik nach 1807. Die Bedeutung der Staatsverschuldung als Faktor der Modernisierung des preußischen Finanzsystems'. *Geschichte und Gesellschaft* 8(3): 367–385.

Schmidt, Christoph (1997), *Leibeigenschaft im Ostseeraum. Versuch einer Typologie*. Cologne: Böhlau.

Schmidt, Eberhard (1980), *Beiträge zur Geschichte des preußischen Rechtstaates*. Berlin: Duncker und Humblot.

Schmidt, Hans (1996), 'Militärverwaltung in Deutschland und Frankreich im 17. und 18. Jahrhundert' in Bernhard R. Kroener and Ralf Pröve (eds.), *Krieg und Frieden. Militär und Gesellschaft in der Frühen Neuzeit*. Paderborn: Schöningh, pp. 25–46.

Schmidt, Peer (2003), 'Der Guerrillero. Die Entstehung des Partisanen in der Sattelzeit: Eine atlantische Perspektive 1776–1848'. *Geschichte und Gesellschaft* 29(2): 161–190.

Schmitt, Bernhard (2007), *Armee und staatliche Integration. Preußen und die Habsburgermonarchie 1815–1866. Rekrutierungspolitik in den neuen Provinzen: Staatliches Handeln und Bevölkerung*. Paderborn: Schöningh.

Schmitt, Carl (1928), *Verfassungslehre*. Berlin: Duncker und Humblot.

Schmitt, Carl (1932), *Der Begriff des Politischen*. Berlin: Duncker und Humblot.

Schmitt, Carl (1950), *Der Nomos der Erde im Völkerrecht des Jus Publicum Europaeum*. Berlin: Duncker und Humblot.

Schmitt, Carl (2017), *Theorie des Partisanen. Zwischenbemerkung zum Begriff des Politischen*. Berlin: Duncker und Humblot.

Schmoller, Gustav (1921), *Preußische Verfassungs-, Verwaltungs- und Finanzgeschichte*. Berlin: Verlag der Täglichen Rundschau.

Schotte, Walther (1911), *Fürstentum und Stände in der Mark Brandenburg unter der Regierung Joachims I*. Leipzig: Duncker und Humlot.

Schrimpf, Heinrich (1979), 'Die Auseinandersetzung um die Neuordnung des individuellen Rechtsschutzes gegenüber der staatlichen Verwaltung nach 1807'. *Der Staat* 18(1): 59–80.

Schumacher, Gijs and Kees van Kersbergen (2014), 'Do Mainstream Parties Adapt to the Welfare Chauvinism of Populist Parties?' *Party Politics* 22(3): 300–312.

Schumann, Dirk (2001), *Politische Gewalt in der Weimarer Republik 1918–1933. Kampf um die Straße und Furcht vor dem Bürgerkrieg*. Essen: Klartext.

Schwartz, Stuart B. (1985), *Sugar Plantations in the Formation of Brazilian Society. Bahia, 1550–1835*. Cambridge University Press.

Schwennicke, Andreas (1996), *'Ohne Steuer kein Staat'. Zur Entwicklung und politischen Funktion des Steuerrechts in den Territorien des Heiligen Römischen Reichs (1500–1800)*. Frankfurt am Main: Klostermann.
Sczaniecki, Michel (1946), *Essai sur les fiefs-rentes*. Paris: Sirey.
Segal, David R. (1989), *Recruiting for Uncle Sam. Citizenship and Military Manpower Policy*. Kansas: University of Kansas Press.
Segura-Ubiergo, Alex (2007), *The Political Economy of the Welfare State in Latin America*. Cambridge University Press.
Sellin, J. Thorsten (1976), *Slavery and the Penal System*. New York: Elsevier.
Sellin, Volker (2010), *Gewalt und Legitimität. Die europäische Monarchie im Zeitalter der Revolutionen*. Munich: Oldenbourg.
Seymour, Michel (1999), 'Présentation' in Michel Seymour (ed.), *Nationalité, Citoyenneté et solidarité*. Montréal: Liber.
de Seyssel, Claude (1961) *La monarchie de France*. Paris: D'Argences.
Shehaj, Albana Adrian J Shin, Ronald Inglehart (2019), 'Immigration and Right-Wing Populism: An Origin Story'. *Party Politics*. Online First: 1–12.
Sheffield, G.D. (2000), *Leadership in the Trenches. Officer-Men Relations, Morale and Discipline in the British Army in the Era of the First World War*. Basingstoke: Macmillan.
Sherry, Michael S. (1995), *In the Shadow of War. The United States since the 1930s*. New Haven: Yale University Press.
Shklar, Judith N. (1991), *American Citizenship. The Quest for Inclusion*. Cambridge, MA: Harvard University Press.
Sieyès, Emmanuel-Joseph (1789), *Qu'est-ce que le Tiers-Etat?*, second edition. Paris.
Sikora, Michael (1996), *Disziplin und Desertion. Strukturprobleme militärischer Organisation im 18. Jahrhundert*. Berlin: Duncker und Humblot.
Sikora, Michael (2003), 'Söldner: historische Annäherung an einen Kriegertypus'. *Geschichte und Gesellschaft* 29(2): 210–238.
Silver, Beverly J. (2003), *Forces of Labor. Workers' Movements and Globalization since 1870*. Cambridge University Press.
Simkins, Peter (1988), *Kitchener's Army. The Raising of the New Armies, 1914–16*. Manchester University Press.
Sinclair, Alexandra and Joe Tomlinson (2019), 'Deleting the Administrative State?'. *UK Constitutional Law Blog*. At https://ukconstitutionallaw.org/
Sitkoff, Harvard (1971), 'Racial Militancy and Interracial Violence in the Second World War'. *The Journal of American History* 58(3): 661–681.
Skidmore, Thomas E. (1988), *The Politics of Military Rule in Brazil 1964–85*. Oxford University Press.
Skocpol, Theda (1988), 'Social Revolutions and Mass Military Mobilization'. *World Politics* 40(2): 147–168.
Skocpol, Theda (1992), *Protecting Soldiers and Mothers. The Political Origins of Social Policy in the United States*. Cambridge, MA: Harvard University Press.

Skocpol, Theda (1993), 'America's First Social Security System: The Expansion of Benefits for Civil War Veterans'. *Political Science Quarterly* 108(1): 85-116.

Skocpol, Theda and Edwin Amenta (1986), 'States and Social Policies'. *Annual Review of Sociology* 12: 131-157.

Skrentny, John D. (2002), *The Minority Rights Revolution*. Cambridge, MA: Harvard University Press.

Slotkin, Richard (2005), *Lost Battalions. The Great War and the Crisis of American Nationality*. New York: Henry Holt.

Smele, Jonathan D. (2015), *The 'Russian' Civil Wars 1916-1926. Ten Years that Shook the Wold*. London: Hurst.

Smith, Timothy B. (2003), *Creating the Welfare State in France, 1880-1940*. Montreal: McGill-Queen's University Press.

Soboul, Albert (1959), *Les Soldats de l'an II*. Paris: Le Club français du livre.

Soboul, Albert (1968), 'Survivances "féodales" dans la société rurale française au XIXe siècle'. *Annales. Histoire, Sciences Sociales* 5: 965-986.

Soifer, Hillel David (2015), *State Building in Latin America*. Cambridge University Press.

Sonenscher, Michael (1997), 'The Nation's Debt and the Birth of the Modern Republic: The French Fiscal Deficit and the Politics of the Revolution: Part 1'. *History of Political Thought* 18(1): 64-103.

Sparrow, James T. (2011), *Warfare State. World War II, Americans and the Age of Big Government*. Oxford University Press.

Speitkamp, Winfried (2015), 'Gewaltgemeinschaften in der Geschichte. Eine Einleitung' in Winfried Speitkamp (ed.), *Gewaltgemeinchaften in der Geschichte. Entstehung, Kohäsionskraft und Zerfall*. Göttingen: Vandenhoeck & Ruprecht, pp. 11-40.

Spreen, Dierk (2008), *Krieg und Gesellschaft. Die Konstitutionsfunktion des Krieges für moderne Gesellschaften*. Berlin: Duncker und Humblot.

Spruyt, Bram, Gil Keppens, and Filip Van Droogenbroeck (2016), 'Who Supports Populism and What Attracts People to It?'. *Political Research Quarterly* 69(2): 335-346.

Starr, Paul (1982), *The Social Transformation of American Medicine. The Rise of a Sovereign Profession and the Making of a Vast Industry*. New York: Basic Books.

Steinfeld, Robert J. (1999), 'Changing Legal Conceptions of Free Labor' in Stanley L. Engerman (ed.), *Terms of Labor. Slavery, Serfdom and Free Labor*. Stanford University Press, pp. 137-167.

Steinfeld, Robert J. (2001), *Coercion, Contract and Free Labor in the Nineteenth Century*. Cambridge University Press.

Stepan, Alfred (1971), *The Military in Politics. Changing Patterns in Brazil*. Princeton University Press.

Stichweh, Rudolf (2000), *Die Weltgesellschaft. Soziologische Analysen*. Frankfirt am Main: Suhrkamp.

Streeck, Wolfgang (2005), 'The Sociology of Labor Markets and Trade Unions' in Neil J. Smelser and Richard Swedberg (eds.), *The Handbook of Economic Sociology*. Princeton University Press, pp. 254–283.

Streeck, Wolfgang and Anke Hassel (2003), 'Trade Unions as Political Actors' in John T. Addison and Claus Schnabel (eds.), *Handbook of Trade Unions*. Cheltenham: Edward Elgar, pp. 335–365.

Stübig, Heinz (1971), *Armee und Nation. Die pädagogisch-politischen Motive der preußischen Heeresreform 1807–1814*. Frankfurt am Main: Peter Lang.

Suri, Jeremi (2005), *Power and Protest. Global Revolution and the Rise of Détente*. Cambridge, MA: Harvard University Press.

Svarez, Carl Gottlieb (2000), *Gesammelte Schriften* edited by Peter Krause in 6 vols. Stuttgart: frommann-holzboog, vol. IV/I.

Swank, Duane (1983), 'Between Incrementalism and Revolution: Group Protest and the Growth of the Welfare State'. *American Behavioral Scientist* (26): 291–310.

Swank, Duane and Hans-Georg Betz (2003), 'Globalization, the Welfare State and Right-Wing Populism in Western Europe'. *Socio-Economic Review* 1: 215–245.

Szlanta, Piotr (2006), 'Der Erste Weltkrieg von 1914 bis 1915 als identitätsstiftender Faktor für die moderne polnische Nation' in Gerhard P. Groß (ed.), *Die vergessene Front. Der Osten 1914/15. Ereignis, Wirkung, Nachwirkung*. Paderborn: Schöningh, pp. 153–164.

Taithe, Bertrand (2001), *Citizenship and Wars. France in Turmoil*. London: Routledge.

Tani, Karen M. (2016), *States of Dependency. Welfare, Rights, and American Governance, 1935–1972*. Cambridge University Press.

Tännsjö, Torbjörn (1992), *Populist Democracy. A Defence*. London: Routledge.

Tarrow, Sidney (2015), *War, States, and Contention. A Comparative Historical Study*. Ithaca: Cornell University Press.

Teubner, Gunther (1997), 'Global Bukowina: Legal Pluralism in the World Society' in Gunther Teubner (ed.), *Global Law without a State*. Dartmouth, Aldershot, pp. 3–28.

Therbon, Göran (1984), 'Classes and States. Welfare State Developments 1881–1981'. *Studies in Political Economy* 14(1): 7–41.

Thiele, Andrea (2014), 'The Prince as Military Entrepreneur? Why Smaller Saxon Territories sent "Holländische Regimenter" (Dutch Regiments) to the Dutch Republic' in Jeff Fynn-Paul (ed.), *War, Entrepreneurs, and the State in Europe and the Mediterranean 1310–1800*. Leiden: Brill, pp. 170–192.

Thomas, Daniel C. (2001), *The Helsinki Effect. International Norms, Human Rights, and the Demise of Communism*. Princeton University Press.

Thomas, George M. and Jon W. Meyer (1984), 'The Expansion of the State'. *Annual Review of Sociology* 10: 461–482.

Thomasius, Christian (1699), *Entwurf der Grundlehren, die einem studioso iuris zu wissen und auf Universitäten zu lernen nötig sind*. Halle: Renger.

Thornhill, Chris (2018), *The Sociology of Law and the Global Transformation of Democracy*. Cambridge University Press.
Thorpe, Rebecca U. (2014), *The American Warfare State. The Domestic Politics of Military Spending*. Chicago University Press.
Tilly, Charles (1964), *The Vendée*. London: Arnold.
Tilly, Charles (1999), 'Where Do Rights Come From?' in Theda Skocpol (ed.), *Democracy, Revolution, and History*. Ithaca: Cornell University Press, pp. 55–72.
Tombs, Robert (1981), *The War against Paris 1871*. Cambridge University Press.
Toplin, Robert Brent (1969), 'Upheaval, Violence, and the Abolition of Slavery in Brazil: The Case of Sao Paulo'. *The Hispanic American Historical Review* 49(4): 639–655.
Torres, João Camilo de Oliveira (2018 [1943]), *O positivismo no Brasil*. Brasilia: Edições Câmara.
Trägårdh, Lars (1990), 'Swedish Model or Swedish Culture'. *Critical Review* 4(4): 569–590.
Trox, Eckhard (1990), *Militärischer Konservatismus. Kriegervereine und 'Militärpartei' in Preußen zwischen 1815 und 1848/49*. Stuttgart: Franz Steiner.
Tsutsui, Kiyoteru and Christine Min Wotipka (2004), 'Global Civil Society and the International Human Rights Movement: Citizen Participation in Human Rights International Nongovernmental Organizations'. *Social Forces* 83(2):587–620.
Tushnet, Mark (1999), *Taking the Constitution Away from the Courts*. Princeton University Press.
Tushnet, Mark (2015), 'Authoritarian Constitutionalism'. *Cornell Law Review* 100: 391–462.
Urbinati, Nadia (2019), *Me the People. How Populism Transforms Democracy*. Cambridge, MA: Harvard University Press.
Van den Heuvel (1982), *Grundprobleme der französischen Bauernschaft 1730–1794*. Munich: Oldenbourg.
Vattel, Emer de (1758), *Le droit des gens ou principes de la loi naturelle*, vol. I. Leiden: Aux depans de la compagnie.
Vidra, Zsuzsanna (2018), 'Hungary's Punitive Turn'. *Communist and Post-Communist Studies* 51(1): 73–80.
Vocke, Wilhelm (1903), 'Indirekte Steuern'. *FinanzArchiv* 20(2): 1–25.
Voelz, Peter M. (1993), *Slave and Soldier. The Military Impact of Blacks in the Colonial Americas*. New York: Garland.
Vogel, Barbara (1981), 'Staatsfinanzen und Gesellschaftsreform in Preußen' in Helmut Berding (ed.), *Privatkapital, Staatsfinanzen und Reformpolitik in Deutschland der napoleonischen Zeit*. Ostfildern: Scripta Mercaturae Verlag, pp. 35–57.
Voigt, Carsten (2009), *Kampfbünde der Arbeiterbewegung. Das Reichsbanner Schwarz-Rot-Gold und der Rote Frontkämpferbund in Sachsen 1924–1933*. Cologne: Böhlau.

Volkmann, Heinrich (1978), 'Modernisiering des Arbeitskampfes? Zum Formwandel von Streik und Aussperrung in Deutschland 1864-1975' in Hartmut Kaelble (ed.), *Probleme der Modernisierung in Deutschland. Sozialhistorische Studien zum 19. und 20. Jahrhundert.* Wiesbaden: Westdeutscher Verlag, pp. 110-170.

Vollert, Michael P. (2014), *Für Ruhe und Ordnung. Einsätze des Militärs im Innern (1820-1918). Preußen-Westfalen-Rheinprovinz.* Bonn: Dietz.

Voltelini, Hans von (1910), 'Die naturrechtlichen Lehren und die Reformen des 18. Jahrhunderts'. *Historische Zeitschrift* 105(1): 65-104.

Von Mises, Ludwig (1902), *Die Entwicklung des gutsherrlich-bäuerlichen Verhältnisses in Galizien (1772-1848).* Vienne: Deuticke.

Vormbaum, Thomas (1980), *Politik und Gesinderecht im 19. Jahrhundert (vornehmlich in Preußen 1810-1918).* Berlin: Duncker und Humblot.

Wallerstein, Immanuel and Sharon Zukin (1989), '1968, Revolution in the World-System: Theses and Queries'. *Theory and Society* 18(4): 431-449.

Walter, Dierk (2003), *Preußische Heeresreformen 1807-1870. Militärische Innovationen und der Mythos der 'Roonschen Reform'.* Paderborn: Schöningh.

Warburg, Jens (2008), *Das Militär und seine Subjekte. Zur Soziologie des Krieges.* Bielefeld: transcript.

Watson, Alexander (2008), *Enduring the Great War. Combat, Morale and Collapse in the German and British Armies, 1914-1918.* Cambridge University Press.

Wawro, Geoffrey (2003), *The Franco-Prussian War. The German Conquest of France in 1870-1871.* Cambridge University Press.

Weakliem, David L. and Anthony F. Heath (1999), 'The Secret Life of Class Voting: Britain, France, and the United States' in Geoffrey Evans (ed.), *The End of Class Politics? Class Voting in Twenty Postwar Societes.* Oxford University Press, pp. 97-136.

Webber, Grégoire (2009), *The Negotiable Constitution. On the Limitation of Rights.* Cambridge University Press.

Weber, Eugene (1976), *Peasants into Frenchmen. The Modernization of Rural France, 1870-1914.* Stanford University Press.

Weber, Max (1921/22), *Wirtschaft und Gesellschaft. Grundriß der verstehenden Soziologie.* Tübingen: Mohr.

Weber, Petra (2010), *Gescheiterte Sozialpartnerschaft - Gefährdete Republik? Industrielle Beziehungen, Arbeitskämpfe und der Sozialstaat. Deutschland und Frankreich im Vergleich (1918-1933/39).* Munich: Oldenbourg.

Weeks, Theodore R. (1996), *Nation and State in Late Imperial Russia. Nationalism and Russification on the Western Frontier 1863-1914.* DeKalb: Northern Illinois University Press.

Weiler, Peter (1988), *British Labour and the Cold War.* Stanford University Press.

Westad, Odd Arne (2007), *The Global Cold War.* Cambridge University Press.

Westerhoff, Christian (2012), *Zwangsarbeit im Ersten Weltkrieg. Deutsche Arbeitskräftepolitik im besetzten Polen und Litauen 1914–1918*. Paderborn: Schöningh.
Western, J.R. (1965), *The English Militia in the Eighteenth Century. The Story of a Political Issue 1660–1802*. London: Routledge.
Wienfort, Monika 2001. *Patrimonialgerichte in Preussen. Ländliche Gesellschaft und bürgerliches Recht 1770–1848/49*. Göttingen: Vandenhoeck und Ruprecht.
Wilensky, Harold L. (1975), *The Welfare State and Equality. Structural and Ideological Roots of Public Expenditure*. Berkeley: University of California Press.
Willems, Emilio (1984), *Der preußisch-deutsche Militarismus. Ein Kulturkomplex im sozialen Wandel*. Cologne: Verlag Wissenschaft und Politik.
Williams, Chad L. (2010), *Torchbearers of Democracy. African American Soldiers in the World War I Era*. Chapel Hill: University of North Carolina Press.
Winnige, Norbert (1996), 'Von der Kontribution zur Akzise. Militärfinanzierung als Movens staatlicher Steuerpolitik' in Bernhard R. Kroener and Ralf Pröve (eds.), *Krieg und Frieden. Militär und Gesellschaft in der Frühen Neuzeit*. Paderborn: Schöningh, pp. 59–83.
Winter, Martin (2005), *Untertanengeist durch Militärpflicht? Das preußische Kantonsystem in brandenburgischen Städten im 18. Jahrhundert*. Bielefeld: Verlag für Regionalgeschichte.
Wirsching, Andreas (1999), *Vom Weltkrieg zum Bürgerkrieg?: Politischer Extremismus in Deutschland und Frankreich 1918–1933/39. Berlin und Paris Im Vergleich*. Munich: Oldenbourg.
Wirtschafter, Elise Kimerling (1990), *From Serf to Russian Soldier*. Princeton University Press.
Wohlfeil, Rainer (1965), *Spanien und die deutsche Erhebung 1808–1814*. Wiesbaden: Steiner.
Wohlfeil, Rainer (1983), *Vom Stehenden Heer des Absolutismus zur Allgemeinen Wehrpflicht*. Munich: Bernard & Graefe.
Wold, Atle L. (2015), *Scotland and the French Revolutionary War, 1792–1802*. Edinburgh University Press.
Wolff, Christian (1754), *Grundsätze des Natur- und Völckerrechts*. Halle: Renger.
Wolff, Christian (1764), *Jus Gentium methodo scientifica petractatum*, reprint of 1764 edition. Oxford: Clarendon Press.
Wolfe, Martin 1972. *The Fiscal System of Renaissance France*. New Haven: Yale University Press.
Wright, Gavin (2013), *Sharing the Prize. The Economics of the Civil Rights Revolution in the American South*. Cambridge, MA: Harvard University Press.
Wright, William E. (1966), *Serf, Seigneur and Sovereign. Agrarian Reform in Eighteenth-Century Bohemia*. University of Minnesota Press.

Xenakis, Stefan (2015), *Gewalt und Gemeinschaft. Kriegsknechte um 1500.* Paderborn: Schöningh.

Yarbrough, Tinsley E. (1976), 'Justice Black, The Fourteenth Amendment, and Incorporation'. *University of Miami Law Review* 30(2): 231–275.

Zaccaria, Giuseppe (2018), 'The People and Populism'. *Ratio Juris* 31(1): 33–48.

Zarate Tenorio, Barbara (2014), 'Social Spending Responses to Organized Labor and Mass Protests in Latin America, 1970-2007'. *Comparative Political Studies* 47(14): 1945–1972.

Ziemann, Benjamin (1997), *Front und Heimat. Ländliche Kriegserfahrungen im südlichen Bayern 1914–1923.* Essen: Klartext.

INDEX

Abolition of serfdom, 32, 33, 92–94, 102, 105–106, 120
Abolition of slavery, 32, 33, 95–97, 106, 121
Absolutism, 60
Act on State Assistance in Childcare, Poland (2016), 209
Administration, governmental, 23, 27, 35, 51, 55, 56, 57, 63, 64, 73
Administration, military, 47, 55, 56, 62, 67
Administrative law, 23, 35, 63–65, 66, 167
Administrative Procedure Act, USA (1946), 167
Allgemeines Gesetzbuch für die Preußischen Staaten, Prussia (1791)
Altenstein, Karl Sigmund Franz Freiherr vom Stein zum, 93
Argentina, 2, 142, 148, 149, 175, 176
Aristocracy, 22, 41, 45, 46, 47, 51, 52, 57–60, 63, 69–70, 73–75
Army
    Conscript armies, 81, 90
    Feudal armies, 46, 48, 49, 50
    Industrial armies, 112
    Standing armies, 49–61, 73–75, 77, 79, 84, 85, 86, 92, 93
Atlantic Charter (1941), 154, 155
Austria, 25, 26, 45, 67, 89, 102, 103, 118, 122, 132, 133
Authoritarianism, 2, 3, 8, 134, 135, 167, 216

Bavaria, 93
Beck, Ulrich, 157
Beveridge Report, 152, 154, 155
Beveridge, William, 157

Bismarck, Otto von, 89
Blackstone, William, 21, 25
Blood, and tax, 42, 54, 82, 84
Bohemia, 58
Bolivia, 5, 166, 199, 203
Bolshevism, 125, 126, 128–131
Bolsonaro, Jair, 206, 209, 210, 211
Booty, gained in war, 53
Brandenburg, 53, 59, 74
Brazil, 2, 5, 95–97, 142, 175, 198, 199, 206, 208, 209, 210–214
Brexit Referendum, 199, 202, 203, 207
Brüning, Heinrich, 159
Brunkhorst, Hauke, 17, 178
Bundesversorgungsgesetz, Federal Republic of Germany (1950), 138

Canada, 120, 138, 154
Castro, Fidel, 142
Cavaignac, Louis-Eugène, 109
Charles VII, King of France, 59
Chateaubriand, François-Auguste-René, vicomte de, 87
Chávez, Hugo, 198, 206
Chile, 94, 142, 149, 175, 176
China, 2
Citizen
    Construct of, 16, 19, 22, 23, 24, 27, 28, 29, 30, 31, 32, 33, 70–71, 77, 79–80, 85, 108, 114–116, 134, 135, 153, 174, 175, 181, 183, 186, 191, 194, 218
    Functions of, 11, 17, 119, 136, 142, 161, 200
    Legal, 19, 22, 23, 24, 27, 28, 29, 35, 38, 70–73, 78, 80, 98, 100, 104, 113, 119
    Political, 19, 30, 31, 33, 36–40, 72, 73, 77–80, 104, 113, 116, 133, 134

Rights of, 23, 24, 72, 78, 82, 85, 98, 175, 180, 181
Sovereign, 17, 31, 33, 78, 80, 97, 113, 115, 116, 133, 134, 135, 185, 192, 218, 219
Citizenship
  Active, 30–32, 35, 70, 72, 73, 78, 81, 82, 87, 98, 99, 215
  And democracy, 8, 11, 30, 34, 35, 37–38, 39, 85, 87–88, 92, 97–99, 108, 114, 118, 119, 121, 123, 124, 133–135, 137, 145, 194, 196, 200, 202, 215, 220
  And popular sovereignty, 9, 16–18, 19, 125, 179, 180, 183, 192, 207, 215, 217, 218, 220
  And the military, 43, 79–89, 92, 94, 96, 97, 99, 100, 102, 105, 106, 108, 110, 112–115, 118, 119, 121, 124, 129–132, 137, 138, 139, 140, 141, 142–144, 181, 218
  As legal form, 19, 23, 24, 78 See Citizen, Legal
  As political form, 30–33, 37–38, 73, 78–82, 99, 119, 125, 129 See Citizen, political
  Demilitarization of, 126, 145, 148, 156, 164, 166, 167, 170
  Militarization of, 113, 115, 136, 144, 170, 212
Civil law, 25, 34, 61, 66
Civil Law Code, Austria (1786/87), 25–26
Civil Rights Act, USA (1964), 106, 139, 173
Civil Rights Movement, USA, 138, 178, 179
Civil service, 32, 52, 161
Civil war, 20, 21, 46, 83, 90, 95, 97, 100, 101, 107, 108, 109, 110, 112, 122, 129–131, 133, 144–146, 170, 177
Class
  And conflict, 128, 149, 152, 153, 156, 163, 164, 211
  And militarism, 52, 57, 71, 112, 124, 129, 148
  And voting patterns, 163

Formation, 32, 111, 115, 151
Weakening of, 124, 148, 151, 167, 169, 179
Clausewitz, Carl von, 56, 86
Codification, of law, 24, 34, 66, 68, 72, 179
Cold War, 137, 139, 140–143, 156, 211
Colombia, 2, 4, 94, 95, 142, 146, 165, 166, 177, 197
Communism, 128, 129, 131, 211
Condorcet, Nicolas de, 114
Conscription, 44, 49, 50, 81–94, 96, 97, 99, 101, 102, 103, 105, 110, 112, 119, 123, 124, 127, 129, 137, 150, 154
Constituent power, 191, 192, 197–199
Constitutional law, 7, 8, 12, 35, 58, 97, 108, 166, 173, 182, 184, 185, 192, 215
Constitutional theory, 14, 110, 189, 191, 193, 219
Constitutionalism
  Authoritarian, 12
  Classical, 20, 191, 193, 200, 208
  Populism and, 10, 12, 189, 190, 193, 196, 204, 216
Constitutions
  Of Bolivia (2009), 203
  Of Colombia (1991), 197
  Of England, 21, 25, 60, 74
  Of fiscal system, 76, 78, 79
  Of France (1791), 34, 102
  Of France (1793), 82
  Of France (1795), 102
  Of France (1958), 137
  Of Germany (1871), 89, 106, 109
  Of Germany (1919), 155, 158
  Of India (1950), 149
  Of judiciary, 69, 77
  Of military, 54, 68, 79
  Of Portugal (1976), 137
  Of Prussia (1848–50), 106
  Of USA (1789), 34
  Of Venezuela (1999), 197
Contributions, military tax, 48, 52, 53
Convention on the Elimination of all Forms of Discrimination Against Women (1979), 176

264   INDEX

Convention on the Elimination of All
    Forms of Racial Discrimination,
    United Nations (1965), 173, 176
Corporations, 27, 48, 58, 65
Corporatism, 131, 152
Courts
    American Supreme Court, 173
    Colombian Constitutional Court,
        166, 177
    European Court of Human Rights,
        173, 177, 203, 206
    Indian Supreme Court, 210
    Inter-American Court of Human
        Rights, 173, 199
    International Criminal Court, 203
Cuba, 142
Czech Republic, 26, 45
Czechoslovakia, 122, 154, 178

d'Aguesseau, Henri François, 21
de Seyssel, Claude, 21
Decolonization, 2, 137, 140, 143, 144,
    164, 178
Defence spending, 142, 150
Demilitarization of, 144
Democracy
    And individualism, 180, 202
    And integration, 11, 12, 32, 40, 72,
        98, 106, 110, 115, 119, 123, 126,
        128, 134, 158, 165, 169, 170–172,
        180, 182, 183, 184, 185, 193–196,
        200, 204, 208, 209, 216, 217, 218,
        220, 221
    And militarism, 14, 41, 71, 85, 87, 92,
        108, 109, 112, 133, 139, 185
    As system of integration, 30, 40, 134,
        193, 194, 215, 219
    Deterioration, 1, 187, 190, 196
    Expansion after 1980s, 1–3, 6, 7, 136,
        176, 187, 201, 217
    Full, 1, 97, 118, 119, 134, 139
    Hybrid forms of, 1, 3–5, 6, 8–10
    Partial, 2, 83, 134, 136
    Theory of, 14, 39, 40, 191, 193, 219
    Transitions to, 2, 3, 6, 7, 121, 136,
        175, 201
Democratization, 2–3, 4, 6–7, 83, 92, 97,
    110, 113, 121, 124, 126, 128, 133,
    136, 145, 165, 171, 175, 176,
    180, 188
Democratizing polities, 136, 138, 145,
    147, 148, 149, 150, 156, 157,
    164–168, 169, 171, 173, 174, 185
Dictatorship, 81, 87, 123, 133, 145
Dubois de Crancé, Edmond Louis
    Alexis, 81
Durkheim, Émile, 28, 98, 115
Dutch Republic, 60

Edict of Fontainebleau, France
    (1685), 20
Education, 32, 138, 140, 150, 151, 162,
    167, 168, 176, 177, 179, 188,
    200, 201
Eisenhower, Dwight D., 140
Emergency Powers Act, Great Britain
    (1920), 132
Employees State Insurance Act, India
    (1948), 149
Engels, Friedrich, 90, 112
England, 21, 25, 42, 49, 60, 61, 68, 74, 85
Estates, of nobility, 21, 25, 45, 55,
    58–61, 67, 73–75, 121
Ethnicity, 164, 165, 166, 169, 170
European Communities Act, United
    Kingdom (1972), 207
European Convention on Human
    Rights, 181
European Union, 7, 171, 199, 206,
    207, 211
Executive legislation, 201, 206
Executive Order 9981, USA (1948), 140
Executives
    Power of, 58, 59, 65, 69, 81, 127, 132,
        154, 207, 212, 213
    Under populism, 6, 197

Fascism, 130, 131
Feudal armies, 47
Feudal law, 43, 60, 93, 120
Feudalism, 24, 38, 41, 42, 43–45, 49, 53,
    81, 82, 93, 95, 112, 115, 182, 186
Fiefs, 42–46, 93
Finland, 118
Fiscal crisis, 75, 76, 78, 79, 82
Fiscal state, 57, 58

INDEX

Fontane, Theodor, 90
Forced labour, 32, 61, 104, 125, 159
France, 13, 20-21, 25, 26, 30, 32, 34-35, 42, 45, 49, 51, 55, 59, 61, 62, 63, 65, 67, 68, 72, 74-83, 86-87, 89-93, 99-101, 105, 106, 109, 114, 121, 125, 126, 127, 128, 132, 137, 138, 152, 154, 192
Franchise, 89, 120, 138
Franchise reforms, 89

Geneva Conventions of 1949, 174
Germany, 45, 89, 90, 99, 106, 109, 118-127, 128, 130, 132, 133, 138, 148, 154, 158-159, 177
Giolitti, Giovanni, 89
Global constitutional law, 12, 185, 215
Global legal system, 215, 218
Global norms, 8, 10, 155, 172, 196, 202-205, 208, 220, 221
Global society, 13, 14, 174, 184
Globalism, and anti-globalism, 209, 210
Goulart, João, 142
Great Britain, 124
Greece, 174
Grégoire, Henri Jean-Baptiste, 114

Habermas, Jürgen, 17
Habsburg dynasty, 50, 76, 93, 94, 125
Helsinki Accords (1975), 136, 176
Hintze, Otto, 55
Hohenzollern dynasty, 74
Holbach, Paul-Henri Thiry, 21
Holy Roman Empire, 21, 52, 59
Horthy, Miklós, 122
Huber, Ulrich, 21
Hungary, 5, 122, 126, 198, 199, 203, 210

Iceland, 118
Ideology, 130, 146, 215
Immigration, 188, 202
India, 3, 5, 8, 149, 155, 168, 198, 201, 206, 210-211, 214
Individualization, 26, 28, 33, 37, 70, 76, 113, 115, 145, 147, 148, 157, 161, 163, 168, 170, 174, 177-179, 183, 185, 186, 194, 200, 202, 215, 217, 219

Institutions
  Central, 46, 111, 215
  Legal, 5, 7, 25, 26, 56, 63, 64, 68, 121, 166, 167, 173, 177, 198, 203, 206
    See Courts
  Military, 56, 96, 144
  Political, 3, 8, 11, 28, 30, 31, 32, 41, 44, 46, 68, 88, 122, 124, 131, 133, 144, 145, 147, 153, 170, 182, 183, 208
Integration
  Individual, 27, 70, 71, 153, 163, 164, 168, 194, 195, 200, 201, 211, 221
  Institutional, 11, 19, 23, 29, 31, 32, 33, 36-39, 67, 75, 80, 98, 99, 111, 114, 117, 127, 133, 134, 136, 137, 143, 144, 145, 150, 151, 159, 162, 163, 164, 169, 170, 174, 180, 181, 182, 183, 185, 189, 194-196, 200, 204, 205, 207, 209, 212, 215, 217, 218, 219
  Legal, 11, 21, 22, 25-28, 31, 34-36, 37, 39, 41, 57, 66, 67, 70-72, 73, 76, 77, 80, 88, 98, 100, 104, 113-115, 117, 121, 136, 137, 143, 145, 183, 184, 185, 215, 216
  Military, 61, 113
  National, 12, 23, 44, 83, 113, 114, 116, 117, 135, 138, 143, 144, 151, 165, 170, 180, 181-182, 185, 208, 213, 214, 220, 221
  Normative, 11, 19, 29, 33, 35, 36, 37, 39, 40, 67, 69, 80, 88, 98, 113, 133, 134, 165, 170-172, 181, 182, 183, 185, 194, 202, 203, 204, 206, 216, 220
  Political, 11, 28, 31, 37, 44, 71, 78, 89, 94, 97, 114, 121, 134, 137, 161, 169, 182, 184, 187, 207, 208
  Territorial, 23, 36
Intendants, French, 61, 62, 63
International Covenant on Civil and Political Rights, United Nations (1966), 136, 173
International human rights law, 173-175, 177, 181
International law, 8, 172-174, 175, 176, 179, 181, 199

International organizations, 5, 6, 7, 171, 199
Italy, 3, 5, 89, 118, 123, 126, 167, 199, 201, 206

Jacobinism, 88
Japan, 3, 154, 167
Jaurès, Jean, 112
Johnson, Boris, 207
Johnson, Lyndon, 173
Joseph II, Holy Roman Emperor, 25
Judiciaries
   And human rights law, 141, 173, 203
   Hostility to, 5, 190, 198, 199
   Power of, 6, 7, 8, 20, 35, 167

Kant, Immanuel, 17, 21, 114
Kautsky, Karl, 112
Koselleck, Reinhart, 14

Labour Code on Industrial Relations Bill, India (2015), 210
Land Law, Prussia (1794), 25, 32, 66
Landesdefensionsordnung, House of Nassau-Siegen, 84
Legal person, 23, 24, 26, 27, 28–29, 36, 66, 67, 70, 71, 76, 77, 115, 174
Legal system, 24, 25, 33–34, 36, 39, 56, 57, 61, 62, 65, 67–71, 77, 80, 98, 104, 113, 115, 116, 117, 135, 180, 184–185, 207, 215, 218
Legislature, 34, 118, 183
Legitimacy, 2, 3, 6, 8–11, 16–24, 29–34, 39, 40, 57, 61, 64, 65, 67, 69–72, 90, 91, 92, 98–104, 106, 107, 108, 113, 115–119, 132, 133, 134, 135, 136, 140, 142, 171, 174–175, 180, 181, 183, 184, 191–197, 200, 203–205, 208, 210, 211–221
Leibniz, Gottfried Wilhelm, 20
Lenin, Vladimir, 112
Levée en masse, 82, 83, 90
Lei Saraiva, Brazil (1881), 106
Libya, 89
Limnaeus, Johannes, 21
Litigation, 35, 167, 168, 177, 179, 180
Locke, John, 21
Luhmann, Niklas, 14, 115

Madison, James, 34, 79, 110
Marshall, John, 192
Marx, Karl, 112
Master and Servant Act, Great Britain (1867), 120
Mercenaries, 46, 47, 50, 57
Militarization, 41, 50, 54, 55, 71, 91, 92, 95, 101, 110, 112–113, 115, 125, 129, 137, 144, 156, 170, 182, 184, 213
Military contracts, 42, 46–49, 50, 51, 53, 61, 62, 70, 81, 84, 85
Military law, 50–53, 61, 62, 97, 103, 125, 132, 174
Military system, 14, 44, 46, 49, 52, 55, 56, 57, 61, 62, 65, 68, 69, 71, 77, 98, 113, 116, 135, 184–185, 218
Militia Act, Great Britain (1757), 49
Militia Ordinance, England (1642), 85
Militias, 49, 81, 102, 109, 122, 142, 143, 213
Minorities
   Hostility to, 122, 139, 165, 173, 198, 214
   Rights of, 140, 165, 166, 198
Modi, Narendra, 198, 206, 210
Morales, Evo, 198

Nation building, 98, 144, 164, 214
National Security Act, USA (1947), 141
Natural law, 20, 21, 22, 65, 66
Nehru Report, India (1928), 155
Netherlands, 53
New Deal, USA, 127, 138, 155, 158
North German Federation, 89
Norway, 118

Obama, Barack, 210
Officers/officer class, 51, 68
Oligarchy, 95
Olympic Games, Mexico (1968), 178
Order Nr. 1 of the Petrograd Soviet, Russia (1917), 129

Papen, Franz von, 159
Paramilitaries, 122, 123, 125, 142, 145

INDEX

Paris Commune, 90, 91, 109
Parlements, French, 59, 63–65, 75
Partisans, 90, 91, 102–104
Peterloo, Manchester, 109
Piłsudski, Józef, 122, 158
Poland, 5, 26, 45, 67, 77, 118, 122, 158, 174, 198–199, 201, 209, 211, 212
Political Parties
 Christian Democratic, 148
 Communist, 112, 126, 142, 176
 Conservative, 112, 211
 Formation of, 31, 110–112
 Social Democratic, 109, 122, 148, 176
Political system, 16, 17, 19, 30, 31, 35, 36, 37, 39, 43, 48, 77, 86, 95, 97, 107, 112, 115, 116, 117, 133–134, 136, 146, 171, 176, 182, 184, 187, 191–193, 198, 208, 209, 212, 216, 218, 219
Populism
 And citizenship, 8, 196, 205
 And constitutionalism, 10, 12, 189, 191, 195, 197, 204, 216
 And democracy, 6, 8–15, 19, 187–191, 196, 197, 200, 204, 205, 214–216
 And individualization, 200, 202
 And nationalism, 4, 5, 198
 And the military, 212
 And welfarism, 201, 209, 210
 Constituent power, 197, 198, 199
 Definition of, 5
 Populist movements, 4, 5, 204, 214
Portugal, 137
Prussia, 21, 25, 27, 32, 35, 50, 51, 53, 55, 59, 62, 64, 65, 66, 67, 68, 74, 76, 77, 79, 83, 89–91, 93, 99, 102, 103, 105, 106, 108, 109
Public spending, 78, 151, 154, 159

Red Army, 129
Religious Peace of Augsburg (1555), 20
Representation, 2, 7, 16, 17, 30, 43, 61, 78, 85, 88, 89, 110, 118, 133, 134, 147, 165, 173, 189, 190, 193, 198, 217
Revolutionary wars in France, 80, 86
Revolutions
 American, 16, 21, 30, 72, 77, 103
 Cuban, 142
 French, 16, 30, 32, 34–35, 63, 72, 75, 77–82, 86–87, 93, 99, 100, 108, 110, 111, 114, 123, 192
 Russian, 16, 119, 126–129
Rights
 Civil, 140, 167, 179, 181
 Constitutional, 139, 140, 167
 Education, 138, 168, 176, 177, 179
 Electoral, 97, 106, 119, 154
 Environmental, 168, 177
 Ethnic, 167, 168, 172, 177
 Fiscal, 26
 Indigenous, 165, 179
 Individual, 160, 161, 165, 167, 172–177, 180–182, 198
 International human, 7, 141, 173–177, 181
 Labour, 172
 Legal, 19, 22, 23, 26, 30, 85
 Minority, 140, 165, 166, 198
 Natural, 66
 Political, 24, 43, 47, 72, 78, 82, 87, 88, 100, 104, 106, 114, 119, 120, 136, 138, 208
 Reproductive, 178
 Sexual, 167, 168, 177
 Subjective, 25, 65, 72, 166
 To health care, 168
 Welfare, 138, 149, 157, 159, 160, 164, 168, 175, 176, 177
Robespierre, Maximilien, 79, 81, 100
Roosevelt, Franklin Delano, 158
Royal Commission on Marriage and Divorce, UK (1956), 159
Russia, 4, 7, 8, 92, 94, 105, 119, 121, 122, 124–129, 137, 164, 174, 211, 212
Rwanda, 144

Sachsenspiegel, 43
Schmitt, Carl, 20, 104, 125, 192
Scotland, 99
Secularization, 20, 22

Serfdom, 25–26, 32, 33, 41, 44–45, 68, 74, 92–94, 102, 105–106, 120, 121, 125, 135
Servicemen's Readjustment Act, USA (1944), 139
Sieyès, Emmanuel-Joseph, 192
Slavery, 32, 33, 41, 45, 93–97, 105–106, 121
Slovakia, 45
Sociology
  Global, 9, 10–14
  Historical, 14, 193
  Legal, 13
  Military, 14
  Of concepts, 14
  Of constitutions, 6
  Of democracy, 9, 10, 12, 19, 214, 217, 220, 221
Soldat-citoyen, 80–83, 84, 96, 102, 109, 113, 119
Sovereignty
  Concept of, 34
  Of state, 50, 54, 73, 75, 76, 103–104, 107, 111, 115, 116, 123, 126, 131, 135, 161, 163, 164, 194, 207, 209, 211, 213
  Popular, 3, 9, 10, 16–17, 90, 91, 108, 113, 125, 156, 171, 179, 180, 183, 191, 192, 198, 199, 203, 207, 215, 217, 218, 219, 220
Soviet Union, 2, 137, 138, 140–142, 164, 169, 176, 181
Spain, 7, 42, 95, 102, 103, 126
State formation, 48, 54, 94, 131, 137, 149, 154, 155, 186
Stolypin, Pyotr Arkadyevich, 121
Students, 162, 178
Subject formation, 18, 97, 149, 152, 157, 160, 163, 166, 168, 169, 176, 182, 185, 200
Subjectivity
  Collective, 107, 112, 115, 135, 152, 157, 163, 165, 168, 170, 181, 185, 198
  Individual, 77, 183
  Legal, 27, 28, 68, 77, 174, 183, 194, 200, 215
  Military, 113
  Multiple, 168, 220
  Political, 8, 17, 18, 19, 31, 38–40, 115, 131, 172, 174, 177, 180, 202, 204
Sweden, 110, 118, 119, 128, 154

Taxation, 26, 46, 53–54, 58–61, 63–64, 75–79, 82
Tehran Conference on Human Rights (1968), 179
Temer, Michel, 210
Trade unions, 146, 147, 148, 149
Truman, Harry S., 138, 140, 141, 149
Trump, Donald, 199, 202, 203, 206, 214
Territorialization, 23

UN Charter, 173
Universal Declaration of Human Rights, United Nations (1948), 176
Universities, 178, 197
Urbinati, Nadia, 191
Uruguay, 95, 176
USA, 1, 8, 83, 97, 99, 118, 124, 127, 134, 136, 137, 138–142, 149, 155, 158, 162, 163, 165, 168, 170, 173, 175, 178, 179, 211

Vargas, Getúlio, 96
Vassalage, 44, 45
Venezuela, 5, 176, 197, 198, 199, 203, 206, 208, 209, 212, 213
Veterans, 126, 127, 139, 154, 158
Violence, 41, 44, 46, 48–49, 52–55, 71, 98, 101, 103, 107, 115, 116, 120, 122, 123, 129–130, 133, 142, 150, 171, 172, 182, 203, 211, 213, 218, 219
Voting Rights Act, USA (1965), 106, 139, 173

War
  Algerian War, 137
  American Civil War, 83, 97
  Franco-Prussian war, 89, 90
  In Germany, 1848–49, 108, 109
  Napoleonic War, 86, 88
  Paraguayan War, 96, 105, 143

INDEX

Revolutionary wars in France, 90, 100, 101, 108
Russian Civil War, 129–131
Thirty Years War, 48
Vietnam War, 169
Wars of Independence in South America, 94
World War I, 99, 118–132, 154, 158
World War II, 41, 137, 138, 153, 154, 155, 173, 184
Warren, Earl, 141
Weber, Max, 42, 43, 99, 126, 128
Welfare democracy, 131, 149, 175, 182

Welfare state, 126, 127, 138, 149–164, 170, 171, 175, 176, 183, 185, 201
Welfare system, 127, 149, 152, 154–155, 157–159, 162, 176, 182, 201–203, 209
Welfarism, and anti-welfarism, 126, 127, 138, 156, 158, 201, 210
Wolff, Christian, 21, 53
World society, 13, 156, 177

Yugoslavia, 122, 174